"Manz reads the larger political, national, and international contexts into the gripping and nail-biting horror stories she tells about the life, death, and rebirth of Santa María Tzejá, a tough little village in Guatemala to which she is emotionally and politically bound for life. More than any anthropologist of her generation, Manz is both ethnographer and compañera." NANCY SCHEPER-HUGHES, author of *Death without Weeping: The Violence of Everyday Life in Brazil*

"*Paradise in Ashes* is a masterpiece. Written with a lucid and sensitive anthropological eye, it is a work of scholarly and literary excellence. There is no happy ending to this remarkable story. Nonetheless, the strength, courage, and hope of the Mayans, poignantly revealed by Beatriz Manz, makes this, after all its horrors, an upbeat, even inspiring, story. Manz brings back to us the best, the most illuminating of the legendary Latin American anthropology." ADOLFO AGUILAR ZINSER, Mexican ambassador to the United Nations and member of the U.N. Security Council

"Much more than the ethnography of a beleaguered village in Guatemala, *Paradise in Ashes* is about how international politics, in this case, the cold war, played itself out within a culture that is every bit as 'foreign' as that of Iraq or Afghanistan. Combining a lifetime of uncommonly solid scholarship with a lively, accessible style, Manz has produced a genuine landmark, blending the local with the global into a compelling new approach to problems that continue to bedevil our world." LARS SCHOULTZ, author of *Beneath the United States: A History of U.S. Policy toward Latin America*

Paradise in Ashes

CALIFORNIA SERIES IN PUBLIC ANTHROPOLOGY

The California Series in Public Anthropology emphasizes the anthropologist's role as an engaged intellectual. It continues anthropology's commitment to being an ethnographic witness, to describing, in human terms, how life is lived beyond the borders of many readers' experiences. But it also adds a commitment, through ethnography, to reframing the terms of public debate—transforming received, accepted understandings of social issues with new insights, new framings.

SERIES EDITOR: Robert Borofsky (Hawaii Pacific University)
CONTRIBUTING EDITORS: Philippe Bourgois (UC San Francisco), Paul Farmer (Partners in Health), Rayna Rapp (New York University), and Nancy Scheper-Hughes (UC Berkeley)
UNIVERSITY OF CALIFORNIA PRESS EDITOR: Naomi Schneider

Paradise in Ashes

A Guatemalan Journey of Courage, Terror, and Hope

Beatriz Manz

With a foreword by Aryeh Neier

UNIVERSITY OF CALIFORNIA PRESS
Berkeley · Los Angeles · London

University of California Press
Berkeley and Los Angeles, California

University of California Press, Ltd.
London, England

© 2004 by the Regents of the University of California

Library of Congress Cataloging-in-Publication Data

Manz, Beatriz
  Paradise in ashes : a Guatemalan journey of courage,
terror, and hope / Beatriz Manz ; with a foreword by
Aryeh Neier.
    p.   cm.   (California series in public anthro-
pology ; 8)
  Includes bibliographical references and index.
  ISBN 0-520-24016-2 (cloth : alk. paper)
    1. Quiché Indians—Crimes against—Guatemala—
Santa María Tzejá.   2. Quiché Indians—Relocation—
Mexico.   3. Massacres—Guatemala—Santa María
Tzejá.   4. Political violence—Guatemala—Santa
María Tzejá.   5. Civil-military relations—
Guatemala—Santa María Tzejá.   6. Ejército
Guerrillero de los Pobres (Guatemala)   7. Return
migration—Guatemala—Santa María Tzejá.   8. Santa
María Tzejá (Guatemala)—Social conditions.   9.
Santa María Tzejá (Guatemala)—Politics and govern-
ment.   I. Title. II. Series.
F1465.2.Q5 M36   2004
972.8105′2—dc21   2003009015

Manufactured in the United States of America
12 11 10 09 08 07 06 05 04
10 9 8 7 6 5 4 3 2 1

The paper used in this publication meets the minimum
requirements of ANSI/NISO Z39.48–1992 (R 1997)
(Permanence of Paper). ♾

To Santa María Tzejá,
to the memory of those killed,
to the hopes that will not die,
to the future realization of those dreams,

and to Harley and Mariela

Contents

Illustrations

Foreword

The 1970s and the 1980s were a terrible period in Latin America. Country after country—Argentina, Brazil, Chile, Colombia, Peru, El Salvador, and Nicaragua, among others—was ravaged by repression and internal armed conflict. The toll in lost lives and in suffering was immense. But it was greatest of all in one of the smaller countries in the region where, for a variety of reasons, it was least reported as it was taking place. We now know that about two hundred thousand Guatemalans, most of them Mayan Indians, were murdered during this period. The overwhelming majority were slaughtered by the Guatemalan armed forces in what a United Nations–sponsored "Historical Clarification Commission" that published a twelve-volume report in 1999 appropriately labeled as "genocide." The number of deaths tabulated by the commission comes close to the known total of all those killed in war and repression during the 1970s and the 1980s throughout the rest of the western hemisphere.

Why was Guatemala so severely victimized? One hesitates to answer such a question for fear of oversimplifying. Yet surely one factor was that, of all countries in the region, it's the one with the largest indigenous population and the country with the most notoriously brutal military force. As the armed forces considered that insurgent forces were rooted in those indigenous communities, they developed a counterinsurgency strategy aimed at disrupting what they saw as the guerrilla base. This was carried out by the armed forces, whose commanders had been trained in the United States, and aided by the organization of paramilitary forces known as "civil patrols," who set members of indigenous communities against each other; through forced displacement and resettlement so as to break up established relationships between residents of a particular community; and through massacres that eradicated entire villages by killing many of their residents and requiring the survivors to flee for their lives.

Many factors combined to shield developments in Guatemala during this period from outside scrutiny. The worst abuses took place in the highlands and distant rainforest regions of the country where the terrain is difficult, where roads and communications facilities were absent, where many different indigenous languages are spoken, and of course, where it was very dangerous to be around while the killing was taking place. During the worst times, there were no Guatemalan human rights organizations to report on developments, and most external human rights monitors only visited for brief periods. Hardly any Guatemalan journalists reported on what was going on in the highlands, and the foreign press corps covering the region focused on the wars in El Salvador and Nicaragua, where the United States was much more visibly and overtly involved. At the peak period of the massacres, during the presidency of Efrain Rios Montt (1982–83), the United States Embassy in Guatemala was effectively a public relations mouthpiece for the armed forces. It was at this high point of the carnage that President Ronald Reagan labeled human rights reports as "a bum rap" and that his Ambassador to the United Nations, Jeane Kirkpatrick, said of the regime committing genocide that it "offered new powers of self-government and self-defense to the Indians" and that Rios Montt's rule "included a strong effort to end human rights abuses by government forces."

Though the full extent of the slaughter in Guatemala was not known internationally as it happened, enough was reported at the time to make clear that a man-made catastrophe was taking place. One of the very few outsiders who ventured into the heart of the most ravaged regions of the country and stayed long enough to observe and understand what was going on during the worst periods was Beatriz Manz. Her role was twofold. She pursued a scholarly study of a remote Mayan Indian community, Santa María Tzejá and its people, and the manner in which the tragic events of the period affected and transformed their village. At the same time, enhancing greatly the risk to her own safety, she consistently spoke out publicly about the crimes that she witnessed, providing crucial information for human rights reports, for the media, and for the United States Congress.

Now Beatriz Manz has written a brilliant book that focuses sharply on Santa María Tzejá and that simultaneously puts developments there into the context of what was taking place throughout Guatemala. Her book exemplifies public anthropology at its best. It combines close observation of a community and its people and a wider-angle examination of the political forces that distorted their lives. The author's scholarly integrity and commitment to the cause of the Guatemalan villagers she writes about are both evident, and neither is compromised in the interest of the other. Beatriz Manz not only explains what happened but also helps us understand what is happening in the postwar period. The result is a book of singular importance. *Paradise in Ashes* is not only the most outstanding work to emerge from the Guatemalan disaster. It also takes its place among the handful of books—such as Elizabeth Becker's account of the Cambodian Holocaust, *When the War Was Over,* Chuck Sudetic's great work on the Bosnian tragedy, *Blood and Vengeance,* and Philip Gourevitch's book on the Rwandan genocide, *We Wish to Inform You That Tomorrow We Will Be Killed with Our Families*—that we need to read and reread to comprehend the terrible era through which we have lived.

Aryeh Neier,
president of the Soros Foundation and
Open Society Institute, former
director of Human Rights Watch

Acknowledgments

I cannot begin to thank all the people who helped me over the past thirty years, inviting me to sleep in their homes in the refugee camps and in Santa María Tzejá, providing meals when little was available, giving extensively of their time, carrying a heavy load on the impassable jungle trails, providing tips and opening networks, meeting in distant locations, even looking after me when their own security was threatened. It would take several pages to thank everyone, and I would still, no doubt, miss many people in Guatemala, Mexico, and the United States. I therefore give one enormous collective thanks to all the wonderful individuals I encountered in this long journey, especially to the people of Santa María Tzejá for their extraordinary support, understanding, and patience. I want to thank specifically the teachers and various committee members; Randall Shea; and Gaspar Quino, who without portfolio, pay, or title became a de facto research assistant. I also need to extend a special thanks to Jesús for his remarkable insights.

I am giving only a few individual thanks to those who helped me in the last stages that transformed voices of villagers, field notes, and library research into a final book. Students at Berkeley, undergraduates and graduates, were instrumental in their assistance. I am particularly indebted to Berkeley's Undergraduate Research Apprentice Program (URAP) and would like to thank Monica Pons, Abbie Lowe, and especially Andrea Valverde. Carlos Bazúa, Neferti Kelly, Abbie Friedman, Gabriela Quiros, and Perla Valdes deserve special thanks. Anne Alleshire went over the interviews and helped organize the appropriate comments into specific themes. Her support came at a crucial time and was truly invaluable. I also want to thank students in the fall 2002 graduate reading seminar for their very useful comments. Several students from Santa María Tzejá at the University of San Carlos in Guatemala City were always available and supportive, especially Edwin Canil and Juvencio Chom.

I am deeply thankful to several friends, colleagues, and former students who read the manuscript and gave me valuable comments, and to those I asked for more precise queries regarding their specific expertise: Charlie Hale, Lydia Chavez, Christopher Lutz, George Lovell, Robert Carmack, Kate Doyle, Nora England, Naomi Roht-Arriaza, Kay Warren, Paula Worby, Luis Losano, Elizabeth Oglesby, Marcie Mersky, Amy Ross, Angelina Godoy-Snodgrass, Elizabeth Lira, and Bettina Prato.

The Center for Latin American Studies at Berkeley has provided a rich intellectual environment for the campus with a highly professional, dedicated, and helpful staff. Many thanks for all their support over the years. Several staff members and colleagues in the departments of geography and comparative ethnic studies at Berkeley were very helpful. I thank Darin Jensen for his first-rate cartographic work in producing early versions of the maps, and Natalia Vonnegut, Donald Bain, and Delores Dillard for the frequent computer help and in general for their infinite patience.

For their friendship and encouragement I want to thank the late Paul and Sheila Wellstone, Aryeh Neier, Jane Olson, Adolfo Aguilar Zinser, Martha Ketchum, Miriam Morales, the late Cecilia Salinas, Margarita and Tom Melville, Stan and Iris Ovshinsky, David and Judy Bonior, Diane Nelson, and for their special enthusiasm, Herb and Marion Sandler.

The "pizzeros"—the Wednesday Berkeley pizza group—is a wonderful and supportive group of colleagues who have kept the weekly pizza tradition alive for many years. Perhaps because we come from different departments and backgrounds but with a common vision made the weekly experience so much fun and never to be missed. The fact that I may have emerged as the best organized—yet the only Latin American in the group—says a lot about the rest of them! The huge Berkeley campus became a small community as we met in each others' homes once a week, with the occasional international visitor.

I want to acknowledge and thank the John D. and Catherine T. MacArthur Foundation for their generous research and writing grant that allowed me to take a year off to prepare the manuscript.

I have great admiration for Rob Borofsky, the visionary editor of the new series in public anthropology at the University of California Press, and I appreciate the fine work of the professional staff at the Press, in particular Jacqueline Volin and Sierra Filucci. Matt Stevens did a superb job copyediting. I have great respect for Naomi Schneider, who saw this book from the first draft through its completion. I am deeply grateful to her for her enthusiastic support.

In Guatemala two people deserve a very special mention of gratitude. First and foremost is Father Luis Gurriarán. I am infinitely grateful for his thirty years of friendship, support, and encouragement. He was always available, always ready to provide an invaluable perspective and deep insights about Santa María Tzejá. Vivian Rivera de Jerez was an exceptional research assistant. Vivian is a hard working, extraordinarily efficient and savvy woman who went way beyond the call of duty. Her skillful and dedicated assistance was crucial in completing this book. I also need to acknowledge her husband, Salvador Jerez, for his help, especially in finding out last-minute details in the village.

I treasured Myrna Mack's close personal friendship and special hospitality. She made her home my home in Guatemala. Myrna helped me understand Guatemala like no one else. The military's cowardly murder of her will pain me forever. Her memory is everlasting. How I wish Myrna could read and comment on this book.

Finally, I want to thank my husband, Harley Shaiken, and my daughter, Mariela Shaiken-Manz. Mariela, while often concerned about my safety when I was away in Guatemala, was always cheerfully supportive and continues to be my champion. Harley has stood by me for thirty years since we first met in the highlands of Guatemala. His support and trust in my judgment never wavered even during traumatic incidents, and he backed my trips even when Marielita was still in diapers. This is what a compañero is all about—he doesn't just provide support, he is totally encouraging. He has followed my involvement with this village since 1973, all the way through the completion of the book. This book truly would not exist without him.

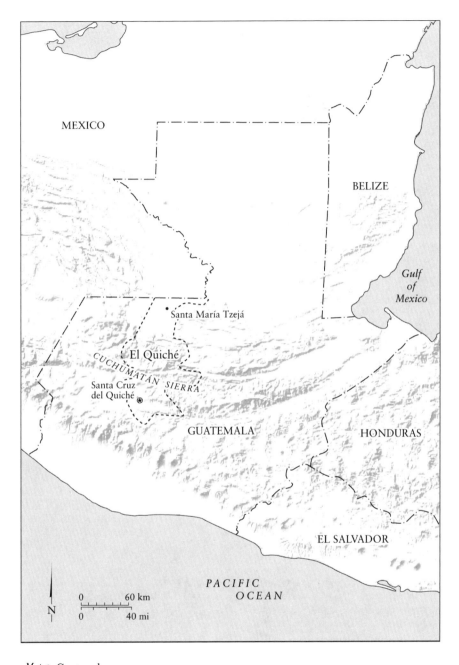

MEXICO

BELIZE

Gulf
of
Mexico

• Santa María Tzejá

El Quiché

CUCHUMATÁN SIERRA

Santa Cruz
del Quiché ⊗

GUATEMALA

HONDURAS

EL SALVADOR

PACIFIC
OCEAN

N

| 0 | 60 km |
| 0 | 40 mi |

Map 1. Guatemala

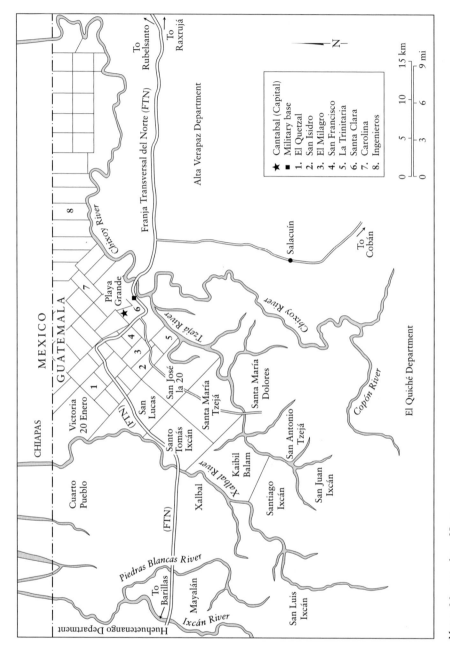

Map 2. Municipality of Ixcán

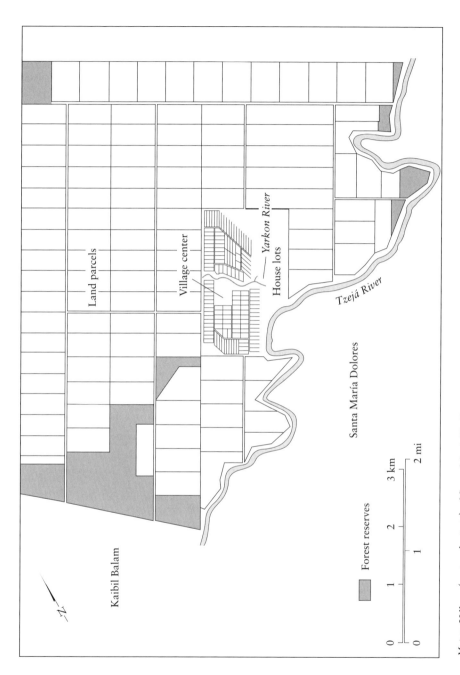

Map 3. Village (or *parcelamiento*) of Santa María Tzejá

Introduction

Near the Mexican border a serpentine path meanders through the dense, verdant rain forest of northern Guatemala, skirting tall mahogany trees and brown hanging vines, traversing the undulating terrain toward the remote village of Santa María Tzejá. Landless Mayan peasants from the highlands made the difficult weeklong, 150-mile journey to settle the village in 1970, building a new life with little more than sweat, hope, and a few antiquated hand tools. Twelve years later, on February 13, 1982, a long column of soldiers traveled that twisted path weighed down with combat gear in the languid heat. Their feet sank in thick mud. The late-afternoon sunlight reflected off their automatic weapons. As they proceeded, hidden sentries from the village watched them approach with deep apprehension.

Already the villagers knew the army had slaughtered all the inhabitants of a nearby settlement two days earlier. So when the sentries gave prearranged signals, the villagers grabbed their children and fled into the sanctuary of the thick rain forest. When the first soldiers entered the village, they found fires burning, food still cooking, and wash laid out by the river. But the villagers had vanished, and only the noise of the troops themselves and the sounds of the rain forest broke the eerie silence. Since the targets of their march had eluded them, the soldiers turned on what remained. Over the next several days, they destroyed what had taken a decade to build. They looted anything of value, slaughtered animals, and torched everything else. Hiding in the rain forest, the villagers—about a hundred families—could hear the staccato bursts of gunfire and see the flames consuming their dreams. During their incursion, the soldiers stumbled across a lone woman, whom they raped, beat senseless, and murdered, dumping her battered body near the village cooperative. When nothing more remained to destroy, the troops packed up and began heading south to the next village. Marching down the path into the rain forest, one of the soldiers heard a dog bark. The troops stopped to explore more closely. They found a cowering pregnant woman cradling an infant and two young boys left in her care, all hiding by the side of the trail. The soldiers yelled at the woman and unleashed a withering volley of gunfire at the small group, killing them all. As they left, a soldier lobbed a hand grenade at the bodies to complete the slaughter. Now on full alert, the troops quickly located a second group. They confronted eight children, their pregnant mother, and their grandmother. The soldiers for a second time began firing mercilessly.

Amid the screaming, the smoke, and the gunfire, several of the children ran deeper into the forest, including a six-year-old boy followed by his older sister. When he reached the safety of a fallen tree he discovered in horror that his sister was no longer behind him. His mother, grandmother, and siblings were sprawled on the ground in a rough circle, disfigured and silent. Many years later he recalled what he saw.[1] "My grandmother had a bullet under her eye, my brother was laying there— the one who had said that he would rather die than be caught by the army." He quietly continued, "My sister, the one who ran behind me when the army began shooting, had a hole in her back. Now I think, maybe she blocked me, because I was in front of her and she was following me. And I turned right at that moment. When I looked back she wasn't there. I think that she gave her life for mine." The soldiers had done more than empty their weapons; they were determined to desecrate as well as murder. "My little sister had her stomach slit open; another sister had no head." He had seen the soldiers search the clothing of their victims for valuables, finding nothing but a few sweets. They took the candy and left the bodies.

The other villagers hiding in the rain forest knew that the army intended to kill everyone. Terrified, they hid among the mahogany trees and the vines for weeks, and then the weeks turned into months. They had no notion of what would become of them. After several months of constant fear, more than half the families made a harrowing forty-mile journey to Mexico, where they would stay for more than a decade. A year after the flight, the army placed those who had remained behind— about fifty families—under harsh military control, literally on the ashes of the original village. To fill out the new village's population, the army brought in a new group of land-starved peasants from the highlands, mainly from the Alta Verapaz region.

This should have been the end of the story, an all-too-familiar Guatemalan tale of displacement and death, another village reduced to blood-soaked ashes. Instead, the survivors refused to give up. They struggled for more than a decade against the longest of odds, the most daunting of obstacles, and ultimately those who stayed behind and those who fled were reunited. Together, they would not only rebuild but prevail. Symbolic of their success, more than one hundred of the community's youth were pursuing professional training and degrees outside the village as of 2002. Nonetheless, appalling human rights violations still plague the country and threaten the village. A 2002 Amnesty International report finds that in the "prevailing climate of impunity," the violations are "so severe" that Guatemala can only be referred to as undergoing a "human rights melt-down."[2] The village is still in the eye of the storm.

This book is the story of Santa María Tzejá. It chronicles the exceptional moments of its birth, destruction, and rebirth over three decades. Santa María Tzejá is not a typical village—if there is a "typical" village in Guatemala—but rather a place whose history embodies the forces and conflicts defining contemporary Guatemala. "It is in remote villages such as Santa María Tzejá," reporter Andrew Bounds observed in the *Financial Times of London,* "that the battle for Guatemala's future is being fought.... [T]he story of Santa María Tzejá speaks eloquently about the country's troubled recent history."[3] The highland peasants who founded the village had been squeezed mercilessly by their lack of land and, given the repressive social structure of the country, had few political or economic options. As a result, they embarked in 1970 on what seemed a desperate, if not foolhardy, attempt to colonize a distant, inaccessible rain forest. Paradoxically, the isolated site they chose became one of the centers of the war that would convulse the entire country in the 1980s. As it turned out, Santa María Tzejá became the first village visited by a small band of men that would grow into the largest of Guatemala's insurgent organizations, the Ejército Guerrillero de los Pobres (EGP), the Guerrilla Army of the Poor.

The sacking of the village in 1982 was part of a larger nightmare inflicted upon Guatemala. The report of the United Nations–sponsored Comisión para el Esclarecimiento Histórico (Commission for Historical Clarification, or CEH), hereafter referred to as the CEH (U.N.) report, concluded that two hundred thousand people were killed or disappeared during the Guatemalan civil war, 93 percent at the hands of state forces and related paramilitary groups.[4] More than six hundred massacres took place, more than half of them in El Quiché province, and during the most intense period of the military onslaught, from 1981 to 1983, as many as 1.5 million people, out of Guatemala's 8 million, were displaced internally or had to flee the country.[5] The displacement included about 150,000 who sought refuge in Mexico.[6] "The massacres, scorched earth operations, forced disappearances and executions of Mayan authorities, leaders and spiritual guides," the CEH forcefully charged, "were not only an attempt to destroy the social base of the guerrillas, but above all, to destroy the cultural values that ensured cohesion and collective action in Mayan communities."[7] The savagery "exceeds the toll in El Salvador, Nicaragua, Chile, and Argentina combined," Stephen Kinzer, the former *New York Times* correspondent in Guatemala, wrote in the *New York Review of Books*. "Ethnic cleansing was practiced on a scale beyond even that of Bosnia." For decades Guatemalans, especially Mayas, had endured living "under a ghastly form of state terrorism."[8]

Fieldwork under fire

I first went to Santa María Tzejá in the summer of 1973.[9] I was a graduate student studying anthropology in the United States. My research that summer was in the El Quiché highlands, centered in the outlying areas of Santa Cruz del Quiché, a place that seemed very far from the rural Chile where I had grown up. Fabián Pérez, a Maya K'iche' man in his early thirties whom I met early on, suggested I visit a new settlement of highland Mayan peasants in a distant area near the Mexican-Lacandón border.[10] I had heard about this region and was interested in the dynamics pushing Mayas to leave the highlands. A lack of land had pressured these peasants first into seasonal work on the coastal plantations and then to colonize the rain forest—a place where land was available because the region was so remote and inhospitable. The first families had come to the Ixcán, as the area is known, three years earlier, in 1970.

I arrived in the village with Fabián Pérez and Luis Gurriarán, a Catholic priest born in Spain, while it was still being established in that summer of 1973. I remember sweltering in the jungle heat, the endless mosquito bites, and being startled by the cries of strange birds and the sight of even stranger snakes. But most of all I remember the spirit and kindness of these Mayan pioneers. After little more than a day I felt I wanted to be connected to this village for years to come. In so many ways, the setting and the people were different from Chile, yet I heard young K'iche' men, the leaders of the settlement project, singing songs by Víctor Jara—the most popular of Chile's singers of the *nueva canción,* or new song—and by Chile's Quilapayún, a folk group in the same tradition. Up to that point everything that I had read or heard in lectures about the K'iche' Mayas had portrayed them as locally centered and apolitical. When I later mentioned to my professor that many K'iche' youth were interested in not only political issues but also international politics, he dismissed my observation as interpreting rural indigenous Guatemala from a Chilean perspective.

The fact that much scholarship in the 1970s and early 1980s missed the growing mobilization and discontent among the Mayas raises a challenge to the narrowness of perspective among many scholars. In contrast to what I had been taught in some graduate courses, I noticed that the peasants were interested in me precisely because I was Chilean; it was 1973, and they were surprisingly aware of the social mobilization and conflict taking place in my country. In the Ixcán rain forest that summer I suspected that a guerrilla movement might be quietly active. Several years later I read the autobiography of Mario Payeras, a guerrilla leader, who related his experience in the Ixcán and recalled hearing the news of Chile's coup d'état in September 1973. It was only then that I realized I had been right.

After that first visit to the village, my inclination was to move to Santa María Tzejá and become a teacher in the one-room schoolhouse that had just been built. I had decided to study anthropology because I thought it was a noble profession, and I envisioned my role as a passionate advocate for marginalized people. I was full of idealism and felt Santa María Tzejá and I were a good match. It was clear from the moment I arrived that the villagers were committed and optimistic about improving their lives. Poverty accompanied by a defeatist perspective would have been unattractive—particularly when the snakes and the mud were factored in— but poverty and neglect coupled with a community eager to move forward seemed just right for me. I thought I might be able to make a difference.

The coup d'état in Chile that September was a sad and disorienting personal blow that distracted me from Guatemala and Santa María Tzejá. When I returned to visit the highlands in late 1975 and early 1976, I was told by a somber Fabián that things had changed drastically since my first visit. A death squad had murdered a dedicated young woman, who had moved to the village to become a teacher, when she was on a visit to Guatemala City; threats from the army had forced Father Luis to leave the village; and soldiers had kidnapped a villager, who never returned.

These tragic events turned out to be only the beginning. By 1976—

in retrospect it seemed almost overnight—my own idealism and optimism had begun to wane. General Pinochet was still in power in Chile, but the repression in Guatemala and the Ixcán in particular was soon to dwarf what took place in my own country. Understandably, the world had become aware and outraged by the human rights abuses in Chile—a country with a long tradition of democratic governments—but no one seemed to care or even notice the escalating repression in Guatemala. It was difficult to explain why the world was moved by one but not the other, especially since the atrocities in Guatemala far exceeded even the horrific human rights violations endured in Chile. In Guatemala, the long, dark night into which the country was descending had only begun—the worst was yet to come. The unimaginable was about to become real.

Observation over Time

Three decades after I first stepped into that clearing in the Ixcán rain forest, I have decided to write a book about the journey of Santa María Tzejá's peasants and the fate of the village. My hope was to capture the spirit of what took place in the village by documenting discussions, arguments, interviews, observations, laughter, and tears. The ethnographic method allowed me the closeness to understand what took place, and time has provided the distance to put it into perspective. I was a participant in and observer of truly remarkable events. My participation grew out of a deep admiration and affection for the village and a commitment to its future. As an observer, I felt an equally deep commitment to providing perspective and, when necessary, to not flinching from the unpleasant either in my interactions with the villagers or in my writing about them. For me it was never really a question of following the role of many traditional anthropologists: distant, dispassionate, inattentive to national or world politics, ostensibly neutral and apolitical. My position might have had a lot to do with the mix of my own personal background and the social violence of Guatemala—exclusion, repression, discrimination, and poverty.

"The idea of an active, politically committed, morally engaged anthropology strikes many anthropologists as unsavory, tainted, even frightening," anthropologist Nancy Scheper-Hughes has noted. "This is less so in parts of Latin America, India, and Europe (Italy and France, for example), where the anthropological project is at once ethnographic, epistemological, and political and where anthropologists do communicate broadly with 'the polis' and 'the public.' "[11] It is also a recognition that being a witness at times demands action, and that failing to witness in these situations is amoral or perhaps immoral. The communities where we immerse ourselves are generally far less able than we ourselves are to expose human rights violations, abuses of power, and repression. The choice is really not between ethnography and activism. Certain circumstances call for an ethnography that is aware of the broader social conditions in which ethnographer and subject find themselves. The research and writing of this book could not have happened without a combination of scholarship and political engagement.[12]

Over time most ethnographers conducting research in Guatemala joined an organization called the Guatemala Scholars Network (GSN), founded in 1982 and still active today, with more than three hundred members from many disciplines and professions.[13] Many scholars in the United States who study Guatemala have been active, concerned, and committed on human rights issues for more than two decades. During the period of the worst carnage, GSN members drafted resolutions at the Latin American Studies Association, the American Anthropological Association, and other professional groups. The GSN organized teach-ins, sponsored visits by victims of human rights abuses, and was instrumental in informing the U.S. Congress and the press about these atrocities. Above all it has been a supportive, convivial association that has kept us in close touch with one another over the years.

Many people—both within and outside academia—have been more fascinated with the ancient Mayan civilization than with the living Mayas. Some archaeologists conducting research in Guatemala at the height of the terror seemed oblivious to what was happening around them. In 1984 archaeologists discovered a well-preserved tomb in northern Guatemala dating back fifteen hundred years. It garnered prominent coverage in the major newspapers in the United States. The *New York Times* ran a front-page article entitled "Untouched Mayan Tomb Is Discovered," which reported on the find and included a photograph and an artist's representation of the tomb.[14] The article related that Guatemalan guards were protecting the extraordinary and valuable site with rifles and machetes. I sent a letter to the *Times* the following day that was published under the title "Mayas Celebrated and Mayas Persecuted."[15] I wrote that "the impression is given that these brilliant pre-Hispanic people left only a fossilized heritage" and questioned, "How will the four million Mayas in Guatemala receive the news?" I wanted to provide a sense of the conditions in which contemporary Mayas find themselves. "Too many are grieving over fresh tombs of kinsmen recently killed. Tens of thousands hiding in the mountains and jungles will not hear of the discovery for some time." I found it ironic that the same army that was littering the countryside with fresh bones was treating ancient bones with such respect and concern.[16]

Even though the record of many ethnographers in Guatemala is laudable, some ethnographers and archaeologists during the late 1970s and 1980s conducted their studies with blinders on. Others selected research sites in new and distant countries. Tracy Ehlers examined seven major anthropological journals in the 1980s and discovered far fewer articles than there once were on Guatemala overall. Those that were published tended to be on ethnohistory or sociolinguistics. "Research published in the 1980s has been emphatically non-policy-based, even though fieldwork was conducted in the midst of crisis," Ehlers observed, inferring that "the reticence of anthropology as a discipline to legitimate policy-based research in Central America stems from a tendency that has characterized the field since its beginnings: studying communities as isolated, timeless cultures that are unaffected by regional, national, and international events taking place outside their borders."[17] The dearth of research and publications in the main journals about the crisis in Guatemala (and Central America more generally) during that period gave the misleading impression that nothing unusual was happening, when in fact a genocide was in progress. One of the more important breakthroughs during this period was the 1988 publication of *Harvest of Violence: The Maya Indians and the Guatemalan Crisis,* edited by Robert M. Carmack, which sought to disclose and grapple with the violence that was taking place.

The absence of publications is one thing, the other is that some failed to see the maelstrom approaching or chose to ignore it.[18] "Many of us who have worked in Guatemala are disturbed about what has come to be called 'the situation,'" Benjamin Colby stated in a review of Barbara Tedlock's 1982 book *Time and the Highland Maya.* "I was disappointed that not even in the history section which talked about rebels of the previous century was there a single mention of what is happening in Guatemala today, where thousands of Indians have been brutally killed by a repressive government in what is now a holocaust. One would hope that all contemporary scholarly contributions on Guatemala, even if only in a footnote, would make reference to this state of affairs."[19] Colby's review in 1988 of another book by Tedlock mentions sympathetically the difficulties of doing research in Guatemala in those years, and that many ethnographers had chosen to take their research to other countries. "[Tedlock] does not give the reason for closing her research on the

Quiché," Colby notes, "but presumably it is that the countryside in Guatemala now has been militarized with troops, government torture, and death squad activity. To do any extended, sensitive fieldwork in those areas of Guatemala today is to risk the lives of one's informants, not to mention other problems of data collection among people who are filled with fear and suspicion."[20]

If some anthropologists ignored the larger forces that were convulsing Guatemala in the 1980s, a controversial contemporary account by David Stoll, *Rigoberta Menchú and the Story of All Poor Guatemalans*, superimposed a distorted and misleading framework on the conflict. What garnered the lion's share of attention for Stoll's book after it was released in late 1998 were the real and imagined discrepancies he found in the widely read oral history *I, Rigoberta Menchú*, the testimony of a young K'iche' woman in the early 1980s, edited by Elisabeth Burgos-Debray. Menchú's story became particularly important when she was awarded the Nobel Peace Prize in 1992. Typical of the media attention accompanying the release of Stoll's book, the *New York Times* ran a front-page story entitled, "Nobel Prize Winner Accused of Stretching Truth." Stoll himself admitted that the inaccuracies he unearthed in Menchú's account are "not a very serious problem." The central issue for him was the fact that "Rigoberta's account is seriously misleading...in its depiction of the social background of the killing [in Guatemala]."[21] For Stoll, the insurgency was neither the "inevitable response to centuries of oppression" nor "a 'last resort' for peasants with their backs to the wall."[22] In fact, he pointed out that "many Mayas felt they were making modest political and economic gains through the Catholic Church and other institutions in the 1970s." The alternative framework he laid out was essentially an apolitical peasantry trapped between a vicious army and a cruel, manipulative guerrilla force all too willing to sacrifice the innocent. Although Stoll recognized the brutality of the army, he nonetheless observed that "in the absence of an identifiable enemy, counterinsurgents tend to retaliate against nearby civilians," in effect arguing that the guerrillas provoked the violence.[23] The context is far more complex.

Stoll's argument is flawed in two important ways. First, he underestimates the ways in which memory may change over time and the reasons why peasants may not trust a stranger. He points out that "the bulk of [his] interviewing occurred between 1993 and 1995,"[24] a decade after the worst violence and when the guerrilla insurgency was near collapse. He conflates the views of the peasants in the mid-1990s with how they may have felt when the rebellion appeared to be growing in the early

1980s. He does admit that "oral testimony from a repressed town like Uspantán could be affected by fear of the army or distrust of the interviewer. That is why I checked what Uspantanos told me against other sources."[25] Evidently, these sources did not include the Central Intelligence Agency (CIA), the U.S. State Department, or the Guatemalan army itself. These institutions had no difficulty understanding the extent of support for the EGP in El Quiché department. (In Guatemala, provinces are known as "departments.") Consider one challenge to Stoll's thesis on the causes of the insurgency. "What [the Ixiles] do understand is that they are poor and that they are so because they live miserably, their work tasks are exhausting and the exhausted land yields little," one well-informed observer commented. The guerrillas were "successful from the very beginning offering the Guatemalan Indians a hope for dignity, something they had not been offered during more than 400 years of humiliation and misery."[26] Who is this critical observer? A naive solidarity activist confusing political orientation with scholarship, a perspective Stoll skewers in his book? In fact, the author, Captain Juan Fernando Cifuentes, was a Guatemalan military officer who wrote a seventy-two-page document published by the military academy in late 1982 to explain why the guerrillas were tapping into such widespread support.

Second, Stoll recounts the conflict in Guatemala with an underlying cold war sensibility. Consequently, there are few comments about the U.S. role in propping up a genocidal military, but considerable commentary about a ruthless left and their manipulative or misguided international allies. Clearly, the insurgents could be manipulative, misguided, and, on occasion, they committed egregious abuses, but that does not mean that the peasants were simply trapped between two equally malevolent forces, or that they could not be agents in determining their own political alternatives. At the heart of this thesis is a yawning logical inconsistency: If the peasantry were caught between two armies, why didn't they simply turn for protection to the far stronger one? Ultimately, Stoll's account becomes a prisoner of his ideology. Consider his comment about the award of the Nobel Peace Prize to Menchú: "Romantic views of the guerrillas are not hard to find in [the solidarity network] milieu, nor the mystique of the noble oppressed Indian. Such assumptions are rarely contradicted by the Scandinavian media, which in Central America rely on young, idealistic freelancers rather than more experienced, cynical correspondents. The resulting haze has allowed European social democrats who fought tooth and nail to shut down revolutionary Marxists in their own countries, to be smitten by revolutionary Marxists from Latin America."[27] The issue is not romanticism or naive freelancers or smitten Scandinavians but rather seeking to understand the complexities, contradictions, and roots of an unusually destructive armed confrontation.[28] Moreover, understanding that the guerrillas had a strong network of support—as Captain Cifuentes discovered—hardly means that one supports the insurgents.

Debates have raged for many years over the role of international anthropologists, mainly those from the United States. The issue in my mind, however, is not so much between international and native researchers, but rather what research is undertaken, and what relation researchers have with the community. Orin Starn has observed that anthropologists missed the deep dissatisfactions in Peru because of academic distractions and the distance between modern Peru and the U.S. academy.[29] Researchers who promote academic disengagement in the field should consider that geographic distance and sociopolitical detachment, ironically, can create their own set of distortions.

Víctor Montejo, a Guatemalan Mayan anthropologist, has observed that non-Mayan anthropologists often go to the field with limited, self-interested reasons. "Foreign anthropologists have studied Mayan culture for one purpose: to write dissertations and to get good-paying jobs at prestigious universities. But let us not forget that, as in the case of the Ladinos, some foreign anthropologists ... have worked for human rights issues also, and have produced books denouncing the genocide suffered by indigenous people (Manz 1988a; Falla 1994)."[30] Mayan scholars have been intensively debating the role of foreign anthropologists for some time, particularly since the unleashing of the war against Mayan communities. "Pan-Mayanists see social science as profoundly political by definition," Kay Warren writes, "and consequently doubt the motives and intentions of foreign researchers who act as if their verbal support for indigenous issues should be accepted at face value." She adds, "What Mayas see so clearly is that linguistics and anthropology are not neutral sciences or nonpolitical ways of knowing."[31] Mayas have argued that "foreign anthropologists evade their accountability to the people they study," noting that it is not acceptable to hide "behind their academic status." Outside researchers should understand that not opposing certain actions gives the appearance of approving of them.[32]

One challenge faced by all anthropologists is documenting violence and atrocities, above all how to protect the individuals and communities. An engaged ethnographer should report about human rights violations in a tone that will allow events as much as possible to inform the reader—a detachment often difficult to undertake, in which I at times don't follow my own advice. "It is more effective to bear witness with restraint rather than with scorn," Primo Levi advised. "The scorn should be the reader's, not the author's, and it is by no means inevitable that an author's scorn will become the reader's."[33]

Guatemala, like most countries intensely studied by ethnographers and archaeologists, has few anthropologists of its own. In the 1980s two outstanding Guatemalans, Myna Mack and Ricardo Falla, made exceptional contributions. They broke the mold confining many traditional anthropologists to a narrower vision that ignored the larger forces shaping community life. Ricardo Falla worked for years painstakingly documenting violence against Mayan communities. As a result, he was forced to do his field research in hiding, with displaced families in the rain forest under the most grueling conditions, with the communities of population in resistance (CPR), or in the refugee camps in Mexico. Tragically Myrna Mack paid with her life for her broader vision. As she left her office in the early evening on Tuesday, September 11, 1990—just blocks from the presidential palace—she was stabbed twenty-seven times by a former sergeant in the Presidential High Command.[34]

Myrna Mack accompanied me on her first, and what was to be her only, field trip to the Ixcán in May 1987. In Santa María Tzejá, despite the exhaustion from the unbearable heat, humidity, rain, and mud, she conducted interviews late into the night with candlelight. After these exhausting days, we would sit under the open sky, tired but unable to sleep, and talk through the day's events—the gossip, the hopes, the dangers, and the possibilities. As we gazed toward the sky, no stars were visible on these hot humid nights; we were enveloped in smoke as forest and fields were aflame, a slash-and-burn agriculture practice in preparation for cultivation. At that time the village was militarized. Palm-thatched homes with stick walls were crammed next to each other in one small area for tighter military control. The poverty was extreme. Mack's field notes were filled with careful documentation and astute observations, displaying a sharp understanding of people and context, a sense of humor and a passion. I wrote in the preface to Ricardo Falla's *Massacres in the Jungle* that while few in Guatemala knew what an anthropologist was, Myrna Mack was always referred to as "la antropóloga Myrna Mack" following her murder in 1990. Now in the most remote areas of the country, as a result of Myrna's death, "anthropology has become an honored, widely known, and admired profession. It has become synonymous with courage, social consciousness, and first-rate scholarship."[35]

Myrna Mack had a love-hate relationship with the profession. She loved the research that brought her so close to the people, but she resented the foreign anthropologists who chose Guatemala for their research and cared little about Guatemalans, "sponging" everything they could with indifference and failing to do anything to help those exposed to injustice and violence. "What is the difference between an American and a Guatemalan anthropologist?" Myrna used to ask friends jokingly. "In America you publish or perish; in Guatemala you perish if you publish!" She could not have imagined how correct she was in her assessment of her country and her work.

In looking over Mack's field notes of our trip to Santa María Tzejá, I find little sense of cynicism or personal political bias. She carefully recorded her impressions, and in interview after interview she copiously wrote what she was told and what she observed: the community organizations, the number of churches, the ethnic groups, the land disputes. Her careful analysis reflected what she was hearing; of one woman she wrote: "La señora did not explicitly recognize who had burned the village and her belongings. In some way, implicitly she blamed the guerrillas. She speaks with disdain of the '*envueltos*.'"[36] She goes on to describe physically the woman and her daughters (Ladinas). Myrna Mack was there to conduct probing interviews, record what she was hearing, and gain a sense of the living conditions and perspectives of the people. She was not there to confirm her own preconceived notions or personal viewpoints. In her opinion, the latter would have been pointless. At times doubt crept into her letters. In one, she wrote to a friend, "What troubles me is that all I do is talk to people. I draw out their sad histories, and that's it. I feel my role reduced to one of extraction." In another, "I still wonder how to give something worthwhile back to the communities.... Can there ever be any hope for them?" She would listen attentively and with compassion. "It makes me realize," she wrote, "that no matter what side you're on in all this, people, especially the people in this region, have an overwhelming need to speak, to tell about their lives, to confide in a sympathetic listener." Dismayed by the suffering, she never questioned the value of her fieldwork, "It was an exciting trip from the point of view of the research, but at the same time you find yourself inundated with sadness at the misery that abounds everywhere. Add to that the impotence of not being able to do anything. We witnessed a tragic case in one village." She ended her letter on an ambivalent note, "You are right; those forays into the interior are a source of strength for me. I feel close to the people there, and those moments make me forget other hurtful things in my life. I have seen new places where beauty and sorrow are intertwined, where there is a silent struggle to rise above pain and despair, to not surrender. But the minuscule changes occur at such a 'low intensity' rate, while the social costs are inordinately high."[37]

I shared Myrna Mack's sense of the way "beauty and sorrow are intertwined." Such was the case in my own research in Santa María Tzejá, surely "fieldwork under fire."[38] I conducted research for years during violent and stressful periods, highlighting the important issue of methodology. Participation and observation took place over an extended period of time and required critical trust, or *confianza*.[39] I was aware of my "*compromiso*" (commitment) and never felt this commitment to a better life for the villagers would interfere with my ability to carry out research. My concerns about the well-being and future of the villagers and my relationships with them hardly handicapped my fieldwork. On the contrary, my concerns contributed to the ease in our interactions and laid the basis for the mutual trust that developed. I assumed that the villagers would discuss my role among themselves and then decide whether to speak with me, while considering the advantages or disadvantages of doing so. They assessed me by checking me out and testing me—not all that different from what an employer does when consulting references. I gave them the time to determine if it was worth their while to include me and to what extent. As with any group, there were differences in perspective: some trusted me from the beginning, others maintained reservations; some liked me, others did not. I too got along and liked some villagers more than others. Though never stated, I felt they assessed my *compromiso*—assessing it by deeds, not words.

I tried to be attentive to their expectations and cognizant of my role. I recognized that placing myself amid a highly charged and violent situation would of necessity involve me in some unexpected, and undesired, ways. Although my fieldwork experience was rewarding, ultimately I was aware of the "inherent moral asymmetry of the fieldwork situation."[40] Nonetheless, I developed long-lasting personal relationships. I never viewed the villagers as exotic but rather as normal human beings—with all their strengths and weaknesses—and that made my research easier and less obscure. The most rewarding aspects of my interaction were those moments—increasingly more frequent—when I was able to have extensive conversations with individuals and, at times, with groups, that reflected deeply on their experiences. Their analytical abilities under conditions of stress were impressive; they saw the positive dimensions of an experience, as well as the negative, and developed carefully nuanced observations. Contradictions or changes in their individual and collective memories were themselves profoundly meaningful. My constant (and no doubt annoying) role as the devil's advocate was soon understood by the most astute as an interest in his or her point of view no matter how inconsistent or contradictory.

Over the years the village's geographical isolation has diminished, considerably influencing perspectives and outlooks. During the initial settlement of the village in 1970, peasants undertook a grueling week-long hike from their old home in the highlands. Later on, when a dirt road was built in the region in the late 1970s, the journey took two or three days by a combination of vehicle and a tough hike through muddy paths. Today the village itself has a dirt road, and under normal circumstances one can arrive there from Guatemala City in one day.[41] The earlier isolation kept the villagers from easily moving and limited their exposure to a wider world. Today half of the villagers have been to Mexico, likely to Cancun and other major Yucatecan cities, by virtue of having been refugees. Young women wear shorts, and dozens of young villagers have made it to the United States. Those who have not migrated north have seen photos and videos and have heard from family members about life and work in California and other states. They talk on the phone, send remittances, and use extensive social networks that are always expanding.[42] Some have been to my home in Berkeley. This transnational experience creates a new reality for the practice of contemporary anthropology. "One of the major assumptions upon which anthropological writing rested until only yesterday," Geertz writes, is "that its subjects and its audience were not only separable but morally disconnected, that the first were to be described but not addressed, the second informed but not implicated, has fairly well dissolved. The world has its compartments still, but the passages between them are much more numerous and much less well secured."[43] The cultural and geographic distance has dwindled. Distant individuals previously described by professionals now reside in translocal communities in the United States and can speak for themselves. With migrations come rising expectations and, at times, crashing disillusionment. Dreams are seldom realized in the short term. Paradoxically, while encounters are more frequent, the technological and economic distance is far deeper. The Internet links some in seconds, while others lack electricity, computers, and schools.

Context: The Land Question and Poverty

The story of Santa María Tzejá unfolds in the context of contemporary Guatemala, a country in which social statistics tend to range between appalling and more disastrous. "Poverty has been a constant in Guatemalan society," the CEH (U.N.) report states, "caused by the unequal distribution of economic wealth, in particular of land, and due to the limited access to education."[44] The best land is dominated by export-oriented plantations. Three percent of the landholdings—large export-oriented plantations called *fincas*—control 65 percent of the agricultural surface, while close to 90 percent of the landholdings are too small for peasant subsistence.[45] Moreover, almost 420,000 people over twenty years of age—about one-third of the economically active population at the time—were without any land at all by 1980 according to the U.S. Agency for International Development (USAID).[46] Thus highland peasants had to work under grueling conditions on hot, humid Pacific coast plantations. The Catholic Church addressed the dismal agrarian situation in a 1988 edict, *The Clamor for Land*. "The clamor for land," the document reflects, "is without a doubt, the loudest, most dramatic, and most desperate cry heard in Guatemala today. It springs from the hearts of millions of Guatemalans who not only are anxious to possess land, but who also want to be possessed by the land." The landless are affected not only economically but also culturally, since their identity is tied to the "furrows, the sowing and the harvests."[47] This document refers to an "inhumane poverty" and a "Calvary of suffering," viewing "the lack of land at the heart of all our national social problems."[48]

A Guatemalan government report on poverty, *El Drama de la Pobreza en Guatemala* (2001; The Drama of Poverty in Guatemala), presents a grim vision of deteriorating economic conditions for most Guatemalans, particularly rural Mayas. The report portrays the vast majority of people as excluded from basic constitutional guarantees, stating explicitly that "they are less citizens because they are poor."[49] Out of a national population of eleven million, six million live in poverty (2.8 million of these in extreme poverty), according to the Guatemalan government.[50] Sixty percent of the population lives on less than one dollar per day and rural Mayas "suffer disproportionately, with nearly three-quarters of them living in poverty," Stephen Kinzer reported in 2001.[51] A U.N. Development Program report notes that nearly 70 percent of the population of El Quiché province is illiterate—a province that is ethnically over 80 percent K'iche'.[52] More than 95 percent of the poor in Guatemala have not attended a single grade of secondary education, and 44 percent have never attended school at all.[53]

The Guatemalan Episcopal Conference stated bluntly: "The illiterate masses are the dramatic expression of the secular injustice that oppresses us. They are the expression of a grand failure as well as the need, always postponed, for an integral development. A society that never wagers decisively on education can never pretend to improve the quality of life of the poor majority, nor obtain peace."[54] Regarding health, Guatemalans have the least chance to live past the age of forty among people in any other country in Central America.

The settlement of forestlands may be undesirable, but for many it is the only alternative. But even this possibility is threatened as the ecological degradation becomes more severe each year. The United Nations Verification Mission in Guatemala (Misión de Verificación de las Naciones Unidas en Guatemala, MINUGUA) states, "When peasants cannot meet the basic needs through the income generated from their land parcels and the low wages received from seasonal employment, they overuse the natural resources, exceeding the capacity of the ecosystem. That implies, moreover, increasing their day's work and consequently a deterioration of their health."[55] Linking economic development to democracy, the government report concludes that "people living in poverty have no commitment to democracy because they see that it does not give them the resources they need to develop as human beings. Without human development there is no full-fledged citizenry and therefore no democracy. In the long term, this situation can make the country ungovernable. Without fear of exaggeration, it is the most serious problem facing Guatemalan society."[56]

Government unresponsiveness and elite intransigence fostered economic erosion. The poor lose irrespective of the state of the national economy or international markets. Between 1960 and 1980, when the economy expanded, Guatemala still showed the lowest social investment and the lowest taxation rate of any Central American country. Not even the surge in coffee markets between 1975 and 1977, along with a 400 percent increase in prices, prompted a change in either social spending or the taxation rate.

The military, no longer content with solely protecting the economic and social advantages of the elite, created a panoply of institutions to safeguard their own interests in the 1970s. One of these was the *Banco del Ejército* (Bank of the Army). With this bank, officers soon helped themselves to large landholdings in Alta Verapaz and El Petén, east of

Santa María Tzejá. These purchases coincided with a project by the USAID to construct a dirt road through what had been an inaccessible area.[57] Even earlier, the rapid growth of the fast-food industry in the United States starting in the 1960s provided large and growing U.S. meat markets. The lands bought by generals quickly became expansive grazing estates for large herds of cattle, and lumber extraction became another quick source of revenue. At this time, foreign oil companies were also successfully extracting oil.

Peasant organizations, trade unions, student groups, and others throughout the country were outraged by military corruption, business sector greed, low tax revenues, and repression. The bribe and the gun seemed to rule jointly. Guatemala had shown its political resolve almost three decades earlier in the wake of the 1944 October revolution, which brought to power the democratically elected government of Juan José Arévalo, followed by the election of Jacobo Arbenz and further political and economic reforms. The overthrow of Arbenz in 1954 as well as the escalating repression of the 1960s severely constricted the process of democratization. However, the decade of the 1970s saw an upsurge of political activity and optimism. In Guatemala City, students, teachers, and workers mobilized, displaying a political resolve and optimism that change was possible. Instead, the murders of peasant, labor, political, and student leaders accelerated in the 1970s, including the killing of two prominent and beloved political figures late in the decade—Alberto Fuentes Mohr and Manuel Colom Argueta. These selected killings had expanded into massacres in the countryside by the early 1980s. "In Guatemala, the state relinquished for many years its role as mediator between different social and economic interests," the CEH (U.N.) report states, "opening thereby a vacuum that lead to a direct confrontation between those who received the benefits, defenders of that established order, and those who were forced to claim their aspirations."[58]

The military's concept of an internal enemy—anyone who was not a fervent military supporter—was accepted by the United States, and the lines blurred between armed combatants, collaborators, sympathizers, and civic democratic participants. Paradoxically, the military assertion that "you are with us or against us" swayed many political activists to a more radical position or exile. Any opponent of the military's antidemocratic regime became a target; silence enhanced survival, but often not even silence was enough. The terror inexorably escalated.

Escalation

The 1960s and 1970s turned out to be a prologue to the mass terror that ravaged Guatemala in the early 1980s. These earlier decades, however, were also a time of profound ideological transformation starting with the radical changes within the Catholic Church throughout Latin America. The Guatemalan Catholic Church became involved in religious organizations such as Catholic Action and secular organizations such as cooperatives and peasant leagues. Religious traditions were challenged and at times uprooted. The Christian Democratic Party—initially a Catholic anticommunist option—also made tremendous inroads and in the 1960s and 1970s was the only national institution to truly have a mass base. External institutions—the U.S. Peace Corps and USAID, among others—became involved in rural development. The transistor radio revolutionized access to information in remote villages, as did fluency in Spanish. New agricultural techniques such as fertilizer and the movement of thousands of highland peasants to the Ixcán impacted the peasantry. Some Mayan communities—the youth in particular—were undergoing important changes. Instead of accepting their fate with resignation, they were becoming active interrogators of their current situation and hoped to shape their own future.

New movements in the Latin American Catholic Church—liberation theology and its preferential option for the poor—produced far-reaching changes in Mayan communities. The new church of the poor focused on addressing the degrading poverty in Mayan rural regions, the dignity of the person, and social commitment. This new approach evolved locally after the bishops' meetings in Medellín, Colombia, in 1968. Subsequently, many within the Catholic Church made a commitment to the poor and to focus on active participation and reflection. They encouraged leaders or catechists to discuss the Bible in a participatory way and to promote social activism. Foreign priests, nuns, and a vibrant network of lay church workers involved communities in new forms of social promotion. They encouraged community participation—including previously marginalized women and youth—in education, health, and communication. These activists also began to address the conflictive issues surrounding land. Agrarian reform programs had been politically out of the question since the Arbenz government's conflict with the United Fruit Company in the early 1950s and his overthrow in 1954. Instead, colonization of remote regions of the country became an alternative and then a goal for the Catholic Church and peasant colonizers. Though these lands were ill-suited for the type of agriculture practiced by peasants to-day—and moreover would become even further damaged by burgeoning population density—these untouched areas fueled the dreams of the landless. Surprisingly, the initial economic results confounded the justifiably dismal expectations of many observers. In the early 1970s, peasant cooperatives flourished throughout the Ixcán, and this success bred a new, spirited confidence that in turn fueled social transformations.

The army took notice. The generals were hostile to independent, mass-based organizing. Their fear was that the organization of students or trade unions in the city or cooperatives among peasants today could lead to more fundamental challenges tomorrow. The Catholic Church itself became a heretofore unimagined target. The first priest killed in Guatemala was a Texan named William Woods (Father Guillermo), who was involved in the Ixcán colonization. His imposing physical presence, manner, temperament, and, above all, his irreverence for the military brought him unwanted attention. (In today's parlance he would be called "a gringo with an attitude.") He is described in the Maryknoll magazine as someone whose "ideas were as big as his heart," a hazard in Guatemala.[59] The army viewed with suspicion his comings and goings; he piloted his own small plane, and they perceived his independent streak as arrogance and defiance. He died in a suspicious plane crash on November 20, 1976, at the age of forty-five. In April 2001—twenty-four years after his death—his remains were finally taken for reburial in Mayalán, Ixcán, one of the colonization sites he formed in the late 1960s. Three thousand peasants participated in the homage, one of them stating, "Now Father Guillermo is with us again. I am happy. All the people are happy."[60]

Before the death of William Woods, Father Luis, who worked nearby in Santa María Tzejá, was persecuted by the army and by the end of 1975 decided to leave the Ixcán. Catholic priests and even a bishop were targeted and killed throughout the 1970s, 1980s, and as recently as 1998. The U.N. commission collected data on a total of "1,169 victims of disappearance, torture and death of members of the church." Of those, "921 were catechists, 17 priests, 27 religious workers, 5 female religious workers and 193 parishioners."[61]

The Guatemalan Conference of Religious Orders (Conferencia de Religiosos y Religiosas de Guatemala, CONFREGUA) reported that between 1978 and 1983:

Ninety-one priests and seventy-eight nuns were forced to leave the country due to death threats. Eight places of religious training were closed, two parish buildings and two religious houses were machine gunned, thirty centers of training for catechists and Christian leaders were closed, seventy parishes were left without priests, two church-sponsored radio stations closed, eight Catholic schools were subject to investigation and police control, all meetings involving evangelization were prohibited.[62]

Juan Gerardi, the bishop of El Quiché province, closed down the diocese in 1980 as a result of the widespread murders of Catholic clergy and worshipers. As CONFREGUA states, even "going close to a chapel had the imminent danger of being labeled a communist and later assassinated."[63]

The Global Context

The local and national themes of this book are framed by the cold war. This global conflict between superpowers shaped the village in far-reaching and unexpected ways. Sixteen years before the first trees were cleared in the rain forest, the overthrow of President Arbenz—the first coup engineered by the CIA in Latin America and the second one in the world after Iran in 1953—strangled the possibility of land reform or broadbased democratic development in Guatemala.[64] The growing political realities of the cold war and the United States foreign policy toward Central America gave the Guatemalan military and economic elites complete license to rule in an increasingly authoritarian way. Anticommunism served to justify and conceal the most heinous of crimes, and the United States—except for the Carter administration—eagerly funneled millions of dollars to military regimes decade after decade, showing no concern for the brutality committed by the armed forces.[65] The battle for global, ideological hegemony had far-reaching local consequences for even the most isolated of peasants.

Throughout the thirty-five-year war, the U.S. government helped train hundreds of Guatemalan military officers in counterinsurgency techniques. Officers attended courses at the U.S. Army School of the Americas in Panama (and later, Fort Benning, Georgia), the U.S. Command and General Staff College at Fort Leavenworth, Kansas, the Inter-American Air Forces Academy, and many other U.S. military training institutions. In addition, the Pentagon sent military training teams of U.S. defense specialists to Guatemala to train their counterparts in the weapons, intelligence, interrogation, logistics, and operations skills necessary for fighting the guerrillas.

In the 1960s, the U.S. military trained the army in counterinsurgency operations, perfecting these tactics later in the decade with the experience gained in Vietnam. This training aided the army in quickly crushing a small insurgent movement sparked by dissident military officers during that decade. The campaign was so fierce and indiscriminate that it alarmed a U.S. State Department official. In a five-page secret memo addressed to the assistant secretary of state for Inter-American Affairs, the writer observed that "people are killed or disappear on the basis of simple accusations" and questioned the criteria for collaboration.[66] The memo also accused the army of brutality. "The official squads are guilty of atrocities," it states, and this disregard for the law "in effect [tells the] people that the law, the constitution, the institutions mean nothing, the fastest gun counts. The whole system has been degraded." The memo blames the United States as well:

> We *have* condoned counter-terror; we may even in effect have encouraged or blessed it. We have been so obsessed with the fear of insurgency that we have rationalized away our qualms and uneasiness....[W]e suspected that maybe it is a good tactic, and that as long as Communists are being killed it is alright. Murder, torture and mutilation are alright if our side is doing it and the victims are Communists.[67]

The memo continues, "Is it conceivable that we are so obsessed with insurgency that we are prepared to rationalize murder as an acceptable counter-insurgency weapon? Is it possible that a nation which so reveres the principle of due process of law has so easily acquiesced in this sort of terror tactic?"[68]

With the inauguration of the Reagan administration in 1981 the interventionist policy toward Central America intensified, especially in Nicaragua. In the case of Guatemala, the State Department made it clear: "The administration would like to establish a more *constructive relationship* with the Guatemalan government. Our previous policy clearly failed to contribute to an improvement of the situation inside Guatemala, while Cuban-supported Marxist guerrillas have gained in strength. We hope changes in the situation in Guatemala will soon permit a closer cooperative relationship."[69]

Soon thereafter, the United States sent a special envoy, General Vernon Walters, to meet with General Lucas García, the head of government in 1981. Walters stated that the United States was intent on helping Guatemala to defend "peace and liberty" and "the constitutional

institutions...against the ideologies that want to finish off those institutions."[70] Yet, according to a State Department memorandum about
that meeting, General Lucas made it very clear to General Walters that
he had no intentions of respecting human rights. General Lucas is described as "amorally rational," a peculiar term, to say the least. "In conversation with General Walters," the memo continued, "President Lucas made clear that his government will continue as before—that the
repression will continue. He reiterated his belief that the repression is
working." The memo then observes, "Historically, of course, we cannot
argue that repression always 'fails,' nor can Lucas argue that it always
'succeeds.' Recent history is replete" with examples of both. Given this
uncertainty, the U.S. government "must now decide whether 'national
security considerations' require that we nevertheless go ahead with security assistance."[71] The answer was affirmative. The U.S. government
rewarded General Lucas by releasing, in June 1981, $3.1 million in mil-
itary sales that had been blocked by the U.S. Congress.[72]

President Reagan was particularly supportive of General Efraín Ríos
Montt, a born-again Evangelical Christian who was responsible for some
of the worst massacres after he seized power in a coup in March 1982.
"On December 4, 1982, President Reagan met with Guatemalan President Ríos Montt in Honduras and dismissed reports of human rights
abuses in Guatemala published by Americas Watch, Amnesty International and others as 'a bum rap,'" Americas Watch pointed out at the
time. "The following month, the Reagan administration announced that
it was ending a five-year embargo on arms sales to Guatemala and had
approved sale of $6.36 million worth of military spare parts to that coun-
try. This sale was approved despite a U.S. law forbidding arms sales to
governments engaged in a consistent pattern of gross violations of internationally recognized human rights."[73] Ríos Montt getting a bum rap?
President Reagan and his administration clearly were not interested in
the detailed information provided by Amnesty International's report
"Massive Extrajudicial Executions in Rural Areas Under the Government
of General Efraín Ríos Montt."[74]

There was no lack of evidence of gross violations of human rights.
Nonetheless, even when the State Department was provided with its own
direct documentation of atrocities attributed to the Guatemalan army, it
gave either the benefit of the doubt or completely whitewashed the military. For example, a 1982 field visit by two State Department operatives
resulted in an internal memo assessing the conditions in Guatemala and
the refugee exodus to Mexico. The memo states that thousands of refu-

gees were fleeing the "effects of the Guatemalan army's anti-guerrilla campaign" and that the refugees "expressed strong anti-government sentiments and claimed to be fleeing the army." This information, however, is not included in the annual report submitted to Congress by the State Department in 1982. Instead, the official report claims that *"clear attribution of responsibility for the death of noncombatants in the area of conflict is difficult."*[75] The State Department claims that due to the remoteness of settlements in the highlands, it was difficult to verify reports of large-scale killings, suggesting that "it has been established that some of the alleged atrocities never occurred," or in "most cases known to have occurred, it has not been possible to clearly determine whether the guerrillas or the army was responsible." The report continues by stating that "where it has been possible to assign responsibility, it appears more likely that in the majority of cases the insurgents, who have increasingly turned to terror in recent months in an effort to force the villagers to support them, have been guilty."[76] No one had better access to the most remote areas of the country than the U.S. government. Moreover, journalists and anthropologists were able, at great risk, to obtain information about army atrocities, some documented with nightmarish details. Headlines in the major newspapers in the United States detailed army barbarity: "Guatemalans Tell of Murder of 300," for example.[77] Amnesty International could not have been more explicit in its 1981 human rights report entitled *Guatemala: A Government Program of Political Murder.*[78] Americas Watch was as forthright in their 1982, 1983, and 1984 reports: *Human Rights in Guatemala: No Neutrals Allowed; Creating a Desolation and Calling It Peace;* and *Guatemala: A Nation of Prisoners.*[79]

The CIA had reliable intelligence information about the political/military conditions in the rural Mayan areas of the country. Through the Freedom of Information Act, some of these previously confidential memos are now available, though many items are heavily excised with black ink. In mid-February 1982—at the time that Santa María Tzejá was being destroyed—a CIA memo stated that the Guatemalan army was reinforcing and getting ready to "launch a sweep operation," adding that "the commanding officers of the units involved have been instructed to destroy all towns and villages which are cooperating with the Guerrilla Army of the Poor (EGP) and eliminate all sources of resistance." This evaluation mirrors the actual events in Santa María Tzejá and surrounding areas. The memo further states:

> Since the operation began, several villages have been burned to the ground, and a large number of guerrillas and collaborators have been killed. (Com-

ment: when an army patrol meets resistance and takes fire from a town or village it is assumed that the entire town is hostile and it is subsequently destroyed.) The army has found that most of the villages have been abandoned before the military forces arrive. An empty village is assumed to have been supporting the EGP, and it is destroyed. There are hundreds, possibly thousands, of refugees in the hills with no homes to return to.[80]

According to the CIA, the Guatemalan army was very pleased with the "initial results," noting that Indian collaborators and sympathizers have been killed. The CIA then observes, "The well documented belief by the army that the entire Ixil Indian population is pro-EGP has created a situation in which the army can be expected to give no quarter to combatants and non-combatants alike."[81]

Another formerly secret document notes:

> The government [of Guatemala] has improved its control over rural areas through a strategic village program in which the rural populace is ordered to move to villages where the army has outposts. A scorched earth policy is then applied in the surrounding area. These tactics have been accompanied by widespread allegations that government troops are regularly guilty of massacres, rape, and mayhem. U.S. Embassy investigations have found that some of these reports cannot be verified, that some of the atrocities reported are attributable to the guerrillas, and that still others cannot be attributed with accuracy to either side. The Embassy does not as yet believe that there is sufficient evidence to link government troops to any of the reported massacres."[82]

U.S. evangelical missionaries were able to travel to conflict zones in the highlands in mid-1982. They generally had close ties to the military government and an explicit antipathy for the guerrillas. Moreover, the government was looking for allies in its efforts to distribute internationally donated food, medicine, and clothing in areas that had come under military control—especially in the "model" villages, tightly controlled, militarized localities. The army was persecuting the Catholic Church, leading to closure of the dioceses of El Quiché province. U.S.-based evangelical churches eagerly filled the vacuum. In one visit between July 5 and 9, 1982, one U.S. evangelical missionary, who had lived in the Ixil region for many years and spoke fluent Ixil, returned for the first time since leaving the area two years earlier and kept a richly detailed diary. He was accompanied by his wife, four dentists from California, and members of the Gospel Outreach/Verbo (Word) Church. The Verbo Church members had "ties to the new President of Guatemala" [Ríos Montt] he notes in his diary. A three-person crew for a Christian Broadcasting Network television program, the *700 Club,* was also there. The missionary's long, straightforward diary is revealing especially since he was supportive of the Guatemalan military government. "The President of Guatemala ordered the Air Force to provide helicopter transport for us and our gear," he writes. "It was a cooperative project in many ways." He repeatedly makes mention of the use of helicopters for military purposes, commenting that "it was the first live war I had actually witnessed, and it left an impression on me." On their first day they saw the bodies of three guerrillas brought in and later "taken to the ditch which serves as a grave for such cases. Someone dumped water on the cement tile floor and swished the blood out. We were glad we'd decided to work in the corridor." As he began to locate some of his old acquaintances (or "believers" as he refers to the evangelicals) and saw and heard about the conditions they faced, he increasingly became concerned and began to question the military's excesses.

The missionaries heard of rape. "Two teenage daughters . . . were prime grist for the 'entertain-the-soldiers' mill in Nebaj, and were virtually fleeing for their lives as well as their virtue." In every home they visited the families expressed fear, especially that many young women were "living in terror day-to-day, assuming [they] would be conscripted for barrack duty." Some of the "believers" had not been heard from for two years, traumatized by the massive population displacement, hunger, and generalized suffering. The U.S. missionary recommends in his diary that the military image "absolutely must be turned around immediately." He recognized "that lots of innocent people are still going to be dying in the area, probably for some time to come." This random killing results "from a generally reprisal-based mentality which slaughters 'the enemy' indiscriminately. . . . In practice, we see a 'shoot first but never mind question afterward' mentality—quite understandable under the circumstances, certainly!—but not really designed to rally people whose loyalties have already been forced to the brink." He continues, "It would be nice if the army could be cautioned not to shoot just because they see [someone] running away, *especially* if it is also obvious that he is unarmed. It would be nicer yet if they didn't even try to chase him. There are lots of good people out in those hills who are simply in terror of the army, as much as they are of the guerrillas. *These* are the people the army is committed to protecting, not slaughtering." He says that "At present, the military image is not lily-white even in town." He is told by a man that "around the first of June, soldiers broke into my house, ransacked it, and took my seventeen-year-old son up to the barracks. They beat him horribly and kept him there for ten days, then threw him out and he managed to get back to the house. He's been in bed ever since, can't eat, has horrible bruises all over, with likely internal injuries since he swells up and has pain every time he tries to eat something." The missionary naively asked the former mayor if there were other cases like that. The mayor responded, "The best thing that man can possibly do is just shut up. If word gets to this present commander that he's telling things like that, it'll be a lot worse for them than it is now." This missionary, with a long history in the region and therefore having earned the trust of many "believers," unfortunately did not feel compelled to decry the military's abuses publicly. He heard a lot: "I could detail some instances of the kinds of things people from Nebaj environs had told me over the course of the last couple of years about suffering at the hands of the army itself." He ponders on a statement made by a local person, "People who are on the army's side now are teetering there, and it wouldn't take much to push them over to the wrong side." Adding empathetically: "I have no trouble at all understanding why a lot of people hesitate to deliberately expose themselves to the mercies of the army," and further, as he relates another abuse after army planes bombed an area, he contemplates, "The army accused [this man] of being a guerilla, which he definitely is not. But if I had been him I think I would have been tempted to consider it!"[83]

I am not sure whether this account or others like it made it to the State Department, the CIA, or the Pentagon. In any case, the U.S. government was far more focused on winning congressional approval for further military aid and crushing the guerrillas than on human rights violations. Likewise, USAID opted to disregard field reports in 1982 that incriminated the army in atrocities in the Ixcán. A three-person team went to Guatemala to evaluate the USAID projects in the Ixcán.[84] It is remarkable how the information provided by the research team's field report became sanitized and edited by the agency in its official published version.[85] Here are several examples:

Original field report: "Three of these 18 settlements (Trinitaria, Santa Clara, and El Quetzal) were exterminated by the military."

USAID's edited version: "Three of the uninhabited 18 settlements (Trinitaria, Santa Clara, El Quetzal) no longer have settlers."

Original field report: "It would have been difficult to anticipate the closing of the project in 1982 by the Guatemalan military and the killings of colonists that took place during the military occupation. The military action caused the failure of one cooperative and inhibited the development of others."

USAID's edited version: "It would have been difficult to anticipate the closing of the project in 1982 by the Guatemalan military and the loss of colonists that took place during the military occupation." [The cooperatives are not even mentioned.][86]

In another official USAID report,[87] the term "evacuation" was used to describe the deadly violence unleashed against the people of Trinitaria and Santa Clara; army massacres were called "military operations." As one of the American authors of the USAID field evaluation said to me with astonishment, "Deletions were made in the 'official' report published by USAID." He then added, "Clearly, they did not want to have us implicate the army in the repression that occurred there." Thus, not even when one of their own settlements, funded with U.S. tax dollars, was exterminated in the Ixcán in 1982, did the U.S. government care to investigate or at least make it known.[88]

A U.S. historian noted:

Washington officials were not pleased with their own creation in Guatemala, but—much as one hesitates to stop feeding a pet boa constrictor— they were reluctant to cut off aid and face the consequences. Throughout these bloody, bleak years, they tried to resolve the irresolvable: extend U.S. military and economic aid so the army could fight the growing revolution, but threaten to cut off aid if the 'rival mafias' did not stop murdering Indians, labor leaders, educators, lawyers, and each other.[89]

Caught between the choice of bolstering the military regime in their internal war and demanding respect for human rights, the U.S. government under Reagan opted to continue supplying the Guatemalan military with economic and military aid. During the Carter administration the Guatemalan military rejected aid that was contingent on respecting human rights. Walter LaFeber put it graphically: the "pipeline had been closed since 1977 because the Guatemalan generals refused to meet Carter's requests to reduce the shootings, beheadings, and torturing of political opponents. By 1981 the generals had not changed, but the U.S. government had."[90] The Reagan administration's thinking was that while the Guatemalan military might be doing unsavory things, they were nonetheless an ally in a larger geopolitical struggle—the cold war.

And finally, a small, personal, but telling example of the obsession of the Reagan administration to undermine criticism of the Guatemalan human rights record. I wrote about a politically motivated murder I witnessed in downtown Guatemala City on June 26, 1986, in an op-ed published in the *New York Times,* "A Guatemalan Dies and What It

Means."[91] Elliott Abrams, the assistant secretary of state for Inter-American Affairs (the highest-ranking position for Latin America) wrote a long response to the editor on July 29. He began by stating that my article "exemplified the *perils outside observers face* in reporting on Guatemala following *short stays* in the country. It also exemplified how *more than one conclusion can be drawn from an observation*" (emphasis added). His letter incorrectly stated that the police were investigating the case, that contrary to my claim the murder was reported in the Guatemalan press, and that the killing was not a political execution. The claim that the police were investigating the murder was particularly ludicrous. I had gone to the national police to report what I saw, and they had no interest in my testimony, a fact that I reported in my article. Abrams also stated that I "unnecessarily attack the motives and capacity" of the government of President Vinicio Cerezo, "and attacks this administration's efforts to help that government succeed." He concludes, "Were Ms. Manz more objective in her reporting she would have focused on the *real meaning of what she observed*—Guatemala needs outside help in combating crime" (emphasis added). I was in fact both thorough and objective in my reporting and sadly became involved in the aftermath of a political assassination. I knelt over the dying, bloody body of a young nineteen-year-old man, whom I was later to discover was an architecture student. Accompanied by Aryeh Neier, then director of Human Rights Watch, I went to the hospital to find out the man's identity. I located the family, attended the funeral, and made myself available to the family to testify on the murder (an offer not accepted by the terrified and heart-broken relatives), and went to the National Police to provide direct witness of the murder and the two murderers (an offer not taken).[92]

Although the cold war affected contemporary Guatemalan history both locally and nationally, one must not overstate the cold war's role. I argue that while this global conflict is key to understanding the fate of Santa María Tzejá, the prime forces behind the onslaught are found in Guatemala's own history and contemporary society. The cold war exacerbated and accelerated, rather than created, the social, class, and ethnic tensions that historically have wracked the country. In the name of anticommunism, elites and the military sought to reinforce their position by tapping into the economic, military, and political support eagerly supplied by the U.S. government. The U.S. government in turn argued that supporting military regimes or military-dominated regimes was essential to provide hemispheric stability.

The effects of military repression traumatized the colonization sites in the north. Yet, while the cold war fueled the devastation, a deeply rooted violence still pervades this society and will require a greater effort than a cessation of fighting—or the end of the east/west global conflicts—to overcome. The U.S. intervention during the cold war, however, provided the legitimization for the Guatemalan army and the elites to unleash further terror against wide prodemocracy and progressive movements. In an effort to root out a small, armed insurgency (less than ten thousand armed combatants) more than two hundred thousand people were killed over a three-decade period. Likewise the insurgent armed groups became an avenue for peasant participation and reaction, although the disaffection pre-dates and runs deeper than the guerrilla conflicts themselves.

This book tells the story of Santa María Tzejá and the rural context in which it was embedded. As with so many other communities, it was gripped by social and economic injustice, racism, land deprivation, political dictatorship, and military repression enveloped by the cold war. The past and future of this village and so many like it inform the fate of a fragile peace in Guatemala. In fact, the future of the country is intertwined with the ability of people like those of Santa María Tzejá to reconcile the trauma of their past and to build a new future. Their tale is one of ordinary individuals who were to display extraordinary determination and courage; they built a new life in the rain forest only to see it consumed by bullets and fire; they walked through this fire, and under the toughest of circumstances they have rebuilt their lives on the ashes. Now they confront the challenges of an uncertain future.

Chapter 1 sets the scene in Santa Cruz del Quiché, the highland *municipio* that would become the point of departure for the journey to the rain forest. I explore the polarized social situation and the land policies that impoverished the contemporary highland Mayas and forced them to work on the coastal plantations. I examine the role of the Catholic Church, especially Father Luis, the priest who inspired the colonization effort and was central in organizing it.

In chapter 2 I discuss the early years of the village, the hardships and hopes involved in settling a remote rain forest. I examine the unfolding of critical events, such as the emergence of a guerrilla organization and the transformation of a military garrison in an isolated region into the largest military base in the countryside. A discussion of the role of liberation theology helps dispel notions that these villagers, while isolated, may not have had a vision of freedom, human rights, and democracy. They in fact had hoped to improve their impoverished conditions, to provide a better life for their children, and to be "serfs no more."

Chapter 3 narrates the intense and painful years between 1978 and 1982. The villagers mobilize, on their own and in increasing cooperation with the guerrillas. The army ratchets up repression, which eventually turns into outright carnage. The narrative centers on Santa María Tzejá but also encompasses the experiences of neighboring communities. The core of this chapter analyzes why peasants were attracted to the insurgency; a variety of reasons involve both broader political critique and the pursuit of immediate needs. Their decisions for the most part were conscious, reflective, and voluntary, although later they felt the pressure of inflated rhetoric from the guerrilla movement coupled with increased army brutality. By the end of this chapter, the village is in ruins, its inhabitants dead, in hiding, or in flight.

Chapter 4 relates the exodus to Mexico and the aftermath of the massacre in the village. The first major divide in the community emerges between those who submit to army-supervised reorganization and those who resist, flee, and end up as refugees in Mexico. The guerrillas' authoritarian side emerges, underscored by their attempt to control the civilians fleeing from the army. The village, a shadow of its former self, includes former inhabitants, beaten down and frightened. The military introduces new methods of village control, including forcing all males into paramilitary-style militias called Civil Defense Patrols.

Chapter 5 looks at the reorganization of the village and the militarization of daily life. The new village is divided between *antiguos*—a group of original settlers now under army control—and *nuevos*—army-recruited peasants desperate for land. The *nuevos*, more favorably inclined to the military, become leaders and are devoted to carrying out the army's orders; the *antiguos* are more passive and comply grudgingly. Raw, grating divisions run through the village. This chapter concludes with the story of Father Tiziano, an idiosyncratic priest who served the area between 1985 and 1992.

Chapter 6 discusses the return to the village of the original settlers who fled to refugee camps in Mexico. The refugees in Mexico negotiated their return, demanding the removal of the new settlers brought in by the military as well as the despised Civil Defense Patrols. A deal was cut to allow the new settlers a graceful exit, and refugees and *antiguos* struggled to overcome their differences and rebuild a "consciousness of community." This chapter ends with reflections by a number of former combatants, highlighting both the complexity of their feelings and a sense that their prior choices were justified.

In the last chapter I assess the short, turbulent history of this village and look at the ways in which villagers recall the past and how they cope with their enduring fear and grief. The chapter examines the elusive, shifting nature of memory itself. The villagers have recaptured their will for a better life, most significantly by establishing a primary and secondary school staffed by teachers from their own village and by reestablishing the cooperative. Their courage is also evident in a lawsuit filed by relatives of the victims against the military for the massacre and other human rights abuses, an act that has brought international attention to the village while sadly renewing incidents of attack and murder. The final message is mixed—celebrating achievements, tempered with sober observations on the vulnerability of what has been gained and the uncertainty of what is to come. The village is prosperous compared to its neighbors, yet enduring poverty and insecurity have led to large migrations to the United States. The book ends with Jesús, the young boy in chapter 2 who descends into the rain forest at the age of eleven with his father and, twenty-six years later, meets the U.S. Border Patrol ("la Migra") in the Arizona desert.

⊹◇⊹

The Highland Homeland

"Viveros de mozos" [Seed beds for serfs].
   Quiché Highlands peasant, describing
   living arrangements in the highlands

The land, breathtaking in its beauty, reflects the turmoil beneath it. A range of high rugged mountains tumbles into western Guatemala from the Mexican state of Chiapas and finally slips into northern Nicaragua, defining an imposing landscape that is the geological core of Central America. Powerful tectonic movements shook the earth thousands of years ago and violently thrust it upwards, molding towering peaks and deep valleys out of sedimentary, metamorphic, and igneous rock. The highest of these massive blocks is the Cuchumatán Sierra, a limestone plateau that spills into Guatemala south of Chiapas at an altitude ten thousand feet above sea level, with occasional peaks soaring toward thirteen thousand feet. Scattered pines and *zacatal,* a montane scrub-grassland, blanket the plateau. Steep slopes, once covered by a verdant cloud forest of pine and oak and laurel, plummet into valleys and areas of serpentine bedrock. Above ten thousand feet, warm, balmy days fade into crisp, chilly nights and, during the rainy season, brief intense downpours herald the evening.

Standing silent witness to the geologic uproar of the past, a chain of volcanoes strings along the Pacific coast from the Soconusco region of Chiapas, through Guatemala, and down the Central American isthmus into western Panama. More than 350 volcanoes—including twenty still active—have thrown up deep ash and lava deposits for thousands of years, transforming the landscape and creating a nutrient-rich, fertile

soil.[1] Along the coastal highway in Guatemala the volcanoes thrust upwards dramatically to the northeast, their abrupt slopes and flattened
peaks overlooking the hot, humid coastal plains. The thunderous power
and unstable nature of the land is still occasionally, sometimes tragically,
demonstrated. A strong lateral shift along the Motagua fault provoked
a devastating earthquake in 1976, flattening entire towns and villages
and killing more than twenty thousand people in the highlands west of
Guatemala City.

The Pacific piedmont and coastal lands are the epicenter of export agriculture—the commanding heights of the Guatemalan economy. In the
last half of the nineteenth century, coffee plantations spread over the upper, cooler elevations in the Boca Costa, or piedmont zone, followed years
later by sprawling sugar plantations at lower, hotter elevations. In the
1960s, cotton plantations extended over much of a hot lowland strip of
land ten to twenty miles wide along the Pacific coast. Today, maps of
Guatemala predictably identify towns on the Pacific coast, but they also
pay homage to the power and influence of the leading plantations—called
fincas in Guatemala—by spelling out their locations and names—Finca
Pantaleón, Finca La Primavera, Finca Soledad, Finca El Paraíso, among
hundreds of others. These fincas developed a vast appetite for cheap, seasonal labor that would transform life in the highlands and define the
country's economy.[2]

The Guatemalan highlands have been home to Mayan peoples for mil-
lennia.[3] When Spanish conquistadors arrived five centuries ago, they encountered a complex civilization—a Mayan kingdom—known as the
K'iche'.[4] Corn or maize was their most important crop; the K'iche' word
for "prepared maize" was almost synonymous with the word for "food"
itself. Farmers used a hatchet (ikaj) and hoe (xoquem) to clear the hills
and mountains near their homes and then turned the soil with a digging
stick (mixquina). Then as now women ground corn on stone metates in
a ritual central to domestic life.[5] While maize dominated the diet, the
K'iche' also harvested squash, beans, chili peppers, and sweet potatoes,
hunted wild game, and raised domestic animals for food.[6] Extended families worked the fields and labored in the home, assigning tasks along
gender lines. Men dedicated their time to agricultural tasks in the milpa
(corn fields); women worked in the house and produced clothing and
home utensils. The powerful K'iche' exacted tribute and traded goods
throughout the region, painstakingly listing in their chronicles the won-
drous tributes they received, such as "metals, precious stones (including

jade), quetzal and other tropical bird feathers, flowered garlands, cacao, gourds, salt, fish, turtles and crabs, and woven cloths."[7] Markets linked people in economic and social interactions; women in particular were ever present selling their goods.[8] Prior to the conquest the K'iche' constructed an impressive center at Utatlán, on the outskirts of the present-day provincial capital of Santa Cruz del Quiché. Few tourists visit Utatlán today—an uncommon detour from the much more famous lowland Mayan archaeological sites of Tikal and Quiriguá.

Soon after the end of the spring semester in 1973, I took off with three other students in a large, black, beat-up American car on a journey from New York to Guatemala. I was going to join the Projecto Utatlán research team in the El Quiché highlands. I was new to Guatemala but full of enthusiasm as research assistant to Professor Robert Carmack. Santa Cruz del Quiché, about one hundred miles northwest of Guatemala City, was then, as now, a faded, sleepy place that drew few visitors, although it lay only twenty miles or so north of the major tourist destination of Chichicastenango. Although it lacked Chichi's famous church, on whose steps K'iche' burn incense, or a busy market overflowing with colorful handmade items, Santa Cruz was nonetheless an important regional center. A three-story clock tower sat atop a drab government building, whose bulk and grim columns dominated an undistinguished central square. Across the square, a small appliance store displayed a working television in its window, attracting in those days an ever present crowd of townspeople and curious peasants from the region. I found a place to stay in a small *pensión* near the central square—Pensión Providencia—owned by Chus Urizar, a man with many other duties. He was a labor contractor for the plantations, a political activist for the extreme right-wing Movimiento de Liberación Nacional (the National Liberation Movement), the owner of the liquor store, and the moneylender for the *enganche,* the advance, or "hitch," peasants repaid by toiling in the plantations.

I contacted the local authorities to begin my fieldwork. I started out with the governor, a stiff military man in his sixties, appointed by the president, himself an aging military man. The introductions told me a lot about the military's power and influence throughout the country. After my high-level visits had been completed, I gave a brief radio address directed to the rural Mayan population in which I explained why the research team was there. Leonardo Zacarías Zapeta, a highly respected Mayan leader, translated my words into K'iche'. He subsequently became invaluable to my research and central to my stay. He and I would trudge to outlying *cantones,* or hamlets, and visit people in their homes or meet with groups of Mayan men, and sometimes women, at the church or community building in a *cantón.*

The central market was a bustling place, but mainly with locals and people from outlying villages rather than tourists. A block away from the square a military base was a commanding presence. The *municipio* of Santa Cruz embodied the economic desperation of highland Guatemala and was home to peasants who would settle the Ixcán. In the early 1970s, about thirty-five thousand people lived in the *municipio*—a little under nine thousand in the town of Santa Cruz itself, and the rest in the outlying rural areas. Eighty percent of the population identified themselves as Mayan and they, like the residents of other *municipios,* viewed themselves as ethnically distinct, with their dress, local saints, values, traditions, fiestas, and dialects. As I got to know people in the *municipio,* they became more and more candid in their conversations with me. Several weeks after I began my research, a group of peasants unburdened themselves, talking about their poverty, their work in the plantations, and their lack of money. In short, they viewed their situation as one of oppression and dependence. Not surprisingly, they wanted land, jobs, schools for their children, and improved agricultural techniques to raise their yields. They used terms such as *estamos bajo el yugo de la tiranía* (we are under the yoke of tyranny). I had expected passivity but encountered a more critical voice, especially from young men.

Guatemala has two main populations whose boundaries often blur: Mayas, generally considered the majority of the population, and Ladinos, either European descendants or more likely people of mixed Mayan and Spanish ancestry (sometimes also referred to as mestizos). At the time of the conquest the distinction was far clearer: one population was the dominant Spanish colonizers and *criollos* (Spanish descendents born in the New World), self designated as *gente de razón*—people of reason— and the other the *naturales*—natural ones, the so-called Indians.[9] Today the distinction between Ladinos and Mayas is complex, ambiguous, and not always easy to identify. Scholars have pointed out that ethnic definitions are fluid, selective, historically inconsistent, ideologically and class motivated, and generally localized. In fact, ethnic identity is often shaped by the group's own process of boundary formation in local interplay. As revealed in the history of Santa María Tzejá, ethnic identity is a dynamic, changing, and for some a politically influenced process. Given my own observations in the village, I will pay heed to Ben Orlove's suggestion that it is unwise to provide an ethnic definition and label; instead it is much more sensible to "witness the different grounds on which these groups encounter one another. [Because] it is in the story of such encounters that identities are made and transformed."[10]

A casual stroll through the outskirts of Santa Cruz del Quiché was enough to reveal the fierce pressures that were squeezing all peasants. The topography of the *municipio* severely limits the land available for cultivation. Rugged eight-thousand-foot mountains dominate its northeastern sections, and deep ravines cut through the landscape. Peasants cultivate corn on slopes tilted at impossible angles. Land-starved residents have stripped large areas of forest, which has accelerated erosion, leaching minerals and fertility out of the soil. By the late 1960s, the land had become so eroded that much of it could no longer grow corn. The small size of the plots and the ravaged fields underscored the economic despair. Everywhere one could see the scars of overuse. "The land was nothing but ruin; it did not produce anything," said Domingo Us Quixán, who lived in the highland area of Joyabaj and then left to settle in Santa María Tzejá. The small size and hilly nature of the fields precluded even the plow, and the lack of cash made fertilizer a dream for most. Nonetheless, like their K'iche' ancestors, peasants laboriously cultivated their tiny plots with the *azadón* (hoe), the *piocha* (pick), and the machete.

Each year survival became more tenuous in the highlands. A highly unequal and unyielding system of land distribution, combined with a lack of other alternatives, trapped peasants in an economic cul-de-sac. Within the confines of the land tenure system, demographic pressures squeezed everyone. Between 1950 and 1964, the highlands population grew by 41.3 percent—an annual rate of about 2.5 percent—fragmenting already small plots and leading to even more intense use. In four departments in the western highlands, *minifundio* landholdings ballooned by almost one-third between 1964 and 1974, according to a study carried out by the University of San Carlos in Guatemala City. In the *municipio* of Santa Cruz, 75 percent of all cultivators lacked sufficient land even for subsistence—the average landholding was 3.4 acres of often exhausted soil, and 22 percent of the peasants had less than two acres or no land at all.

Some peasants lived on communal lands, although this arrangement was becoming rarer; others lived on large farms in the highlands owned by an absentee wealthy Ladino. The logic was simple and the consequences inescapable: by the 1960s and 1970s, the small highland plot compelled its tenants to work on the owner's coastal plantation. "We lived in the land owned by the *patrón*," Pedro Canil said. "We were there at his good will. His name was Carlos Herrera." Herrera had seized "a large extension of land in the highlands," according to Pedro, in which thousands of families had lived. He also owned several *fincas* on the coast. "So the deal was this," Pedro matter-of-factly stated. "We could live on his land in the highlands, and in return we had to go twice a year to work in the *fincas*. Thus, he didn't have to bother looking for labor.... We already knew the date, the year, the month, when we had to go work on the *fincas*." Pedro Tum, a short man who lost the vision in one eye and wears the years of hard work on his face, elaborated: "The three years I attended school in the highlands awoke me a little and allowed me to see the injustices around us. We had barely eight *cuerdas* [less than an acre] of land. The land was poor, full of stones." The misfortune of the peasants proved to be economic opportunity for the landowner. "[Our land] was the leftover land that the *patrón* did not use for cultivation." Pedro Tum continues, "He used it as a warehouse for his *mozos* [servants]. There he would put his *mozos* like working tools [como herramientas de trabajo]. The season for plantation production would come [in August], he would take them out. The season is over [in March], he would store them." Should one of the laborers want to work on another plantation, the highland *patrón* would swiftly kick him and his family out of the highland property. One person described the living arrangements in the highlands as being "*viveros de mozos*" (seed beds for serfs). These migrations separated families and disrupted labor-intensive work that needed to be done in the highlands, such as repairs in the house. The migration of the whole family interrupted schooling and exposed everybody to the diseases that were rampant in the plantations.

These *fincas de mozos* in the highlands date back to the early twentieth century. Carlos Herrera purchased several landholdings in El Quiché, and the Herrera family, more significantly, owned several plantations on the Pacific coast as well as Pantaleón, the largest sugar mill in the country. One of the highland *fincas de mozos* was the twenty-thousand-acre Chuacorral estate purchased in 1923 by "coffee and sugar baron [and ex-president] Carlos Herrera." This was one of the first *fincas* targeted for expropriation during the Arbenz reform period. "The *finca* was expropriated in November 1953 but then returned to the Herreras by the counterrevolutionary government in September 1956, with the 'protective' proviso that 'the *mozos colonos* have a right to remain in the same conditions they had prior to the application of [the agrarian reform].' "[11] Powerful wealthy landowners, such as the Herrera and Leal families,

owned dozens of *fincas* in key locations. Thousands of peons would reside in the large *fincas de mozos.*

Compounding the problems stemming from a lack of land is the
scarcity of credit and resources. Almost 90 percent of agricultural credit
went to large and medium-sized operators in the early 1960s, especially
the coffee and cotton plantations. The government agricultural extension, the Service for the Development of the Indian Economy (Servicio
de Fomento de la Economía Indígena), reached only 1 percent of the indigenous rural population. W. Arthur Lewis, the Princeton development
economist, provides insight into the perverse incentives to the government for not providing technical aid:

> The fact that the wage level in the capitalist sector depends upon earnings
> in the subsistence sector is sometimes of immense political importance,
> since its effect is that capitalists have a direct interest in holding down the
> productivity of the subsistence workers. Thus, the owners of plantations
> have no interest in seeing knowledge of new techniques or new seeds con-
> veyed to the peasants, and if they are influential in the government, they
> will not be found using their influence to expand the facilities for agricul-
> tural extension.[12]

Few nonagricultural jobs existed in the *municipio.* The most common
home industry was the braiding of palm leaves into *trenzas* used for making hats. It was common to see K'iche' women braiding at their market
stalls or men braiding as they walked through their fields. An experienced
person, working quickly, could braid a roll per day, netting about five
cents. The hats themselves were produced in El Salvador, and the production was showcased there as development of local, small industry.
Some peasants supplemented their income by working on the land of more
prosperous neighbors, earning between thirty-five and sixty cents a day.
During the harvest season, peasants hired themselves out carrying either
the crops of their neighbors or firewood to the market on their backs.

The once self-sufficient highlands were compelled to import food by
the late 1960s, often grown on *fincas* from the south. Unable to survive
on tiny, exhausted plots of land and with few local possibilities, the
K'iche' peasants faced their only alternative: the dreaded seasonal migration to the coastal plantations to harvest the cotton, sugar, and coffee.[13] The little money earned would be spent almost immediately to survive, causing new debt and ensuring yet another trek to the *fincas* for the
following season, a debilitating and inescapable spiral. In July, a month
or so before the corn harvest, when grain reserves are low and cash even

lower, labor contractors would show up to recruit workers for the plantations. The deal was simple and onerous: the contractor might offer an advance of half a month's wages in return for a signed contract to work a certain number of days during the harvest. By first having to work off the advance and the contractor's 10 percent commission, the worker was, in effect, bound to the plantation regardless of conditions. Three-quarters of the migrant workers in one survey received these advances in 1965–66.[14]

While the labor contractor might provide the advance, the most effective recruiters for the plantations were the deteriorating conditions in the highlands. More than three-quarters of the labor force came from the northwest Mayan highlands; by 1969 more than 60 percent came from the two departments of Huehuetenango and El Quiché alone. During the 1968–69 harvest, over half of the economically active population of these two departments made the trek to the coast.[15] Some were transported in open, flatbed trucks, feeling every rock and rut on the tortuous roads; others took buses or walked all or part of the way.

I heard so much about the plantations that I decided to visit one in 1973. Despite having grown up on a farm in southern Chile, I was unprepared for the experience. The plantation owner—a *cañero* (sugar cane producer)—was driving a large late-model Ford Galaxy 500 when we left Guatemala City early in the morning. The descent from the city happens quickly as the cooler highlands become a lush, humid, tropical terrain with steep volcanoes jutting up to the north—geographically and socially severing the Mayan highlands from the wealth of the rich plantations. After passing the town of Santa Lucía Cotzumalguapa, we followed a truck on which thirty or so migrant workers were precariously hanging onto wobbly, wooden sides, or to each other, to keep their balance. We wound up on the Pacific Highway, a busy two-lane road, where trucks, buses, cars, bicycles, and pedestrians jostle for space. Other trucks stacked with sugar cane shuttle from *fincas* to *ingenios* (sugar mills).[16] Finally, we turned right onto a narrow gravel road that would take us to the heart of a sugar plantation. Tall trees lined either side of this private road, providing shade in the late-morning heat in a scene eerily reminiscent of plantations in the antebellum South. We approached a roadblock at which armed guards stopped all vehicles except, of course, the one driven by the *patrón*. Once on the plantation, we passed the homes of the rancheros or permanent workers with their walls of bamboo sticks, a turquoise-painted Catholic chapel, a one-room school house, a store, and an administrative building where workers were receiving their pay from a tellerlike window. We then pulled up to the plantation quadrangle dominated by the owner's house—*la casa del finquero*. A long, open veranda along the front of the house overlooked a deep green, perfectly trimmed lawn bordered by large tropical trees with bright pink, red, and white flowers. Sitting in comfortable patio chairs one could look out at gigantic blooming bougainvillea vines in infinite colors, bushes along the fence with large red flowers and large verdant green leaves. The sounds of crickets, birds, and frogs completed the exotic setting—not enticing, but profoundly strange and something I had not experienced before. The porch faced the entrance road, offering a view of the comings and goings on the plantation. The air was humid and hot. The *patrón* sipped Chivas Regal on the rocks under the veranda's roof while the afternoon tropical rains poured down. It all seemed—and was—a world apart, spatially and temporally.

The luxury in the midst of this poverty carried a price. The plantation owner employed several heavily armed guards twenty-four hours a day and always carried a handgun tucked into his belt. During meals he would place the black gun on the fine white, perfectly pressed Swiss linen tablecloth. In their conversations, the *patrón* and his friends tended to rail against social change—no matter how modest—as "communism." They referred to *Time* magazine as "communist" and President Richard Nixon as part of the vast international communist conspiracy evident by his 1972 trip to China. Racism laced all conversations. Mayas were slow, lazy, ignorant, and would never rise to the level of Europeans. The *"indios"* liked the way they lived and did not want to change their way of life. Outsiders failed to understand this and came to Guatemala only to stir up trouble. While I had only spent a short time in the highlands by then, that was already significantly more time than any of the *finqueros* I was meeting. The landed elite usually live in well-off walled neighborhoods in Guatemala City.

I was very aware that my access to this segment of Guatemalan society was unusual. The *finquero's* wife was a distant relative of mine. At the time of my first trip to their plantation I was viewed with amusement and as naive. I spent time with this family both in the *finca* and at their home in zone 10 in Guatemala City and through them met several German and Swiss *finqueros,* as well as a few Guatemalan landowners.[17]

During my 1973 visit the *finquero* gave me several tours of the plantation on his jeep or on horseback, but I was never taken to the place where the highland migrant workers lived. I had heard about these structures—the *galeras*—from the Mayas in the highlands and very much wanted to see them. Early one morning, I put a camera in my bag and walked down a road that the *finquero* had failed to take me on. I came face to face with why we had never driven down it. The *finca's* housing conditions were appalling and reminded me of a classic piece of writing by C. L. R. James: "[People were] housed like animals, in huts built around a square planted with provisions and fruits.... These huts were about 20 to 25 feet long, 12 feet wide and about 15 feet in height, divided by partitions into two or three rooms. They were windowless and light entered only by the door. The floor was beaten earth; the bed was of straw, hides or a rude contrivance of cords tied on posts."[18] James was not describing contemporary Guatemala but rather slave quarters in Haiti in the early nineteenth century. What I saw on the *finca* that morning was surprisingly similar, except there were no fruit trees. The *galeras,* large, open sheds capable of housing up to five hundred people, were dilapidated structures covered by corrugated steel roofs and lacking much privacy inside.

Villagers from Santa María Tzejá recalled their housing on the *fincas.* "[We are housed] as if we were pigs," one woman said matter-of-factly, recalling the *galera* in Finca de Los Tarros, "that is how we sleep there, fifty people, some this way, some that way, and the fires in-between. There are no beds. We sleep on the very ground." These crude structures also lacked sanitary facilities, electricity, running water, even outer walls for protection from the torrential tropical rains. The floor was often packed earth, which quickly turned into mud during downpours. While people compared their living conditions to those of animals, I visited a plantation where bulls were housed in far better conditions. The animals, shipped from Texas, had a structure made of cement with metal roofing, kept clean by a team of workers.

The plantation was a breeding ground for contagious diseases, and many workers became seriously ill with diarrhea, malaria, dysentery, respiratory illnesses, and chemical insecticide poisoning. Children were especially susceptible and vulnerable to an early death. Diego, Santa María Tzejá's traditional medicine-nurse, reflected on becoming deathly ill one season. "I got a very high fever when I was working in the *fincas.* I was about to die," he stated. "I barely made it back home to the highlands. I was going to die, but God did not want me to. I sweated a lot when I got home, and then I got better." His recovery, however, was not enough to let him break free of the cycle. "As soon as I got better I went back to work again," he commented. "That is how life would go on. That is how it was in Finca San Antonio Sinache."

Work on the cotton plantations was considered the worst. The heat was more intense, rations more meager, the lodging pathetic, and constant, indiscriminate pesticide air-spraying of the fields common. Peasants repeatedly told me that they would rather die than go back to harvest cotton again, yet they invariably returned. No matter how horrible the conditions, the cotton *fincas* had enough workers at harvest time. Pedro Lux, a weak, elderly man who spent his best years toiling in the plantations, recalled that workers were unaware of the consequences of the fumigation at first. "When the cotton plant was at a certain height, they would come and fumigate," he said. "We heard there was a law that stated there should be no fumigation while workers were in the fields. But they did not respect that." While the fumigation was going on, he continued, "we would play games and throw ourselves to the ground as the planes flew overhead. All those fumes would fall over us. Then we would yell, as the plane left, 'The war has ended, *muchá!*'" he recalls laughing. "Sometimes they would fly over while we were having lunch."

To make matters worse, the harvest was occasionally meager. "They would keep checking you, to see how your quota was coming along," said Pedro. "If you were not producing, they would cancel your credit at the *finca* store. Then we had to pay up front for the corn." The sixty-cent daily salary seemed to vanish. Workers repaid the contractor's advance and used the rest for transportation, medicine, and food. At the end of the season, many workers would return to the highlands empty-handed. "We would leave for the plantations around January 15 and would return for Easter in the month of April or sometimes we would not return until May," Tomás recalls. "Then in August it was our turn to go to the coast again. That is how our life was spent going around, going around, and there was no change up ahead, just the same situation, no money, nothing."

The contempt for the Mayas was obvious not only on the plantations but also in a pervasive racism exhibited by the Ladino elites in the highland towns. I often heard young Ladinos—even children—calling K'iche' elders *muchacho,* or boy, and observed the pain a proud father had to endure in front of his family. Encounters with the local Ladinos, whether in pharmacies, government offices, hospitals, or simply along the road, were fraught with insults and humiliations. From an early age, K'iche' children were exposed to the culture of contempt, discrimination, and segregation. Adding to the insult was the injury of central government policies. Investment in infrastructure or schools in rural areas ranged from haphazard to nonexistent. Moreover, while parents sacrificed to send their children to local rural schools, the schools betrayed the dream. "Ignorance reigned completely," Pedro Tum recalled. "None of us knew how to read or write." He paused for a moment and then continued, warning with mock severity, "Beware of the peasant who learns how to read because he will rebel!...It wasn't until later that I noticed that they did not want us to get an education, because they were afraid that if we learned we may be able to read the laws, the articles about our rights, and that we could strike."

Miguel Reyes, a Ladino peasant leader with curly black hair and an easy sense of humor, admitted that while Mayas may have faced more direct discrimination and constant insults, his experience was not that different from that of the K'iche' when it came to schooling. In El Palmar, a poor Ladino village in the highlands, the school only went up to the third grade, and that was the least of its problems.[19] "There was only one teacher, and she attended more to her husband than to her students, because this guy was a nonstop chain-smoker," Miguel observed, managing a smile. "Her job was to roll cigarettes for her husband, so she would leave us there, without worrying at all about us." He continued, "The twenty-eight letters [of the Spanish alphabet] written on the board stayed there for months. She would only open the school for us and then command, 'Children, study!'...She would come back ten to fifteen minutes before twelve and tell us, 'Put away your chalkboards,' because back then we used individual chalkboards on which you write with a little piece of plaster....That's why I think we aren't good for anything. And she was well entrenched in her post because she lasted fourteen years as a teacher, making cigarettes for her husband! At that time it was difficult for us to do anything about it because no one paid attention to the students to help us learn." The third-graders may have been neglected but they were not unaware.

Sitting across from Miguel as he told the story, Alejandro Ortiz, a K'iche', started laughing. He joked that at least Miguel was exposed to the alphabet, whereas he would have been lucky to have seen the five vowels. "When [the teacher] arrived she sent me away to get firewood. She only cared for the children who are from the towns. The rest of us who are indigenous, she just tells us to get firewood and water," he recalled. "During the recess she tells us to go play. After recess she calls us back and just gives us a book. She doesn't even teach us the twenty-eight letters, or the vowels. She just puts books in front of us to read and makes us all read together as if we were in church. The smart ones learn a little bit. When my father comes, she tells him, 'Your son is smart, he's learning!' But in reality I'm not learning, I didn't know anything. I was in school like this for a while, without learning anything. So my father noticed that I was not progressing and he told me, 'Let's go to work, because there's no means to pay for you to continue studying!' 'That's O.K.,' I told him." Later things improved somewhat for Alejandro. "Then, when I was fourteen years old I trained to be a catechist. I did learn some letters there, from a priest whose name was Bartolo, in San Andrés. He arranged for us to learn how to read and write, and there I learned a few letters. In school I didn't learn anything. That's how my life went."

Not surprisingly, many highland rural children never became literate, even if they went to school for a couple of years. What the schools did convey was contempt, and this the children picked up and, all too often, internalized. These perverse values fueled what Pierre Bourdieu has called "symbolic violence," the intimate sense that the social order is both natural and pervasive.[20] Many teachers made it clear that it was a waste of everyone's time to teach these children; the knowledge would be of no use to them in the long run. Teachers were unavailable in remote corners of the *municipio*. "Since we live away from the village in a small hamlet, we didn't know there were teachers," Candelario Quinilla remembered. "That's how we grew up. There is nothing in our hamlet. We didn't even know what a teacher was."

Pedro Canil, who listened to the conversation about schooling, emphasized the overarching problem of racism against Mayas. "I want to talk a little bit about discrimination against the indigenous people," Pedro abruptly interjected in one conversation. "In the past, we indigenous people were not treated like humans. They looked at us as if we were animals, with no need to learn or earn money." As is the case with animals, "they made us work hard. If they wanted to, they would pay us; if they didn't, then they wouldn't. They only gave us a little bit to eat, just so that we wouldn't die, right? Just to keep us alive so that we would continue working another day."

The racism the Mayas endured had deep roots. In the recollections of many peasants, the ruthless presidency of General Jorge Ubico (1931–44) stands out in particular. Although some Mayas benefited and admired Ubico, poor peasants tend to remember him for his demagogic power and toughness. "My father said when President Ubico was in power people were forced to complete the big [national] work projects," Pedro Canil said. "People had to walk for many kilometers to go build roads, while carrying their own food with them; that's how the situation was before." Pedro Lux said of that time, "My mother told us that sometimes she didn't even have corn to prepare my father's food. I think they had to borrow it, because my father was really poor, we didn't have much land. So my mother would work all night long making the food, toasting the tortillas so they would last a little longer." While on the job, the conditions were harsh. "The rule was that there would be no breaks, you had to be careful not to sit down or stop for a little while, because the overseers had orders to hit them."

The renowned British author Aldous Huxley noticed the public labor performed by the Mayan workforce under Ubico. "Not far from Sololá we passed a group of Indians working on the road," he observed in *Beyond the Mexique Bay* (1934). "Two or three soldiers, rifle in hand and with fixed bayonets, were superintending the operations. Convicts? Not a bit of it: taxpayers and volunteers. Most of the Indians still pay taxes in labour, and when any considerable job needs doing, the authorities send word to the neighboring villagers that they have need of so many volunteers. The soldiers are there to see that the volunteering spirit does not cool down."

Huxley rather remarkably appears to justify the practice. "Volunteer labour at the point of the bayonet—the notion, to us, is extremely distasteful. But, obviously, when you are confronted with the urgent problem of domesticating a wilderness, you cannot afford to be very squeamish in your methods of getting the work done." As bad as conditions were, Huxley expected that following generations would enjoy the fruits of this labor. "The development of an undeveloped land will ultimately (we hope) be of good to all the inhabitants. But this potential good cannot be made actual without a large amount of systematically applied human effort." Huxley then goes on to compare the backwater Ubico dictatorship with the glories of the British empire. "Every colonial power has found itself obliged to systematize the efforts of its subjects by compulsion. Naked or in disguise, as slavery or in some less brutal form, forced labour has everywhere been employed in the development of wild countries. And it is exceedingly difficult to see how they could have been developed without it."[21] However, in the case of Guatemala, the country did not develop even with forced labor.

The Vagrancy Law, proclaimed in 1934, institutionalized the practices Huxley wrote about and reflects only one of a long line of measures to control and extract labor from the native population since the Spanish Conquest.[22] Ubico presented the Vagrancy Law as a more modern or humane means of involving the Mayas in the larger economic needs of the country's elite. In fact, this new enactment was more a matter of intensifying the mechanisms for using the indigenous population rather than a modernizing step. Prior to the Vagrancy Law, Mayas were subjected to debt servitude or peonage to a particular plantation or *patrón*. With the new law, a peasant could choose "freely" where to work by contracting labor with a plantation. A "vagrant" was any person who was not working on a plantation, fully employed elsewhere, or not planting a specified number of acres of land. Every peasant had to carry the *libreto de jornaleros,* a passbook that recorded a worker's labor, showing the annual labor performed. Each person with insufficient land had to work one hundred days per year (if he had at least ten *cuerdas* under cultivation) and 150 days if the person did not have any land planted. Theoretically a person could chose his place of mandatory work. The *finqueros* would register compliance with this law in the peasant's *libreto*. If the national police found a person had not worked the mandatory number of days, the individual would either be imprisoned or assigned work in a public works project until the obligatory days were completed. As a result, the large plantations, especially those growing coffee, were assured the labor force needed during boom times, and the government was assured the labor needed for public works. Ubico also instituted a central government tax for road construction. Those who could not pay the tax had to work for at least a week on public roads. Reflecting the repressive character of this law, General Ubico made the Ministry of Labor an adjunct to the National Police. Plantation owners were also given de jure police functions, which they had been assuming de facto all along.[23]

The Vagrancy Law remained in place until President Juan José Arévalo repealed it after the democratic election of 1944. While the formal legal structure had changed with this repeal, the underlying dynamic of the economy did not. As the 1960s drew to a close, highland peasants— weak, exhausted, malnourished, and fatigued—still were caught between the poverty of the highlands and the exploitation of the coast. The most enterprising, generally the young, began to look for options. "When we got to the age of eighteen or twenty we began to think that we couldn't go on living like this," Pedro Canil explained. In this environment, the very possibility of access to new land carried a magic ring. "We heard people were organizing to go to the Ixcán in search of land," Pedro said. "When we heard that, we didn't think twice about it. We went straight to the place to register our names." Alejandro Ortiz told a similar story. "The reason why I came [to the Ixcán] is because we are poor. We had no land. Six months out of the year we worked in the plantations on the coast. Sometimes we were not even paid. We would just work and get no money." Ricardo also said his family had no land at all. They were sharecroppers, meaning they turned over half of the harvest to the landowner. "My parents [went to the Ixcán] because of their experience on the plantations," he said, "because of the hard work, the mistreatment, the low wages. It was very hard for them to survive because of the big family we had. They did it for their children, so that some day we would have a place to live." Pedro Lux was one of those who hesitated joining the colonization effort. Despite having so little he felt he had so much to lose. He told Father Luis who was organizing the effort in the late 1960s, "Father, I would like to go but haven't because I am poor." Luis responded, "You are poor? Well, that is the reason why people are going there." Those words, Pedro explained, "gave me courage and I said to myself that is true, that is why people are going. I will go also. Once I got home I made up my mind, and eight days after getting back from the *fincas*, we decided to leave for the Ixcán."

Pedro Tum described the growing awareness of their predicament as "a consciousness of poverty." He stated that "one feels that consciousness because the exploitation was enormous." People became aware that their parents' land was insufficient, he recalls, and dividing it further among grown children meant moving from misery to desperation. The land produced increasingly lower yields, and although some peasants began to apply fertilizer in the 1960s, the cost for most was prohibitive. The purchase of fertilizer required a loan from a plantation contractor, and then the debt had to be paid off with labor at the plantations. "This is how we would end up, that was our life, never getting out of debt," Pedro Tum bitterly stated, having tried that route. "All our lives paying debts and nothing for us to keep. That is why we felt the need to come look for land, even though it was tough." The challenge for him and his family was to move from a "consciousness of poverty" to a consciousness of cooperation and hope—to be part of a community.

The dismal economic realities facing highland peasants in the 1960s— a symbiotic combination of scarce land at home funneling them into debilitating work on the coastal plantations—were embedded in a larger social and political context. Unyielding elites exercised a stranglehold over both the economy and the political system. "The anti-democratic nature of the Guatemalan political tradition has its roots in an economic structure, which is marked by the concentration of productive wealth in the hands of a minority," the report of the U.N. Commission for Historical Clarification, or Comisión para el Esclarecimiento Histórico (CEH), pointedly concluded, consequently forging "a system of multiple exclusions, including elements of racism" and "a violent and dehumanizing social system."[24] This deep-rooted system of repression has been referred to as "structural violence" and has been aptly described as a "political-economic organization of society that imposes conditions of physical and emotional distress, from high morbidity and mortality rates to poverty and abusive working conditions."[25] State social policy exacerbated deep-rooted inequality rather than alleviating it, particularly in the wake of the overthrow of President Jacobo Arbenz in 1954.

The government never acknowledged the deteriorating plight of poor Guatemalans, even during periods when resources were available to do something about it. In the two decades beginning in 1960, for example, Guatemala recorded unprecedented economic growth while taxation and government social spending nonetheless ranked last in all of Central America, a region hardly known for its progressive vision.[26] Not surprisingly, mounting social problems combined with shrinking political options proved to be a volatile combination that finally erupted into armed confrontation in 1962 in the eastern Ladino-dominated part of the country. This revolt was crushed by 1968 without major change occurring in the Mayan highlands. The United Nations report attributes the conflict to the government's "reluctance to promote substantive reforms that could have reduced structural conflicts" as well as to "the closing of political spaces, racism, [and] the increasing exclusionary and anti-democratic nature of institutions."[27] While repression blanketed the entire country, military operations and paramilitary terror were largely unleashed in Guatemala City, the south coast, and eastern areas. The victims were rural organizers, ordinary peasants, schoolteachers, student activists, professors, and those perceived as guerilla sympathizers.[28] Although the peasants in the highlands were not the direct targets during this period, the repression was intense, vicious, and effective. It gave terrifying notice of what could be in store for those who in any way challenged the existing order.

While armed conflict flared in Guatemala during the 1960s, the Catholic Church throughout Latin America was experiencing a profound, at times wrenching, set of changes. These developments were particularly radical for Guatemala because historically the church had focused its spiritual attentions on the next world while it acted as a solid pillar of the status quo in this one.[29] In the aftermath of World War II, the church sought to strengthen and extend its mass base to fend off troubling new competition, both ecclesiastical and political. To answer the growth of Protestant fundamentalism and to dampen more radical peasant politics, the church formed the Catholic Action movement in 1948. As the cold war unfolded, Pope Pius XII (1876–1958; elevated in 1939) engaged in what he viewed as a global, spiritual battle of cosmic importance, calling on the Catholics of the First World to go to Guatemala to save the country from communism.[30] These new foreign priests and nuns—many imbued with traditional idealism and a sense of historic mission—became integrated into Catholic Action and were warmly welcomed by Colonel Castillo Armas, the right-wing CIA-backed leader of the 1954 military coup.

As part of this movement, the Missionaries of the Sacred Heart (Misioneros del Sagrado Corazón) in Spain went to Guatemala a year after the overthrow of Arbenz. The first three priests who arrived in the department of El Quiché faced a daunting challenge and an impossibly large area: eight thousand square kilometers and 250,000 people scattered over the rugged mountains and deep ravines. The church's practices were typical of the time: distant, centered on spiritual issues, and mystical to the core. These Spanish priests were not simply politically conservative, but reactionary, according to the evaluation missionaries made of them years later. Several of the priests that went to El Quiché were admirers of General Francisco Franco and his fascist ideology (politically as well as ecclesiastically). But what they experienced in Guatemala had a profound effect on them. Some were so shocked by the grim poverty and desperation that they returned to Spain after a short while, but for others the underlying idealism and sensitivity that motivated them to come in the first place led them in an unexpected direction. They focused on the plight of the poor and grew to be a vital part of the community. When the church went through its own revolution, they were ready.

The Second Vatican Council (1962–65) and the Episcopal Conference of Medellín (1968) fueled the growth of liberation theology, a doctrine committed to the plight of the poorest and most dispossessed. This "preferential option for the poor" emphasized *concientización* (consciousness-raising)—a process of educating and involving people in struggles to improve their lives. The church sought to give voice to the dispossessed and relate the lessons of the scriptures to the daily lives of the poor. Beginning in 1968, in isolated peasant villages, in crowded urban slums, in *cantones* throughout the highlands, activist clergy, nuns, and priests interacted with their parishioners in new ways. Symbolic changes embodied bold messages: the priest now spoke in Spanish as he faced the congregation rather than saying mass in Latin with his back to the parishioners. He spoke about the hardship, the indignities, the desolation people confronted in their daily lives and how faith could be key to challenging their exploitation and improving their condition. A frequently posed question was, "What would Jesus do if he were here?" But also, "What would Jesus, who gave his life for us, expect of us?" The answers became a vehicle to inform the struggle for change.

Many of the most far-reaching changes took place on a local level. Catechists—local peasants trained to impart spiritual knowledge to their neighbors—were in charge of organizing their own village or hamlet. Like a Christian base community, peasants in these *cantones* met to reflect on the Bible. Unlike the old church, where the priest was the only person who spoke, this new church allowed—in fact demanded—discussion and participation in the local language. The promotion of schools inspired young people to be part of a growing religious and social movement. As one of them said, "We began to open the Bible." The Bible began to make sense as a guide to daily life and as a spiritual document. All the activity in the village meetings flowed into larger meetings that brought people together from throughout the diocese on market days or Sundays to analyze their progress, coordinate the next steps, and plan future events. Intensive courses scheduled over several days ranged back and forth between spiritual and immediate issues and often provided much-desired practical training. The more people learned, the more they wanted to learn.[31]

The Casa Social in Santa Cruz del Quiché, a one-story concrete building with a large inner courtyard near the center of town, emerged as a hub of activity and excitement in the late 1960s. Occupying half of a square block, the building's nondescript appearance was infused with life by the constant movement of individuals, groups, and, at times, entire communities through its rooms and central courtyard. One group came to request the construction of schools, another group wanted to form cooperatives; several villagers sought to build soccer fields, others simply desired to be part of whatever was happening. Given the scarcity of priests and nuns, the catechists were at the front lines of the highland movement.

A remarkable Spanish priest inspired the colonization of Santa María Tzejá. His life embodied the social and historical forces transforming the church during those intense years. Father Luis Gurriarán, a priest of the Missionaries of the Sacred Heart, came from a comfortable background in Galicia. One of his cousins inspired him to become a missionary priest. "When I was a kid, this cousin—who had been a missionary around the world—would come to visit my house," he wistfully recalled. The initial attraction was adventure, but a deeper, more spiritual, inspiration soon followed. At the age of fifteen he entered the seminary to study philosophy; when he was ordained in 1958 at the age of twenty-five, he was anxious to leave Spain. In the wake of the 1954 military coup, the church hierarchy and the government in Guatemala were aggressively recruiting from among the most conservative, anticommunist, pro-Franco clergy. Luis Gurriarán fit the bill. His congregation had a mission in El Quiché staffed by a dozen priests. "I came to follow in the footsteps of the traditional Spanish missionaries," he remembered. "I had that conquest mentality—to introduce the Christian faith." Initially, he viewed his role as telling the impoverished peasants of this world about the wonders of the next. "Social matters had not been discovered yet," he observed dryly, adding, "I at least had not discovered them." What did he think he was going to find in the New World? "Well, I did know that the people were poor. What I didn't know were the causes of poverty and exploitation, or that the poverty was in great part due to the years of colonialism," he recalled. "From the vantage point of today, I can see that there was a certain culpability, not only from the Spanish kingdom, but a certain moral responsibility on the part of the church." Instead of meeting that responsibility, "the church allied itself with those in power who subjugated or enslaved the peoples of the Americas. That realization was a surprise or an awakening to me."

The awakening inspired change. "I had no other alternative than to figure out how I was going to rearrange my ideas," he observed. "That meant to bring about a radical change in my mind-set and therefore find the way to aid people in changing their conditions." Within the diocese of El Quiché, others had already arrived at similar conclusions by the late 1960s. Luis found a strong movement in which the missionaries felt that preaching the gospel to a "poor, exploited, oppressed, ignorant population" was not enough. The movement was, in effect, telling people to "wait for the kingdom of heaven and to continue being subjected to the current situation." Instead, these priests increasingly viewed the gospel as the path for people to guide themselves to liberation. *Concientizar*—to elevate their consciousness—meant to aid people in organizing themselves. As Luis remembered his own transformation, "I came to evangelize the Indians of Guatemala, but in the process of getting to know them they evangelized me."[32]

In the populous El Quiché highlands the young clergy of the Missionaries of the Sacred Heart began with modest education and peasant organization projects in the 1960s. Carol Smith remarks on the critical role played by Santa Cruz del Quiché in those years: "Indians from different parts of the department" studied "at the secondary school in Santa Cruz del Quiché, and as students had initiated their activism in the Departmental capital." Several associations were formed, "with conspicuously Indian claims that centered its action on undermining oppression and discrimination in the cultural sphere, thus accelerating the consciousness of Indian identity. It operated primarily in Santa Cruz del Quiché and Quetzaltenango."[33] Middle-class and educated Mayas in the highlands became instrumental in promoting change and introducing a vision of a new society. The Catholic clergy, nuns, and well-positioned professional local Mayas worked with the rural population with initially modest aims: making immediate conditions a little easier, a little better. One example was organizing cooperatives in the highlands, especially in areas such as Huehuetenango, Quetzaltenango, El Petén, and El Quiché.

Principal among these cooperatives were credit unions to deal with the near total absence of credit for peasants. Prior to credit unions, the only way to obtain a loan was through the plantation labor contractor, which bound a person to work on the plantation. Other moneylenders charged extortionate interest of up to 20 percent monthly, initiating a never-ending circle of indebtedness. The new cooperatives charged 1 percent annually. The priests also formed consumer cooperatives that allowed peasants to buy better-quality products at lower prices and receive the correct measurement and weight. At the end of the year, the profits were shared among the cooperative members. And, most important for the future of Santa María Tzejá, an agricultural cooperative was formed in the late 1960s to find unsettled national land to colonize. Peasants throughout the highlands would hear by word of mouth, or from Father Luis directly, about the agricultural cooperative project and the potential to find unsettled land in the lowland rain forest to the north.

Excited by the possibilities and the enthusiastic response of people in the highlands, Luis wanted to sharpen his skills and develop new ideas. He left Guatemala in 1962 and went to the Atlantic coast of Canada, where he enrolled in an intensive nine-month program on cooperative training and social leadership at Saint Francis Xavier University, in Antigonish, Nova Scotia. This area of Canada was known for a large, well-developed cooperative movement, he recalled, and he became immersed in the classroom, farms, and main streets of Nova Scotia. Cooperatives had become a vital part of the community back in the Guatemalan highlands. Several years later, when he was expelled from

Guatemala for the first time, he wasted no time in returning to Nova Scotia to continue building his skills. Later, he would study cooperative administration at the University of Wisconsin as well as at the Credit Union National Association. He worked hard in the classroom and sought to absorb the lessons of what he saw in the field. His greatest passion, however, was the possibility of applying the experience in rural Guatemala.

While Luis and many others in the church were instrumental in promoting the cooperatives in the mid- and late 1960s, they thrived because the peasants themselves both wanted and needed them. He may have planted the first seeds, but the villagers were inspired to nurture and tend the crops. The K'iche' shaped the cooperatives according to their local needs and built them in a way that captured traditional practices. They were hardly strangers to communal work, and this cultural familiarity aided the effort considerably. Luis contributed, in his view, the formal mechanisms to organize and the experiences he brought from other countries. "A cooperative is an enterprise that has to be managed by its own associated partners *(asociados),*" he emphasized. "Most of the K'iche' peasants did not have experience in this type of enterprise. Thus to guarantee success of a cooperative required a serious training process before joining." He is quick to point out that the cooperative he was promoting was "not just an issue of business training—economic and administrative training—but above all training regarding social issues."

The benefits for the peasants around Santa Cruz del Quiché were obvious and immediate. The competition, however, did not go unnoticed by the local Ladino and K'iche' merchants and was hardly welcomed. Father Luis was threatened and accused of being a communist. The organization of these cooperatives created such a furor among the small businessmen in the area, as well as the government, that in 1965 Father Luis was asked to leave the country by the Guatemalan military government. In response, Catholic Action activists organized the first massive demonstration in Santa Cruz against the governor. Several members who were also cooperative leaders were kidnapped. Luis's expulsion and the kidnappings provoked a huge response throughout El Quiché province. The Christian Democratic Party saw this as an opportunity to ally itself with progressive political forces and show its relevance and solidarity. A large group representing Catholic Action went to the capital to expose these abuses to the Guatemalan Congress. The individuals detained were released, but Luis was not brought back. In part the politicians could correctly say that this was a church matter. Indeed, the bishop of Sololá and the superior of the Sacred Heart order were in agreement with the expulsion. This incident was significant in that it highlighted the growing force of Catholic Action, especially the role of Mayan intellectuals.[34]

Assessing the impact of Luis's expulsion, the Catholic Church of El Quiché stated: "The main objective of the priest's expulsion was the destruction of the cooperative movement that he had initiated and promoted in El Quiché. However, the real consequence of the expulsion was the growth and strengthening of the movement. A year and a half later, the study circles and the precooperative groups had multiplied."[35] In Santa Cruz, the savings and credit cooperative grew from twelve hundred to two thousand members, quadrupling its capital and by 1971 was the largest in the country. Three years after the expulsion there were eighteen cooperatives—ten savings and credit, six consumer, one industrial, and one agricultural.[36]

When Luis returned from exile in 1966, he rolled up his sleeves once again with the same commitment and enthusiasm and began organizing workshops at the Casa Social in Santa Cruz del Quiché.[37] Luis's commitment and faith in finding solutions to the land problem inspired many peasants. By the time I arrived in 1973, Casa Social seemed the liveliest place in town. Located at one corner of the building was Radio K'iche', where broadcasters would transmit news and programs of interest to the outlying *cantones* in K'iche'. The airwaves were filled with announcements of meetings, workshops, Bible study groups, and visits to their *cantones,* as well as a variety of courses, especially literacy classes. Given that local Ladinos did not speak K'iche', they took a while to figure out the political content of some of these broadcasts, which is probably why they went on as long as they did.[38]

At Casa Social, Luis and others (clergy and lay social "promoters") raised larger questions in the context of specific organizing strategies: What basic problems do peasants face? How does one promote locally based development projects? What is the relationship of Christianity to cooperatives and social change? The discussion of cooperatives ranged from an analysis of broad social issues or political conditions to local accounting practices. Discussions covered the causes of poverty, the policies of the government, the unequal distribution of land, exploitation, lack of organization, or lack of employment. Amidst all of this "they made sure we learned the rules of the cooperative," Jesús remembers. Manuel recalled that he learned "the seven principles of the cooperative," and he recalled with some awe the "long, big pamphlet" in which "we found out the cooperatives were formed in Europe, and what advantages they brought to the poor...what obligations one has and what rights one has, all of that." Underlying all these discussions was the value of unity to confront problems.

These talks would often wind up on the issue of land. People frequently asked, "What can be done to obtain land?" "Some recognized that the cooperatives were helping us to become more aware of the reality and to resolve some of our problems," Luis recalled. "The fundamental problem was always how to resolve the land problem. Others would say, 'A few years ago there was an effort toward an agrarian reform that was drowned in blood,' referring to the aftermath of President Arbenz's overthrow," he continued. "Could it be that we will never be able to obtain land? That we will never be able to work and be free peasants, owners of our own future? The idea to find land somewhere in the country began to surge. The leaders were aware and determined in this effort. Willing to go all the way, no matter what, to achieve their objective to find land."

The cooperatives focused on economic issues, especially those pertaining to land issues, and therefore centered on men. At times the discussions became more personal, probing addictions—especially alcohol—and their resultant calamities. Nuns would bring women together to discuss hygiene, health care, and child care. Local promoters conducted training sessions in health, education, and adult literacy. The promoters took great pride in their activities and approached the classes with an impressive seriousness. The catechists of Catholic Action, who tended to be young K'iche' with literacy and Spanish-language skills, were the obvious choices to promote and introduce these programs in distant rural areas. This role in turn increased their standing—more secular and more modern—in these communities. The Catholic Action movement is not without its critics, including self-criticism from within the diocese of El Quiché. A self-righteous, if not narrow-minded stance, and at times a certain aggressiveness created deep divisions within El Quiché province.[39] Nonetheless, the confidence of the young catechists grew, as did their expectations of more rapid change. To them it was as if blindfolds had been removed. I remember spending long hours talking to K'iche'-educated youth in the early and mid-1970s. They would talk about both local and national matters with ease. Radio had changed their access to world events, and they wanted to know about President Salvador Allende in Chile and other international news. On the plantations, truck drivers raised questions about Jimmy Hoffa in the United States. This new consciousness provoked a reaction from the local Ladino and some Mayan elites. The greater the opposition from the local power structure, however, the more determined these young people would become. The hostility demonstrated they were having an impact.

Through it all, Pedro Lux recalled, the workshops at the Casa Social brought people together. Those who came usually did not know each other before but they found they shared a lot in common; above all, the desire for land of their own and better living conditions. "There were people from Canillá, Zacualpa, Joyabaj, Cunén, from many *municipios*," Pedro said. The workshops, the classes, the cooperatives did not simply talk about unity. They created bridges between individuals and groups and molded a sense of engagement in a common cause.

By 1967 there were 145 rural cooperatives in the country involving more than twenty-seven thousand peasants.[40] The classes might teach people rudimentary accounting or the principles of sanitation, but most important, the experience fed a sense of confidence and ability. Nonetheless, the elites still ruled, the land continued to erode, the military remained in power, and the dreaded seasonal migration to the plantations did not stop. Within this context, however, some were no longer content to accept the conditions in which they found themselves. These highland peasants now had organized a cooperative and were ready for change—to put into practice what they had prepared themselves for in all the cooperative workshops. On the other side of the mountains, in the hot, humid, dense rain forest, there was land. The area was inaccessible, the land ill-suited for long-term agriculture, the tools limited to axes and machetes, but despite all the formidable, seemingly insurmountable obstacles, the land had one outstanding characteristic: It was available.

In 1969, with the support of the Catholic Church and several Mayan organizers, one hundred peasant families from various highland *municipios* in El Quiché came together and formed the Zona Reyna Multiservice Agricultural Cooperative with the purpose of colonizing the jungle. The people came from the *municipios* of Joyabaj, Zacualpa, Chinique, Canillá, Uspantán, Cunén, San Pedro Jocopilas, Santa Cruz del Quiché, and Chichicastenango. Most had received training and gained some experience working in local cooperatives. With courage, apprehension, faith, and excitement they would soon begin their remarkable journey.

chapter 2

✦◡✦

Settling in the Promised Land

As 1970 approached, the prospective settlers were awash with conflicting emotions: hope mixed with dread, optimism laced with
apprehension, excitement fueling a deep determination. They
knew they were about to leave the familiar refuge of their highland
homes. They were saying good-bye, perhaps forever, to a place where
their fathers and mothers had tilled the land, where they had spent their
childhoods, where the morning mists were familiar, and where for generations their ancestors had walked the cool mountain paths. Their destination was a distant, uncertain place they had nonetheless begun to call
the "promised land." This new place was by all accounts an inhospitable
rain forest, but it represented their own piece of land and, therefore, a
sliver of hope for a better future. They had few illusions about their difficult journey ahead, but they knew that success would mean an end to
their despised trek to the plantations and their deepening poverty in the
highlands. They were taking a gamble, the most important of their lives.
With scarce resources, they had little room to fail.

Considerable planning and coordination had already gone into the
project. All the classes, discussions, and endless meetings at Casa Social
had laid a sturdy foundation. The classes had given them practical skills
that they would draw on heavily in the years to come; the discussions
and meetings deepened their political awareness and provided a sense of
the challenges ahead. Most important, the extensive preparation taught
the families to work together. They developed a strong cooperative spirit
and a deep sense of solidarity that would bind them together and give
life to their dreams. Amid the hardship of the rain forest, poor Maya and
poor Ladino strangers drawn from different highland *cantones* would
forge a community.

In the months before they left, Father Luis and the other leaders of the cooperative worked with personnel from the government's Instituto de Transformación Agraria (INTA, National Institute for Agrarian Transformation) to locate unsettled national land. They thought about two areas in an isolated northern region for settlement: one in western El Petén province and the other in the Ixcán in northern El Quiché province. The Maryknolls already had aided in colonization projects in the western part of the Ixcán, known as Ixcán Grande, and in the western section of El Petén. Luis and the members of the agricultural cooperative thought the closer, southern Ixcán region, known as the Zona Reyna, would be an appropriate site for colonization. With the aid of INTA engineers and Israeli topographers, the cooperative located the best place for the center of the village. The communal land and buildings would occupy the center, surrounded by 116 house lots of one hectare each, and with an outer circle of parcels of twenty-eight to thirty hectares for cultivation. With this approach, every house would be near the center, and parcels for cultivation would be located further away. The entire layout was organized into four sectors.

The initial plan called for small groups of a dozen or so people to migrate to the colonization site in rotations lasting for several months. On these rotations, they would clear the land, lay out the village, and then return to the highlands when another group would take their place. The men would clear the rain forest—hacking through the dense foliage with machetes and felling old *ceiba* and *conacaste* trees with axes—and build the communal buildings; one or two women would accompany each work brigade to prepare the food.

All the settlers remember the day, even the moment, when they or their loved ones left the highlands. The younger children recall tearful, apprehensive good-byes to fathers, uncles, brothers, and sisters and the stories they told and retold when they returned. Those who went will never forget the extraordinary experience of the tough week-long journey—the rugged mountains, the descent into the unfamiliar rain forest, the brown, surging rivers, the kindness of strangers, the bone-numbing exhaustion, the inescapable heat, and finally the intense joy and satisfaction of arrival. Manuel Canil recalled the difficulty of slogging through mud that at times would reach their knees. "We almost couldn't take it any more with the mud and the plagues of insects," he said. "We also had to make sure we wouldn't get lost." While the rigors of the trip savaged their bodies, their spirits remained full of wonder. "We did not become disheartened," he insisted. "We had to get there. We had to go see what that land was like."[1]

Consider the stories of Jesús and Valentín, two of the initial K'iche' settlers. Jesús, an eleven-year-old boy at the time, recalls the moment his father decided to go. His father, who had been orphaned at the age of four, had endured a lifetime of backbreaking work as a peasant and a woodcutter, but had little to show for his efforts. Weathered by the unforgiving sun of the cotton plantations and hardened by the tough life in the highlands, he looked older than his years. One day he simply had had enough of a perverse, debilitating combination of shrinking resources and increasing anxiety and made the decision to see the colonization site. While Jesús's mother was apprehensive, the youngster was amazed and excited. Years later he recalled the events so vividly that they seemed to have happened the day before. "My childish dreams and fantasies made me want to know a new way of life," he remembered. Being the eldest, he was able to accompany his father. "A few days before we departed," he recalled, "my father traced a map on the floor with a charred piece of wood, showing the places we had to go through to get to the jungle." His young imagination avidly followed each black line on the floor, imagining trails through the rain forest and mysterious journeys down rivers. His mother painstakingly packed *totoposte* (toasted corn tortillas), *tzocom* (tamales), a little cornmeal, sugar, salt, coffee, and chilies. They also took along an axe, a machete, and a saw, as well as a few pots and pans and some clothes. "I tried not to notice my mother's pain and worry, and left happily with my father," Jesús recollected, wondering how his enthusiasm survived in the face of this anxiety.

As they left the house in the cool hours before dawn in mid-1970, they heard the crow of distant roosters from houses on the hilltops and the response of other roosters echoing the call from houses nearby. The smell of burning wood provided a familiar reassurance to the morning, and they saw smoke rising from rooftops as they walked. They encountered several people who wished the father well but pleaded with him to leave the young son behind. The journey was too dangerous, they warned, and the son would have to leave grammar school. Jesús would have none of it— he was eager to go—and, in any case, his father needed him on the trip. "All of the arguments weren't enough to convince me to stay," he stated. "My dreams were worth more, above all to live in the promised land!"

In search of these dreams, Jesús and his father walked with a quiet determination to the rutted field where the buses stopped on the edge of Santa Cruz del Quiché. As they arrived, the first sun rays began to break over the fields and the surrounding mountains. The two of them crowded aboard an old school bus—six people squeezed into each row, some carrying large sacks, others holding a chicken or small pig. As the old bus belched fumes and its axles bottomed out on the deep ruts in the road, Jesús and his father watched the familiar countryside recede on their way to San Miguel Uspantán. That night they slept under the stars in the town's square. The second day they once again rose before sunrise feeling the cool, familiar mountain air and began what would be a grueling eight-day walk. "Before I thought that the world ended where the horizon was," Jesús recounted. Now he was taking the first steps into a whole new world. They traversed the spine of the craggy Cuchumatán Sierra, hiking on narrow trails and trudging through *milpas,* or cornfields, that reminded them of what they were leaving. His father was pressed down by the eighty pounds attached to his forehead with a *mecapal,* or tumpline, walking with the measured rhythm of experience, while Jesús struggled less deftly with twenty-five pounds on his back. The heavy weight caused them both to strain on the steep climbs and made it difficult to keep their balance on the descents. Jesús remembers clutching at anything in order not to "fall like stones to the bottom of the ravine."

Soon the familiar vegetation of the highlands began to change to the more lush, unfamiliar plants of the lower elevations, and Jesús began to marvel at the sight of "orchids and moss, the songs of the Guardabarranco birds, which gave a touch of beauty," to the otherwise demanding journey. Occasionally they heard wild boar or a tiger running through the underbrush or the flapping of wild turkey hens in flight. Toward dusk they listened to the strange, distant sounds of macaws and parrots. At night the damp warmth of the jungle enveloped them and they listened to night mammals scurry across the rain forest floor or scamper up its trees. The sounds of unfamiliar tropical birds announced the coming of dawn. Along the way they encountered Ixil traveling salesmen who provided welcome information about what awaited them ahead. As the path meandered through the rain forest, they continued walking under the thick green jungle canopy, continually swatting away insects and remaining alert for the red and black rings of deadly coral snakes. On occasion, they reached the end of a tired day near the house of a Q'eqchi' family who would give them *posada* (a place to repose) under a thatched, makeshift cover. In these simple dwellings, they noticed with amazement the skins of wild boar or jaguar.

By the sixth or seventh day, their bodies were overcome with fatigue, hunger, insect bites, and blisters; they were slowing down and increasingly drawing on reserves of courage and hope. They confronted new challenges: thick, heavy mud that gripped tired ankles, trails they had to hack open with machetes, rushing rivers of unexpected colors, suffocating heat, and swarms of bugs. Their horizon now was a few yards, if that, and they feared getting lost. On occasion, the distant crow of a rooster or the clucks of chickens announced a nearby human settlement. On the eighth day, about four hours from their final destination, Jesús and his father reached a small cluster of thatched-roofed houses of Q'eqchi' settlers in Santa María Dolores. "All I remember are the tops of the trees," Jesús said, reliving the overwhelming exhaustion of that moment, "but we kept walking until we arrived at the Tzejá River. I was so tired I didn't want to keep going, but I had to do it." The sight of the Tzejá—a name that derives from a K'iche' word, *tzii' ha'*, which means water-dog or river of the otters—and the knowledge they were close to their destination revived their spirits and jump-started their energy. "The river made me feel not so tired because it told me that when we were in the new colony we could come here to bathe, swim, fish, and those thoughts motivated me through the last kilometers of the trip," he said.

At last they reached the newly named Santa María Tzejá in the dense rain forest. "In the afternoon hours we had arrived in a clearing made by the first settlers who had come ahead of us," he remembered, "and there we observed three huts built out of *pamaca* palm branches and sticks. Three families were living there: two were from Zacualpa, the other from Canillá." The settlers who had arrived a few months earlier came out to greet them, to hear news from the highlands, to commiserate about the journey. "One woman gave us *atole* to drink and some tortillas," he said. "Then they struck up a conversation about the long journey, remembering their own suffering, because all of the families had to make the same long trip." The next day work began in earnest. Jesús's father scouted for trees, especially the highly valued mahogany, to use for the public buildings in the village center. Others began clearing the area and preparing the land for cultivation. In the early morning, the sounds of dull axes hitting century-old trees could be heard among the cries of the birds. The settlers built their homes from the wood they cut and the abundant palm leaves nearby. "There was a lot of hard work that had to be done manually, without the help of machines," Jesús remembered. "On many occasions we had to make our own tools out of wood, as our ancestors had done. We made spades, wedges, wagons, and others tools." At the end of the day when the work was done, Jesús and his father took in the wonder of where they were. "There was no noise that did not emanate from nature," Jesús recalled. The shades of green seemed endless; the rivers were mysterious and forceful; the vistas were close-up, leaving to the imagination what might unfold beyond. It was a place that demanded reflection and admiration. It seemed so distant from everything—and "everything" was generally dreadful. By contrast, the promise of the Ixcán was awesome and inspiring.

Unlike Jesús, the young Valentín was not able to make the journey with the early rotating groups, but his father and uncles did. Valentín remembered when they returned in mid-March 1970. "We all rushed to meet them. After greetings we walked them to the house. My brothers and sisters and I, with immense happiness, didn't give my father time to rest or drink." Instead, they overwhelmed him with questions: "How was it? What is the place like? How far is it? Did you see any animals? And so on." His father was "infected with happiness and forgot how tired he was, and while he ate he narrated everything he had seen." He began recalling the journey, "the trek that would get us to that sacred place." His mother immediately interrupted, asking "What is there that makes you call it a sacred place?" His father responded, "I call it sacred because I cannot compare it to the lands from here." He then elaborated to his rapt audience on the streams and the fertile land that produced two harvests of corn per year without fertilizer. He told them about the animals— armadillos, *pizotes,* wild boar, deer, raccoons, tigers, *dantos, tepescuintles*—and told them trees were plentiful—mahogany, cedar, *hormigo, conacaste, granadilla.* "The rivers are full of fish," he continued. "In those lands you can plant and harvest anything." This bountiful nature made it sacred, like the Garden of Eden, and now they would be able to move there after all they had endured.

After four months or so of clearing and building, Valentín's family, the first complete family to settle the site, arrived in May 1970. They felt that the hand of God, like a miracle, had touched and guided them. Soon more families came. The trip was especially difficult for mothers who carried their children on their backs. Some of the women had never been to the Pacific coast plantations and thus had not experienced the suffocating heat and humidity before, let alone the swarms of mosquitoes, ticks, and other strange jungle insects. Their clothing—heavy, long *corte* and *huipil*—awkward on the narrow, overgrown trails, and walking barefoot made their journey even more difficult. Moreover, one woman recalled they had to contend with "snakes and wild animals we didn't know" and, as a result, "we were quite afraid." Another woman agreed, adding a bit more optimistically, "but little by little we became used to the place." A third was even more positive, "We went with good spirits in spite of the hardships, because there we knew we could live." The chil-

Figure 1. The Quinilla-Taperio family, the first complete family to settle in Santa María Tzejá, arrives with companions at the shores of the Tzejá River, 1970. Valentín is in the center, with a ceramic jug to his left. Photo courtesy Father Luis Gurriarán López.

dren suffered the most, however, with the change in climate and the exposure to lowland forest diseases.

Early on, securing food supplies was difficult. Caritas, a Catholic relief organization, donated corn for the early months; people also scoured nearby settlements in the Ixcán to buy maize. The first journey was to the small, already established community of Xalbal on the other side of the Xalbal River. After this trip, they returned with seventy-five-pound bags of maize on their backs, crossing treacherous rivers and sinking into the mud with the added weight. In May 1970, the settlers had burned enough of the forest debris so they could begin cultivation for the first time, a momentous event for all who were there. On that date the village of Santa María Tzejá was truly born. When they plunged their digging sticks into the earth and began to plant, they knew their new life had begun. "We were happy," one villager states. "No more worries; there is maize, there is food. There is life."

Miguel Reyes, a Ladino peasant from El Palmar, arrived in 1972 more than two years after the initial settlers. He recalls his heart sinking when he first saw the rain forest and realized the work needed to clear the area. "I almost changed my mind," he said. It rained torrentially and when they began clearing near the Tzejá River, "there were so many mosquitoes it looked like a cloud. In one hand we had the machete, in the other a branch to hit our backs to keep the mosquitoes away." At the end of the day they were soaked and mosquito bitten. The work would have been difficult under any conditions, but now "the rains were relentless. We did not finish the work we had expected to do in the forty-five days. The river rose a lot, it flowed nonstop in every direction into the jungle." The topographers (who were going to set the borders of the settlement and measure the land parcels) could no longer work, so Miguel and others had to carry the heavy topographical equipment back to the highlands. On the way out, Miguel remembered, it rained so much that by the time they reached the first settlement, Santa María Dolores, the mud and water sometimes were up to their knees. They were grateful if they found a chapel or *ermita* (a rough palm shelter), where they could take shelter from the downpour at night. Otherwise they huddled under the nylon tarps they took with them.

If Miguel Reyes had misgivings, they were fleeting. All he had to do was remember the rocky, dry, eroded land in the highlands that could no longer sustain his family. Now he had the possibility of fertile land in the rain forest. The year before moving to the Ixcán, his family slid into disaster. The entire *milpa* they had planted had dried up, an increasingly frequent occurrence. They had no choice but to head to the Casa Social in Santa Cruz to explore the possibility of settling in the lowlands. But by 1972 there were only five openings for the nine families from El Palmar who wanted to resettle. Eventually, however, some of the 1970 settlers could not adjust to the hot, humid climate and the rigors of their new life and abandoned the effort at colonization. This opened space for all the poor Ladinos from El Palmar. Although these families were the last to come, they nonetheless were required to take daily classes on the principles of cooperatives. "No choice," Miguel said firmly, about the no-nonsense requirements. "At four in the afternoon you had to be there for the classes, every day! That is how we became trained." The trainers were Fabián, Luciano, Mario, Cruz, Esteban, and Father Luis, all seasoned colonizers.[2]

Miguel and the other Ladino families from El Palmar were a minority in the new predominantly K'iche'-speaking village, but they were as poor as the K'iche' in the highlands, and their dreams were the same. I asked Miguel how it felt when he arrived in Santa María Tzejá. "In the beginning we felt a lot of pressure," he responded. "We felt that they did not trust us. The problem was that we did not understand what they were saying, but we could see them talking." I ask what he meant by being "pressured." He replied, "We had no voice, we could not express ourselves at all, we were too few—the majority rules." Since they could not speak K'iche', they could not fully participate. "In the beginning we felt badly, and they wondered if we wanted to take advantage of them, but that was not so," he said. "Then after awhile things changed. There were no differences among the people that are here. Our children marry their children. We are all mixed."[3] Their training clearly smoothed the adjustment for the Ladinos. "We knew from the classes we attended in Uspantán about the big Mayan movement," he said. "We knew that Catholic priests and nuns were helping the indigenous people. There were literacy classes." He was also aware of the growing tension between clergy and the government. "Nuns and others were threatened," he emphasized. What prepared the Ladinos most, in his view, was the fact that "we had taken classes in catechism, and we were no longer so proud. What we wanted was land and not problems, the same as everyone." The historic mistrust between Mayas and Ladinos would have proven far more difficult to overcome without the intense effort of the church. Miguel, years later, would become a key leader in Santa María Tzejá and in the refugee camps in Mexico.

The isolation of the village and the cooperative aided in the integration. Individuals could not succeed if the village failed, and the fate of the village rested on cooperation and participation. Settlers could not remain in the village without integrating. Constant meetings, discussions, and collective decisions defined their lives. The best ideas and best behavior would win, not the biggest bully. Ladinos, in any case, were vastly outnumbered. With time those among them who were the most capable rose to positions of leadership.

The cooperative, inspired and organized by Father Luis, laid the basis for a community and became the soul of its success. Later, it proved instrumental in obtaining funding from international nongovernmental organizations (NGOs). When a U.S. organization provided cattle for the cooperative, those who received breeding cows were obliged to give others the offspring so that every cooperative member could start off with several animals. This donation provided milk, meat, and extra cash. Once everyone was secure with several cows, each member could sell or breed animals as they wished. A Kansas-based organization, Wings of Hope, provided the cooperative with a single-engine Cessna plane and a volun-

teer American pilot. Without these common projects the isolation and atomization of the basic family unit would have been far greater due to the
absence of extended families and ancestral links at the colonization site.

The communal spirit guiding the cooperatives was familiar to these
settlers. "I learned from my parents, even though they had no education,"
Pedro Canil remembers, "that when a family has a downfall, one must
always help. We are born with, we carry with us, a consciousness to aid
and care about others. It is one's duty to provide aid." Gaspar adds,
"When someone dies and leaves a family in crisis, we all come together
to pray a rosary, to make a collection, to give some food." The cooperative became central to the functioning of the community, facilitating
business projects and resolving social conflicts. The work in building the
cooperative—particularly the training and the classes—energized the villagers' interest in learning. By 1973 they had built a school and had their
own adult-literacy promoters. In the village, there were always courses
on agronomy, hygiene, how to run a cooperative, health care, children's
care, and Bible discussions. The value of working together ran through
all the disparate classes.

The spirit of optimism that inspired the cooperative also infused
Shalom Alehem, a youth religious group that Luis organized. Thirty-eight
young men and women joined the group, which had a profound, life-
long impact on many of them and the community itself. Former members say the group's goal was "*concientizarnos*" (to raise our consciousness) and to create solidarity. In the process, they met kindred young
people from other provinces at regional and national gatherings. "Shalom
Alehem helped me to awaken my mind," Pedro Tum remembered more
than two decades later. "It made me see my Christian duty through the
Bible, through the word of God." But, in the spirit of the liberation theology, the group went well beyond religious teachings. "[Shalom] made
me see that there was much to do to achieve a change so that I no longer
have to live the way my father did," Pedro Tum continued. "I am a little better off than he is and my children are better [off] than I am. And
the children of my children will be excellent." Pedro reflected for a moment and then added, "To this day my experience in Shalom is still of
value to me." The organization broadened the horizons of its members
considerably. "[Our parents did not have] the opportunity to enrich their
knowledge, the ability to study their human rights, or other knowledge
that would help them to rise above the ignorance we have been subjected
to," Gaspar commented. Villagers recall that their parents had never
learned or even heard the term *derechos,* or rights. "They did not know

they had rights, and even less the concept of universal human rights."
People like Gaspar and Pedro Tum felt that prior to going to Santa María
Tzejá when they had lived in *cantones,* they had been totally marginalized and isolated from others. Paradoxically, in the geographically isolated village they had the opportunity to organize, develop friendships,
promote discussions, and become more connected to others in the same
situation through the national youth meetings. The social promoters in-
stilled confidence in the Shalom Alehem youth. When asked for the translation of Shalom Alehem from Hebrew, one former member replied,
"May peace be with us," rather than the more accurate "May peace be
with you." And for him the meaning was that "we wanted to feel as a
united community, even though people came from several *municipios,*
here we came to find each other." They were always encouraged to work
in unity and aspired to make Santa María Tzejá a "model community."
The fact that the concept of community emerged through unique circumstances in a new village made it more conscious, real, and strong.

One member of Shalom recalled his days in the highlands working
for one of the wealthiest families in Guatemala, the Herreras. After the
grinding labor and pervasive mistreatment, his experience in Shalom was
very emotional. Most villagers never experienced equal relations with
Ladinos in the highlands, he said, while in Santa María Tzejá, where the
Ladinos were only 10 percent of the population, they lived as brothers,
intermarried, and became godparents for each others' children. They began to feel much more positive about themselves. "We learned to read,
and with that we were opening the Bible," Pedro Tum observed. "That
helped us." In fact, it was more than "opening" or reading the Bible.
They began to interpret it and understand the ways in which it related
to their daily lives. They invited youth of other communities, and they
in turn were invited to attend *encuentros,* or retreats, of three or four
days. They learned "that Jesus was not in agreement with injustice, with
the bosses. He announced the Kingdom of God on earth, not in heaven
when we die. Before we were told to pray looking up to the sky, but the
Kingdom of God has to be won here on earth with peace, justice, solidarity. We also have to struggle ourselves to get out of ignorance," Pedro Tum emphasized. They learned about concepts of rights, to "discover
them, to interpret them. We began to understand that we needed to make
changes in our lives, both in terms of religion as well as in a social and
political sense," he added. Some members of Shalom Alehem went on
scholarships to Catholic (boys' and girls') boarding schools and attended

the Escuela Nacional Comunal Indígena in Chichicastenango. In a few years, they made crucial decisions and took part in the village's destiny.

Prosperity but No Security

The village of Santa María Tzejá was founded in the spirit of community. Given the magnitude of the obstacles and the scarcity of resources it should have failed. In fact, many predicted and some wished it would fail. Instead, this long-shot undertaking became a surprising success. The settlers built a landing strip and bridges; they constructed paths and simple homes. In the center of the village they built a large structure for the cooperative, as well as a school, a multipurpose room for community meetings, a clinic, and living quarters for the volunteers. At the heart of the village, they constructed a chapel with a roof of palms and walls made of small tree trunks. Already by 1973, as the community slowly began to prosper, they had built a more elaborate church with a sheet-metal roof and walls of fine mahogany. Nearby, they leveled an area and laid out a soccer field.

I was impressed with all they had managed to do in just a couple of years. I arrived in a small single-engine plane that had taken off from the grass landing strip on the outskirts of Santa Cruz del Quiché. As I flew over the Cuchumatán Sierra and then over the rain forest, a dense green canopy below stretched endlessly to the horizon, covering everything except for the occasional brown river snaking through the forest. Trails were invisible from the air, and I looked out the window in awe at how the settlers had traversed this formidable landscape. We landed south of the Tzejá River, and from there we proceeded on horses, crossing the river toward Santa María Tzejá. The most impressive dimension of the village was the spirit that pervaded so much of daily life. The houses, for example, were simple structures, made of thin tree trunks tied together and palm roofs, but many also had small flower gardens. At dusk, there was always a gathering at Luis's house to play the guitar and sing. I still remember the haunting lyrics of some of the songs. The *nueva canción* (folk protest music) from Chile was being heard in this corner of the continent. Some lyrics came from romantic *rancheras*— "where are you going, alone in the city"—about the pain of urban loneliness. The success of these pioneers, 116 families at the end of the first year, served as a beacon to others in the Quiché highlands, often desperate and with far less preparation. In 1970 there were five thousand people in the Ixcán.[4]

Within two years, there were ten communities of the same size as Santa María Tzejá or even larger. By 1975 as many as ten thousand people were living in the Ixcán, and by 1982 the population had risen, according to some estimates, to around forty-five thousand.[5]

In the land parcels the villagers cultivated the corn, beans, and rice that would sustain them. The fields, unlike their exhausted highland plots, did not need fertilizer. In the house lots they planted oranges, banana, pineapple, tangerines, and yucca. They raised pigs, turkeys, chickens, and cows. Their diet immediately improved, and the days of buying corn were soon behind them. "I remember we used to talk about the fact that we will never have to work for a *patrón* again," Gaspar stated. "We are now working for ourselves." The ability to meet immediate needs led villagers to consider longer-range economic possibilities, especially commercial crops. In this endeavor, they faced tough new challenges. "Anything grew on the land, but we lost a lot of what we planted due to the lack of roads and the difficulty of bringing crops to distant city markets," Jesús commented. Despite these setbacks, the settlers persisted. "With the passage of time, we began to experiment with new crops according to the strength and ability of each person," he recalled with pride. "We began to plant cardamom, coffee, cacao, *achiote,* pineapple, sugarcane, and a variety of other spices." Cardamom became for them a "green gold." The spice, first harvested in the mid-1970s, commanded a good price in the international market, especially the Arab countries, reaching five hundred U.S. dollars per *quintal* (one hundred pounds).[6] And initially the village had few competitors. Since the cooperative had access to a small plane, the crops could be taken to Santa Cruz del Quiché or directly to Guatemala City. Building on the village's experience along with the cooperatives of Ixcán Grande, Ixcán cardamom producers later organized into a regional organization. Within a decade—by 1980—the 116 families in Santa María Tzejá were selling cardamom and had about one thousand head of cattle, a source of cash as well as food.

But not all was tranquil. A vague, deepening unease hung over their success. One undemocratic military government after another was the norm. In the Ixcán, the military began harassing settlers around 1969–70 because of the presence of individuals in the region who had been associated with the Rebel Armed Forces, a guerrilla group from the 1960s. A few years later, the military unleashed selective killings of leaders and was closely watching the settlers and the priests who organized the colonization, notably after a new guerrilla group began operating in the region. Father Luis, however, claimed the military harassment preceded the insurgents. "When we came to this area on January 5, 1970, the army was already kidnapping people, such as the *cacique* [chief] of Santa María Dolores, Pedro Ical," Luis said, referring to a neighboring community. "We succeeded in having him freed. There were no guerrillas then; but there was a military detachment by the Tzejá River near San Antonio. Then they moved the detachment to Ascención Copón. We had to pass by there—right in front of the boots of the army."

In that same year when some villagers were returning from Xalbal, they encountered an army helicopter. The soldiers said that they wanted to check Luis's "camp" and ask him questions. Disturbing rumors also spread through the village. Relatives in the highlands made occasional comments that some were suspicious of the goings-on in the Ixcán. Soldiers charged that the peasants who went to the Ixcán were bandits, delinquents, terrorists, outlaws, communists, guerrillas, or all of the above. "At that time we did not know them [the guerrillas]," Gaspar stated, but still the rumors about the Ixcán were disconcerting. "What I want to emphasize is that the military occupation of the Ixcán occurred before the guerrillas were here," Luis stated. "Some say the army came because the guerrillas came. [In fact], the army came before the guerrillas, because they had that ambition, because they realized these were rich lands. Then the guerrillas came and the military presence increased, leading to the total militarization of the region." Luis was referring to military officers who became very interested in the region just east of Ixcán and by the late 1970s had in fact acquired large expanses of land, turning them into pasture for raising cattle. Luis said that "the soldiers were drunk; they fired their weapons; they did not respect anyone."[7]

What made the settlers especially anxious was the delay in receiving titles to their land parcels located on national lands. Officials from INTA, the most significant governmental agency for the colonizers, informed the settlers that even though some had provisional titles, no one would receive permanent documents for twenty years or so. Some did not even receive provisional papers. Miguel Reyes complained that insecurity over land ownership was not just a village issue, but a national problem. "They gave not only to one but sometimes to two or three—or who knows to how many peasants—the same piece of land!" he angrily stated. "So it becomes a mess to straighten out. To whom does this belong? Mr. Braulio Flores from [the government's] INTA office said one should be patient. But to this day [1998] there are parcels in the name of the nation," that is, they don't belong to an individual.

Adding anxiety to aggravation was the government's suggestion that the parcels were too large and ought to be subdivided to allow more peasants to settle the area. In the mid-1970s, USAID had begun a large colonization project called Project 520 just north of Santa María Tzejá. "Those peasants were subjected by the government to do things only as the government and the military said," Felipe Canté insisted. Project 520 parcels were much smaller—about a third the size—than those in Santa María Tzejá, underscoring fears that the government might deliver on the threat to subdivide the village's parcels (thirty hectares in Santa María Tzejá versus ten hectares in Project 520).

In the early years the settlers had a good relationship with the government's agrarian agency and remember a few local officials as being helpful. When the settlers went to make their payments for the land parcels at the office in nearby Buenos Aires, however, they received either nothing or a slip that hardly resembled a receipt. When the villagers questioned the scraps of paper, they were told the papers were "provisional" receipts. In a country where everything is demonstrated by showing a document—often heavily laden with embossed stamps and elaborate symbols—the peasants feared having no "official" proof of their payments. Worse yet, they became increasingly uneasy about the "provisional" tenure of their land parcels. They feared that INTA's administrators were pocketing the money rather than sending it to Guatemala City where the payment would be duly recorded. There were discrepancies between INTA records and what the settlers claim they paid. In some cases in the Ixcán, the parcels were still registered as unoccupied national land because no payments were ever officially recorded.

In 1974 a government agrarian administrator, Máximo "Chimino" Contreras, stated specifically that the land parcels for each family in the first four *parcelamientos*, Santa María Tzejá, Kaibil Balam, Santiago Ixcán, and San José la 20, were too large. This announcement came at the time that San Lucas and Santo Tomás Ixcán were being laid out for settlement. These government bureaucrats felt that if the land-parcel size was kept as originally defined, the available land could not accommodate all the people from the south coast and the highlands who now wanted to colonize the Ixcán. After the first pioneers showed they could succeed, landless peasants from throughout the country began descending on the northern lowlands. Aware of that potential deluge and eager to keep the Ixcán colonizers in check, the government threatened to divide the original parcels in half. This threat prompted a heated discussion at a cooperative meeting. "We couldn't let this happen," Domingo

Us Quixán asserted. "Our families are growing each time more and more." Felipe Canté proposed that "we should try to pay off the parcels as soon as possible so as not to give the INTA authorities a chance to divide them up, because that is their plan." Some settlers decided to go directly to Guatemala City in the late 1970s to make payments, but they were sucked into the slow, grinding gears of INTA's bureaucracy. The agency would not accept their payments, claiming that the parcel was in someone else's name, or it was still registered as national land, or that the records couldn't be found, or some improbable combination of all three. It became clear that INTA wanted to keep the land situation as uncertain as possible to give the bureaucracy maximum leverage. After making four costly, difficult trips to deliver a mountain of requested documents, Felipe Canté concluded that the agency was wasting his time. "I told the employees of INTA," he recalled, "that they were all legally irresponsible, that they only wanted to make money. Even though they made me get my papers notarized four times, they never wanted to legalize my parcel." He then reflected and added, "I don't know, perhaps it was the policy of the government to leave us without documents, without titles, so they could take the land away from us later on."

Amid a burgeoning anxiety, a little-noticed event took place that would reverberate throughout the rain forest for decades. A small group of armed men silently slipped into northern Ixcán from Mexico on January 19, 1972. These fifteen Guatemalans were survivors of the counterinsurgency war in eastern Guatemala in the mid-1960s. Their organization did not yet have a formal name but they called themselves the Nueva Organización Revolucionaria de Combate (New Revolutionary Combat Organization) and subsequently the Edgar Ibarra front (named after a student leader of the 1960s).[8] "Our clothes were torn to shreds as we pushed our way through the dense vegetation—we avoided cutting a path so as not to leave a trail," Mario Payeras, one of the participants, wrote a number of years later in *Days of the Jungle*. "When, balancing carefully so as not to topple over, we descended to the bed of a ravine, our boots sank deep into the mire and there we were, stuck." Those few among them who knew the jungle sought to teach the others the rudiments of survival. Only one of the fifteen ragged recruits knew how to use a *mecapal*, or headband; for the rest it "was a nuisance: it would slip down, cutting off our vision."[9] After several months of battling the vicissitudes of the jungle, they came on a small settlement of six families near the Xalbal River.[10] There they were told about a larger vil-

lage several hours away that had a weekly market. As they left, they sur-
veyed the jungle in front of them. Mario Payeras, a future leader of the
group, described the scene in his memoir:

> One morning, from a small rise, we looked out over the panorama of the
> jungle. It was the month of the *tamborillo* tree, and its yellow blossoms
> spread unforgettably before us. To the south, awesomely close to the sky,
> were the great peaks of the northern Chamá range, an objective still be-
> yond our reach. There, several miles to the north, we were sure there were
> Indian settlements where guerrilla armies would be organized in the fore-
> seeable future. We allowed ourselves to dream a while, but our reality was
> the jungle with its dangers, its loneliness, and its huge distances.[11]

With meager resources and vast ambitions, this makeshift column
promptly got lost on the confusing, overgrown trails of the rain forest.[12]
After a day or two they arrived at their destination, Santa María Tzejá.
It was 1972 and what was to become the Ejército Guerrillero de los Pobres (EGP, Guerrilla Army of the Poor) was entering an established village for the first time. Payeras wrote about their encounter:

> After a brief look around Santa María Tzejá, we returned to the jungle,
> having spent almost all our money in the village store. In order to mislead
> possible informers, we had, on our arrival, pretended to be an antiguerrilla
> patrol and had also pretended to force the traders into selling to us, al-
> though such was not the case. But thanks to such stratagems, the enemy
> could do little more than note our presence in the area.[13]

The EGP's ideology was complex and eclectic. It combined intellectual Marxist roots with a focus on the most egregious problems facing
peasants—land and indigenous discrimination among others—and
adopted important elements of liberation theology. The ideology tended
to vary depending on to whom you spoke and when. The leadership
identified with the Cuban model, and their emblem was Che Guevara—
the Latin American revolutionary icon. A Guatemalan military officer,
intrigued by the success of the group among the rural population, credits their focus on relevant local issues. They do not speak to the indigenous peasants of "Marx, Lenin, Mao, Fidel, or Che," but about their
poverty, their long history of exploitation and discrimination. The officer
also credits the EGP with understanding early on the Mayan culture,
learning the local languages, and thereby winning the confidence of the
population. The very name, Guerrilla Army of the Poor, this officer ac-
knowledges, "represents the mystique that propels them." The EGP "has
reminded and made them conscious of their whole historical process, and
offered them a dignity they have never encountered from the governments

who have always seen the indigenous people as a subgroup, backwards and brutalized by ignorance and alcoholic consumption." Not surprisingly, "the civilian population shuns and refuses all collaboration with the military."[14] In 1999 I interviewed the author of this military document, Captain Juan Fernando Cifuentes. He mentioned that the military high command, as part of a propaganda campaign, always referred to the guerrillas as terrorists, delinquents, or criminals and failed to examine the source of their success. This error, he stated, delayed an appropriate strategy against the EGP until it was almost too late.

The guerrilla group's first visit to the village left an indelible impression on their commander, César Montes (Macías). "As I am telling you this I can almost see everything as it was happening," he told me almost three decades later. He too remembered getting lost on the paths meandering through the rain forest. Finally, the exhausted unit arrived at the banks of the muddy Tzejá River, where they spent the night. The next morning they walked across the hanging bridge and headed for the village center, located on an elevated section of the *parcelamiento*. For them this was a rather large village, not a hamlet. More importantly, the cooperative store was full of merchandise—all the things that would make their improvised and arduous conditions more bearable. Montes says that given Father Luis's reputation, they expected to find a Spanish conquistador, say a Hernán Cortés or Pedro de Alvarado: someone who was strong, muscular, rough, mean looking, and gray. "Anyone who did something beneficial or noble for the people was made to seem a giant in their eyes," Montes recalled. Luis was such a giant, in spirit and commitment, if not in physical stature. I asked Montes if Luis had been friendly to them. "No, not particularly," he replied. "But not unfriendly either. He received us with some apprehension or misgivings. Our arrival, we could tell, had worried him." It was obvious why Luis was apprehensive. "He said to us, 'The army will come,'" Montes remembers. "I told him to tell them everything, that we were here, and the village was forced to sell what we demanded." As they were talking in the early morning hours, the daily radio transmission from the military base in highland Santa Cruz del Quiché began to come in. "So I said to Luis, 'I will accompany you,'" Montes recalls with a grin. "I sat right in front of him with the rifle pointed to his chest and I had no doubt that if it had been necessary I would have fired it." The atmosphere was tense as the static from the radio interrupted the quiet of the morning, and the conversation began. "The colonel began asking for the weather and Luis responded, 'humid with such and such temperature,'" Montes relates. "I became concerned at that moment.

What if they have a previously designated password by which the priest would let the colonel know that we are there? Then the colonel asked specifically about our presence there. I held my weapon firmly and stared straight at him. Luis responded, looking at me, 'I wouldn't know, how would I identify them? What do they look like?' " The colonel proceeded to describe the rebels as long-haired, dirty, smelly, bearded—an unflattering but largely correct description of this disoriented band. Luis calmly responded that the group should not be too difficult to identify. With that, the daily transmission ended.

The rebels then went to the store and, as prearranged, pretended to force the cooperative members to sell them things.[15] Luis went along, as did the person in charge of the cooperative at the time. Montes asked Luis to change a one-hundred dollar bill, the only money he had. In those days even paying with a twenty-quetzal bill would have been difficult, but dollars, let alone a bill that large, presented a significant, if not surreal, problem. At first, Luis thought he was joking. But, in reality, this turned out to be the only bill the unit had left. "Who would have believed that we were risking our lives without a rearguard, pursued by the Mexican army from behind and the Guatemalan army in front, no social base, lost, without help and with nothing else but a one-hundred-dollar bill?" Montes reflected in amazement. Luis, still in disbelief, changed the bill, and provided lots of small-denomination quetzales in return. All the guerrillas felt good about this first encounter and made plans for future contacts and purchases at the store using a code. Luis asked how he would know the purchases were in fact for this group. Montes responded that the code would be the "colmillo del tigre" (tiger's fang), which he remembered to this day. The guerrilla leader was impressed by the determination of the highland peasants and the Spanish priest. "Anyone who lived in the jungle needed to have not only tremendous physical strength, but more important, huge inner strength," he observed. "The Ixcán jungle consumes you, there is malaria, diarrhea; it just consumes you. But people came from all over the country to obtain a parcel in the promised land."

After having breakfast and completing their purchases, the insurgents climbed in a *cayuco* (a dugout canoe) and took off down the river. Some villagers went to the banks of the river to wave them farewell. The *cayuco*, however, had been used almost exclusively to cross from one side of the river to the other. The Tzejá River was notoriously dangerous, and this heavy, unwieldy boat was certainly not suited for novices who knew neither how to maneuver it nor the intricacies of this rushing, turbulent river.

Not surprisingly, the *cayuco* overturned not too far down the river, and it was only a miracle that everyone in it survived. The wet, startled survivors managed to make it to the shore, but lost many of their new purchases. The river fiasco seemed an inauspicious beginning.

Although the guerrillas remained only a short time in the village, their visit struck a chord with some of the residents. Their presence seemed to echo elements of liberation theology and its "preferential option for the poor." Given the social history of Guatemala and the persistent economic and social conditions, the guerrillas were planting seeds in fertile soil. The insurgents did not always find such a receptive village.

The settlement had not happened in a vacuum. Only the most energetic and optimistic went to the Ixcán. That said, even many of those who went could not withstand the constant effort and the consistent optimism that it took to remain. The colonization was part of a major mobilization and activism. These settlers had not gone to the jungle with a political tabula rasa. They had distinct opinions about the military and their forced recruitment and abuse of power; they knew the governments were undemocratic; they knew about work in the plantations and the privilege of the land-holding elite; and they knew how Mayas were treated and perceived by society. Many of them had short-wave radios and listened to Radio Havana Cuba or news about Allende's Popular Unity in Chile.

They went to the rain forest with particular impressions about the military, the oligarchy, and politicians. On the other hand they had no prior experience, one way or another, with insurgent groups and therefore were relatively open-minded. The insurgents spoke in terms similar to those of the priests, the nuns, the students, the social promoters, and the political activists back in the highlands. These experiences could be uplifting, hopeful, and inspiring. No doubt they watched Father Luis's reaction, as well as the Mayan professionals working in the village at the time. If these community leaders were not overly alarmed, neither were most of the villagers.

From these decidedly modest beginnings, the EGP slowly grew over the next several years. After a little more than two years in the jungle, they numbered about fifty men in 1975 but had fired only a single shot in combat.[16] The leadership decided that the time had come to make a dramatic public debut. They made a decision to begin "armed propaganda actions" as well as executions that would bring them public notice and redress local grievances.[17] Politically, their aim was to recruit the local peasant population, especially the Mayas, who they calculated would identify and sympathize with these selective assassinations and become cadres in the insurgent organization. To be more mobile and flexible, the force of fifty divided into three smaller units. Also, the guerrilla commanders sought to limit their actions "so that the enemy's reaction would not exceed either what the people were prepared to understand or what we were capable of withstanding and defending at the local level."[18] In this calculation they were fundamentally and tragically mistaken.

On May 28, 1975, one of the guerrilla units executed Guillermo Monzón, a peasant and military commissioner from Xalbal who had been a tractor driver working on the landing strip. Monzón, who had a working relationship with INTA, had sought to ingratiate himself with the local military and government authorities. He tended to flaunt his allegiance to the army and frequently displayed his smugness; it was not surprising that many local people mistrusted and disliked him. The guerrillas mercilessly executed him on the banks of the Xalbal River.

A few days later the insurgents began a much more ambitious and visible action. Finca La Perla was a coffee plantation near the Ixtupil River on the northern spur of the Cuchumatán Sierra, about a two-day hike from Santa María Tzejá through thick jungle paths and over irregular terrain. The military had warned Luis Arenas, the owner of the *finca* as well as Finca San Luis Ixcán, about a possible guerrilla attack. The "Tiger of Ixcán" (as *finquero* Arenas was known) was ruthless, arrogant, and had a murky past, not atypical for large landowners in this area. He had obtained several large *fincas* as rewards for past political and military exploits. He first made a name for himself during the 1954 CIA-backed coup that overthrew the Arbenz government, after which he was given La Perla.[19] Arenas had founded the Anti-Communist Unified Party in 1952. During the repressive military government of Carlos Arana Osorio (1970–74) he was given charge of the development agency of El Petén. He had a reputation for cheating and mistreating Indians, forcing them to open trails and clear the forest for the cultivation of coffee and cardamom, and reportedly employed deception, forced indebtedness, and virtually any pretext or intimidation to recruit a large labor force. Often he used military helicopters to ferry workers onto his *fincas*. His overseers were said to resort to whips if necessary to keep workers in line. The isolation of the area made the abuse of the Mayan workforce, with all its racist overtones, more agonizing and ruthless than plantation work elsewhere in the country.

On June 7, 1975, several hundred workers were waiting patiently in line for their fortnightly pay by the administration building of Finca La

Perla. Intermingled in the crowd were four members of the EGP carrying concealed, antiquated pistols. They could have been military commissioners or even secret guards of the *patrón* and so did not attract undue notice. Given the large number of people from distant places who worked at *fincas* throughout the country, it was easy for the strangers to go unnoticed. Their dress was typical of the area, rubber boots and straw hats. One of them was a dark-skinned man with a beard; another was tall and light-skinned. At 4:30 P.M. two men appeared near the pay window while those in the line entered the offices where Arenas was located. They pointed their guns at him and ordered, "Do not move, hands up, we come for Mr. Arenas, to avenge the blood of the workers who have been mistreated and abused."[20] To those outside they said, "We are not going to harm you—get to the ground face down." At that point they fired six shots at Luis Arenas, three at his chest and three at his forehead. Afterward the guerrillas spoke to the people in Ixil, identifying themselves publicly for the first time as the Guerrilla Army of the Poor and taking responsibility for having killed the "Tiger of Ixcán."[21]

The execution touched a raw nerve with other landholders and infuriated the army. A few days later, on June 10, about nine o'clock in the morning, planes carrying paratroopers—something never seen before in the area—flew over the Xalbal colonization settlement, west of Santa María Tzejá. The army paratroopers quickly surrounded the center of Xalbal's village and rounded up the villagers. They then took out a list of names that had been supplied to the army months earlier, it was believed, by Guillermo Monzón (assassinated by the guerrillas only days earlier). They read the names out loud. All knew the consequences would be catastrophic, but all felt powerless to act. Three men on the list were present: Sebastián Felipe, a Mam Maya from San Ildefonso Ixtahuacán, and Juan Tomás and his son, Chuj Maya, from San Mateo Ixtatán. These settlers were supposedly guerrilla sympathizers. The soldiers marched them away, and they were never seen again. Fifteen people from Xalbal were kidnapped in the next few weeks, and none ever reappeared. Other villagers were tortured, beaten, intimidated, called "guerrilla motherfuckers," and forced to guide soldiers in sweeps of the area. News of these developments spread to every corner of the Ixcán region. The army took over the offices of INTA in Buenos Aires (near Xalbal and Santa María Tzejá) where a landing strip was located. As someone from Santa María Tzejá stated, the army had been harassing them ever since they arrived in the rain forest, but after the assassination of the "Tiger of Ixcán," the army began a far uglier process, "the rustle downwards" toward the settlements in the Ixcán. Over the next six months, thirty-five cooperative members from the Ixcán were tortured, killed, or disappeared.

Among the disappeared was twenty-two-year-old Santos Vicente Sarat of Santa María Tzejá, who was kidnapped on July 25, 1975, and never reappeared. He came from the lowland area of Mazatenango, and his wife, Rosa Botón Lux, was from a village in the municipality of Cunén. They met on a south coast plantation. In 1972 Rosa's father heard about available land in the Ixcán and moved with the young couple to Santa María Tzejá. Santos was nineteen years old at the time and a skilled carpenter. While several others in the village were becoming interested in the guerrillas, Santos was decidedly not political. Although no one can explain precisely why the army kidnapped him, he is remembered as proud, independent, and self-assured, all qualities capable of provoking the army. "He was a simple carpenter," recalls Pedro Tum. "His kidnapping was quite a blow for the community and we did nothing about it at the time, because then we were less experienced," although it is unclear what they could have done.

Rosa recalled the fateful day the army first came to their house, June 12, 1975. The day began in a busy, ordinary way. "I was making tortillas for lunch when I noticed the soldiers surrounding the house. So I asked Santos, 'Why are the soldiers surrounding the house?'" Santos was working in the carpentry shop—a simple room next to the house. Most villagers were taking care of their daily agricultural work in their own land parcels. Santos remained as usual somewhat indifferent, remarking, "Who knows why they are here or what they want," according to his wife. He continued his work, paying little attention. Rosa thought, "Perhaps the soldiers are thirsty," and suggested to Santos that "it may be a good idea for you to offer them some water." "You can't offer them water," he matter-of-factly replied, slightly annoyed. "There are too many, its not just one, how are you going to give them water?" While he and his wife were talking, "four or five soldiers sauntered into his shop" and began taunting him. "What do you do with so much money?" they sneered. "Why are you making all these tables?" He responded that he was a carpenter and making tables was his job. "To support myself," that is why the tables are made, he told the soldiers. While most of the soldiers kept the dwelling surrounded and five or so were with him in the shop, "with the guns pointed at him," seven others entered the house itself. They began to ransack the family's few possessions, turning everything upside down—dishes, pots, clothing, the bed, even the zinc roofing sheets. By now they were screaming at Santos to show where he had hidden things. Rosa said that "he continued working and did not pay attention to them." "Nothing was left intact," Rosa recalls. They asked if he had done his military service and to show his *cédula* (identification). The soldier in charge said, "Ah, con razón [no wonder]!" when they found out he had not been conscripted. The soldiers remained "for about two or three hours, and when they left they were very angry." The anger was likely a combination of frustration over the *finquero*'s murder a few weeks earlier, their obsession with having to find culprits, the apparent arrogance displayed by Santos, and not being able to find any incriminating evidence or money in his house.

Rosa was nervous and alarmed after the visit. Santos in contrast showed little sign of being affected by the bullying of the soldiers. She remembers questioning him, "Aren't you afraid?" And he would say, "How is it that I am going to be afraid if I am not doing anything? I have done nothing, I know very well that I have done nothing wrong, I owe them nothing and have not done anything against them." "He just did not pay attention to them," Rosa recalled. Later he told her again he was not afraid of the soldiers. "It is the weapons they carry, the uniform, that is what makes us be afraid," he said. "They, the soldiers, are just men like me." Instead of calming her, she said, "I felt a shudder," and, if anything, her fear escalated.

One villager, Bartolo Reyes, offers a different interpretation of what happened and why Santos was kidnapped a few weeks later. According to Bartolo, Santos reacted angrily to the search of his house, an unusual behavior for a peasant facing the army. Soldiers often invaded houses, but most peasants dealt with it by staying quiet, terrified of provoking the soldiers. Santos, however, insisted that the army had stolen a pen when they ransacked his house and that if they did not return it, they should pay for it. As if this challenge was not enough, he also complained when the soldiers threw a trunk of clothes out of the house, supposedly telling them, "Don't throw my wife's clothes away, or if you take them and you want to wear them, go ahead, take them and put them on," an offensive statement to macho soldiers and something that would have been very provocative. "He went to complain to the lieutenant the next day about his pen," Bartolo explained. "The lieutenant paid him for the pen. And then about a week later they came and kidnapped him."

The common wisdom is that the army took his outspokenness as a sign he was involved with the insurgency. Bartolo claimed that either the lieutenant or a soldier spat back to Santos, "You must have gotten upset for a reason," and that is why the soldiers returned and took him away. What is certain to Bartolo and to everyone else in the village is that Santos had nothing to do with the guerrillas. In those days there was barely any contact or collaboration on behalf of anyone. "I am sure he never even saw the guerrillas," says Bartolo, "because he was always going to sell his little tables and chairs. He probably never even talked to any of the guerrillas, making it less likely that the guerrillas could have had any influence over him." No one thinks that someone maliciously denounced Santos to the army, a common occurrence in many other villages later on. Hardly anyone thinks he may have been mistaken for someone else. Rather he was targeted because of his independence—he asserted his rights to the army.

Rosa describes what happened the evening of July 25, about two weeks after the initial visit. At the end of an ordinary day, when the traumatic memories of the soldiers' first visit was dulled by the rhythm of everyday life, Rosa, Santos, and their one-year-old daughter went to sleep early, around seven o'clock. A heavy tropical rain was falling. They were sound asleep when they heard voices outside. They groggily thought it could be dawn, but it was only about nine o'clock. They wondered who could be outside. Santos was waking up slowly when they heard a man scream, "Get up!" and then, "Come outside, you will come with us right now." Before he could respond, the soldiers rushed into the house and grabbed Santos. Rosa was terrified. She had no time to light a candle and could not see how many there were, but she knew they were violently dragging her husband out of the house, not even giving him time to put his shoes on. It was still pouring rain as they disappeared into the night. She could hear the dull thuds of boots, leaving her with the impression that many soldiers were involved, and they were dragging her husband to the center of the village. Rosa huddled in her house with the baby, paralyzed by fear and vainly waiting for Santos to return. In retrospect, she regrets that she waited some twenty minutes before she ran to alert her parents. Her father scolded Rosa for not having come sooner, although this hardly would have made any difference. He insisted he would have asked the soldiers why they wanted Santos or at least inquired where they were taking him. Her father felt strong and sure of himself, as did her husband. After Rosa told her tale, her father grabbed a flashlight and ran to the center of the village. He noted the footprints of the boots in the mud and followed them first to the chapel and then to the priest's house. Many soldiers had stayed in the village earlier that day, but by this time of night they had all left. The next day a military helicopter landed in the parcel of Martín Chajal, about two hours from the village center, and people later assumed it had come to take Santos.

After Santos's abduction, Rosa and her parents began the somber journey to look for him—a bitter journey similar to that taken by tens of thousands of Guatemalans since then. "We began to inquire," she said in K'iche' with grief still choking her voice years later. "We were very sad." She would patiently wait for someone to come by on various paths in the rain forest. "We would ask anyone that came by," she said, "By any chance have you seen my husband?" With the scraps of information she was getting here and there, a fuller picture of his seizure began to emerge. The stories weren't promising. "Santos was taken by the soldiers," she was told. "People said that there were many, many soldiers, that they were laughing. The soldiers were happy. They sang and yelled." Others said Santos was not taken immediately to the military base, but rather was tortured in the fields.

"We were very sad. We would ask anyone that went by the path if they had not seen my husband." Twenty days after his disappearance "a young man came walking down a path" from the direction of Santiago Ixcán. From a distance she noticed "he was walking very slowly." When he got closer to Rosa, who was standing with her baby strapped to her back, she observed that he was visibly in pain, a result of beatings he had suffered. She had already heard from people in San José la 20, a village north of Santa María Tzejá, that three young men had been kidnapped by the army. Given that Santos had not appeared, everyone assumed that he must have been killed along with the other three. "But here I saw this young man coming toward us," Rosa thought, feeling a rush of horror at his battered condition, but a surge of hope that her husband too might be alive. "Perhaps this is how it will be with my husband," she hoped. "Perhaps he will also come soon." Rosa, a quiet, shy woman, nonetheless asked the young man where he was coming from. "I am coming from work in my parcel," he responded tersely. "I told him, 'That is not true,'" Rosa said. "I implored him, 'Please tell me.' I was crying. I was very sad. I said, 'I know the army took you, isn't that true, that the army also kidnapped you?'" Then, she asked the question that consumed her entire being. "By any chance did you see my husband?" But the young man continued to insist, "No. I am coming from work."

After witnessing Rosa's deep, uncontrollable sobbing and trembling as she used her apron to wipe her tears, the young man finally relented and told her, "The truth is, yes, I saw your husband. Yes, your husband is there [in the Santiago Ixcán army base]." Rosa stopped crying and became excited as her nearly extinguished hope seemed to flicker. "Oh God, maybe he will come back! Perhaps he will come this evening!" she exclaimed. It was the first time in almost three weeks that someone had actually seen her husband. She wanted to believe that she too might see him again, that he might be released just as this young man had gotten out. The young man made Rosa promise she would not tell anyone. "I will tell you a little, but you can never, never, never tell anyone," he insisted. "Do not talk to anyone about it because this is very dangerous. They will kidnap me again and then they will kill me. They will kill me." The young man then disclosed some painful details. Rosa recounted that "he said he saw my husband when Santos was dragged in one evening. The young man had been kidnapped a few days earlier. Santos had been kept several days in the parcel [of Martín Chajal] where they tortured him," Rosa recalled being told. "His feet were destroyed. One leg was broken. He had no shoes on and had a lot of thorns in his feet. They had made him walk a lot even though his leg was broken." Santos talked to the young man, describing "his life before being taken by the army." The young man told Rosa that her husband was still at the Santiago Ixcán army base, but that he was in such bad shape that he doubted he would ever come out. "They will not release him. He will not come here, he is already in bad shape [muy castigado]," he said sadly. I asked Rosa if she understood that comment to mean that they were going to kill him. She looked at the ground, a rush of tears flowing down, and in a very low voice she whispered, "Yes."

When he found out that Santos might still be alive, Rosa's father rushed to the military outpost in Santiago Ixcán. "He went twice to look for him," Rosa stated. "He spoke with the soldiers, to tell them that Santos is a hard worker, that he doesn't do anything bad. The soldiers told him to leave, or they'll take care of him too, and that is how they got my father out of there." After two tense inquiries her father became deathly afraid. The soldiers treated him especially roughly the second time. He was terrified. They didn't deny they had Santos, they simply dismissed his query, emphasizing it was subversive and dangerous to even ask. They made it clear that his next visit would be his last. With anger and regret, he resigned himself and never inquired again about his son-in-law.

While everyone in the village had quickly become aware of Santos's disappearance, they did not take action or respond collectively. "In those days we were a little slow, asleep, we just let this incident pass," reflected Miguel Reyes. The disappearance was baffling, since nothing about him

Figure 2. Rosa Botón Lux, left, in 2003 with daughter Delia Virgen Vicente Botón, age twenty-seven. Rosa's husband, Santos Vicente Sarat, was the first victim of army kidnapping. Photo by Beatriz Manz.

indicated why he would have been the first to be kidnapped. Some attributed the killing to the general "rustling downward" in the wake of the assassination of Luis Arenas in 1975.

To this day, Rosa and her daughter, now in her twenties, do not know what happened to Santos, nor do they know where his remains might be buried. The only memento she has is a tattered photo of a happier moment. Santos is dressed in a yellow shirt with a serious look. He is holding his only child in his arms. Rosa is to his right. They are standing in front of the house where she spent her last moments with him. She has looked after that treasured photograph since 1975.

In the aftermath of Santos Vicente Sarat's disappearance, life seemed to return to normal in the village, at least to all outward appearances. Women still ground corn for tortillas before dawn; men walked to their fields in the morning and returned tired in the afternoon. But an unmistakable fear had slipped into the community. The settlers were no strangers to racism, abuse, and contempt, and they knew the army could be brutal. Now they were seeing the first signs of a frightening paradox whose details would only become fully clear in the coming years: Their very isolation in a remote area of the Ixcán had placed them in the center of the trauma that would convulse Guatemala. One villager somberly recalled in 1987, "Some even thought of returning to the highlands, but how could they, given the poverty there? So no one returned."

News of other instances of military terror quickly spread through the rain forest. In nearby San José la 20, more disappearances took place, and then six months later another political murder occurred. A few days before a major earthquake, the highly regarded teacher and principal of the Santa María Tzejá elementary school, Raisa Girón Arévalo, became the second village casualty. *El Gráfico,* the main Guatemala City newspaper, had a front-page headline and photo of Raisa on Tuesday, January 13, 1976: "Young Teacher Found Tortured and Strangled: The victim was the principal of a rural school in El Quiché; was kidnapped Saturday."[22] As a young woman, Raisa and thousands of others were involved in an organization of high school students, FUEGO (Frente Unido de Estudiantes Guatemaltecos Organizados, or Guatemalan United Organized Student Front), which was even more active than the university student association. Raisa emerged as a highly regarded leader of the group that mobilized many large peaceful demonstrations in the streets of Guatemala City. Luis remembered Raisa as a member of a Guatemala City youth group called Kato-jó, which means *Ven Señor,* or "Come Lord." Luis invited her and several other university students to Santa María Tzejá in 1973 to promote the first meeting of Shalom Alehem. She became enchanted by the village and the settlers. She thought that this was a place where she, an active student leader from the city, could really make a difference. Luis wanted to establish a grammar school that would offer a pedagogy of liberation—schooling that would be relevant to peoples' lives as well as dedicated to the community. Raisa asked Luis if she could return to run the school. She was the ideal candidate because this was not just a job; it was a conviction, a mission, a passion. She immersed herself in the community; she was creative, full of ideas, and inspiring. She was confident and fearless, qualities that were both noticed by and anathema to the military authorities. "Raisa Girón Arévalo was a good-hearted teacher," Pedro Tum observed. "She had good thoughts, a good heart, and she cared about the poor." Pedro saw something religious in her work and was also aware that she had been a principal at a school for the blind before coming to the village. "She took Jesus as her example. Jesus favored those who were suffering. Jesus made miracles with the sick and the blind." For Pedro, Raisa's teaching was part of liberation theology. "We cannot make miracles, but with the Bible we can teach to read, we can open the eyes of the blind," he continued. "There are blind, Jesus said, that do not see. But there are those who have sight but don't see. So, that is what Raisa was involved in: opening the eyes of those who do not see to give life to those eyes."

Everyone in the village associates the assassination of Raisa with a chance encounter with César Montes, the guerrilla commander. On one of the guerrilla incursions into Santa María Tzejá in 1975, a unit took over Father Luis's house while he was visiting relatives out of the country. Raisa was in a neighboring village teaching adult literacy. When she returned to the village and entered the house, she unexpectedly came face-to-face with Montes, who had also been a leader in the student group FUEGO in the capital. Neither could hide their joy and amazement at this surprising encounter, and they greeted each other warmly with hugs and quick kisses to the cheeks. Many people witnessed the meeting, among them a fellow teacher named Julio, from Cobán, Alta Verapaz province, who was teaching in Santa María Tzejá. Villagers assume that Julio informed the military about this friendly encounter; he then slipped out of the village and never was heard from again.

Not suspecting anything, Raisa went to Guatemala City to petition the Ministry of Education for a replacement for Julio, assuming that the teacher had simply quit. As Raisa and her cousin approached her own house in Guatemala City on January 11, 1976, she was grabbed by some men. Her body was found dumped by the side of the road in the Anillo Periférico in the early morning hours of January 13. Twenty-seven years old, she had been strangled to death. Her frightened family did not demand an investigation.

The military terror was also targeted at priests. Father William (Guillermo) Woods, from the Maryknoll order, who had organized the settlement of peasants in the western part of the rain forest in the late 1960s, was the first victim. On November 20, 1976, his small plane went down on a return trip to the Ixcán, in an accident that was widely attributed to the military. It was the first time that a priest in the Ixcán, in fact in all of Guatemala, had been killed. César Montes recalls that both William Woods and Luis Gurriarán had told him that they would never help the guerrillas, but neither would they denounce them. Montes remembers when Luis was unable to return to the village after 1975, people would say to the guerrillas, "We feel like orphans without the father. But now that you are here, we feel like brothers. We will work with you to keep alive the memory of Father Guillermo as well." Seeing that the guerrillas did not threaten Luis or William Woods, made the villagers more comfortable with the insurgents.

The army interrogated Father Luis in 1975 and came to the village several times asking for him and searched his house. They made it known that he was considered a communist dressed as a priest. Luis was overseas when Raisa was abducted and killed. As a result of these events he decided that it would be unsafe for him to return to the Ixcán. Instead he became a parish priest in the tourist highland town of Chichicastenango, until Bishop Juan Gerardi closed the diocese in 1980. He did not return to Santa María Tzejá until 1994 — nearly a twenty-year absence.

Amid the growing repression there were other sources of anxiety. What had been an isolated area unexpectedly found itself in the eye of the storm. In the late 1970s the government built a dirt road called the Franja Transversal del Norte (FTN, Northern Transversal Strip). Funded by USAID ostensibly to help small farmers, the road ran from the eastern part of the country, around Puerto Barrios, and then westward toward the Ixcán. Army generals and wealthy land speculators, with advance information about the road, raced to acquire large landholdings in the neighboring departments of Alta Verapaz and El Petén, where they set up vast cattle ranches. In fact, so many military officers bought ranches that the area was dubbed "the strip of the generals." Peasants viewed the FTN as a mixed blessing. "Always, where there is an access road," observed Miguel Reyes, "this facilitates the army to corner people." Gaspar remarked that "to walk seven days with a load on your back, yes the road was a relief, but then when you see the consequences one says: 'On the one hand it comes to benefit us; but on the other hand it comes to harm us.'" In contrast, Pedro Canil maintained that at the time he didn't give the road much thought and, to the extent he did think about it, only viewed it as positive. "I didn't think then that it could have something to do with repression, that it could bring us bad consequences. But of course the ambitious ones, the ones who come behind the road, they surely would see how to get in here."

The consensus emerged that the road was being built for rich landowners. Now that peasants had demonstrated the area was useful for permanent settlement, international donors were supposedly funding a road to help small farmers, but peasants feared that these powerful ranchers, mainly high-ranking military men, would sooner or later seize their land. Once the land belonged to the ranchers, the settlers worried that they would again become a source of cheap labor. It would return them to the century-old dependence. This scenario, according to the peasants, ex-

plained why the government did not give them titles and wanted to subdivide the parcels; with less land the peasants were more likely to work
for wage labor.

Ironically, the international funds for infrastructure development had
been given in the name of the peasants. In fact, the USAID Project 520
was called the "Small Farmers' Project." In the long run, should the military and the elites have their way, the settlers thought, the ultimate
beneficiaries of the colonization would be large landowners. The government was claiming that the value of the land had increased, but the
way the peasants saw it, their own efforts had boosted its worth. The
higher land values also explained why, in their view, the government was
not giving them permanent titles. If someone seized the land, the villagers
surmised, they would have no legal recourse and would be subject to expulsion. All the work, all the sweat, all the hardship would prove to be
in vain.

If these developments were not enough to make the peasants apprehensive, oil companies began prospecting on their lands in the mid-
1970s.[23] The companies evoked an agreement with the government and
never asked the settlers for permission to explore. Here again bitter experience led the villagers to fear dispossession. If oil was to be found,
these international companies would surely take over, and the peasants
would be powerless to prevent the seizures. The oil companies, however,
proved both a benefit and a curse: their presence made villagers even more
worried over land rights, yet the companies were also the only source of
employment in the Ixcán. While Santa María Tzejá's peasants had
achieved basic food self-sufficiency with corn, bean, and rice production,
and were beginning to earn some money from cardamom, they lacked
cash. Thus, some peasants viewed the oil companies as an opportunity,
a risky one to be sure, but an opportunity nonetheless. The wages were
higher than the minimum wage, and the companies paid overtime. "[I
had] no money, nothing," Pedro Canil says. "When I was told that it
was my turn to go work in *la petrolera*, that was a great relief for me,
because I did not have a cent to buy things. That helped us to get out
from under. There was no work here. No one paid you for work....In
the beginning we did not have anything to sell." Others disagreed on the
long-term benefits of the oil companies. "I did not think it was a benefit
for us, for Guatemalans, for the poor, because the oil is not refined in
Guatemala," Domingo Us Quixán remarked. "It goes to another country, gets refined, and then returns. Then, we Guatemalans have to buy
it. This is a great loss for Guatemalans." Others were concerned that the

oil companies would despoil the land and possibly seize their parcels. Gaspar felt that many were unconcerned when the oil companies were drilling in Rubelsanto and Tortugas in the neighboring department of Alta Verapaz and elsewhere in El Petén. Then they saw the activity solely as a source of paid work. "But when they got a little closer, when they began drilling in the wells near San Lucas, I began to worry," Gaspar maintained. "Rumors already circulated that when the oil companies come they don't respect your parcels, whoever is the owner, they invade it. They don't care." Parcels were destroyed in San Lucas, some said, and it was unclear if the company paid for the damages. "What if later they take the land away from us?" Gaspar questioned. "Maybe the companies will pay the government, but the peasants will once again be at the mercy of others, of those who can pay for the land." Experience fed their worst fears of being exploited and losing the independence they had sacrificed so much to achieve.

By 1976 Raisa was dead, Santos Vicente Sarat had disappeared, Maryknoll priest William Woods was dead, and Father Luis could not return to the village. The death of admired people and the persecution of Luis underscored who the army was after. The lesson peasants learned was that their friends were the military's enemies.

chapter 3

The War Finds Paradise

The growing presence of the guerrillas and the resulting escalation of military terror created a tense, nightmarish situation in the Ixcán. It is too simplistic an analysis, however, to simply link military violence with guerrilla growth. "Even without subversion the army is abusive," Pedro Lux told me, "because they have always had the power, they have the weapons."[1] Nonetheless, the army unleashed a far more extensive and brutal campaign of terror against civilians to dampen guerrilla expansion. The villagers of Santa María Tzejá, distant from the turmoil of the south coast and Guatemala City, found themselves at the epicenter of a conflict that would convulse the country.

As we have seen, the ragged band that was to become the EGP stumbled on Santa María Tzejá early in its wanderings through the Ixcán and only two years after the founding of the village. This encounter and its aftermath raises a critical question: Why do peasants support an insurgency?[2] José Napoleón Duarte, the centrist Christian Democratic head of the ruling junta in El Salvador in the early 1980s and a perennial favorite of Washington policymakers during the Reagan administration, offered a down-to-earth analysis. While not a scholar, Duarte was to spend the defining moments of his political career fighting a guerrilla movement. When a *New York Times* reporter asked him two decades ago what provoked the insurgency in El Salvador, he stressed that poverty and repression fuel rebellion. He told the reporter, "Fifty years of lies, fifty years of injustice, fifty years of frustration. This is a history of people starving to death, living in misery. For fifty years the same people had all the power, all the money, all the jobs, all the education, all the opportunities."[3] For Guatemala one should add five hundred years of racism, exclusion, and contempt against the Mayan people.

In this chapter I explore the forces that shaped the attitudes of the villagers toward the insurgency and the voices of those who became guerrilla combatants. I interviewed most of the key participants at length; some on a number of occasions over a period of several years. A personal trust developed that allowed villagers to speak with remarkable candor about their lives and their relationship to the insurgency.[4] With the passage of time, a valuable perspective was gained: it highlighted the ways in which their attitudes evolved as history unfolded and their distance from the early days of the insurgency increased.

The larger context of the conflict informs what took place in the village. In defining this context, a number of comprehensive human rights reports emphasize the bloody intersection of the structural problems of Guatemalan society and the repressive actions of a violent authoritarian regime. Monsignor Próspero Penados del Barrio, the archbishop of Guatemala, writes in the introduction to the report from the Recuperación de la Memoria Histórica (REMHI, Recovery of Historical Memory Project) that "people joined the insurgency out of their desire to bring about a more just society and the impossibility of accomplishing it through the established system."[5] The report finds that, paradoxically, military repression fueled the insurgency. "Faced with increasingly indiscriminate repression," the report states, "many people saw the revolutionary movement as a means of bringing about change and realizing their demands for justice and freedom."[6] In other words, the ruling elites made violent change far more likely by making peaceful change impossible.

The guerrilla organizations had also learned from their disastrous experience in the 1960s. In the following decade "some guerrilla organizations adopted strategies to expand their bases and incorporate large numbers of people into their military support structures," the REMHI report observes, finding that "these strategies had a strong influence on community dynamics." Although many peasants flocked to their cause, when necessary "the guerillas used violence to eliminate army collaborators and, on other occasions, to eliminate the opposition in zones under their control."[7] By the end of the 1970s, the guerillas "were able to amass a formidable support base," and "when the EGP's first regular military force penetrated southern El Quiché, a large percentage of the population was waiting for it."[8] The EGP leadership was surprised, if not overwhelmed, by what took place. "Far from a repeat of the earlier cycle of winning people over and organizing them," the report continues, "the EGP's political cadres and combatants were increasingly astonished by their overwhelming reception and the speed with which the population organized itself based on the guerrilla-proposed model."[9] The intellectual roots of the reception were deep. "The organizing that had taken place in the seventies, with the substantial involvement of certain sectors of the Catholic church, had something to do with this," the report maintains.[10]

The Opposition Grows

The activities of the EGP in the rain forest took place at a time when social conflict was accelerating throughout Guatemala. New protests were filling the streets and mass movements were forming in the 1970s, challenging the ruling elites in visible, unprecedented ways. In 1976, soon after the murder of Raisa Girón Arévalo—the teacher at Santa María Tzejá—a catastrophic earthquake violently shook Guatemala, leveling large parts of the province of Chimaltenango. The response to this natural disaster revealed the corruption and political rot afflicting the country. Almost immediately, villagers heard of the impressive self-organization of peasants in the relief efforts, but they soon saw that even a natural disaster does not affect the rich and the poor in the same way. The settlers of Santa María Tzejá decided to show their solidarity by sending maize to the victims of the highland municipality of Joyabaj, where they had many relatives. When the maize arrived in Santa Cruz del Quiché, however, the army forced the villagers to take it to a military warehouse. "Why continue sending maize if it is going to land in the warehouses of the military?" a villager observed. "The military is not allowing us to deliver it to the victims in Joyabaj." Pedro Canil reflected about the social fallout from natural disasters. "When you think about it, who suffers most from natural disasters?" he questioned. "It is always the poor. Any mishap of nature, we are the ones who suffer most. Then, international aid comes, and who controls and benefits most from that aid? The most-clever ones since the aid travels only half the road. At the end, the poor are even poorer and the rich even richer!"

The same year the earthquake shook the highlands, the Comité de Unidad Campesina (CUC, Committee of Peasant Unity) began to emerge as a broad-based national movement. Its ranks included peasants and agricultural workers, Mayas and poor Ladinos, the old and the young, women and men. The CUC drew on an eclectic mix of ideas and experiences, including liberation theology and the cooperative movement. Initially the group organized secretly to minimize repression, but its message of justice and change touched a nerve throughout the country. After two years of quiet organizing, the CUC burst forth on the national scene at the May Day demonstrations in the capital in 1978. The organization ballooned to 150,000 members at its peak and was particularly strong in its place of origin, around Santa Cruz del Quiché. As tensions intensified during the early 1980s, the group moved closer to the EGP.

While the CUC was forming, the Ixtahuacán miners held a widely supported strike and march across the country from Huehuetenango to Guatemala City in 1977. One young K'iche' man from the highlands remembered the march as the first mass political activity he had seen. "By the time we heard about the miners of Ixtahuacán they had already begun the march," he recalled. "We organized as a show of solidarity. We went by the road in Totonicapán and waited for them there with food and other things. It was the first time that I saw the participation of women and children." Not only was the march impressive, it inspired new people to challenge the status quo. "Many of the people who came did not belong to any organization at that point, and because it was a very large march everyone was commenting about it; it started a discussion among the people."[11]

The military backlash was not long in coming. In May 1978, the same month as the large CUC demonstration in Guatemala City, the army violently lashed out at peasants demanding rights to their land in Panzós, Alta Verapaz. Soldiers fired into an unarmed crowd, slaughtering more than a hundred people and wounding three hundred more.[12] News of the massacre rapidly spread throughout the Ixcán. "We live in a place where the same thing could happen," Felipe Canté remarked in Santa María Tzejá. "We knew that the army had tried to repress the peasants whenever we protest for our rights or our dignity. The army is never on the side of the peasants." Pedro Canil also reflected on the Panzós incident. "I never thought the army would totally violate the laws, the constitution, that they could do the things they did because they have the weapons in their hands," he said. "I never thought they would step all over the laws as if they are worth nothing." The massacre provoked a demonstration of eighty thousand in Guatemala City, the largest protest in more than two decades, only to be followed by an even larger demonstration of one hundred thousand people a year later. The bloodletting also underscored the insurgents' warnings that the army was brutal and that the Mayan population itself would soon become the target.

By 1980, confrontation and repression were both clearly on the rise. In January, K'iche' peasant-activists and urban supporters seized the Spanish Embassy to protest the human rights violations in the country-

side. Among them was Vicente Menchú, father of 1992 Nobel laureate
Rigoberta Menchú. Guatemalan riot police stormed the embassy, resulting in a fire that left thirty-nine people dead. Only a protester, Gre-
gorio Yujá Xona, and the Spanish ambassador survived. Escape from the
flames, however, did not mean escape from the terror. The surviving protester—a peasant—was kidnapped from his hospital bed, murdered, and
then dumped on the campus of the University of San Carlos. Hundreds
of thousands of people somberly and defiantly came out for the funeral
of those who died. One of the participants at the funeral, a K'iche' leader
of the CUC, recalled that "people became very emotional as we carried
the coffins outside." During the demonstrations, he wore a handkerchief
over his face to hide his identity. "We could see then, very clearly, the effect that the massacre had had on people from all sectors of Guatemala,"
he said. "There were many people in the march who had never been part
of an organization, who had never been to a demonstration before, who
had never been interested before. These people had come to the march
and were yelling slogans with everyone else." In his view, the demonstration sent a clear, uncompromising message. "This uprising against
the government revealed the depth of the anger that people felt about
what was happening in the country."

The size and intensity of the demonstrations in early 1980 created a
condition of near panic among the elites in Guatemala. The burgeoning
mass support for the opposition, however, bred overconfidence on the
part of many, including students, urban workers, guerrillas, and peasants. In retrospect, it is clear that while widespread anger was pouring
forth, it did not necessarily translate into a support for an insurgency.
Guerrilla leaders, however, misread escalating demonstrations and increased support as signs of near insurrection. At the same time, the military terror was intensifying, crushing any thought of challenging the status quo. A highland activist said that more than a hundred people were
kidnapped immediately after the march on the Spanish Embassy. Also,
a CUC organizer stated that the organization "needed to decide what we
were going to do in response to the government's actions," in particular
if they should continue with a planned February strike on the south coast.
"We had been planning it for five or six months and decided to go ahead
with it," he stated. As one striker put it, "The massacre in the embassy
acted as a spark that set off the strike." The labor stoppage in February
1980, in the middle of the harvest season, was far stronger than most
expected, and it became the largest strike of its kind in Guatemalan history, not surpassed to this day. Some eighty thousand workers, highland

migrants and lowland permanent workers, Mayan and non-Mayan, stopped working. Pacific coast plantations ground to a halt. The CUC had demanded a $5 daily wage in the countryside and, in the end, the plantation owners agreed to raise wages from $1.10 to $3.20 a day. Plantation workers had demonstrated the power of effective organizing and direct action. The CUC had spread fear among the *finqueros* as they realized the unthinkable: One organization could bring together those who historically had been kept divided. In response, widespread disappearances began on the Pacific coast within days. "Twenty-eight unionists were assassinated or disappeared from the time of the strike to 1983," according to the CEH (U.N.) report.[13] In response, the CUC had to go underground.

The growth of social movements in Guatemala took place in the turbulent context of Central America in the late 1970s and early 1980s. In nearby Nicaragua the Sandinista guerrillas had succeeded in toppling a far more entrenched dynasty in 1979. In El Salvador the guerrilla Frente Farabundo Martí de Liberación Nacional (FMLN, or Farabundo Martí National Liberation Front) was becoming a real force with large urban and rural support despite a ferocious military onslaught and United States direct intervention. On March 24, 1980, Archbishop Oscar Arnulfo Romero was assassinated while saying mass at a chapel in San Salvador. Social upheavals and indiscriminate repression both were escalating throughout the region. The Guatemalan insurgents and many supporters thought that if victory had already taken place in Nicaragua and seemed possible in El Salvador, why not in Guatemala? This proved to be a tragic miscalculation.

The Slow Beginning of the Insurgent Movement

This intense optimism among the insurgents in the early 1980s was far different from the slow, cautious beginnings of the 1970s. After their initial arrival in the rain forest near the Mexican border, the guerrillas slogged through the unforgiving Ixcán from village to village, seeking to win the trust of the villagers slowly, respectfully, secretly. They would briefly "take over" isolated hamlets and bring everyone together to hear a message in which they hammered at unremitting exploitation and pointed to armed struggle as the only viable avenue for change. Jesús, later critical of the guerrillas for their tactics, remembered the first time he saw the insurgents in Santa María Tzejá in the early 1970s. "I was about twelve years old. They talked to us at the church. They said they were struggling for all of us, the Indians and the poor, and for that reason it was important that we help them, that we participate in the struggle. They talked about the injustices in Guatemala, racism, discrimination against the Indians. It was obvious to all of us in the church that they were talking about the reality that we lived every day, that they were speaking the truth. When I heard what they said, I felt a moment of freedom, and I saw that some of the others felt the same way. I was impressed and liked what they said."

Initially, the insurgents weren't seeking mass conversions but rather small numbers of committed and politically informed individuals who would join them for the long haul. They wanted to build a tough, dedicated infrastructure, recruit by recruit, capable of withstanding the ravages of a prolonged war. At first the guerrillas would ask villagers to collaborate with food and information; the next step would involve more activity, political education, and possibly weapons training. The lowest level within the insurgency was the Fuerzas Irregulares Locales (FIL, or Local Irregular Forces). These recruits would be given specific tasks, such as informing on the army, collecting food, acting as couriers or guides, transporting goods, and approaching relatives and neighbors. The next level was the Comité Clandestino Local (CCL, or Local Clandestine Committee), which included five people from the village and indicated a more intense commitment, followed by the Dirección Regional (Regional Command), which oversaw several villages. The military units were organized into fronts named after historical revolutionary leaders. The Ernesto "Che" Guevara front was deployed in the Ixcán, the Ho Chi Minh front operated in the Ixil area, and the Augusto César Sandino front was in the southern highlands.

In Santa María Tzejá, more than fifty men and women out of a village of 116 families joined the EGP on one level or another and received training in a guerrilla camp in the Ixcán or in Mexico's nearby Lacandón jungle. Those who joined the FIL and some who were in the CCL remained in and around Santa María Tzejá. Of those who became combatants, most participated in the Ixcán-based Ernesto "Che" Guevara front, although none operated in Santa María Tzejá itself. Among those who remained in the guerrillas for several years, some ended up in either the Ho Chi Minh front in the Ixil area or the Augusto César Sandino front in southern Quiché or in Huehuetenango. Some were assigned to the Fuerza Móvil, a mobile response unit that moved from one combat zone to another: from the Ixcán to the Ixil area, back to the rain forest, up to Huehuetenango, and then to southern Quiché. The EGP cadre from Santa María Tzejá played various roles: local support, political work at the level of the CCL, combat, directing logistics for an entire front, coordinating supplies; one villager even served as bodyguard to EGP commander Rolando Morán. Some stayed in the guerrilla forces until the demobilization in the mid-1990s, but most left after a few years.

At first glance, the insurgents seemed to confront an insurmountable obstacle to organizing in villages such as Santa María Tzejá: peasants had land. Moreover, these peasants did not depend on plantation wages and had little direct contact with the government or the army. However, peasants joined the insurgency for complex reasons. In later years, after the peace accords were signed in December 1996 and the demobilization of the URNG (Unidad Revolucionaria Nacional Guatemalteca, or Guatemala National Revolutionary Unity) in early to mid-1997, former combatants reflected on the meaning of the insurgency in profoundly different ways. Most former combatants tend to be proud of their participation while others, even those who remained in the guerrilla forces until the end, express deep criticisms of the strategies pursued by the insurgents. Whether they feel the decision to join was the right one or rue their choice with the clarity provided by time and experience, former combatants nonetheless take pride in having made the choice themselves. No combatants I spoke with said they joined because of force or manipulation. On the other hand, some regret their involvement in retrospect. A few noncombatants claimed to have collaborated because of threats. Peer pressure was obviously a factor for some, and in the later stages, threats were made against the holdouts.

Sabas, a philosophical twenty-six-year-old Ladino villager who grew up in El Palmar, was the first recruit from Santa María Tzejá. An informal leader in the village, he was an admired catechist. After the demonization of the guerrillas by the army and the elites, he was surprised when they arrived at the village: they seemed like ordinary, decent people. Most important, they lacked the arrogance and contempt of the military. He remembered the insurgents giving clear, well-delivered talks that could at times be inspiring. "These talks awakened an inner interest in me to know more about them," he said. The second time the insurgents entered the village, in 1974, Sabas was explaining the Bible to people at the church when a young man approached and asked if he could address the group. "I will never forget that," said Sabas. "I remember it most of all because of the courtesy he showed. They were not violent. I listened. I did not talk to them personally. When they left, I felt good. I was impressed and had a curiosity to find them." He would not have to wait long. "Later on that same year I was walking down a path in the parcel and I ran into three of them," he said. "They greeted me by asking, 'How are you?'" The insurgents then asked Sabas's permission to talk briefly. "We spoke for about ten minutes, we didn't talk long," he said, but the experience "led me for the first time to want to struggle, to do something. I didn't know what or how. There was a spark but without a path yet."

The path would soon be laid out. A year later, a message reached Sabas that the guerillas who had talked to him before wanted to see him again. He eagerly went. The insurgents gave him material to read—itself a new experience—and then came back quietly but regularly to discuss it; "and so time went by," he reflected. After this slow, patient preparation, Sabas finally joined the insurgency in early 1976. "I did not join them as an adventure," he explained, "or because I felt disillusioned about something, or because I was looking for something without values. No, it was not because of that. I thought about it a lot." He slipped out of the village one day, telling only his father about the dramatic turn his life was taking. In his new role as an active member of the insurgency, he was given a weapon and was trained in military tactics. "What was more interesting to me were the social issues," he emphasized, mentioning his background as a catechist. Once he joined, he began to contact other selected people in the village; friends, informal leaders, the most independent, the most capable. Many villagers joined the insurgents early on because Sabas was an admired person, someone they looked up to. The fact that he is Ladino may have been less important, except to demonstrate that Ladinos were willing to risk their lives in an attempt to bring about radical change in Guatemalan society.

Among the recruits were Mayan men and women who had studied at the Escuela Nacional Comunal Indígena and lived in the boarding school for indigenous children in Chichicastenango. When the diocese and the Catholic schools closed down in 1980, the students from Santa María Tzejá went home and became involved in one way or another with the insurgent movement. Like Sabas, they had been members of Shalom Alehem. The process was slow and cautious, so much so that those who wanted to join outright were seldom accepted immediately. "People always had to go through training, and then there would be a selection," Sabas stated. "From ten who were interested in joining, two or three would end up being selected." Collaboration was clandestine. Often villagers did not even know of a relative's involvement.

Braulio, a K'iche' Maya, joined the insurgency at the beginning of the 1980s. Initially he had planned to join for a few months; once in the ranks, he decided to stay for a year, and after surviving that tough first year, he said to himself, "I might as well stay forever." One year flowed into the next, and he wound up remaining in the ranks for sixteen years, until the demobilization in early 1997. "I didn't even feel how the years went by, five, ten, fifteen," he reminisced. "I was conscious of what I was doing, I was there voluntarily, and I knew it was a just struggle and that my contribution was important."[14] The depth with which the guerrillas explained their history impressed him, and the history made him want to join. Moreover, for Braulio as well as many others, the learning experience itself was important. Despite the privations and hardships, he learned to read and write and gained the experience of living with different ethnic and social groups, from Mayan peasants to urban Ladinos. The fact that Braulio was single allowed him to make a full commitment, and when he later married a fellow combatant, Candelaria, his ties to the cause deepened. His unit wound up in the Verapaces in the blood-drenched years of 1982–83. I asked if the thought of quitting didn't cross his mind when he found himself amid this carnage. "No," he answered firmly, "that was not my thinking. For me it was 'win or die.'" He was a political organizer, had already led a unit, felt he had to set an example, and did.

Francisca, a twenty-two-year-old K'iche' woman, married and mother of a little boy and girl, joined the EGP in May 1980. At the age of eleven she had already begun working in the plantations prior to her family settling in Santa María Tzejá. Interviewed in 1986 while a combatant, she explained that in the first year she did small tasks for the insurgents. "The *compañeros* explained the situation, and I decided to become a combatant," along with her husband, she said. "They spoke about the rich, the exploitation, that we don't even speak Spanish, we cannot even read or write and so on." She said she became afraid to be detected by the army. Someone had come looking for her husband and that had frightened them. They left their children in the care of Francisca's in-laws, and she and her husband left the village to join the insurgent forces.[15] Asked about her personal expectations, she repeated a familiar rhetoric: "As the *compañeros* say, the society we have in Guatemala is capitalist, and we want to put a revolutionary society where we will all have the same."

Figure 3. Guerrilla wedding, 1990. With weapons nearby, Candelaria
Montejo, a Popti' Maya speaker, gets some final touches to her hair
before her wedding to Braulio Ralios Mejía, a K'iche' Maya of Santa
María Tzejá. Both are now actively involved in Santa María Tzejá and in
projects in the municipality of Ixcán. In 2003, Candelaria was running
for municipal office in the next election as the number-two person on
the ticket of the former guerrilla organization, the URNG; in the
mayor's absence she would fill the post. Photo courtesy Braulio Ralios
Mejía.

Güicho joined the insurgents while still a teenager to "struggle against oppression." "The most important [reason] was the never-ending poverty," he said, pausing a moment and then continuing, "as well as the discrimination, exploitation, and the bad distribution of land. My family and I were very poor, and because of that I became a combatant when I was fourteen, in 1981." Again, I brought up the fact that the settlers of the Ixcán had sufficient land. "Even if we had land or a place to live," he responded, "we weren't well off. We were always poor as we are now. We had economic problems. The land that we had was of poor quality. That's why I thought about joining the struggle, no matter how hard it is, but it will be worth it, I said to myself." He too is proud of the fact that the decision was his. "I consciously decided to join the organization," he stressed. "From the day I joined until today, I have not changed my mind about that." He also emphasized that "the people who had joined the guerrillas acted voluntarily, and I felt the same way."

"I was twenty-five years old at the time [I joined]," Tencho remembered. "I was young and strong, with no illnesses. I understood the reasons for the struggle when the guerrillas explained to us that it was important to make war on those who governed and on their army, to put an end to the injustices that the people were suffering, and take power." Tencho pointed out that villagers joined the insurgency for different reasons, although few in his view were manipulated. "Some [joined] on account of army threats, others because they couldn't figure out where else to go," he related. "Others for interests of power, and so on. What is true is that the war started because of the poverty in which people lived. Fortunately there were men to lead it."

María also challenged the notion that the guerrillas pressured peasants into joining, although she did admit that some people claimed that happened. "For the most part the people volunteered, because at that time they had no other choice but struggle, to make war," she said. For María, peasants in Guatemala were trapped between powerful landlords and an abusive, ruthless military and therefore had little alternative but to turn to the guerillas. "Because more and more [peasants] realized that the big landlords took their lands," she explained, "also because of the disgraceful attitude of the army. You would hear about them abusing women, especially young girls." Later on she elaborated, "There are rumors that some were forced [to join the insurgents], but that wasn't true in my case. I thought that with my support [the movement] would be stronger." Others who were of military recruitment age worried that the army might forcibly induct them, so they "preferred to join the guerrillas and not the army of the government," Pedro Tol noted. "Otherwise, we [would have to] come to kill our own kind." He added that he had heard negative comments about the guerrillas, "Then I saw how they lived, I talked to them and joined. I thought then if the majority of the people joined we would be able to change our unequal situation."

Ricardo was curious about the ideas that seemed to inspire the insurgents. He had some doubts about their program in the late 1970s but was not afraid to engage the guerrillas with questions. "I would ask them about equality for all. Would that be possible? Would a guerrilla victory bring changes in people's lives?" he remembered asking. "They would answer 'Yes, there would be changes, there would be land, better wages.' In those days the big landowners controlled so much land. People were wandering from one place to another without even being able to build a little house somewhere." Despite lingering doubts about some issues, he became convinced the insurgents would carry out a sweeping land reform throughout the country, and he felt, as did others in the village, that large structural changes were needed.

The success achieved by the villages made them all too aware of what they still lacked. "It is not true that we were well off," Emiliano commented. "To be well off means to have a nice house with a cement floor, to have some animals, peace of mind, to have legal titles to your property, and money to buy a few things. I did not have that." He sarcastically commented that he certainly could not say, "Thanks to the army now I am well off." He pointed out that larger economic concerns were at issue. "The little cardamom we had was sold to intermediaries at an exploitative price," he continued. "A pair of pants, a machete, axe, boots, all had to be bought at the price of the exploiter. You can see the discrimination and exploitation. The sellers would just say, 'Buy this hoe at such a price and that's the end of it.' And what could one do?"

No Longer a Prolonged Popular War

The EGP radically changed the method of recruitment in the Ixcán following the Sandinista triumph in Nicaragua in 1979. The EGP leadership interpreted the Sandinista success as showing not only that victory was possible but that it could occur in the near term. "With the triumph in Nicaragua and the advances in El Salvador," Sabas stated, "the initial strategy of a prolonged war was forgotten, and things began to accelerate." As a result, recruitment became far more aggressive and the standards for joining the insurgency were considerably loosened. Although committed cadre such as Braulio or Güicho joined during this period, many others were less sure of exactly what was taking place or why they were joining. "If three people came to make a contact, and all three wanted to become combatants, oh well, the three would join," Sabas recalled with regret. "The [guerrillas] lost all sense, all security, all secrecy." Another villager commented that the guerrillas "would talk to someone two, three times, and, whether he got it or not, they would dictate what he had to do, even if it was still beyond his comprehension." Anxious to expand their ranks rapidly, the EGP lowered the age of new recruits, incorporating boys under fifteen and girls as young as eleven or twelve. The guerrillas saw this as a now-or-never moment to move forward, and villagers were responding enthusiastically, creating a volatile and illusory mix. "There was a lot of support from the population; it was massive," Sabas observed about the Ho Chi Minh front in the Ixil area. "When there were talks for the units, people would come out of everywhere, from *aldeas* (hamlets), everyone, men, women, children." This outpouring fed the excesses, in his view. "We never thought initially that children should participate in the war, but then with all the disorder that happened, the guerrillas would say, 'Everyone, children, elderly, everyone will participate in the war.'" Whatever the guerrilla excesses regarding recruiting children, they paled next to the ferocity and viciousness of the army. The military would say, "'That child is a guerrilla,'" Sabas recalled. "A child in the womb of the mother was already a guerrilla. So they applied the scorched earth, because not even the seed was to be left." Thus children, along with everyone else, would be tortured and murdered.

Domingo joined the insurgents during this period of mass recruitment when he was only fifteen. For him, as for others, the personal merged with the political as he became part of a military and political movement. "The guerrillas told me it's important to collaborate, and that if we wanted to, the doors were also open to be a combatant right away and take up a rifle," he said. "It was the only alternative we had. After three months I went. I had no father. I lived with my sister. My mother had gone with another man. So I said, 'I am going,' and that is how I went to the mountains." Domingo, who felt like an orphan prior to joining the EGP, remained in the organization until the demobilization more than fifteen years later. His unit became his family as well as a political cause, and both defined his world. He trained in Cuba, was wounded several times in bloody clashes with the army, and wound up at one point disconnected from his unit for a few years. In fact, he heard about the demobilization only by chance.

Jerónimo became a combatant after witnessing the destructive violence of the army. "I saw that my father collaborated [with the gueril-
las]," he remembered, "but when I really felt like joining [them] was
when I saw the burnt houses in Santa María Tzejá in 1982." He bitterly
recalled that "the [soldiers] were always chasing us with the purpose of
exterminating us." His anger, however, was infused with idealism and
a sense victory was possible. "When I joined the struggle I did think of
a revolutionary victory," he said. "I thought Guatemala needed a
change, with all citizens having rights and obligations." He then went
on to detail what he meant, enumerating a surprisingly extensive and
sophisticated set of changes. He spoke of "social and economic equality, security, social justice, respect for human rights, education and health
care for all, infrastructure work financed by the government in all corners of our nation." He wanted to see a society in which "there would
be no racial discrimination or exploitation." Despite an optimism that
would prove illusory about winning, he had few illusions about how
difficult the struggle would be. "I agreed that those changes needed to
be made, that is why I decided to give my time and shed my tears and
even give my life to bring about change." He felt that given the army's
actions, "We could not continue to live without weapons, we needed
weapons to defend ourselves."

Juan had been involved with the CUC in the highlands and in the plantation region. He moved to Santa María Tzejá in the late 1970s where
several of his brothers had settled. In the village he met Florencia, whose
entire family was collaborating with the EGP. They became a couple, and
he joined the insurgency. "I felt it was a struggle that was for the whole
country," he stated. "It was a popular war. The combatants don't earn
anything. They are not doing it to earn a salary, but to respond to the
people." Juan admitted he had land but pointed to those who did not,
particularly the people who worked on the coast as he had done. "Exploitation dominates the country," he charged. "There is no democracy.
That's why it's better to collaborate [with the guerillas]." I asked why people would risk everything by joining the guerillas, suggesting perhaps they
were pressured to do so. Juan reacted with a mocking expression in his
bright eyes. A person who thinks that, he responded, "doesn't think of
his fellow creatures, his *pueblo* [people]. He doesn't care about others who
do not have land." I repeated the thesis that people were trapped between
the army and the EGP and that some may have been deceived or manipulated by the guerrillas. I ask him directly if he was forced into joining.
Sitting in front of me, Juan was looking down while I was talking, lis-

tening intently, and he took his time answering. He finally raised his face slowly, and I noticed a slight grin. He broke the silence with a single word, lingering on each syllable: "Voluntariamente!" I just stared at him for a few seconds, and then he continued, "With my five senses!" Spontaneously I burst into laughter and asked him, "Which five senses are you talking about? Let's see, hearing, sight, smell, touch, what else?" He also laughed and then replied, "The brain, that," pointing to his forehead, illustrating that he had rationally and consciously made the decision. He was proud of the fact that he and others had made that choice and spoke with deep sadness about the army's actions. Those who were tortured and murdered were the most admired people, he stated, the people who were the least selfish, the best prepared, and the most giving. As the terror unfolded, the villagers rejected the military with even more fervor.

Florencia was pregnant and already had one infant when she left the village to join the revolutionaries. She said her husband, Juan, had told her, "Are we just going to stay here? We have to struggle. If we don't struggle we are going to stay here, and here we will leave our life having done nothing." Soldiers were coming to the house to check on them, and so the entire family left and joined the EGP. Florencia's father had decided that it was too dangerous to remain in the village. "He told us," Florencia recalled, " 'For years I have given my life to the rich; now I have to give my life for the poor.' " Florencia stayed in the guerrilla camp and was trained to give medical care. The EGP found a family to look after her one-and-a-half-year-old son. She did not become a combatant, although all her younger sisters did. After Florencia and her family left for Mexico and ended up in a refugee camp in Quintana Roo, the EGP reestablished contact with her. "They invited us to attend meetings and named me to do some [political] work and plan tasks, but all of this was clandestinely." She said some of the work in the refugee camps was with the women's organization Mamá Maquín. "The main objective was to make women conscious that we have the same rights as men," she said, and get the refugee women politically involved for the future return to Guatemala.

Villagers joined the insurgents for various reasons, depending on the year, the context, and personal circumstances. Some participated for a few years, others stayed for more than fifteen years, until the peace accords and demobilization. A vast difference existed in the depth of commitment. Six main reasons for joining the insurgency ran through the interviews and discussions over several years. Some combatants touched on all of them while others dwelled on one or another. Notably absent were issues related to the United States, the cold war, or redefining a political or economic global system.

First, many peasants expressed a pervasive and well-founded anxiety of losing their land to the army or the oligarchy or both, a concern fed by the uncertainty of land titles in the village. As peasants, land was central to their existence and land had always been a highly charged issue in Guatemala.

Second was the "paradox of success": the more villagers prospered, the more they chafed against the weight of an unresponsive and brutal social system. Success exacerbated the tension between growing confidence and frustration over repressive forces that choked their efforts. As a result, some peasants came to want deeper structural change, not just a parcel of land. "To have a parcel does not mean we have everything," Pedro Tol remarked assertively. Several other former combatants indignantly rejected the notion that they were well-off because, unlike other peasants, they had sufficient land. They challenged the notion that land should be the whole criteria for an acceptable standard of living and pointed out that they, too, like others in society, had greater aspirations. "As far as losing one's life in the struggle?" one person remarked. "Well, anyhow you are dying of hunger, and illnesses."

A third reason for joining the insurgency was rooted in the difficulty of peaceful change. Attempts at reform in Guatemala, no matter how modest, risked running afoul of a rigid social structure and a deeply authoritarian state with severe, frightening consequences. Paradoxically, the risks inherent in seeking moderate change made radical transformation all the more plausible. If you might be murdered for joining a cooperative, why not join the guerrillas? Tencho, echoing the REMHI report, found the roots of the conflict in the fierce tension between the injustice of Guatemalan society and the closure of avenues for peaceful change. "The struggle wasn't born because the [guerrillas] wanted it," he remarked. "No one would want a war, rather [the war came] out of necessity. In Guatemala those who govern have been committing injustices, oppressing, discriminating since the Spanish conquest." When asked many years later (in 2001) why the message of the insurgents seemed to resonate, Father Luis responded in a characteristically straightforward way. The people listened to the guerillas, he said, "because they were poor and because they felt threatened by the army."

Fourth, the villagers' new understanding of liberation from the Bible, as the REMHI report underscores, provided the moral underpinnings for their vision. These values transcended immediate self-interest and looked toward achieving a more equitable and democratic society.

Fifth, the escalating military terror frightened many but fueled the recruitment of others to the insurgency. Defense against the army and revenge for its atrocities fused into a powerful recruiting tool for the rebellion. After the early 1980s, in particular, peasants began to join in fierce anger at army atrocities, seeking both protection and retribution through the insurgency. In sum, it felt safer to have a gun in your hands.

Finally, as the insurgency reached critical mass, peer pressure played a role in participation. Some, particularly the very young, joined because everyone else was getting involved and because of the initial excitement and adventure. Others participated—although not as combatants—because their peers seemed to be going along or because of implied or real threats. This group joined quickly and was more likely to leave quickly.

Social and Political Collisions

The insurgent forces grew substantially throughout the countryside and in the urban areas: among peasants and university students, workers and professionals, trade unionists and catechists. As the decade began, military-sponsored kidnappings and assassinations escalated—well-known political figures, trade unionists, students, and leaders more generally—laying the groundwork for the coming massacres that would wipe out entire villages. When army atrocities increased sharply in the early 1980s, the terror cast an increasingly dark shadow over the Ixcán. The CEH (U.N.) report indicates that almost half the documented massacres in Guatemala occurred between 1980 and 1983, the period when the country was ruled by General Lucas García and then, after a coup, by General Ríos Montt. At first, the violence was targeted: it struck down the most respected, the most talented, the most energetic, and the most independent, and then it degenerated into mass slaughter of the Mayan population. "After the death of our *compañeros* in the Spanish Embassy we held a mass," Domingo Ixcoy, a founder of the peasant organization CUC from Xesic, a *cantón* near Santa Cruz del Quiché, remembered. "People came from all over. Three of the leaders killed were from Santa Cruz del Quiché." He recalled the surge of activities—meetings, demonstrations, and leafleting—during January and February of the new decade. Soon after, the army began to lash out without mercy at local leaders and communities. Fabián Pérez—a highly admired catechist, K'iche' leader, and another founder of the CUC—was to become an early victim. "Fabián was well known all over the region because he had worked with the cooperatives and because he was part of the central directorate of Catholic Action," Domingo stated. Fabián was also a key organizer of the cooperative in Santa María Tzejá and served as the critical link between the village and the highlands. Fabián had encouraged me to visit the Ixcán in 1973 and accompanied me there. As tensions throughout the highlands escalated, he and many others joined the EGP. Fabián was an effective leader, president of his chapter of Catholic Action, and he worked with the cooperative, three factors that would have drawn the army's attention. Domingo recalled, "Fabián Pérez left Santa Cruz del Quiché around four in the afternoon to go home [on April 9, 1980]. As he was passing the ruins of Utatlán [an ancient K'iche' Mayan site] on his bicycle, masked men emerged and killed him right there. It was the first terrorist death in the area." The murder was an incalculable loss, inflicting both widespread fear and anger throughout the highlands and severing a key connection between Santa María Tzejá and the rest of the country.

Fabián's funeral drew hundreds of people, some from distant villages. "The funeral was a very political event," according to Domingo. "People were very upset. Our response to the murder also served as an example to other villages. The repression was growing but so was the resistance." During the funeral, helicopters created panic by flying provocatively low with machine guns sticking out on both sides. About four hundred mourners were caught on a flat plain, with no place to escape. Some tried to disappear in the cornfields; children screamed and cried in horror; some began to run toward the chapel about a kilometer and a half away. As the helicopters roared above the funeral line, many fell to the ground. When people arrived at the chapel, soldiers parachuted to the ground, setting off further panic and scattering mourners in every direction. Despite the army's attempt at intimidation, the funeral was a major sign of defiance. Soon after his burial, Fabián's widow and some of her children fled to Nicaragua; in the end, most of his children wound up joining the EGP back in Guatemala.[16]

Murders and disappearances had become more common by 1980. In response, some peasants began to seek out the insurgents. Some who joined felt the insurgency might both protect them and challenge the army. The army remained overpowering, vicious, and feared, but it had ceased to seem invincible. The fact the military no longer fully controlled the situation, however, made it even more brutal and genocidal. One teacher from Chichicastenango, who volunteered for the fire department, recounted how hundreds of bodies were found in ravines and cornfields in 1981–82. The soldiers were acting as if they were "out of their minds, like crazy," he remarked, not even burying the bodies, to underscore the terror. He told me in 1987 while teaching in Santa María Tzejá, "I could show you places in the *cantones* around Chichicastenango where I know there are hundreds of bodies. And this was happening in Santa Cruz and in Sololá and in Chimaltenango, everywhere." News of these killings in the highlands spread to the rain forest, and word of the atrocities in the Ixcán traveled rapidly to the highlands, creating a climate of anger, fear, and hatred.

In Santa María Tzejá, the EGP forces were operating openly by 1980. Villagers soon realized that practically everyone was involved in one way or another with the insurgent forces. Previously clandestine training became more open, as did other insurgent activities. When another act of terror occurred in a neighboring village around 1981, a unified, confident village publicly responded. "Rubén Alfaro was kidnapped by the army in Santo Tomás," Bartolo Reyes recalled. "The guerrillas organized the demonstration—a march to defy the army so they would not continue with their kidnappings." Miguel Reyes remembers the march well, although he maintains the villagers themselves organized it. "People came from Santo Tomás to let us know that not only had Rubén Alfaro been kidnapped but also a man by the last name of Pinto," he said. "Those who guided the march were not the armed guerrillas, but Don Florencio and 'at your service,' yours truly, Miguel Reyes."[17] He stated proudly that they "headed the march because we along with others had attended a training workshop on social promotion at the Rafael Landívar University.[18] When we got word about what happened we called a meeting immediately and invited people from Santa María Dolores to come. They asked for a march permit from the military detachment and forty-seven people from Dolores joined." The military responded, he remembered, seeking to dissuade them from the march. "We were meeting and ready to go when a military officer came by helicopter to tell us that it was no longer necessary for us to go because the problem had already been resolved. But we said we would still go just to see." Although Rubén Alfaro, the kidnap victim, never appeared, the commander of Playa Grande came to listen to the villagers' grievances. "The commander left and said he'd look into it and see if [Alfaro] was in some military detachment," Miguel Reyes reported. "[The commander] returned once again to inform us that it was impossible to find him. He said we didn't take note of who may have taken Alfaro. The people responded, 'Tell us, do the guerrillas have helicopters?'" Miguel continued, insisting that "the demonstration would have been even bigger but the word never got to the other side of the river in time—to Ixcán Grande. By the time they wanted to join us, we had already returned to our village."

The strong community spirit in Santa María Tzejá forged a common attitude toward the military. In neighboring villages, especially those founded by USAID in the mid-1970s (known collectively as Project 520), some villagers provided information to the army and, as a result, peasants were killed, tortured, or disappeared. The very possibility of informers exacerbated suspicions and divisions, and trust itself became a casualty of the conflict. The nature of these villages tended to reflect their history. USAID would announce that land was available, and those who came would have little in common beyond the need for land. Some came from the Pacific coast area where they had received land as part of the government's agrarian reform program in the early 1950s, only to have it taken away after the overthrow of Arbenz, thereby catalyzing their politicization. Others came in search of land and had not participated in mobilizations or organizations. They lived together, but few mechanisms existed to draw people toward a common vision. In contrast, Catholic Church–run cooperatives such as the one in Santa María Tzejá placed an emphasis on creating a community spirit, developing solidarity, and establishing rules that would bind people together. These villagers had a particular vision of the Bible and its relation to their lives, providing a moral sensibility that both informed their everyday actions and the village institutions. The deadly consequences of division in the villages around them reinforced their determination not to replicate the splits of other communities. Whether someone was skeptical or embraced the insurgents wholeheartedly, informing the army was not an acceptable option in Santa María Tzejá. "In this village either no one is involved with the guerillas or everyone is," a colonel commented to a villager in frustration around 1981, adding ominously, "We shall find out which sooner or later." In nearby villages, such as Santa María Dolores, the military was not unsure.[19] The army was exasperated with Santa María Tzejá, suspecting that the village was exceedingly well organized. Commanders often sent soldiers dressed as civilians or as guerrillas to a village to obtain intelligence information. On one occasion two men—pig buyers— arrived in Santa María Tzejá. They talked to people, hung out, and expressed interest in buying pigs. The villagers eyed these strangers suspiciously and quickly put two and two together—they were army agents. They grabbed the two men, tied them up, and held them in an outdoor cell. They then proudly went to the nearby army base to tell the commander that two guerrillas had come to their village, that they were pretending to be buying pigs, and that the villagers—not wanting to have anything to do with delinquent subversives—had captured them and were going to kill them. The military officer panicked and rushed out with soldiers toward Santa María Tzejá. While wanting to commend the villagers for their good deed, he nevertheless chastised them, "You cannot kill them, that is not for you to do, we do the killings." The officer arrived and went straight to untie and free the very frightened "pig buyers." After calming down, the colonel looked at the straight-faced villagers and thanked them, stating he would take care of these two men. The soldiers and pig buyers marched off together, and strangers no longer came snooping around the village.

This incident was not the first or the last time that the villagers either played dumb or showed a faux patriotism and an ostensible loyalty to the military. A military manual on psychological operations discusses the role of "rumors" in carrying out psychological war. As an example it cites an incident that occurred in 1977 in Santa María Tzejá.[20] The village's cooperative was meeting when the military patrol entered the village. The officer, taking advantage of the gathering, asked the president of the cooperative if he could address the group. According to the manual, the president of the cooperative "refused to let [the officer] speak, stating that *he had information* that the troops operating in the region were not Guatemalans, but Central American mercenaries." This rumor had been planted. "This response demonstrates," according to the manual, "the effectiveness of the *bola* [rumor], which was created precisely to create these results and uneasiness in the region."[21] The president of the cooperative in 1977 later told me that he did not remember this incident but said it was not uncommon for them to act that way. When I mentioned that it appeared in a military manual as an example of the effectiveness of rumors, he just laughed, adding that their own response had been effective for the village, at least for a while.

As the conflict escalated through 1980, the EGP slid into more authoritarian behavior, making impatient demands and peremptory commands. Bold, often wildly unrealistic, pronouncements began to rule the day. " 'What we had was politics, now we will act militarily,' " Pedro Tum reported the EGP saying. " 'We will face the army. The soldiers who come in here, here they will stay; an airplane that comes, here it will stay.' " With the pressure building, "the people assumed the guerrillas knew what they were doing," Pedro said. In any case, the EGP leadership was in no mood to accept challenges to their tactics. When some peasants offered support around 1980–81 but wanted to know when they would obtain weapons to fight, Pedro maintained the guerrillas responded, "No, no, no. You don't worry. Who is speaking over there?" They poked fun sarcastically asking if the person who spoke, Manuel Canil, was related to General Lucas, the president at the time. Tragically, Manuel Canil was to lose his family in the massacre about a year later. Pedro Canil claims that by 1981 people had begun to refer to those who questioned the guerrilla tactics as timid. "From that day on," he observed, "even if people were not in agreement with some tactics, they would say nothing; they would not say its either good or bad."

On Sunday, August 17, 1980, the guerrillas committed an act that stained the memory of all who witnessed it. Most of the villagers were in church celebrating Sunday services, Federica recalls. Andrés Ixcoy, dressed in a yellow shirt, was playing with his musical group on the left side of the altar as he often did. When the time came for the prayers, two heavily armed men walked in from the back of the church warning that everyone should remain calm, that they were looking for only one man. They called out Andrés Ixcoy's name. In a suddenly hushed church, he answered, "Here I am," and when he saw that they were armed he knelt down and began to pray. The two men asked everyone to leave and to congregate by the basketball court next to the church. There the guerrillas staged an impromptu political/military meeting while a terrified Andrés Ixcoy stood by the side of Father Luis's house near the church. Federica remembers that his face was very sad. He wasn't looking at the people, she recalled; his head was hanging down. Next to him were two of his children, his son, Felipe, and his oldest daughter, Margarita. The guerrillas charged that he was an *oreja* (spy) for the army.

Rosario Castro, Ixcoy's widow, and their daughter Margarita spoke with me about the assassination almost a decade later.[22] Their accounts differed in some details from what Federica described but not in the essentials. "Andrés liked songs of glory to God, and he always participated in the church service," Rosario mentioned in another discussion in 1999 after she had returned with the other refugees to Santa María Tzejá. "He did not like the guerrilla organization. He rejected the guerrillas. He did not want to join them or have anything to do with them." The daughter added that outside the church, "The guerrillas and my father began to argue, because he did not accept what they were saying—some kind of accusation against him, that he was a spy of the military. They said they were going to kill him. At that point he tried to escape and was running, while he was running they fired at him. It took until he got by the stream until they were able to hit him, and he fell." Rosario and Margarita stated that he was executed because he did not want to become more involved with the insurgents, although he had provided modest food aid when asked.

I discussed Andrés Ixcoy's assassination with many villagers over a number of years. The responses were complex and reflected many deeper feelings about the insurgency, although no one felt comfortable with the guerrilla actions that tragic day. In general, villagers felt that the execution may have been a mistake carried out by "undisciplined local EGP units." The villagers tended to blame EGP excesses, human rights abuses, and misguided strategies on local or regional cadre while leaving national commanders off the hook. Their assumption was that these actions were not intrinsic EGP policy. Although most villagers believe Andrés Ixcoy had not been a spy, a few imply that had he been an *oreja,* the assassination would have had a purpose. During this period, villages around Santa María Tzejá were suffering horrendous repression. Well-known, highly respected, and well-liked men and women were kidnapped, assassinated, tortured, and raped throughout the Ixcán as a result of informers. Some villagers implied that while Andrés Ixcoy may not have been a spy, his behavior was at times strange and unexplainable. "He went frequently to Santa María Dolores [a village with a military outpost]," one villager commented. "From what I've heard this was the reason why many people from the guerrillas suspected that he was an *oreja* for the military. Why did he go to Dolores every Saturday?" From these accusations, it was not a major step to a rumor that on one occasion Andrés Ixcoy turned over a list of names to an army officer in Dolores.

Vladimiro, who was captured by the army two years after the assassination of Ixcoy and was forced to work for the military for several years, reflected about that period many years later. "There were army *orejas* in the community. They passed on information to the army. They were not very successful because they didn't pass on too much information. There wasn't that much. Yes [the guerrillas] killed Andrés Ixcoy. He was the only one [from the community] executed by the guerrillas. He really was an *oreja.* They advised him to 'change his ways,' but he didn't. He didn't change, and they killed him." He continued, "That was the good thing about the guerrillas. They killed him and left his body there so that his people could bury him. In contrast, the army would burn the bodies so they would be unrecognizable, nothing would be left. During that time

Figure 4. Rosario Castro in 2003, at age sixty-three. She is the widow of Andrés Ixcoy, who was killed by the guerrillas in Santa María Tzejá in 1980. She spent twelve years in refugee camps in Mexico with her children. Photo by Beatriz Manz.

[in the Ixcán] the smell of burning human flesh was present all day long." According to Vladimiro, the army also left bodies strewn in the jungle. Relatives would find skeletons with just skin, or pieces of cadavers after animals had devoured them.

An apparent pullback by the army toward the end of 1981 fueled the guerrillas' boldness. Despite their confidence, however, the rebels were well aware that the troops would return. The insurgents began to prepare the population in the Ixcán, including Santa María Tzejá, for the army's counterattack, recommending that tunnels be built in case of air raids and that food be stored in the land parcels. Villagers dug and camouflaged deep holes on jungle paths, placing sharp sticks in traps to impede the army's advance.[23] The guerrillas became the de facto authority in the village, a new reality that took some by surprise, but flowed from the military situation on the ground. In this tense environment, the village became more isolated. The army confiscated the village truck, seized merchandise transported by river, prohibited normal travel in and out of the area, closed markets, and drove foreigners and NGOs out of the region. Those villagers who were inimical or indifferent toward the guerrillas had no alternative but to do as the guerrillas ordered.

As tensions increased, the guerrillas could be ruthless in asserting their authority. In late 1981 they killed Armando, a man from Cobán who operated the wood-burning cardamom drier, charging him with being an army informant, although no one could exactly confirm the indictment. The guerrillas sought to bring him to the center of the village for a public trial; he resisted and was killed by a stream near the center of the village. The guerrillas also warned the cardamom pilots from Cobán to stop flying into the area. Nonetheless, soon after the warning a small plane flew over the village several times and then headed toward the army base in Playa Grande. After this flight, the guerrillas killed the next pilot who landed and fired at another pilot who flew in to retrieve the dead pilot's body.[24] The insurgents then ordered the landing strip sabotaged to prevent more planes from arriving. These killings provoked two reactions from the settlers: some maintained that it was acceptable, even necessary, to kill informers in a time of war or innocent people might be killed. The majority, however, were more critical, arguing that the accusations could be false, reflecting *envidia,* or personal jealousy or animosity, and they rejected the takeover of the village by the insurgents. The reaction to the closing of the landing strip was surprisingly subdued, considering that now the villagers were far more isolated. Without air access, the only way to leave the village involved using the Chixoy River, which put travelers under tight military control. The guerrillas said the sabotage was necessary to prevent the air force from landing in the village, an explanation that made little sense since the large air force planes could not land at the airstrip and helicopters did not need it.[25]

The guerrillas began instructing the population in defense plans. They established a "system of fixed sentries," posts commanding a view over the thick forest canopy and the paths leading to the village. The sentries were an early warning system, trained to detect any unusual movements and warn the villagers immediately. If they saw imminent danger, they were to make noise with homemade bombs of tin cans, or by firing shots or throwing a grenade. The insurgents also instructed the villagers on civil defense and survival in the rain forest. "The tunnels made us feel more secure in case of a bombing attack," a peasant stated. "We needed to be prepared. When Dolores was bombed we used [the tunnels] because we thought they would also come here to bomb." In the land parcels the people built *buzones* to store food, clothing, and valuable documents such as birth certificates and *cédulas* (identification cards). "The *buzones* helped us a lot because thanks to that we had some food reserves when we had to live in the forest," another villager commented. "The army did find some of them and burned them. Others were never found." When asked if those who were not fully on board in terms of collaboration with the insurgents would also build tunnels and *buzones*, this villager replied, "Yes, because the airplanes and the helicopters did not distinguish who was a collaborator and who was not."

EGP leaders who were sent to the village played an unusually important role, defining the insurgency in the minds of many villagers. One of these leaders, Adalberto, broke the *varas* (sticks that were a traditional symbol of authority) that the municipal mayor passes to his local assistant, the *alcalde auxiliar*. He did this in front of everyone, an act meant to underscore the political control of the insurgents. "From now on the auxiliary mayor will no longer have authority here," Adalberto proclaimed at a meeting in the house lot of Gaspar. "Instead, those who are directing the war and those directly named by the people will lead, because this is a popular war. We are hereby declaring that we have begun the war against the illegitimate authorities and we have started the takeover of power by the people." After declaring Santa María Tzejá a "liberated village" (and within the EGP given the nom de guerre Karakovia), the EGP repeated the act in other neighboring villages. Carlos, another EGP guerrilla leader, took over control of Santa María Tzejá at the end of 1980. He seemed to become a lightening rod for local resentment and animosity. Pedro Tol, a combatant under Carlos's command, described him as arrogant and a liar, prone to exaggerate the number of army casualties to enhance his own reputation in the eyes of his superiors. Carlos, a member of the Dirección de Frente (Command Front), was responsible for both the military and political activities of the area and thus played a critical role with the civilian population. Most think he was a Ladino from Chiantla in Huehuetenango Department. He is described as rather tall, muscular, and thin, with straight black hair and a dark complexion. His rotted upper front teeth gave his smile a menacing presence. Years later he appears to have deserted, and some claim to have seen him working with the army.

By late 1981 the Ixcán was about to descend into a poisonous darkness; the military repression would escalate into wholesale slaughter. The army sought to extinguish any thought of challenging its power through unimaginable violence against civilians. Villages were not caught in a cross fire between contending armies; they were the targets in the military's gun sights. The officers who ordered massacres surely descended to new levels of depravity, but the depravity had a purpose: It was meant to induce submission and to embed fear, distrust, and disunity into the character of everyday life. The demonic manner in which people were butchered and the highly visible ways in which their cadavers were left, charred or unburied, was meant to scar the living. The historic racism against indigenous people further fueled the process. Ultimately, the military made no distinction in villages between the strongest advocates of the guerrillas or their adversaries, between combatants or civilians. All peasants in targeted areas were held responsible for the insurgency, and all would be made to pay the price.

The stage was set for a major confrontation by early 1982. The army was no longer coming into the area, and an uneasy calm seemed to settle over Santa María Tzejá. The EGP units operating in the area mistakenly interpreted the calm as a sign of impending victory, and the army's withdrawal added to their sense of strength. Many villagers, previously apprehensive, began to think that the military might fall as it had in Nicaragua. Despite the confidence, the insurgents possessed few weapons themselves, and no guns were given to the villagers other than a few to the sentries and other key people. The EGP maintained they had matters under control, according to several villagers, asserting that the war would last another "three months, at most, and that victory would be obtained quickly." The EGP appeared confident, if not arrogant, displaying little patience with peasants raising questions about a possible military response. Miguel Reyes recalled, "There were some villagers who wanted to sell their cattle to buy weapons to fight, because this was the moment for everyone to support the EGP militarily, but the EGP responded, 'No, because here the war will not last.'"[26] Miguel continued, "Well, when you heard that you gained confidence. You thought, 'Well it will not be so hard, or if it was going to be hard it will be hard for a little while.' For a lot of people it was confusing." Although many villagers were nervous, Pedro Canil recalled that the EGP would assure them there was no reason to worry, "'Nothing will happen to you here,' the EGP would say, 'Here we are to protect you. In a few days this whole area [Ixcán] will be declared a liberated zone. When the army comes to kill you, all you have to do is go hide in the jungle for a few days and we will confront the army.'" Pedro continued, "And we believed that. But now we know that was just politics so the people would stick with them. Who would have thought then that the army would freely enter here and do whatever they wished with the people?"

The brief lull proved to be the calm before the fiercest of storms. In early February the army began to move against villages just to the northeast of Santa María Tzejá. The word of the atrocities spread quickly, and a deep fear gripped people throughout the Ixcán. The army marched into La Trinitaria on February 10 and butchered every person they encountered in the village, even merchants from other villages who were there by chance. The soldiers surrounded the village and then opened fire, killing everyone. The murderous staccato sound of automatic weapons was followed by an eerie silence, the smell of gunpowder mingling with the smell of death.[27] The soldiers continued south on the jungle trails toward San José la 20. Many people had already been killed in this village, so when the army arrived it was deserted. Not to be deterred, the soldiers set the village on fire.

After torching the village—twelve kilometers north of Santa María Tzejá—a column of about 150 heavily armed troops marched southwest down the winding path to Santa María Tzejá. At about the same time, some say, another column of soldiers moved north in the direction of Santa María Tzejá, eight kilometers away, after a destructive rampage in Santa María Dolores. On the path near the outer border of the smoldering San José la 20 and the boundary of Santa María Tzejá, anxious sentries from the village—members of the FIL—were on the lookout. When they caught sight of the troops, they gave prearranged signals— whistles and hand signs. Sentries frantically ran down the four major paths in the village, passing the word from one house to another and yelling that the army was on its way. As the troops approached the houses of the village, a small EGP unit threw a grenade and fired some shots, perhaps to give the villagers more time to flee.

Alerted that the troops were approaching, terrified villagers dropped everything and fled, especially after they heard the grenade so close by. The village they abandoned seemed frozen in time: clothing was scattered over rocks by the river, fires for cooking continued to burn, radios played music, chickens and pigs wandered by houses. Although they were frightened, most villagers thought that the army would move on when they saw a deserted village, and the residents would be able to come back to sleep in their houses that night, or at most in a day or two. One man put on his old shoes, not wanting to ruin his new ones in what he thought would be a brief flight into the rain forest. Young children were particularly horrified, unable to comprehend the fear that suddenly consumed all the adults. Fleeing villagers ran through branches, cut their feet, ripped their clothing, and bruised their bodies, propelled into the forest by their fear. Some may have wanted to grab a few more treasured possessions but realized seconds could mean the difference between life and death.

The first soldiers entered the center of the village around four o'clock on Saturday, February 13, 1982, a typically hot, humid afternoon. They camped in the village that night as villagers huddled in different places hidden in the rain forest. Several soldiers dragged a marimba from a house and began playing, the cheerful sounds echoing through a rain forest riven with fear. All the villagers had managed to escape except Vicenta Mendoza, whom the soldiers seized and held in the village that night. The next day the army began to loot and then destroy every building: the school, the priest's house, the cooperative, the cardamom drying structure. Groups of marauding troops moved down the paths ransacking and torching all the homes they encountered and slaughtering animals with guns and machetes. Villagers could see the smoke rising over all they had built. A small guerrilla unit fired briefly (with uncertain effect) on the soldiers in the center of the village.

On the second day, after the soldiers had brutally raped Vicenta Mendoza—a mentally retarded woman—they murdered her, dumping and partially burying her bleeding, limp body near the cooperative building. Weeks later the rains made it easy to spot where she had been dumped, a grisly reminder of the horror that had taken place. At night villagers could hear the soldiers celebrating—laughing and roasting meat for supper—while they themselves were sleeping in the jungle, hungry, not able to cook, soaked from the torrential tropical rains, their children coughing and crying. Once again there was marimba music.

On February 15 a group of men went to survey what was happening and to try to recover some badly needed food, and, if possible, to untie pigs and give water to the animals. Several silently climbed a small hill where they could view the center of the village; they left their families hidden in several groups in the dense foliage close to a trail that lead to Santa María Dolores in the southern part of the village near the Tzejá River. Unexpectedly, the men on the hill saw an army patrol heading south down a path toward the Tzejá River in the direction of their families' hiding places.[28] A helicopter was also flying overhead. Crouching in fear in the jungle undergrowth, trembling mothers had stuffed rags into the mouths of their infants so they would not cry. As the last soldier passed, a small dog barked. The column immediately halted and turned back to investigate. They soon located a pregnant woman, her infant, and two boys left in her care. Meanwhile, Pedro Lux and his son Ángel Lux ran to warn their family that an army column was on the way. Running desperately through the forest, Ángel, the little boy, was nonetheless too late. He heard the soldiers yell something at the terrified woman and children, indicating without doubt that the troops knew they had run across a group of unarmed civilians, and then he listened in shock as the soldiers emptied their weapons into the cowering group.[29] As the bleeding bodies lay on the ground, a soldier threw a grenade to finalize the carnage. The unit then began examining the area more thoroughly, quickly locating a second group of eight children, their pregnant mother, and a grandmother. The soldiers moved against them with indescribable fury, firing their weapons at point blank range. The soldiers ripped open the pregnant woman's stomach and tore out her unborn baby. A little girl who had not been killed in the fusillade of bullets was tossed in the air and bayoneted. A young boy, Edwin Canil, managed to run and hide behind a fallen tree trunk, becoming the only witness to a bloodletting that wiped out his world. "I remembered what we had been told to do if the army came," he later said. "There was a lot of noise, smoke, everyone was screaming, my sisters," he recalled tearfully. "I continued running any way I could. My goal was to get out of there. I was not afraid. When I was running I turned my head and saw one of my sisters was following me. I continued running. I turned my head again. My sister was no longer there. I stopped and I hid behind a fallen tree trunk." He had jumped into thick, sharp brush that was cutting his skin. From there he observed the carnage. "The army killed them all. Perhaps they did not notice when I fled. I do not understand why. I saw it all. I saw it well. My baby sister was crying. A soldier took out a knife and opened my little sister's stomach and threw everything out on the ground. My sister no longer cried." Finally the soldiers left after looking for anything of value on the bodies. "Then I only heard that no one was speaking, no one was making any noise. I came out from under the tree trunk. They were all dead," he recalled and then described the scene. "One sister had no head, I don't know, they burst her head with automatic fire. They were all lying around like a wheel. I was around them. My mother had been shot near the nose, below the eye. My brother, who had said he would rather be dead than be caught by the military, he was dead. My sister, the one who was following me, she had a hole in the back." He then reflected, "Now I think, perhaps she covered me. It is likely that when they fired at her, those bullets did not hit me. I think she gave her life for me."[30]

Edwin Canil, surrounded by the bodies of his family, now became very frightened. "I wanted to get out of that circle that curled around me, and when I wanted to get out of there, I couldn't, I was so afraid." Six-year-old Edwin became frozen, he had never seen or imagined anything like what he was witnessing. "I observed each one of them. No one was speaking anymore. Finally I got out of there! I went back to where I had been hiding. When I got to the tree trunk I felt bad. I went back again where the dead were. I stayed there again and watched them, but this time I did not go in the middle of the wheel, I was too afraid. I looked at them."

He is not sure how long he remained in his hideout, but eventually he began searching for a jungle path. He arrived at the place where the whole family had slept the night before, but no one was there. "I was left alone in the forest! I didn't know what to do. If I screamed the soldiers would hear me." He headed to a pasture, and though he was frightened he looked up. "In the hut we used to store corn, there they were, the soldiers were sitting there. A helicopter went around and around overhead." When the military had finally left, little Edwin began to scream calling for his father. "I was getting very frightened because it was getting late." There was no way for Edwin to know if his father or the others from the village were alive. "I did not find my father until the next day. When he saw me, he asked if only I was alive. Oh God! I told him what happened. He just cried and cried."

The news of the massacre spread fast even though the population was dispersed and hiding. Many had heard the gunfire and the screams. The hundred or so families made an immediate, drastic decision to kill all their dogs to avoid a repeat encounter with marauding soldiers. No one had any doubts that they all would have been murdered had the army been able to locate them. The villagers were apprehensive about going to the site of the carnage, fearing the army may be waiting for them. Manuel, Edwin's father, said, "I couldn't go there right away. I don't know why. Truly I couldn't. About five days later I went, they were still hurled there. On top of each other, swollen, I could not recognize them." He quickly covered the bodies with a few branches. About a month later, on a Sunday, they returned to bury them. "We put one on top of the other in two deep holes. Some this way, some that way, then on top. We buried them in that same place because we could not take them out." I asked him what they were like. He looked down and cries, "Decomposed, just skeletons, all that is flesh you cannot see, worse yet, the little children. I could not bear it, I could not bear being there, the pain was so great, it was a tremendous sorrow." Manuel Canil barely managed to finish the sentence.[31]

The bloodletting was hardly over in the Ixcán. After the savagery in Santa María Tzejá, a column of troops headed in the direction of an-

other nearby village, Kaibil Balam.[32] The column of troops arrived at
Kaibil Balam on February 27, 1982.[33]

In neighboring Santo Tomás Ixcán the evangelical Protestants gathered in their chapel to pray, certain that the army would not kill them—
given that Catholics were generally identified as the enemy. While most
of the villagers fled, the evangelicals felt that they had no reason to run
and what they needed to do at this crucial moment was to place their
fate in God's hands, certain that He would protect them. Nonetheless,
the army was in no mood to ask questions of loyalty, to make excep-
tions, to think twice. Soldiers set the chapel on fire. As one villager from
Santa María Tzejá stated, "They began to pray, the army must have
thought 'how pretty,' and they grabbed them all. They surrounded them,
opened up with machine guns and then set the chapel on fire. Ten families, sixty-five people were killed. The sin in those days was to live here
even if you were not with the other side [with the guerrillas]. Nobody
could explain, 'I am a Guatemalan.' "

After the murderous rampage through the Ixcán, Santa María Tzejá
as well as countless other villages lay in ruins, the broken bodies of neighbors and friends lay scattered on the ground, houses and animals were
decimated, a decade of hard work lay incinerated, and dreams were shattered. Hiding and fearful in the rain forest, the terrified residents of Santa
María Tzejá knew that simply to survive would be a victory. And they
slowly and painfully began to plan their survival. Children and the elderly suffered the most. For others the army's carnage produced further
rage and even more determination to fight. Many youth signed on as combatants. The village had taken sides with the insurgents, but the army had
broken the most basic rule of combat: to distinguish combatants from
civilians. It is estimated that in the Ixcán between one thousand and twelve
hundred civilians were killed by the army between 1975 and 1982.[34]

chapter 4

Ashes, Exodus, and Faded Dreams

I n the early morning hours of February 16, 1982—the day after the massacre in Santa María Tzejá—the intense heat of the sun began enveloping the rain forest as it did on any other day. The sounds of birds in the forest and the smell of the thick, verdant vegetation had not changed. Something, however, was eerily, tragically different that sad morning: no human sounds at all. No noise of children playing, no yelling across a field, no chopping wood, no morning laughter, no grinding of corn, no smoke, no cooking. The clearing at the center of the village was a blackened scar; the embers of the torched buildings were now ash. Smashed personal belongings littered the trails. The foundations of buildings were covered with debris. Santa María Tzejá lay smoldering and its inhabitants either had been murdered or had fled into the rain forest.

The families who had survived were huddled in terrified groups in the jungle wondering where they might go and what their future would hold. It had not yet sunk in that they were becoming part of a vast magnitude of displaced people. "Estimates of the number of displaced persons," according to the CEH (U.N.) report, "vary from 500,000 to a million and a half people in the most intense period from 1981 to 1983, including those who were displaced internally and those who were obliged to seek refuge abroad."[1] Some families were captured by military units; others, worn down by the jungle and debilitated by their fear, intentionally or unwittingly surrendered to the army. For the first time since they had settled the village twelve years earlier, a divide driven by enmity would separate the villagers between those who wound up in army custody and those who eluded the military and became refugees; an ugly question re-

Figure 5. Women with their children in the Maya Tecún refugee camp in Campeche, Mexico, in 1988. They gave birth while hiding and fleeing from the army; all but one of the children born during their flight survived. Photo by Beatriz Manz.

mained about who collaborated with the officers and the results of that collaboration.

Half of the families of the village, about sixty families (some 300 people), would make the arduous trek over the border to Mexico, some within days of the massacre, others after a month, still others a year or so later, ultimately joining 150,000 people who sought safety in Mexico. Another group, about forty families, came under military control either because they returned to the site of the destroyed village or were captured by soldiers. During the period in hiding, women gave birth to six children.

Five separate groups spilled across the border to Mexico at different times.[2] The first was composed of the families of victims of the massacre. One family fled within two weeks of the destruction of the village, in February 1982. When they arrived in Mexico there were few refugees and no international agencies to aid them. The Mexican *ejidatarios* (peasants) received them, gave them work, sometimes in exchange for food. The Catholic Church in Chiapas, led by Bishop Samuel Ruiz, was the first Mexican institution that tried to locate and aid the Guatemalans. The second group, mainly Ladinos, left in March, followed by the next group in May. While the EGP was promoting the exodus in Ixcán Grande until mid-1982, their policy apparently changed by August. The guerrillas set up *retenes* (checkpoints) in La Catorce according to Miguel Reyes, who was in the fourth group. They refused to allow people to head north to Mexico, holding them up for nearly a month. Asked to explain why the guerrillas interfered with their exodus, Miguel caustically responded, "They had no basis and no right whatsoever." He then reflected for a moment and continued. "It appears that those guerrilla groups believed that they had control over the civilian population and that they could make decisions as if they were an authority. Quite obviously, the affected people could not do anything against them. Even though they complained, they accepted submissively the order not to continue out of fear of being killed. Perhaps the guerillas were afraid of being left alone, without popular support, if the people went to Mexico to seek refuge in massive numbers. On the other hand, neither did they have the military capacity to stop the massacres, nor the scorched earth tactics of the army."[3] Incredibly, the guerrillas told the villagers in those devastating months that "victory was going to be achieved in three months." When the insurgents were asked for weapons, they admitted not having any to give. After the people in this group were finally allowed to head to Mexico, they discovered to their amazement that some guerrilla leaders from elsewhere had already sent their families across the border to safety. This understandably created deep resentment.

The last group, about thirty families (some 150 people), remained in the rain forest, determined not to abandon their dreams. "As a consequence of the massacres," the CEH (U.N.) report notes, speaking about Guatemala as a whole, "the population massively fled to seek refuge in Mexico, where they maintained their ties to the EGP. Thousands of others stayed within the country but hidden in the mountains, where they formed the Communities of Population in Resistance (CPR) of the Ixcán (CPR-I) and in the Sierras (CPR-S)."[4] Under the toughest conditions this last group from the village waited for the military to leave and hoped, however much in vain, that things might improve. While living concealed in the forest for over a year, they managed to grow food in hidden fields and harvest their crops.

These holdouts were well organized and developed a division of labor that involved even the children. They posted sentries around the clock to monitor approaching army patrols. In fear of bombings and strafing from the air, they cooked at night to avoid telltale signs of smoke during the day and washed and dried clothes discreetly so as not to be spotted by helicopters. They trained their children to be quiet and prepared them for quick escapes. Everything was collective and shared. Living deep in the rain forest was draining physically and psychologically; constant pursuit by the army and the exposure to the harshness of the rain forest produced serious weakness, illnesses, and emotional strain. As noted by the CEH (U.N.) report about similar groups elsewhere in the country, "Life in the mountains meant constant movement, in part to avoid the soldiers or the patrollers, in part to search for food, water and, above all, to find refuge. The constant movement under the shadow of death and terror made it enormously difficult to subsist."[5]

After thirteen months, pushed ever deeper into the forest, these last thirty determined families were still hanging on in March 1983, not wanting to give up and reluctant to admit that the hope of the past could evaporate so quickly. Though strong and tenacious, the will of these families finally crumbled when they witnessed their own relatives, neighbors, and friends forming parts of large, army-organized bands of peasants, at times numbering in the hundreds. These groups, living under military control (most had no other choice), ventured deep into the forest to destroy cornfields. The fields had been tended carefully over many months and were close to being harvested. This act of sabotage and destruction was a particularly cruel blow to the families who had tended the fields, since fellow villagers and even relatives were involved. The fact that neighbors and relatives were involved in identifying the hidden locations, and in the destruction of the crops, is what made it so psychologically devastating, in addition to being materially devastating.

Jesús took charge of the last group, who remained in hiding in the forest for a year. In 1980 he had been forced to abandon his studies at the boarding school in Chichicastenango; soon after he joined the EGP as a political organizer, adopting the nom de guerre Nelson in honor of Nelson Mandela. "We never considered the wild animals or snakes in the jungle much of a threat," he said. "We didn't even have time to think about them. We felt safer in the jungle than the possibility of encountering the army." Nonetheless, he admitted, "That was the hardest thing I have ever lived through." When all their food had been destroyed and they were reduced to eating even the peels of the bananas, roots, and herbs, they finally decided to head to the Mexican border.

Deeply demoralized, they began the demanding trek north to Mexico and exile. With their hope of returning to the village shattered, they could no longer endure the wracking hunger, the weakness, the debilitating disease, the emotional drain, and the constant persecution. Walking single file on the narrow jungle trail, they carried their children on their backs. They had nothing else to carry after more than a decade of sacrifice in what they thought would be "the promised land." As the group made its way through the rain forest, perhaps some remembered the trek they had taken little more than a decade earlier to found the village. Jesús was now twenty-four in 1983, married and with an infant daughter. This time their haggard column grew in numbers as they made their way on overgrown paths, skirting large trees, and slicing through underbrush. The goal was not the dream of a new life but a struggle simply to survive. They were a column of desperation—fearful, exhausted, and sick, ghosts of their former selves—but nonetheless still determined. "We were more than five hundred people in total from three villages. It was a very long column, a true path of silence [un verdadero camino del silencio]," Jesús related. They had to move with caution, clandestinely slipping through to avoid army patrols. Along the way local guerrilla irregular forces (Fuerzas Irregulares Locales, or FILs) aided them, carefully scouting for army movements and pointing the way. "We did not speak. We only communicated by signs." As they reached the border on March 26, 1983, they were so relieved, Jesús remembered, "we jumped like rabbits." It took them five days to reach the Mexican border about fifty miles away. Hungry and thirsty they stumbled into a wide clearing at Chajul by the Lacantún River, where tens of thousands of others were already in refugee camps organized by the U.N. High Commissioner for Refugees.

When I visited the refugee camps in Chiapas, first in 1982 and then in 1984, one of the most painful episodes related by the last group of refugees was of their fellow villagers who had "gone with the enemy." They did not want to hear about the horrors other villagers may have faced when forced to guide the army to their hiding places. Above all they were upset that when their former friends and neighbors were unable "to deliver us to the assassin army, they destroyed our corn fields." They spoke about how difficult it had been to cultivate and take care of the maize while in hiding, plant by plant, and then their neighbors, fellow peasants, annihilated the fields when the maize was close to being harvested. The people in hiding may have been mobile; the corn was not, and they needed the corn to survive.

One unusual family decided neither to leave the country nor to submit to military hands. Emiliano and Adela and their children sought to remain in hiding in Guatemala no matter what might come. They first went up to the Ixil Mountains for a few years and later returned to the Ixcán with a small group, eventually joining the Ixcán CPR. I asked Emiliano why he didn't go to Mexico like the others. "I just didn't feel like it, [No me nació la voluntad]," he replied. "My *compañera* supported me. I would say to her, 'Lets try to hold up.' And when I would get desperate and demoralized, then she would encourage me." He then added, "And so the years went by. We were wandering from one place to another from February 13, 1982, until May 16, 1994." Once Emiliano and Adela had decided not to live in a militarized village nor to go into exile, they adapted quickly despite the extreme hardships. Surprisingly, he remembered some positive elements of the experience.

Most of the people in the CPRs were Mayans. Emiliano and Adela are Ladinos, originally from El Palmar. Born in 1943, Emiliano had lived in Ojo de Agua, El Palmar (located in Uspantán, the municipality that Nobel Peace Prize laureate Rigoberta Menchú comes from). He and Adela were among the last settlers to come to Santa María Tzejá with their family, not even checking the place beforehand. "I didn't even know if it was far or nearby. My *compañera* would ask, 'Are we about to arrive?' I would just tell her, 'Ay, God only knows, because I have no idea how far this place is.'"

Emiliano had joined the military service in the 1960s. While the law stipulated an eighteen-month service, he served twenty-two months of his own free will. While most K'iche' avoided the roundups forcing them into the military draft, he explained that he joined voluntarily, and therefore initially was suspected of being on the side of the army. Actually he felt that having been in the army, and knowing their thinking, actions, and discipline, helped him make some decisions. "Since I had been a soldier before, I knew a lot about military discipline. When they say, 'do this,' that has to be done. So I said to myself, 'Better God take my life in the jungle than die at the hands of the military.'" Emiliano has always been outspoken and a rebel—as he called himself. He left no doubt that he joined the military voluntarily, but also that he later joined the guerrillas voluntarily. He said that the first time he saw the insurgents from a distance, he was not sure if they were soldiers or guerrillas, but then one of them declared that they were the Army of the Poor. He responded in a characteristically cynical fashion, "Oh great, so you will get the poor out of their misery! [Ah, que bien, van a sacar a los pobres de sus penas.] They started right away with their *rollito* that the army this and the exploitation that and slavery this and that. That is how I started to get to know these gentlemen."

Emiliano explained how people lived and worked in the CPRs. The land was worked collectively in this western area of the Ixcán. They formed well-organized communities in the safest areas (although the land parcels belonged to people who had fled for Mexico from that region). He said everyone had to work and had assigned tasks, even children. "There was discipline. We all had to work because we all had to eat," and this was understood. "The normal routine," said Emiliano, "was to work from 7:00 A.M. to 3:00 P.M. in the collective cultivation. Then after 3:00 P.M. we were free to work or not work in individual production. Sometimes I did not get home until 6:00 P.M." The plantings were varied. "I would plant some sugar cane, bananas, yucca, clean up a bit. That was one's own. We called that '*chascada*' [gratuity] because all that production was for my family. What we had left over we would give away." He continued, "When you get used to collective work, it's really great." He said a person was in charge of organizing the tasks for the CPR. If someone did not go to perform their work in the fields, they had to inform that person and detail the reasons.

I asked him if he had managed money over the years in the CPRs. "No, we didn't need any," he responded quickly and somewhat haughtily. "We could not go to a market to buy anything. We had no soap, salt, axe, machete, hoe. That is why some people had to give themselves up." Their clothes were often rags, but he said, "We resisted. That is why we called ourselves the communities in resistance." The CPRs managed to survive for more than ten years and eventually negotiated their "coming out into the open." Emiliano and his family took these difficult years suffering hunger and illnesses with remarkable aplomb. Referring to his journeys alone or with other families in the CPRs in the Sierras and in the Ixcán, as well as a few months in Chiapas, he said with a sense of pride, "I am glad. I have had different experiences."

Despite some positive feelings, Emiliano and Adela deeply regret the price their children had to pay. On June 24, 1982, they ran into a military unit who fired on them. Although they managed to escape, their daughter Inés was hit in the leg and their son Eduardo was hit in the back. Three years later, on October 1, 1985, around four in the afternoon, they were surprised again, though fortunately not captured, by another unexpected patrol. Everyone ran, as they had so often planned, and hid deeper in the forest. When Emiliano and Adela came out, to their horror, they could not find their twelve-year-old daughter, Inés, who had been shot in the earlier incident, or their seven-year-old son, Julio. They desperately began looking for the two, their hearts sinking. They ran to the place where the children would have known to hide; they returned day after day to check the *buzón* where food was hidden, but there was no sign of them. The parents' frustration and fear rose. Finally, Emiliano and Adela tearfully accepted the fact that the military had seized the children. They hoped, even believed, that the children might still be alive, as the military usually dumped the bodies of those they killed in visible places. Two women and a man had been killed in that raid, their bodies left where they fell. Emiliano and Adela and their remaining children found themselves alone. Adela gave birth in those years and in total had nine children.

The story did not end there. It turns out the two children had been captured by civil patrols, a paramilitary force set up by the army. Ten years later Emiliano and Adela located Inés and Julio and learned a little about their intervening years. They were taken, along with a woman who was captured, to the military base in Playa Grande, then to Nebaj. The son eventually went to live with a relative and the girl went to find work in a home in Barillas, Huehuetenango. After reestablishing contact, Inés and Julio went to visit their parents in Santa María Tzejá in the late 1990s. Sadly, the experience did not go well. After twenty-five days they told their parents that they wanted to leave because the years had made them strangers and they did not like the village. It also became painfully apparent to the mother and father that "they lost their love for us [nos perdieron el cariño]." Inés had told one of her siblings, "I feel that they are not my parents."

Interviewed in Huehuetenango in 1999, after the visit to Santa María Tzejá, Inés, a shy, very thin woman in her late twenties, claimed to feel no affection for her parents, whom she thought had abandoned her. She had also convinced herself they were dead. "I have affection for Nubia [the woman with whom she has been living and working for many years]." She explained that she did not feel comfortable with her parents, nor did she like Santa María Tzejá when she went to visit them. It was unclear if she did not remember much of what happened to her at the military base or if she simply didn't want to talk about it. Nubia, her surrogate mother and grandmother of Inés's two children, kept a watchful eye nearby. It is very likely that Inés's two children were fathered by Nubia's only son. Inés said that it was the civil patrols who captured her: "Those who grabbed us were not soldiers, they were civilians, they were normal men, they were paid to find people that are with the guerrillas." First they were taken to the patrollers' village for two or three days, and then they were delivered to the soldiers. "A helicopter arrived and we were taken to Playa Grande [the military base]." She thought that either smoke or clothing left to dry in a pasture field had revealed their hideout.[6] She thought she was held in the military base for five months. While she had told others she had been raped by a lieutenant, she did not mention that incident. "They took a lot of photographs. They showed us that they were not bad, that those were just lies of the guerrillas. If the soldiers were bad they would have killed us when they grabbed us. But no, they were good, especially in Uspantán, they gave us breakfast, lunch, and dinner. They did not do bad things either." She said that the soldiers asked a lot of questions daily. "How did the guerrillas live? How many are there? What are their names? How did they get food? Did they work? And so on, a lot of questions, but there were things we would say and things we wouldn't say, right?" She elaborated that she did not tell them "how they [the guerrillas] taught us to use weapons, even though they were made of sticks." Although she was only twelve years old, she apparently sorted out what to tell the military and what to withhold. She continued, "Other things we would not say. What for? Right?" For example she did not tell the military that the guerrillas taught them how to hide, to escape in case of an army attack, how to move by crawling, and taught them how to write on a piece of wood with charcoal. What was her opinion of the guerrillas? "Likewise, they are not bad, they work, they did not make us work, only to give them food depending on how many there were. We got more or less eight *guerrilleros* per family, and we gave them breakfast, lunch, and dinner." She thinks she was with the guerrillas for two years, more or less. At the time of her capture there were six families living together, she recalled.

The first news of her parents came as a total surprise. "I was in a village about one hour from Nubilá. When I returned, Doña Nubia said, 'They came for you.' I asked, 'Who?' and she said, 'Your father and your mother.' 'That is a lie,' I said. I had in my head that I was never going to see them again; imagine, it had been some time since I had seen them [ten years], since I was six [she had, in fact, been twelve]. Nubia said, 'Yes, it's true, all the people live in the village again.' I couldn't believe it, I just couldn't believe it." She did not see her parents on that visit but did send a letter to them. Eight days later they again made the two-day journey over land to visit their daughter. "We spoke a lot with my father and my mother, because I did not know them anymore. I had in my head that I was never going to see them again," she repeated. The normal parent-child bonds and affection had been broken, especially for Inés.

The son felt somewhat closer to the parents. The parents told them about their life since the terrible day when they lost the two of them.

After all this Emiliano was unusually open in interviews.[7] Given his own natural curiosity, he seemed to enjoy the longest conversations, responding and asking questions as well. He said the people who lived under military control "were angry at the army. Yet, they would not express what is in the bottom of their thinking." He explained that when villagers speak favorably of the army and against the guerrillas, "they just say that for political purposes. They need to take care of the forced alliance with the army. Inside them they guard their real sentiments." When told that one hears that people respond to interviews by expressing positive views about the military and negative of the guerrillas, he quickly responded, "The truth is that of one hundred people interviewed by a person who is not known to them, five may be sincere, and ninety-five will say negative things regarding anything that has political content."

By early 1983, the second phase in the story of Santa María Tzejá had begun. The refugees in Mexico were devastated at hearing about the new army-imposed political and social organization, and they assumed their former neighbors were willing accomplices, an ethos in which the army's values defined the values of the village and in which the cooperative spirit they had nurtured so long was shattered. The refugees found it hard to accept that the same people with whom they had built a hopeful community were now following every military order; not only had they destroyed their food, but they were forming civilian patrols, providing intelligence information to the army, going on search-and-destroy operations, raising the flag, and marching at orders from the soldiers. An individualistic, atomized existence defined the social mores of village life.

Given the various phases of the exodus over more than a year, the refugees from the Ixcán in Chiapas were scattered throughout the Lacandón forest along the border with Guatemala by the Lacantún River. In April 1984 the Mexican government forced the relocation of the refugees to Campeche and Quintana Roo. The refugees were in no mood to go, having been uprooted once already and desiring to remain close to Guatemala, but their resistance was futile. While the relocation splintered many communities, the people from Santa María Tzejá sought to be relocated together, despite the fact that they were not necessarily from the same ancestral *cantón*. Most ended up in the sprawling Maya Tecún camp in Campeche. When Maya Tecún filled, a few families who resisted the relocation longest went to Quintana Roo. A handful of families—

those who were most concerned with maintaining their ties and support for the insurgents—refused to be relocated and blended into the Chiapas population.

The refugees aided each other materially as well as psychologically. The Catholic Church was an important presence in solidarity with the refugees as well as the international agencies that were there. In the camps the villagers met regularly with the larger refugee population, attended workshops, and moved on to more advanced seminars. Despite being dislocated, they felt a measure of control over their lives. The camps were dynamic, even though the large ones were filled with people from all over the northern regions of Guatemala who spoke different Mayan languages and came from different cultures.

Most significantly, the villagers from Santa María Tzejá made a conscious decision to remain in touch and hold their own meetings even if that required sending a representative to other states in Mexico to notify others about decisions taken in one camp. Democracy and the cooperative spirit had taken root and grown in this new soil. The refugees elected leaders, formed a variety of organizations, such as the Permanent Commissions (Comisiones Permanentes, CCPP)—an organization integrating refugees from various camps to negotiate for an eventual return— and Mamá Maquín, a refugee women's organization. Villagers from Santa María Tzejá soon emerged in the Mexican camps as leaders to represent all the Guatemalan refugees in Mexico.

Miguel Reyes, an active member of CCPP, played a key role in the years leading up to the successful return of the refugees from Santa María Tzejá and the reunification of the village in 1994. The leaders of both organizations were initially influenced by the insurgents, but there were other influences as well. "It was very helpful that most of us were all in the same camp," he said. "That aided the preparation of the people. In Maya Tecún we had a lot of workshops about our rights, as well as religious workshops. Catechists participated actively in a new organization called the Acción Cristiana Guatemalteca [Guatemalan Christian Action, ACG]," an ecumenical organization promoted by the pastoral agents of the Guatemala Church in Exile. This group was very well prepared. They had a clear purpose and strategy. They knew their rights and how to struggle for these rights. One of their goals, according to Father Luis, was to promote, "from a Christian perspective, the conditions for the return." At the same time, the ACG was also involved with the displaced population among the CPRs inside Guatemala. Just as the Catholic Church had played a crucial role in the 1960s and 1970s in the highlands of Guatemala, it was performing a similar role in the refugee camps in the 1980s. From the first days when the people from Santa María Tzejá arrived in Mexico, the Catholic Church, headed by the extraordinary Bishop Samuel Ruiz, provided material aid and spiritual comfort. The liberal church therefore retained a solid reputation and credibility among the refugees. "The Guatemalan Christian organization in Mexico was an effective instrument in promoting the return to Guatemala," according to Father Luis, but inside Guatemala, "some bishops such as in El Quiché, viewed this organization as too liberal and placed obstacles to its future work in Guatemala." Displaying an extraordinary unity, vision, patience, pragmatism, and negotiating strategy, the refugees in Mexico were determined to see their goals of return become reality.

Living over the Ashes

While a number of families were already in relative safety across the border in Mexico, other villagers remained in Guatemala and emerged from hiding out of a combination of desperation, poor information, and misguided hope. The people hiding together in the northeastern area of the village (known as Sector II) heard on the radio that General Ríos Montt had taken power via a coup on March 23, 1982, and had proclaimed an amnesty, offering them a thin patina of hope. Ríos Montt, whose name was to become synonymous with blood-drenched slaughter and a merciless scorched earth policy, had been the presidential candidate of a political front headed by the Christian Democratic Party (Partido de la Democracia Cristiana, PDC) less than a decade earlier and had won the 1974 election.[8] Shockingly, given what was to come, the leading military commanders viewed Ríos Montt as a reform candidate at the time and therefore prevented him from taking office. Instead, the high command installed a more compliant and dependable General Kjell Laugerud into the presidency in one of many such frauds since the overthrow of President Arbenz in 1954.

Several days after the March 1982 coup, Vladimiro sought to escape with his wife Angelina and son to their highland homes. Vladimiro, originally from Patzún in Chimaltenango, had worked as a nurse in Santa María Tzejá since 1975. He had come originally in response to a request from the cooperative to the Ministry of Health for a health worker or nurse to run the community clinic. When he and his wife made the decision to come out of hiding and return to Patzún, they did so without telling anyone their intentions. They needed to act quickly because Angelina was pregnant and close to giving birth. After hearing on the radio that General Ríos Montt had taken over, he happily declared, "Well fella' [muchá]! The suffering is over. The PDC has gained control and that is what we were hoping for!" Moreover, Vladimiro's father had been a loyal PDC local leader in the highlands. Seizing this tenuous sliver of possibility, Vladimiro and Angelina headed in the direction of Playa Grande hoping to catch a ride out of the region to what they hoped would be safety in the highlands.

They never made it very far. Almost twenty years later, in his native highland town, he was hesitant to be interviewed, quite clearly reserved, confused, and apprehensive. Without the presence of Father Luis he likely would have refused to sit down to a conversation and insisted he did not want his real name used. He had received no news from Santa María Tzejá since he had left in 1982. Vladimiro is remembered as an outstanding nurse, a good neighbor, and the first person to leave those in hiding and involuntarily fall into the military's hands. Soon after he became an army collaborator and nurse.

On their way out of Santa María Tzejá in 1982, Vladimiro and Angelina approached San José la 20, which was deserted and destroyed. "When we passed there, a man who knew us and who was hiding came out," he recalled. "He was frightened. He asked us, 'Where are you going?' 'That way,' I said [out of the Ixcán]. 'Don't go there, because you will surely die,' said the man. 'Well we are going that way and we'll see what happens.'" Vladimiro and Angelina continued towards Playa Grande, the only way to leave the region. He was not worried, because he had heard the military broadcasting news of the amnesty on the radio.

A civil patrol unit captured both Vladimiro and Angelina as they tried to board a truck. They were a step away from escaping the killing fields on the road between San José la 20 and Trinitaria, two destroyed villages. The patrol asked for their documents, which they did not have, and then dragged them, terrified and downcast, to the military base in Playa Grande. "They took us to the army base. They took our things. They tied me. They hit me. At the army base they kept me blindfolded, lying over the sand," Vladimiro remembered. "At three in the morning it was cold. We did not even have a plastic sheet to cover ourselves. But nothing. And the food, God help me! The food was water. I ate peels of watermelon, peels of bananas, peels of pineapples, in order to survive. My wife was kept in another place. She got some food. The soldiers ate meat, to us they would give only half a tortilla."

During the first three days he was completely exposed to the scorching sun. The prisoners had their hands tightly bound, making them feel even more vulnerable. They felt as if they were being burned alive. The beatings were constant. In the following days his fear increased as he saw what was happening to others. "I remember there were sixty-four men from everywhere in the Ixcán. From Xalbal, from Mayalán. They had all been captured by the army. Little by little the group got smaller and smaller. Daily they would take a few, four or five. They were told, 'Sign here. You are free.' " Instead of releasing them, the soldiers would bind their arms and load the traumatized peasants on a vehicle. "They would tie them, put them into a jeep with a can of gasoline, and then take them away." Vladimiro and the other prisoners could well imagine the destination, and he soon found out what took place. "One day the captain showed me a place where they put their heads on a tree trunk, and with one machete stroke they cut them off," he recalled, still wincing at the thought. "Then, they would throw the people in a huge hole, some of them with their heads still hanging (not totally cut off) and then burn them." The captain sharply told him: "This is what will happen to you if you do not put in your batteries [si no te ponés las pilas]; if you don't react quickly." Each day the initial group dwindled, and terrified new prisoners were dragged in to replace them. "You just thought, 'When will my turn be [to be killed]?' " he stated. The purpose of the tortures and intimidation was military intelligence. "The army wanted me to tell them about guerrilla operations. I said to them, 'Sorry, but I know nothing. My mission was to cure people, not to kill people. I know nothing.' "

While he was at the army base he saw people from Santa María Tzejá. "Yes, there they were, but thank God, they came out alive from there, little by little they came out," he said. "Yes, they were tortured, of course, they were very thin, and food? There was no food. Well, perhaps there was food, but the prisoners did not get any. The prisoners were tied, they would put them in water, they would shock them with electric cables." His tortures were not as severe by comparison. "No, I was not shocked. They would only throw me in the water and beat me. I was tied up for about three or four days totally exposed to the sun," he recalled. "I remember one day two officers came and began to kick me. I pretended to be dead so they would stop kicking me. They kicked me. They threw me in the river. I said, 'I am innocent! And I will prove it you. I will show you.' " Vladimiro then began to cooperate with the army and inform on others. Dressed in army uniform and put at the head of a column, he guided the army to the jungle hideouts.

He confirmed that it was not possible to resist the tortures or to avoid implicating others. "Oh no! It was very difficult not to talk [to collaborate]. One had to say something. Accuse others. Some of the names were already there. There were controls in Playa Grande, so when the people passed by and were stopped to be checked, the names were already on the list. So there they would stay. That was because they were already accused by others." And, with countless desperate confessions, the army's list of "subversives" grew longer and longer. "The truth is that any person who falls into the hands of the military provides some names [implicating others]." Those captured by the army were not always sure what information the interrogators already had. The army was not interested in people fingering those who were obviously of no use to the military, and the interrogators further warned the captives, "If you lie or mislead when you accuse, it will be you that we will fuck."

I had heard that his wife, as well as other women captives, had been raped at the base. "Oh yes," he said about women being raped, but he does not know or did not want to acknowledge that his wife was among them. "The soldiers themselves told me that they raped." He insisted his wife had told him she had not been raped. His willingness to cooperate and his reputation as a superb nurse are probably why his life was spared. Several villagers mentioned that they understood his situation and are neither scornful or judgmental about it. He had to do what he had to do "for the love of life," one person remarked.

After being severely beaten and tortured, he told his tormentors he would work with them, but he insisted he told the officers that although peasants were living in hiding near the village, they were innocent of any wrongdoing. "I said to the captain, 'It may be good to go save those people.' 'Is that so?' the captain responded. 'Yes,' I told him. Then the captain said 'Let's smoke a cigarette.' He gave me a cigarette. I smoked. 'Well' he said. 'We will organize a patrol.'" After this exchange, he told the captain, "If you want I can go show you where the guerrilla camps are located." Just before arriving in Santa María, the army column stopped. Vladimiro recalled the scene. "Soldiers were coming from all four cardinal points. From Kaibil, Dolores, and we from San José, others from Santo Tomás Ixcán. It was like a pincer movement. So I said, 'What will you do now? Are you going to massacre?'"

Some villagers say they saw Vladimiro wearing a military uniform and that he had his hands tied behind him when he entered the village with the military. Later on villagers saw him dispensing medicines to soldiers. Vladimiro remembered the agony of searching for both guerrilla and civilian camps. As he led an army column down the serpentine paths through the jungle, sweating profusely in the intense heat and humidity, he felt consumed by anxiety, guilt, and fear. He assumed or at least hoped the camps he knew had moved, and he had no intention of finding new ones, he claimed.

He knew the guerrilla camps very well, given his own involvement with them. He admitted, "I used to go there. About fifteen combatants would come, then they would leave. That was the place where my wife was before the [February 1982] massacre. We had gotten the information that practically the entire Canil family had been killed." As they were walking, Vladimiro pointed out to the military patrol he was guiding, "Here there had been one," but the camp had obviously dispersed. "One used to be here, here it was," he told the captain. "But God is so great. We went very close to camps where there were people [civilians], it's just that I had forgotten about it. And it was from here to there [about 150 meters]." He then recalled what happened the next day. "Yes, there had been people there, and we went to get them, but they had just left. The cooking fire was still going." Had the soldiers discovered the camp with the people in it, he observed, "for sure there would have been a massacre!" Further in the dense undergrowth, another camp was hidden nearby; the soldiers noticed the site, but the inhabitants had just fled. Vladimiro said they could still see them running from a distance wearing olive green. He said that while he was with the army, "There were massacres everywhere, in the whole region of Ixcán. All day long during that period, one could smell the odor of burning human flesh."

Vladimiro reflected on the ideological war the army was waging in the Ixcán. "They tried to change the minds of the people, to change their ideas," he remembered, "but the people were not paying attention." He admitted that indeed most people were as influenced by the guerrillas as he was. "The army did not want those ideas," he said. "They wanted the people to be on the army's side. But since [the people] didn't pay attention, they opted for the massacres." To illustrate the mentality of the army, he mentioned the horrifying incident in Santo Tomás Ixcán that took place soon after the massacre in Santa María Tzejá. The soldiers incinerated ten evangelical families. "People did not want to leave. Their response was, 'No, we are not involved with anyone, neither with the army nor with the guerrillas.'" Their faith in the army would have tragic consequences. "All ten families were burned alive," acknowledged

Vladimiro, "The army said, 'Ah, Evangelicals, you are all liars. We know that you are involved.' "

Vladimiro wondered what his future would be. He hoped at some point the soldiers would let him and his wife and son leave since he had cooperated. "I wanted to leave, but the military would not let me. Only once they let me leave, but alone." The army held his wife hostage and only allowed her to leave after he returned twelve days later." Reflecting on the brutality of 1982, Vladimiro drew a distinction between the insurgents and the soldiers, paying the guerrillas a backhanded compliment. "If the guerrillas had a problem with a person, because of some error, they would tell that to their face," he said. "Not the army. The army tortured and even killed, without investigating." He brought up the case of Andrés Ixcoy. "The guerrillas told him not to do that [to pass information on to the army]. Don't get involved in that. Seven times they told him, but he did not pay attention. The army does not try to find out if a person is guilty or not. The army was more violent. The guerrillas checked things out and were more calm." Vladimiro felt that the guerrillas had a just cause. "Ah, it was just, but the military are managed by the rich and they have other ideas," he said. "They have always wanted to have the people under their thumbs. So long as the people remain poor, they will always have more control. The guerrillas did not achieve what they wanted. That is it. They wanted to improve the standard of living for everyone. That is difficult. How do you achieve that?" At the end of the conversation he paused, looking physically drained, and then broke down in tears, as did his wife. He pointed to his seventeen-year-old daughter, who was born in the military zone of Playa Grande—a very difficult birth a month after he and his wife were captured. Her name is Milagro Esperanza (Miracle Hope). "I saw [her birth] as a miracle . . . and as hope. This is hard. That is why I gave her that name," he said. "But," he took some time, "it's all behind us now." He stopped crying and continued more positively. He felt good that a nurse from Comalapa congratulated him saying, "You will always be remembered [as a good nurse]!" She told him, he proudly recalled, "Your name is not dead. It has history." His wife, Angelina, still crying, signaled she had nothing to add. The experiences of Vladimiro at the army base were similar to those of others from Santa María Tzejá who also became guides for the army. Routinely soldiers conducted brutal interrogations to squeeze information out of even the most reluctant captives. Despite his protests to the contrary, Vladimiro most likely provided significant information about the village to the military, although under great duress.

The Ríos Montt coup and proposed amnesty, which prompted Vladimiro and Angelina to return to Patzún, had sparked a discussion among many of the families hiding in the rain forest about whether they might be able to return to Santa María Tzejá and begin rebuilding their lives. "Our idea was not to give ourselves up to the army [*entregarnos*], or to surrender [*rendirnos*]," a villager emphasized many years after the calamity, "but to go back to live in our village and have a normal life without being bothered by one or the other." At the end of April 1982, a little over two months after the massacre, a group of men went to see if either the army or the guerrillas were occupying the village. Since neither was there, several men proceeded to collect anything that might be salvageable, particularly zinc roofing materials, to rebuild their homes in the lots near the center of the village. While they were in the village two helicopters unexpectedly flew overhead. Since just weeks before helicopters were strafing and bombing them, they immediately pulled out white handkerchiefs to show they were civilians and peaceful. The helicopters ominously circled over them several times. At first, they descended fast and menacingly, hovering above the ground for a closer look, and then finally flew off in the direction of the army base at Playa Grande. The villagers returned to the land parcels where their families remained in hiding and excitedly told everyone the army had come and done nothing. They then made a decision to return to Santa María Tzejá. Almost all the families hiding together in Sector II chose to come out of hiding on May 3, 1982, the day of the Catholic feast of the village and the date in 1970 when the first families settled. The villagers viewed returning on this date as a symbolic act, a good omen when they were desperately in need of good omens. They thought the war might be over for them and that both sides, the army and the insurgents, would leave them alone. Three families from Sector II were not convinced and chose not to go along; two families hiding in the western area (Sector III) joined the group. A total of thirty-one families walked out of the rain forest that day and headed to the center of the village to set up their homes in an open area, demonstrating they had nothing to hide. Unlike the way in which they had lived on their previous individual lots, they crammed about four to five families per lot. They built their houses with whatever they could find: zinc roofing material, nylon tarps, palm branches, and sticks.

The respite was short lived. Three days later, on May 6, a column of about three hundred heavily armed soldiers hiked down the path. A lieutenant ordered all the villagers to assemble in the center and then brusquely asked, "What happened here? Why were you hiding?" Nicolás

Vásquez claimed that he answered, "You know what happened. The army came to kill us and to burn our houses." This answer seems far too sharp and accusatory given the circumstances, and he likely responded in a more circumspect and respectful way. The lieutenant, according to those who were present that day, answered that the villagers were mistaken. "It was not the army that did this," he shot back. "It was the guerrillas who came to kill you and burn your houses." The witnesses recall that even though they knew indisputably that it was the army who destroyed the village, "We said nothing because we were afraid." The lieutenant then added, "In any case, all of that is behind us. There is no longer war. The government gave an amnesty. Now there will be a new order." He ordered all the villagers to move their houses even more tightly together into one location cleared of trees and slightly elevated. The villagers rebuilt their temporary huts in this area, and about fifty officers and soldiers pitched their tents immediately next to them. The balance of the troops set up camp in an outlying section.

After the coup that brought Ríos Montt to power, tactics shifted, at least in this area of eastern Ixcán. In early 1982 soldiers sought to annihilate everything they encountered. They were not particularly concerned with occupying an area. After Ríos Montt, the army sought to "search and capture" the population and maintain control over an area. Using captured villagers or collaborators as guides who knew the hideouts, the army would surround a group and capture them. If anyone ran, the soldiers would fire at them. Troops located many families from Santa María Tzejá on these search-and-capture operations and took them to the military base. On several occasions in the chaos of the capture, families became separated, some for as long as twelve years.

One of these cases occurred when the army, guided by villagers from Santa María Tzejá, surrounded a group. When the families realized what was happening and began to flee, the military started shooting. Emilio Tojín and his little daughter María Elena ran and survived; his wife, Tomasa Pérez, and the smaller children were captured. Emilio went into exile to Mexico; Tomasa was taken to the military base, where she was subjected to the same appalling treatment as other women prisoners. She had collaborated with the EGP, and her name was on a list in the army's possession. It was not until several years later that each heard the other had survived the attack. I carried tape recordings and photographs back and forth. After the return the couple got together again, but with considerable strains.[9]

Figure 6. Magdalena Tum, in the Maya Tecún refugee camp in Campeche, Mexico, in 1988, shows the scar from an army-fired bullet that hit her arm. She thanks God it did not hit her heart. Photo by Beatriz Manz.

Units concentrated on "emptying" a region of its population, destroying all food sources and infrastructure, and then resettling the people under tight military dominance. The tactics are reminiscent of the Spaniards' arrival in Hispaniola centuries ago. C. L. R. James charges that Europeans introduced "artificial famine" by destroying the cultivated fields to subjugate the population and "starve the rebellious."[10]

As part of its consolidation of new areas, the army began in mid-1982 the "beans and bullets" project, providing "protection" and food for those under its watch, with aid from the United States. The military initiated food-for-work projects throughout the countryside, using food as the bait to induct starving and homeless peasants into building infrastructure and to further regiment their lives through new military institutions. These tactics were aimed at crippling support for the insurgents. In this new phase, the military strategists waged an ideological war on the captives as well as seeking to control them physically.

Figure 7. Tomasa Pérez holds photos of her daughter María Elena and husband, Emilio Tojín, in Santa María Tzejá in 1988. She had last seen them in 1982 as they ran away, barely escaping the bullets fired by the military. The family had been discovered while hiding in the forest. Photo by Beatriz Manz.

Figure 8. Emilio Tojín and his daughter María Elena listen to a tape-recorded message from Tomasa in the Maya Tecún refugee camp in 1989. They spent twelve years in refugee camps in Mexico. Photo by Beatriz Manz.

The day after the army took control of some of the villages, in May 1982, Chema Cux and Juan García were coming out of hiding. Soldiers captured them on their way toward the village and brought them to the area where the other thirty-one families were camped together. Around that time two others, Diego Larios and Juan de la Cruz, sought to check from a safe distance what was going on with the families who had come out of hiding. Troops detected their presence and seized them. Unlike the other two, who were found in the open, these two had been caught hiding and were therefore far more suspicious. They were not put with the other families but rather forced into a temascal—a Mayan traditional sauna constructed of stones and clay in the form of an igloo. The hot temascal was suffocating, and after a few sweltering and anxious days, the two planned their escape. When soldiers noticed them running at night they fired at them, killing Diego Larios on the spot; Juan de la Cruz managed to escape.

The families who had returned to the village then confronted a dark moment. An officer ordered everyone to assemble in the center of the village where a helicopter waited. Under an intense sun, people stood very still and quiet as a soldier began to yell out names. As a name was called, the person stepped forward. All the men and women who were called were young, and it quickly became clear to the villagers standing on that forlorn field that the army had a list of those involved in guerrilla activity. No explanations were given, and the horrified families did not dare ask anything for fear that they too would be taken. Ten people were shoved into the waiting helicopter, and a second was loaded soon after. Nineteen people were grabbed in total.[11] The helicopters flew ashen-faced prisoners to the military base at Playa Grande.

After the cowed villagers arrived at the base, soldiers dragged them off the helicopters, separating men and women. Troops tied up the prisoners, beat them with fists and slammed them with rifle butts, provided practically nothing to eat or drink, and began brutal, systematic torture. As a preview of what would lie in store for the newly arrived villagers, people from other places huddled on the floor silently or softly moaning. Some were bleeding; others looked vacantly into space. Blood-stained ropes that had bound previous victims were scattered on the floor. "People were there from San Lucas, Santiago Ixcán, Kaibil, Paraíso, La Pita, even from Salacuín," a villager stated. "Some of these people would be at the base two or three days, then they would disappear. We thought they took them to kill them." Sometimes prisoners from Santa María Tzejá were packed in a room with a roof and walls made of tin. "It felt

like an oven," one person recalled. "It was unbearable, it made us faint."
The suffocating heat, the stench of the festering wounds and sweating
bodies, and the gnawing hunger weakened and demoralized them. Soldiers took them one by one to be interrogated about guerrilla activity,
particularly the names of collaborators. Those who provided the least
information were the most severely tortured. Officers and conscripts subjected Mayan people to particularly venomous assault, both physically
and verbally. Near death, prisoners would be dragged out into the yard
and kept under the blinding sun without water and in near starvation.
The soldiers created a grotesque chamber of horrors in which many of
the tortures were self-inflicted. Thirst-crazed peasants under the unrelenting sun in the yard would drink their own urine. Soldiers would tie
a penis to a bent leg so that as a peasant stretched he would submit himself to excruciating pain. Victims could hear the screams of men and
women in shacks next door as well as see mutilated corpses dumped onto
the back of trucks to be discarded near the Chixoy River. Conscripts took
villagers from Santa María Tzejá to the river and tortured them under
water. Women were kept in separate rooms where they were repeatedly
raped and tormented. One soldier after another would swagger into the
places where the women were kept, and then other soldiers would take
their turn. This horror and humiliation would go on for hours. Troops
held two women from Santa María Tzejá in separate rooms and especially abused them for long periods. Indigenous women are very reluctant to talk about these gruesome experiences and certainly not in detail. When asked directly, the women from the village responded in
general terms, providing few specifics about the rapes, preferring not to
revisit their abuse but making clear their tremendous resentment and hatred against the army.

These nineteen who were seized provided the military with considerable information. "Surely once that group was taken by the military,"
one villager stated, "they told everything to the army, such as the structure of the guerrillas in the village." That explains, he continued, "why
someone like Xan, who was a leader of the guerrillas in the village at the
time, would have been so severely tortured, while Nicolás, who was not
involved at that level [got a lighter treatment at the base]." Another villager provided a similar interpretation: "Nicolás was also involved, but
as soon as he cooperated and denounced others and gave information
about what he knew, then the military gave him a recompense. As they
say, 'It is like selling your people,' then you begin to be one of them and
you are respected [by the army]." Miguel Reyes was convinced that those

"courageous ones" who did not cooperate with the army were the ones most cruelly treated. He added that some, even if they knew a lot, refused to say much and pretended not to know, often at great cost.

Vladimiro was one case of many from Santa María Tzejá who collaborated with the army after February 1982. Nicolás, according to some, also became a military informer. A former member of the guerrillas, he had received weapons training in one of the most important guerrilla camps, located in Mexico's Lacandón jungle and known as Nicaragua Libre (NL). While Nicolás was in the hands of the military in mid-1982, he is believed to have provided significant information early on. Allegedly, using Nicolás as a guide, the Guatemalan military asked their Mexican counterparts for permission to search for this significant guerrilla camp on Mexican territory. "It was not convenient for the Mexican military to declare there were Guatemalan guerrilla training in its territory," Bartolo Reyes, a leader in the Mexican camps, recalled with a laugh. "So the Mexicans told the Guatemalan military, 'You have from this time to that time,' I think it was something like from eight in the morning to noon [to find the camp]. After that time they had to leave Mexican territory, even if they had not found anything." Bartolo said that a Mexican civilian who owns a river launch was involved in the operation. This Mexican individual was obviously sympathetic to the Guatemalan insurgents, or at least hostile to the military, because of their reputation. He revealed to Bartolo what had happened. "The *lanchero* [a river motor-launch driver] moved very slowly [down the river]. The motor was at a low speed in order not to advance much. When they got more or less to the *pica* [a light path formed by walking through the forest] where they would have had to go in, and Nicolás would have had to guide them, the driver suddenly accelerated the motor. His intention was for Nicolás to get lost and therefore to be unable to recognize the spot." The speed of the boat caused the desired confusion. "The Guatemalan officer said, 'Where? Where is it?'" Bartolo related. "And Nicolás quite confused and squinting his eyes this way and that way would say, 'Around here.' The Guatemalan officer would keep on asking, 'Around here, where?' He became impatient. 'Where? Where is it?' The Mexican who was traveling with the group soon lost patience. 'Alright, that's it, time is up. Let's return,'" Bartolo remembers him saying. "And they were not able to find the place. Nicolás looked like a fool," Bartolo said roaring with laughter.[12] Had the army succeeded in finding this critical camp it would have been a major development in their counterinsurgency war and an incident that would have involved Mexico.

While the nineteen men and women were at the army base, the rest of the villagers at the site of the destroyed village were wondering what their fate would be. The soldiers established tight control that no one dared challenge. During the daytime, if villagers asked permission, they were generally able to bathe in the river, fetch water, or go to the center of the village to retrieve things. When villagers asked permission to go to the parcels to gather food, army recruits would always accompany them. "While they said it was for our protection," one villager commented, "it was to keep an eye on us." Though it was the time for planting, they were not allowed to plant or even prepare the land for cultivation. When they were talking among each other, officers or soldiers would stand nearby to monitor the conversation. Cooking had to be done all in one place. At night the control was absolute, and no one could move.

One day, three brave families decided to risk escape in the daytime despite the fact that Diego Larios had already been shot dead for the same offense. They believed staying might prove the more dangerous option, especially since many of their friends had been taken to the military base. After carefully observing the rounds of the sentries, they requested permission to collect water and roofing material, leaving all their belongings behind so as not to arouse suspicion. When the families were at a safe distance, they disappeared into the rain forest, finding their way to a camp where others were still hiding.

The escape infuriated the commanders. Immediately after, on May 20, they ordered all the remaining villagers to walk to Playa Grande under military guard. This long, sad march included civilians from other places who had been caught by the military. Once the villagers arrived, they were kept in *galeras*—large open communal structures—near the Chixoy River. These villagers still had no idea what had happened to those who had been taken by helicopters to the base. They were often called to meetings where soldiers would constantly ask about the whereabouts of those who had remained in the jungle. The officers would question, "Where are they? Why did they hide? You know where their camps are located. Tell us where they are so we can go get them and tell them there is no longer a war." The officers made it clear that their own return to normality was tied to their providing information. Their information would enable the military to control the area, allowing villagers in turn to resume their normal life. But the villagers would always say that they didn't know where they were, one villager proudly recalled. "At least we never gave information when we were in the meetings all together. Who knows if someone gave information to the army when they were alone!"

The military routinely told people in captivity that their relatives were dead, often using specific, grim detail. Gaspar, who successfully fled to Mexico after a year in hiding, told how he had been reported dead to his relatives living under military control. "They told my sister that we were in a meeting with the leadership of the guerrillas near the Cantil hill, the soldiers surrounded us all and killed absolutely everyone," Gaspar said. "A lot of people lost hope to see their relatives alive again," he added. In addition to demoralizing people, the military employed the same psychological tactics to convince villagers to "go to the side of the army and forget about everyone else." Once again the lesson was that support for the guerrillas brought death as a consequence.

Aided by information extracted through torture, the soldiers returned to the village accompanied by guides to capture those who remained in hiding. Alejandro Ortiz recalled, "On June 24—I remember the date well because it is Saint John the Baptist day—the army captured us, five adults and fourteen children." His young son ran as the army surrounded them, so the soldiers started firing wildly—at one point he jumped over the body of a woman hit by bullets. Alejandro did not know what happened to his son, although the probability was high that he had been cut down by bullets. Likewise, the son assumed his entire family had been massacred.[13] The families from Santa María Tzejá were kept in Playa Grande almost a month and were then released, at least in part as a result of a visit by journalists from Guatemala City.[14] Initially, they were taken to Carolina and left there with nothing. A month later, in mid-July, they were relocated to Ingenieros (both near the Mexican border), where they were given some land, although it was well past the time for cultivation. A few families, about a dozen in all, were given land nearer the road in a place called San Francisco. Many speculate that this better location— near what was later going to become Cantabal, the municipal capital— was given to those who collaborated with the army and provided useful information. While in detention in Playa Grande the collaborators supposedly also received better treatment, better food, and even money. "The land they received in San Francisco was like an award for their collaboration with the military," charged one villager.

In late 1982 and early 1983, the army organized large bands of peasants recruited from throughout the region to search and destroy corn fields and all edible foodstuffs, laying waste to a pivotal resource for the insurgents and those peasants still in hiding. In addition to wiping out the fields, they destroyed the *buzones* (drop boxes) and *trojes,* hiding places containing food, documents, and personal belongings. The military took

a few villagers as guides and then organized marauding peasant bands totaling more than three hundred peasants from different communities to
lay waste to the fields and storage areas. Few who participated in this action want to talk about it, most pretend not to understand the questions
or deny their involvement. Deep shame exists about what took place, and
even those who avoided participation do not like to name those who did.
For peasants, the razing of cornfields and the desecration of land had special significance: It destroyed a sacred plant and strangled the source of
life. The results were devastating for those enduring a harsh life in the
jungle, never far from discovery and always struggling to survive. These
villagers had managed to plant corn and beans that would provide them
with sustenance for the months ahead. Now, their future was annihilated
by peasants like themselves, often by relatives and neighbors. The mili-
tary-led actions against the food supply of those in hiding, however, were
meant to reward as well as to punish. Hundreds of heads of cattle were
taken to those villages whose civil patrols had provided help in the campaign. The future mayor of Cantabal, Jerónimo Villeda Lemus, allegedly
received many heads of cattle, later becoming the richest rancher in the
Ixcán. A few villagers, such as Chema Cux, reportedly gained from these
roundups, becoming the wealthiest peasant in Santa María Tzejá. Last
but not least, cattle were taken to the military base.

Ak'el was one of the villagers who had participated in the destruction
of the cornfields. He had been involved with the guerrillas and was one
of the nineteen taken by helicopter to the army base. Soon after, he became a guide to locate families in hiding and for the destruction of the
milpas. Later he enlisted in the army. Ak'el and his father were unfriendly
and uncooperative in the village. One of Ak'el's sisters became a young
combatant with the insurgents and broke with her family. He was often
criticized by the villagers in the refugee camps as mean-spirited and a
traitor. During my visits in the 1980s and early 1990s, while the village
was still militarized, Ak'el made a point of staying away from me. I had
been warned to be careful about him because he informed the military,
allegedly, even about the questions I asked. In 1999, however, I decided
to send a message that I wanted to interview him, his father, and one of
his sisters, whom I had been told was one of the young women most
abused at the army base. Ak'el, a K'iche' Maya in his mid-thirties, with
sharp features, short black straight hair, jet-black eyes and dark skin,
showed up at the assigned time and place. He was wearing a tight white
T-shirt featuring the Ixcán military zone. The whiteness of the shirt made
his arms look darker. His shirt and rolled-up short sleeves displayed his

muscular arms, chest, and abdomen. His wide belt buckle consisted of five bullets—a recently favored design in the region.

I explained that I wanted to hear from him about what had happened at the military base and in the months that followed the massacre in 1982. He said when the helicopters landed at the military base, an officer explained why they had been selected. The army already knew about his involvement with the insurgents, and the officer made it clear that they wanted information about others. "So we said to them, 'OK, that's fine,'" he matter-of-factly stated. "We saw that what they wanted was information about how the guerrilla operated; the network of communication the guerrilla had, and a whole bunch of information. Who collaborated; who are the messengers, that is what the captain wanted to know. How many were involved in the village."

Ak'el told me that he had provided no information and had not implicated anyone. This response, not surprisingly, is what everyone has said who was taken to the army base. He admitted that when the military asked something they obviously already knew, such as his own involvement, he would respond, "Yes, I said, I collaborated, I never denied that. 'OK,' the captain said, 'in what did you collaborate?' I would say, 'They asked for tortillas, salt, sugar, pineapples, oranges, bananas, all kinds of food.' Then the captain asked, 'And why didn't you come to the military to inform us?' I told him, 'because the guerrillas said to us, and that was true, that they would kill us.'"

Those who cooperated with the military, Ak'el admitted, received better treatment and the hope of returning to their village. They were given food, they were told that there was a hospital and medicines, they were taken to bathe. He stated that he and his father were kept at the military base for two weeks and that "since we gave all the information that they wanted, they sent us to Carolina and told us they would give us a parcel in Ingenieros [sites north of the military zone near the Mexican border]." He then elaborated, "The army said, 'We are going to Tzejá to corner the guerrillas and push them to Mexico. We are going to kick the shit out of them, and then if it is calm in Tzejá we will let you return there.' They promised us that. So at one point they came from S5 [civil affairs of the military] and asked us, 'How many of you want to return to Santa María Tzejá,' and they made a list."

Ak'el continued, "We went out on reconnaissance operations, the army ordered us." Then I asked rather unexpectedly, "And you went to cut the *milpa*?" He coughed and was visibly uncomfortable and surprised by the directness of my question. I waited for his answer. "So it is," he said finally. "How did the military know where the *milpa* cultivation was?" I asked. "That *milpa* was of the guerrilla," he responded, correcting himself by adding, "well, not of the guerrilla exactly, but of those who remained in hiding, those who decided not to come out, and they all planted corn. Then the order came from the military [to cut it] and after that they left for Mexico." He said that they destroyed all sources of food, not just the corn.

While clearly reluctant and uncomfortable at points, Ak'el was willing to continue with the interview, unlike his father, who I spoke with later that same day, who became upset and agitated at the questioning about his participation in the destruction of the *milpas* and then pretended not to understand. The interview with the father, an old and ill man who had difficulty speaking Spanish, went along more or less until it touched on the question of the *milpas*. First he claimed not to understand my questions, and as I persisted he became visibly upset, angrily demanding, "Why are you asking all these questions? For what end?" as if haunted by a mixture of anxiety, guilt, and anger at me for aggravating a long-festering wound.

In December 1982 some families—those who felt most secure in doing so—lobbied the army to allow them to travel to Santa María Tzejá to harvest the cardamom, their most valuable cash crop. They knew the cardamom was ripe and expected a plentiful harvest. Moreover, the price was high because of the displacement and upheaval in the region, a potential cash bonus seeping out of their misery. The military allowed twenty men and two women (to cook) to go, accompanied by soldiers, and several weeks later gave permission for a second group to make the journey. By early February 1983 the majority of the thirty-one families had returned to the village with the goal of being allowed to stay. A tragic incident a month later, however, caused most to reconsider, and only twelve families chose to remain. Several adults and children had gone from the village to Playa Grande to sell their cardamom. On their way back, a guerrilla unit unexpectedly stopped them on the path and began asking questions. The guerrillas may have suspected that the villagers were looking for *buzones*. At one point twelve-year-old Pedro Juárez, son of Pedro Juárez Hernantó, bolted from the group and did not stop running when the guerrillas yelled at him to halt. They fired as the villagers looked on in horror, and a bullet ripped through the young boy, leaving his limp body by the side of the path. Making matters worse, the only other son of the distraught father had joined the guerrillas as a young man and had been killed by the army in Alta Verapaz. The grieving father has harbored deep resentment against the guerrillas ever since the younger son was shot, charging he was killed deliberately.[15] Others think the guerrillas may have tried to scare the boy, but the bullet mistakenly hit him. No one excuses the action. In fact, villagers are unanimous in criticizing the irresponsibility of the guerrillas.

Circumstantial evidence exists that the guerrillas may not have meant to kill the boy. In another instance the insurgents encountered Manuel Saquic, a widely disliked early army collaborator and alleged cattle thief. Given his reputation, the guerrillas treated him harshly, making him kneel down. "Now what do you have to say?" asked the guerillas, according to a villager. "They taunted him, they laughed at him, and humiliated him. But they let him go and did not harm him." Manuel would have been a far more likely candidate for execution, the argument goes, than the young boy who died. Alternatively, the possibility exists that different guerrilla units were involved, with some being more ruthless than others.

In an effort to gain allegiance and cooperation, the army began employing crude psychological tactics (later these "psychological operations" would become more sophisticated and effective). They told the villagers that the guerrillas were obviously trying to extract revenge on them for having deserted the insurgency. Despite the fact the guerrillas were practically gone from the area, an officer insisted he had found an identification card belonging to a guerrilla, who the army claimed had come very close to firing at the group. Looking down at the identification card, he asked if anyone knew a person by that name. The name allegedly was that of a well-known combatant with the EGP from Santa María Tzejá. Not content to limit the evidence to a single identification card, the officer also produced a notebook, deliberately left behind by the guerrillas, he said, containing names of those who had collaborated with the insurgents. The clear message was that the guerrillas were trying to implicate their friends and relatives or former allies. Some villagers immediately rejected the story as a dangerous, nonsensical ruse; others, however, became demoralized. If their former neighbors in the guerrillas were now after them, they might as well put their fate completely in the hands of the military. Some may also simply have wanted to believe the identification card and notebook stories to make their own collaboration more justified.

One of those who took the army's story to heart was Nicolás. The army claimed that insurgents fired shots when Diego Larios and Juan de la Cruz fled. "When the army went to see from where the shots had been fired they found a notebook in a napkin," Nicolás recounts. "In that notebook were all the names of the people from here, from San José la 20, and from Santa María Dolores." What was the meaning of this discovery? "The way we interpret that was that the [guerrillas] did that so that all of us would be killed," Nicolás added. "It was their way of letting the army know that all the people were involved with the guerrillas.... It was not that it fell as they were fleeing, but that intentionally they left it behind." Others, such as Miguel Reyes, challenge this account. "There are many explanations about that notebook," he maintains. "It could have been nurse Vladimiro's notes for medicine control. It is likely that the army took that notebook from the medicine box hidden in Don Pablo Herrera's parcel, when they caught people there. There was a huge shootout there." It is also possible that the notebook belonged to the army and contained the names of villagers involved in the insurgency collected from torture victims. Emiliano also objected to the army's version of the meaning of the identification card. "I noticed that the guerrillas never had IDs or documents on them," he said. "They had other kinds of credentials in their backpacks, but not the official identification, in case they would fall in combat." Emiliano added, somewhat mockingly, "It would be more likely that the guerrillas would leave behind their weapons than their backpacks! This is all part of the army's strategy to confuse the population." Whatever the explanation, it is clear that the villagers now in military hands were haunted with fear, depleting all of their psychological reserve.

A year after the destruction of the village, the battered survivors who remained in Guatemala would soon see a new, divided village emerge—what the army would call a "model" village.

chapter 5

A Militarized Village

On the charred remains of the villages it had incinerated, the army began to resettle the Ixcán. It sought to impose a military model on the very structure of village life—what the generals began to call "the new Guatemala."[1] Beginning in 1983, "Army strategy toward the displaced population was designed to bring it under military control," according to the CEH (U.N.) report; "amnesties were offered and those who accepted were resettled in highly militarized communities."[2] In Santa María Tzejá this new approach combined three elements that were more or less introduced simultaneously: the army brought large numbers of new settlers into socially atomized villages; established strict military controls and new paramilitary organizations, such as the civilian self-defense patrols (patrullas de autodefensa civil, or PACs); and set in motion "psychological operations" to win the allegiance of the peasantry in the conflict.

As part of this new strategy, the army decided to recruit new settlers to Santa María Tzejá in 1983. These settlers would create a base of loyal supporters who owed their land to the army and, at the same time, weaken the social cohesion of the village, thereby undermining the possibility of unified, independent action. Radio programs began running in targeted areas of the country, such as the Verapaces and Huehuetenango, trumpeting the fact that land was available in the Ixcán. In response, hundreds of desperate peasants, predominantly Evangelicals and their pastors, descended on the rain forest in flocks.

The army also had peasant collaborators in this resettlement process, including some of the original settlers. Chema Cux, who had become an army ally soon after he was in military hands, was named patrol chief. He offered to recruit new people to move to a militarized Santa María

Tzejá to meet the army's condition of filling up the village for him or any other of the original settlers to return. He and a few other K'iche' managed the resettlement for the army. Chema, as the new authority, offered people employment on his land and, knowing the military was encouraging the occupation of vacant plots, told them land was available. In the process, he amassed cattle—allegedly becoming a cattle thief—and cash, in contrast to most other villagers who barely had enough to eat.[3]

The new village would once again consist of about one hundred families. All the new arrivals—now about 60 percent of the village—became known as *nuevos* (new ones). Although some came from Huehuetenango, Baja Verapaz, and other places, most came from the area around Cobán in Alta Verapaz.[4] These *Cobaneros*—about thirty families in all—were Evangelical Christians and spoke Pocomchi' and Q'eqchi'. The "new" village was now divided by seven ethnolinguistic groups and five different religious denominations. In addition to the Pocomchi' and the Q'eqchi', other ethnolinguistic groups included K'iche', Chuj, Mam, Q'anjob'al, and Ladino/Spanish-speakers. The original settlers now composed only about 40 percent of the village and referred to themselves as *antiguos* (the old ones, or original settlers).

The military gave a pass to all the *nuevos* to enter Santa María Tzejá because, as one of the villagers stated, they wanted to give away "the land parcels of the people who had left for Mexico, were still resisting in the jungle, or were combatants."[5] Soldiers told the *nuevos* that the parcels were "vacant" and that the National Institute for Agrarian Transformation, or Instituto de Transformación Agraria (INTA), would give them land titles. This strategy not surprisingly fostered considerable conflict. "Community conflicts over land tenancy," as stated by the report from the Recovery of Historical Memory Project, or Recuperación de la Memoria Histórica (REMHI), "while part of the history of rural communities, are currently strongly influenced by the effects of displacement and militarization and by the repopulation policies implemented by the army as part of its counterinsurgency strategy."[6]

When I first visited the restructured village in 1985, I was stunned to see a depressing combination of extreme poverty and social atomization. All the houses were jammed cheek to jowl, nearly touching in every direction, yet the families were wary and socially distant. The reconstructed village was now organized in a far different way; it was a tightly controlled, militarized area. This "model village" was patterned after the "strategic hamlets" of the Vietnam War. Rather than being able to live in their lots, the people of Santa María Tzejá had to construct houses in

Figure 9. The militarized village of Santa María Tzejá in the 1980s. After destroying the village, the army demanded that all the houses be rebuilt in a small area in the center of the village, rather than on the original house lots. Photo by Beatriz Manz.

the center of the village where no dwellings had been located before, except the house of Father Luis. This new settlement pattern was a hardship—people were distant from their farming land and packed together—but the army would tolerate no alternatives. Even to inquire about returning to their original lots brought individuals under suspicion. Sabas, a combatant at the time, described the mood during this period. "Today life is difficult," he observed. "There is no freedom to live where they want or work when they want in the parcels." The army kept a close watch as well as a tight rein on the population. In addition to the civil patrols, in which conflicting loyalties still simmered beneath a veneer of obedience, the army had military commissioners who informed and spied on fellow villagers.

Many villagers believe that Ak'el, who had joined the army, was a paid informer. "Every week he goes to the military base to inform about what is going on in the village," one villager insisted. "He is an effective collaborator of the military." For a while the army deployed a detachment in the center of the village to keep an eye on things and to remind everyone, as if they needed reminding, who was in control. When the military commanders felt confident enough to withdraw the troops, the unit would still return unexpectedly, thus villagers could never be sure as to when the soldiers might show up.

The CEH (U.N.) report details the widening net of army control at the village level throughout Guatemala. "The most important mechanisms for ensuring control of the resettlements were: the organization of people in the PAC, the military appointment of the mayors and auxiliary mayors, the creation of the Interinstitutional Co-ordinators to ensure military control of state and social institutions at all jurisdictional levels, the expansion of the army's civil affairs (S5) activities that included psychological operations to 're-educate' the people, and the construction of model villages in the most conflictive regions."[7] The REMHI report estimates that nearly half a million Mayas wound up in "[militarized] rural communities based on an exorbitant level of social control."[8]

The high command sought to build allegiance from peasants to cement its military control utilizing the psychological operations of its civil affairs (S5) units. "The army captured people to get information," Domingo Ralios, a young man who had been held captive at the army base explained. "They would torture people, but they also wanted to change the ideas people had. They would say our minds were infected with the sickness of communism."[9] In this effort at garnering control and loyalty throughout the country, the army would either send displaced people back to the site of the original village, if military control could be assured (such as the case of Santa María Tzejá), or would relocate them to "model villages" in new localities where the military presence was even more intense. The more typical model villages, such as those in the Ixil area, were located far from the original communities. Army planners laid them out in grid form, set up with strict controls and sought to monitor villagers' every move, including entering and exiting the village. With grim-looking watchtowers overlooking a barren landscape covered by tightly packed dwellings, these settlements appeared more like run-down prison camps than villages. In the ones I visited in 1983, loudspeakers summoned people for reeducation classes or called them to work on military projects such as building an airstrip, constructing a road, or working on an army base.[10]

In Santa María Tzejá, the military spoke of a new army, a new village, and a new relationship between the two. "They would tell us this was a new army that wanted what was best for the people," Alejandro Ortiz recalled. "But we knew that they continued killing, massacring, and persecuting those who did not want to surrender to them." The new rhetoric was undermined by the vivid, consuming memories of the massacre, the destruction of the village, and all the cruelty that had been inflicted by the soldiers. The purpose of the terror, the CEH (U.N.) report maintains, "was to intimidate and silence society as a whole, in order to destroy the will for transformation, both in the short and long term."[11]

Villagers received military training; they had to raise and salute the flag every morning, learn military hymns, and master disciplined military formations and slogans. At the army base, or when soldiers came to the village, the residents had to listen to speeches as part of what the military called "psychological operations." The military sought to construct a new past, one that portrayed the army as the savior from the monstrous guerrillas rather than as the perpetrator of the destruction. "They would tell us we had to participate in the patrols, we had to defend our lands, defend our houses, defend our family, so that what happened in 1982 will not happen again," Ricardo remembered. "They said, 'the guerrillas destroyed your houses, burned your cultivated fields, came to kidnap many people, took them out at night and killed them.' Those talks did not have an effect on me. I was very clear as to what had happened. But I had to listen." The commanders made it explicit that the patrols were needed to "help the Guatemalan military to look after the peace and security of the citizens in general, considering that the territory is too large for the military and civilian authorities alone to be able to provide security."[12] In Ricardo's case it was particularly ironic for him to hear that he needed to defend his land and his crops, since his family had returned to the village only to discover that the army had given their land to a new settler.[13] Nonetheless, "If you did not do as the army said, you would be considered a collaborator of the guerrillas," Ricardo recalled.

The army's psychological operations could be sophisticated. They brought up issues that at times resonated with a captive, distressed population. They would say, for example, "Were you not living here peacefully until the guerrillas came to stir things up? And what happened to their promises? Did they protect you or did they run and abandon you?" Many claim they had to listen but did not necessarily believe, or certainly did not believe, everything. Some say they were aware the army was manipulating them. Nevertheless, the military's ideological offensive did have an impact. Suspicion eroded trust, atomization supplanted cooperation, and military discipline choked openness. What was left was guilt, resentment, apathy, indifference, silence, complicity, feelings of abandonment, anxiety, and fear. Even if someone understood the military's psychological efforts, they nonetheless felt a sense of shame at having become accomplices—although at times unwillingly—in the tactics they carried out at the direction of the army.

At the same time, the relationship between the *antiguos* and the *nuevos* was rocky and tense, exacerbated by deep cultural, religious, and language differences. The five different religious affiliations and seven languages coexisted uneasily in this small village. The *antiguos,* who were K'iche', looked down at the Pocomchi' and Q'eqchi' and found them backwards, gullible, and far too ready to side with the military who had given them land. In retrospect, these divisions proved to be a blessing in disguise for the *antiguos*—in fact for all the original settlers. In the long run, their resentment, even contempt, for the newcomers, left open the possibility of reunification with their former neighbors who had fled to Mexico.

Deepening the divide between the *antiguos* and the *nuevos* was the profound difference in their frame of reference: the *antiguos* measured the present against a dream they had achieved and seen incinerated; the *nuevos* compared their situation to their landless desperation of yesterday. While the *antiguos* might be subject to military control, they were realistic, rather than enthusiastic, about this new arrangement. They recognized, at the point of a gun, the overwhelming power of the army, but they bitterly complained among themselves about much of what was taking place: the civil patrols, the restrictive demands and controls, the raising and lowering of the flag, the military salutes and standing at attention, and so on. They were far more cynical than the *nuevos* about the patriotic appeals. Many had relatives in the refugee camps as well as in the ranks of the guerrillas and did not feel particularly threatened by the insurgents. Rather than building a new, safer village, they viewed the military efforts as attempts to control their lives and extract unpaid labor and intelligence about civilians and the guerrillas.[14] In sharp contrast, the new occupants were happy to have land, and that was their most important and perhaps only consideration.

The army compelled villagers in the "new" Santa María Tzejá to join the civil patrols, a new paramilitary institution incorporating most men between the ages of fifteen and sixty. The military aggressively sought to use the patrols to rip apart and then restructure social relations throughout the countryside, implanting its values and strict control at the most basic village level. As the CEH (U.N.) report noted, the civil patrol's objectives were to "control physically and psychologically the population,"

Figure 10. Marta Castro, who arrived in the militarized village in 1984, grinding corn in a house typical of the time. Photo by Beatriz Manz.

citing the army's plan "Firmeza 83" to "influence the population psychologically" so that villagers will "repudiate [the guerrillas] and create a people-army unity, aimed at locating still active enemy organized bands."[15]

During 1982–83, one million peasants were conscripted into the civil patrols, practically the entire rural adult male population.[16] The patrols were meant, according to REMHI, "to seal off communities from potential guerrilla penetration as well as remove the guerrillas from areas where they had already established a presence."[17] The REMHI report continues, "The civil patrols worked with the army to pursue and capture people fleeing in uninhabited areas; these often became mass round-ups.... They also carried out selective detentions in their communities. Another civil patrol activity was to search for alleged guerrilla collaborators whose names appeared in previous prepared lists."[18] In many cases, "the patrols would show up accompanied by neighbors who had fingered people in the community."[19]

These new paramilitary groups extracted a high social cost. "The CEH counts among the most damaging effects of the confrontation those that resulted from forcing large sectors of the population to be accomplices in the violence especially through their participation in the Civil Patrols (PAC)."[20] On one level, the patrols "deeply affected values and behavioral patterns, as violence became a normal method of confronting conflictive situations and promoted contempt for the lives of others."[21] The REMHI report elaborates, charging that "obligatory participation in the Civilian Self-defense Patrols (PACs) shattered community life. The patrols' militarized hierarchical structure imposed new forms of authority and a new set of rules and values distinguished by the possession of weapons and the use of force."[22] On another level, Judith Zur points out that the civil patrols "developed from the army's desire to reorganize the countryside in its own image."[23] She argues that the army sought to use the patrols "to control interpersonal relationships, something which had eluded them as far as the Indian population was concerned."[24] The officers demanded twenty-four-hour civil patrol shifts of all adult males and most boys in their teens.

The forced patrol service was not compensated, exacerbating the economic burden on villagers. The peasants were not given food or clothing, and they themselves had to build the *garitas* (stationary checkpoints). Moreover, if someone missed his shift due to illness or absence from the village, he had to pay for a replacement. Patrollers were ordered to accompany soldiers on several days of search-and-destroy operations, at times dressed in military uniform and interspersed in the military column, which placed them in great danger. At other times the military would request a certain number of villagers to work at the army base or on other military projects.[25]

Service in the civil patrols underscored the difference in attitude between *nuevos* and *antiguos*. The *nuevos*, many of whom had served in the army, were more likely to view the patrols as voluntary, while the *antiguos* viewed them initially as a necessary requirement to their return to the village and then as a mandated burden. "The civil patrols surely are not voluntary," Ricardo reflected in the early 1990s, in a widely shared sentiment. "They are called voluntary, but they are forced, they are obligatory. Because whoever does not comply with the shift is called a collaborator or member of the guerrilla. And, of course, everyone is afraid, because from one moment to another, [the army] could kill you." Army officers instructed all the patrollers to look for guerrillas and pass on information on any suspicious activities to the army, including reporting on fellow villagers.

Ricardo, whose Spanish is very fluent, said the army's speeches always referred to the guerrillas as terrorists and delinquents. He gave some examples of the officer's message. "Well, when the army came, more than anything they tried to convince people," he said. "They would say, 'The delinquent terrorists are people from other towns or countries, and they only want to destroy the communities. They are people who do not want economic development, only to destroy.'" How could this fate be avoided? Ricardo quotes the officer as saying, "For that not to happen you must comply with your obligations. You yourselves have to protect your families, your homes, your lands. The military cannot do it alone, because it is not able to protect all of Guatemala."

The *antiguos* and the *nuevos* tended to behave very differently while on patrols. "The army would ask us to go look for foot tracks," Nicolás recalled. "[They told us] we should go quietly, not to smoke, break things, because it was a risk for us, because if the guerrillas detected us they would attack. The *nuevos,* who were in charge, would follow all the instructions and would tell us 'You must do it like this.' But *antiguos* would talk loudly, smoke, break branches, make as much noise as possible," to alert the insurgents that the patrol was coming. Most of the *antiguos* knew the guerrillas were not going to attack them and therefore had no interest in alerting the military to the guerrilla presence. Some *antiguos,* especially those who had benefited from the militarization or had a special grudge against the guerrillas, may have been more inclined to cooperate with the army, but these were few in number.

The patrol shifts stretched through twenty-four hours, typically running from six in the evening through the next day.[26] The patrollers spent most of the time in the *garitas,* monitoring the movements of anyone coming or going. The patrollers would stop strangers, asking them for identification papers and the all-important permission slip from the military, or the village patrol chief, to be traveling beyond their own village. They would ask where the person was coming from and where they planned to go, recording the information to pass on to the military base. The patrols also monitored the villagers themselves. Once the villagers were allowed to work in their parcels again, they had to go by the *garita* so those on duty could write their names in a notebook. (I often thought in those years that producing lined notebooks must have been one of the growth industries in Guatemala.) At the end of the day, the villagers had to report that they had returned from their parcels.

The military set up a garrison in the village in 1983. After that oper-

Figure 11. Juan Osorio in 1988, at 6 A.M.,
fatigued after spending the night performing the
mandatory twenty-four-hour civil patrol shift.
Photo by Beatriz Manz.

ation was accomplished, military patrols would show up every twenty or thirty days, and then, by the mid-1980s, the military would show up less frequently, though always unannounced. Early on in 1983, the soldiers would meticulously check the amount of food a villager was taking to the parcel—literally counting the number of tortillas—to ensure that no one else was being fed. Each time an army unit would come to the village they would gather everyone together and give them a pep talk. If people didn't feel like going out on patrol, the soldiers would warn them ominously of what had happened in 1982. If someone had to leave the village on a trip, they had to receive written permission (or a safe-conduct pass) and pay for a replacement for their patrol shift. The patrol chief would write the safe-conduct pass, which the person had to display at the dozen or so civil-patrol or army checkpoints they might encounter. The date of departure, destination, purpose of the trip, and return date would all appear on the slip. It was like getting a visa to travel within their own country. If for some reason a person lost his or her identification or safe-conduct pass, the consequences could be severe, if not fatal. People in the countryside in the 1980s were considered guilty until proven innocent, and the "guilty" were harshly punished.

On several occasions I spent long hours at the *garita,* in part because little else was going on in the village, and also because I was sure to catch a dozen villagers in one place, themselves quite willing to kill time and talk. Even the *nuevos* began to view the patrol shifts as a waste of time and a burden. Quite regularly, when I slept on the benches in the open village chapel at night, the patrollers would come in and sleep there as well, often carelessly leaving their rifles pointing in my direction. They would cheerfully comply when I would complain about the location of their guns. I would grumble, "Do me a favor and turn your weapons the other way, it's not pleasant to be eyeing that cannon from here!"

The military provided the civil patrols with rudimentary training. Some of the *antiguos* would laugh when asked, "Didn't you tell the military you already received guerrilla training?" There were also special officers in charge of political "indoctrination," as several villagers called it. The indoctrination largely consisted of telling people they had to defend their lands and prevent the return of guerrilla support and strength. Ricardo explained that many of the *nuevos* who were new to the area did not know exactly what had taken place. Others, who had been army recruits participating in the counterinsurgency campaigns in the region, not only knew there was vacant land but also why. Above all they did not want the land taken away from them.[27] "Those who did not have an opportunity to get to know the guerrillas, of course, they believed everything they heard," Ricardo said. "We were told that the guerrillas were terrorists, they raped women, stole chickens, stole the crops, they were savages, had no conscience, bothered their daughters, kidnapped people, burned houses, and did all kinds of barbarity." But those "who had suffered at the hands of the military, they of course did not believe a word of it," he continued. "Among friends we used to say, the soldiers see a lot of civil patrols but they must ask themselves, 'Are they really convinced morally or are they simply fulfilling a requirement?'" According to the *antiguos,* only a few of them were committed patrollers: Manuel Saquic, José Quixán, Juan Reyes, Chema Cux, and the Pachecos, especially Miguel Pacheco. And among the *nuevos,* about half were on the side of the military, the other half did not care about politics and just wanted to work their land and take care of their families but had to do as their leaders demanded. Some of the "committed" patrollers were harsh even on their own neighbors, not tolerating late arrival to shifts and reporting any suspicious behavior, no matter how minor, to the military base. It became common practice for a patrol chief to spread rumors about an individual he did not like, hoping for some personal gain for himself while causing fear, military punishment, or even death for the victim.

Ak'el mentioned that any leaflets or *mantas* (banners) left by the guerrillas had to be taken to the base, otherwise the military would consider the villagers collaborators with the insurgents. Military commissioners had to report to the military base every two weeks to receive what even some military commissioners thought of as "indoctrination." Despite the regular attendance, none of the commissioners seemed to remember much of what those lectures were about other than the constant emphasis on the evil nature of the guerrillas. A number of commissioners were outright cynics who obviously tuned out after the first few lectures, but even Ak'el and those who were more amenable to the message, strained to remember what those long, rambling lectures were about. "At least those of us who suffered first hand did not believe [what the army was telling us]," Ricardo said. "We were conscious and sure of what we saw. Who is going to believe something like [what the army was saying]?"

Ricardo, whose family had been the first to settle Santa María Tzejá in 1970, had joined the guerrillas in the late 1970s. But, after spending a few years in the insurgency and sensing that "the situation was getting critical and very dangerous," he returned to his original highland village in 1981. From there he went to work in the *fincas* on the south coast. His family, except for his brother Valentín, joined him there.[28] After spending the worst years away from Santa María Tzejá, Ricardo, his parents, and siblings decided to return to the village in 1985. They were dismayed by what they encountered.

"My father loved his parcel of land in Santa María Tzejá very much," Ricardo said. "So he got a statement from the *finca* proving that he had worked there so he could present that to the military authorities in Playa Grande. I also got proof that I had been working in the *fincas*. So I came back. No sooner had we walked to the village than the chief of the civil patrols came to question us. He demanded, 'You must go to the *garita* with all your documents.'" Ricardo did not recognize this man, Ricardo Cuc Xol, a *nuevo* from Cobán who had been given land, had become chief, and was the new authority in the village—that same village that his family, along with other K'iche', had settled and organized.

The authorities in the village were no longer elected. Instead, they were appointed by the military based on army criteria such as obedience, loyalty, and sympathies with the military—not community-recognized social qualities. Now Ricardo's family not only lost their land but had no hope of recovering it. It quickly became clear that the military government favored the Q'eqchi' occupiers of his father's land. The contrast could not have been more striking. The Q'eqchi' chief of the civil patrols was intimidating. "And so, with what purpose did you come here?" Ricardo said he was aggressively asked after Cuc Xol examined all his documents. "I responded, 'I was from here, that is why I am coming.'" These chiefs had all been former soldiers in the military." Soldiers knew there was land available because they had taken part in the massacres and displacement. However, while some of the *nuevos* had been recruits in the army and participated in the military offensive, most had not served in the army.

In the late 1980s, the army named Ricardo to be the military commissioner in the village. It is not clear if the army was aware of his past involvement with the insurgents. The new position exacerbated his personal conflicts, yet the military appears to have had at least a short-lived influence on him. He warned a relative, who he knew maintained contact with the guerrillas, to watch out because this information had to be passed to the military. "Now there are no uncles, no parents, no cousins, it's all the same, so watch out," the relative said Ricardo had told him.[29] Ricardo implied that if he did not carry out the orders to inform the military, he himself would be implicated. There is no evidence, however, that he ever informed on this relative. In fact toward the end of his "term" he provided a safe conduct pass for a relative in the guerrillas who was secretly visiting Santa María Tzejá. Ricardo was torn by his involvement with the army. Over the years I talked to him, he would reveal wide shifts in perspectives. Often I wondered if he really believed what he said or was simply repeating it without much reflection, or perhaps he had lost trust in everyone, especially an outsider like myself.

While Ricardo was the military commissioner in 1989, I asked him about his duties and what happened every time he had to go to the military base. The former member of the Local Irregular Forces, or Fuerzas Irregulares Locales (FIL), tended to recite minispeeches.

"The military tells us that the army and the people have to work together to save the fatherland. They told us about Nicaragua, Cuba, and Russia. Those are communist countries, and you know what happens in those countries? They make pants for everyone, lots of them, and give them to the people, all the same color, olive green."

I cannot resist asking: "Same size?"

"All the same."

"What if they don't fit? Look at me, what would I do?"

He grinned, "I don't know, they don't care if it fits or not, all have to be the same.... There is no freedom there. They work together, they call it collectivism, all have to work, and there are no wages. The army says we have to see that that does not occur here and for that the PACs must cooperate with the army."

Nicolás, a former guerrilla FIL member, had also brought up Nicaragua in a conversation in 1987. "Look what happened in Nicaragua," he warned. "Thank God that didn't happen here." I ask, "What happened in Nicaragua?" Nicolás answered, "The officer at the base told us that in Nicaragua everyone dresses the same. You cannot have a wife, no religion is allowed, all the harvests go to the state, you cannot own land, anything. Thank God that didn't happen here." I looked at Nicolás, sitting by me. He was very thin with his front upper teeth missing, though he was only in his early thirties, his pants were torn, and he was wearing old shoes with holes in them. He was putting endless hours into the civil patrols, and he was risking his life without pay, all of this negatively affecting him and his family. The shifting viewpoints of Ricardo and Nicolás in the 1980s compared to their positions in the 1990s reveal both the successes and failures of the army psychological operations.

Amid this suffocating supervision and fear, peasants still managed to maintain contact with the guerrillas, especially with their relatives, providing token collaboration. "The army hoped that in the end the PAC would provide total control," Emiliano said, "but it was not able to do it, because the collaboration was maintained. Not even the hardest blows the army gave were able to change the conscience of some in the civil patrols. They were not able to reach the heart of the people. A lot of what people say is just from the lips out, not from the heart, it should not all be believed." Sabas, a combatant for sixteen years who left the ranks disappointed, said civil patrol units were never a military threat to the insurgents. He added that if a civil patrol unit had decided to engage the guerrillas it would have been a problem, not because of the military threat but rather that the guerrillas did not want to attack the civil patrols and risk antagonizing the civilian population. In contrast, the combination of military and civil patrols could be devastating to the guerrillas since the local patrols knew the terrain and were highly effective guides.

During the early years of the militarized village the civilian government and the military were intertwined. As a result, villagers felt totally vulnerable. If they were tortured or if their relatives disappeared or were killed, there was absolutely no recourse. When Vinicio Cerezo, a Christian Democrat, was elected president in 1985, it brought the appearance of a civilian in office, though little changed in the day-to-day life of rural communities. A small difference, according to one villager, was that "we heard about human rights." Of some comfort were foreigners beginning to visit the village. When I returned in December 1985, it was the first visit by an outsider who knew the village's history. Subsequent regular visits by the Needham, Massachusetts, Congregational Church and international NGOs provided a modest sense of security.

The intrigues and suspicions that coursed through the village also affected the attitudes toward outsiders. The *antiguos* felt my visits between the village and the refugee camps helped considerably in the reestablishment of communication with their relatives and former neighbors. They looked forward to what I brought with me: painstakingly written letters, emotional cassette-recorded messages, and treasured photos. In contrast, the *nuevos* charged that I was with the guerrillas, an agent of Father Luis, a leader of the refugees checking up on conditions and paving the way for their return. These charges escalated to the point that in 1987 I received a threat stating I would be killed if I came to the village again.[30] From the safety of the United States the threat would seem absurd and surreal; standing in the Ixcán it was frightening and all too plausible. I knew I had to confront the suspicion and the innuendo and do it quickly. As reluctant as I was to go to the military base, the trip was absolutely necessary to challenge the rumor and show that I had nothing to hide. When I went to Playa Grande voluntarily to confront the commander about these charges, the whole episode was followed with intense interest by the villagers—accusers and supporters. In retrospect, it may have provided a ray of optimism to the villagers to see that I was willing to challenge the threat, and that it was never carried out.

My trip to the military base came after some *antiguos* had come to warn me by a path near San José la 20 that I was being associated with the guerrillas. Several *nuevos* had boasted publicly that they would not let me into the village and would meet me with machetes and guns. At this time defense minister General Héctor Gramajo was designing a new military campaign dubbed "Fortaleza 87" (Fortitude 87). The Ofensiva de Fin de Año (year-end offensive) in the north of the country was a massive show of strength aimed primarily at the Ixcán area. It mobilized more than thirty-five hundred troops in two battalions. The command was in the hands of the Fuerza de Tareas Kaibil Balam.[31] According to the CEH (U.N.) report, the 1987 offensive involved "the greatest number of mobile troops that would be known in the war, with similar intentions as the offensive of 1982."[32] It was a tense time. American Chinook helicopter pilots were ferrying Guatemalan troops to the Ixcán.[33] There were daily military bombings and shootings right outside the municipal capital of Cantabal. The guerrillas were taking over villages, stopping vehicles on the roads, and engaging in combat very near the military base. The insurgents had boldly conducted propaganda meetings in two villages near Santa María Tzejá during my stay in April and May 1987.[34]

While Myrna Mack and Liz Oglesby stayed nearby, I walked to the gate of the massive jungle military base.[35] Dozens of soldiers guarded the fortified entrance protected by a heavy steel bar. Lookout posts seemed to be everywhere, with guns at the ready. As the soldiers watched in amazement at my approach, I suddenly realized how odd I must have looked. Wearing the only clean clothes available, I was dressed totally in pink—blouse and pants—except for heavy, muddy hiking boots. I kept on walking, trying my best not to show my nerves or lack of preparation. I mustered all my courage to assertively say, "I need to talk to the commander." I noticed the soldiers were baffled by the request, and that increased my confidence from zero to slightly above zero. The sentry took a long time to figure out what to do next. Finally he said, "un momento," and consulted with a superior among those behind him. Then another soldier came with a wooden pad and paper and asked, "What is your name? Is the commander expecting you?" I gave my name, which took him forever to write. I pretended to be either amazed or amused that he could not quite get it, moving my head to the side as if by looking at his sheet I could help him along. My face no doubt also expressed slight contempt and annoyance at having to waste my time with this. To the second question I said confidently and with a slight smile, "Oh, yes, the commander is expecting me." So off they went with the sheet. I stood there for probably fifteen minutes or longer, fully aware that by now even more eyes must be looking at me.

Several soldiers returned and stated that I could come into the base. They manually raised the heavy steel bar as if I was a vehicle. I walked past several sprawling barracks, knowing that thousands of soldiers were stationed at the base. I was escorted into one of the buildings and told to sit in a waiting room in the commander's quarters. At this point I was beginning to get more nervous, in part because I did not know what to expect next.

The door opened and in walked Colonel Guido Abdala, the chief of the Ixcán, zone 22, military base—the new commander about whom I had already heard so much. His neck seemed as thick as a tree trunk, and his large muscular arms hung away from his body as he walked. His hands were so enormous they seemed double the size of normal hands. We shook hands and I felt—the only time in my life—quite petite. After a friendly greeting, he offered me tea. I went straight to the point, expressing that neither he nor I, of course, wanted to waste our time. "I am here to do research, and I am coming to tell you that people are saying I am a guerrilla." "Oh no," he said showing complete surprise. "That is it," I said, "that is what they are saying. Any idea why they might be saying something like that?" I asked. "There is much ignorance, there are so many rumors all the time," he commented. "What are the source of these rumors?" I replied. "Who knows, the people make these things up," he responded. I then pointed out, "I don't think so, people don't just make things up, perhaps it was suggested or the rumors were planted. In any case, I cannot work under these conditions. Perhaps you can do something about this?" He made a suggestion. Since I was an anthropologist, why didn't I study the languages of some people on the other side of the Chixoy River (a safer place and, not coincidentally, closer to the military base) and forget about Santa María Tzejá. I smiled and said something to the effect that his suggestion was intriguing. I actually liked the idea that he might think I was a linguist and not a cultural anthropologist. That seemed to be less threatening to the military, I thought.

Perhaps he assumed all anthropologists studied languages or excavated thousand-year-old Maya sites, and then again, he could have just been pulling my leg to see how I would respond. One easily became paranoid in the Ixcán, double- and triple-guessing anything. Does he know who I am or not? Does he know what anthropology is or not?

The soldier in camouflage walked in with a tray and, to my total amazement, with what appeared to be a fine Venetian tea set. I asked Colonel Abdala about his term in the Ixcán, about his views of the war, about the guerrillas. He showed me a map with pins: one for each of the areas of guerrilla concentration, others where their radio station was located, a mountain area stronghold, and of course the Ho Chi Minh front, the Ernesto "Che" Guevara front, and the Augusto César Sandino front. I left the base satisfied that I could continue my work. When I confronted the three Q'eqchi' ring-leaders back in Santa María Tzejá, they denied any role in calling me the "head of the guerrillas" or making the threats against me, adding jovially while drunk, "But look, you know, if you come to visit again, my house is your house!"[36]

The army had a tendency to denounce certain priests bitterly, especially Father Luis. These priests, according to the officers, were linked with the guerrillas and sought to manipulate the people into collaborating with the insurgents. The army was equally critical and condemnatory toward Guatemala City–based human rights organizations such as the Mutual Support Group and the Guatemalan Widow's Organization. "Be very careful not to get involved with them, because they are the right arm of the guerrilla," Ricardo remembered being told. "They are pure guerrilla." Vladimiro recalled that the officers at the base always referred to Father Luis as the person responsible for the guerrillas in the region, calling him the "Commander of the Ixcán guerrillas."

From Venetian Gondolas to Jungle Canoes

The army terror against the Catholic Church grew so extreme in El Quiché that Bishop Juan Gerardi did the unthinkable: he closed the diocese in 1980, the first such closure since the church arrived with the Spanish conquest. When the church reopened, the diocese sent its first priest back to the Ixcán in 1985, the Venetian Father Tiziano Sofia. If not exactly humble and pious, he was a man for the moment and seemed to reflect a bizarre, surreal element that ran through these troubled times. He welcomed the challenge.

Tiziano's role during the counterinsurgency period in the Ixcán is a crucial, if unusual, part of the evolving drama. Without him, the overpowering military domination might have seemed harsher and created even further suffering and hopelessness. With Tiziano, the villagers from Santa María Tzejá—part of his parish—could find at least symbolic support. With no civilian government, no democratic institutions, no judicial system, Tiziano provided a small semblance of hope. The officers, for their part, put up with his eccentricities because he was no threat to the military and they knew it. Yet psychologically, Tiziano, perhaps unknowingly, provided comfort amid despair. He stood up to the military.

Tiziano, who was in his early sixties, came from the Salesian order and was fearless, energetic, authoritarian, and arrogant. Moreover he was a builder. The Ixcán had just been designated a municipality, and the first town, Cantabal, was getting off the ground, or more literally, off the mud. Had he not been a priest he would have likely wanted to be an architect. He had great design vision and was demanding in his construction projects. He was able to collect money all over the world for his missionary work and used these funds to build projects with free labor from impoverished militarized villages throughout the Ixcán. His role in the Ixcán embodied elements of feudalism in a contemporary context. Unfortunately for the ecology of the jungle, he loved mahogany, which put him in competition with the desires of foreign merchants and colonels for marketing that precious red, hard wood throughout the world. As a result the mahogany trees were practically decimated in the Ixcán in the mid- to late 1980s, including Santa María Tzejá. Buyers and illegal speculators, with the protection of the military, invaded the zone with large electric saws. For weeks on end one could hear the piercing sound of the saws cutting the ancient trees. A constant procession of large mahogany rafts floated down the Tzejá and Chixoy Rivers toward Playa Grande, and from there the logs were trucked to the Caribbean docks of Puerto Barrios for shipment.

The depletion of natural flora for housing material was also a growing problem. The *nuevos,* insecure about their tenure in the village, saw no benefit in replanting palm needed for thatch roofing material. The *antiguos,* concerned with day-to-day survival, also saw no purpose to reforesting, especially since the growth would take many years to provide them with any short-term benefits. Who knew where they may be living in a few years, or even if they would be alive?

Father Tiziano demanded labor from the villages. He never failed to

Figure 12. Deforestation as a result of cattle raising, population migration, and timber extraction—for example, of mahogany, as in this 1990 photo—was severe, especially during the period of militarization. Photo by Beatriz Manz.

Figure 13. Mahogany rafts going down the Tzejá River in 1988, headed for the intersection of the Chixoy River, the Playa Grande military base, and the Northern Transversal road. Photo by Beatriz Manz.

combine a Bible workshop with a heavy dose of construction work. When I stayed with him in Cantabal in 1985, he had a modest church and parish house with a thatched roof, but he boasted about his big construction plans: a hospital, a carpentry shop, a new church, dormitories, a large parish house, and a sawmill. All these projects represented his vision of development, and he did not tolerate criticism in general and specifically of his top-down and centralized development projects. In contrast, village projects were not particularly interesting to him. As we walked around his property in Cantabal at the edge of what was to become a bustling frontier town in the middle of the rain forest, he complained of the lack of a work ethic among the local peasantry. As he described his ambitious projects—in the middle of a sentence, having spotted incorrect hammering—he would bark in his Italian staccato accent, "No! No! No! How many times do I need to tell you? How many times? When are you going to learn?" he asked, as the shy, disconcerted, and embarrassed peasant replied with a sheepish smile. "I am getting tired of telling you how to hammer." He would yank the hammer away from the semi-frightened peasant and say, "This way. Can you see? This way. How many times do I need to tell you? I do not want to tell you again. Do you understand?" I would become quite uncomfortable as if by association one might become a party to that bellowing. Tiziano would then continue with the sentence, as if he had just inserted a comma. He remembered exactly where he had left off. He could never miss an opportunity to correct ineffective labor. His tours always had a purpose. He wanted to know if I could raise money; he wanted to show off his projects; he wanted sympathy for having to deal with this unskilled labor. He felt the people had no initiative and were basically lazy. Never mind that while he was saying this he was not putting any sweat into the work himself.

"In the construction jobs, sometimes we go hungry, because the food he gives us does not fill us up," one villager from Santa María Tzejá commented. "He doesn't give us tortillas, but a food that he calls 'polenta.' And he says, 'You are just pigs! You eat too much, as if you were animals! In order to work it is not necessary to eat so much. The Italians just eat polenta. They eat less than you, but they work harder!'" The villagers couldn't figure out what polenta was made of, although it looked and tasted to them suspiciously like pig feed. He would receive food donations by the tons from Europe and then benevolently provide these rations in exchange for labor.

No one hated Tiziano more than the local merchants. "He declared war on the merchants because he installed his own store," a villager commented, "he sells all kinds of stuff and the competition is fierce. The merchants are protesting against him and even denounced him legally, because the *padre* wanted his store to function without a business license." Another villager added, "He gets a lot of free things so he can help the people: clothing, food, corn and beans by the thousands of pounds." He continued, "I remember one time he went to Puerto Barrios to pick up several truck loads of things for the people. He would not give that out as gifts, but he would sell it in the store. Perhaps he sold that to finance his grand construction projects." Tiziano felt that it was not a good idea to give out things for free; it would create dependency and bad habits. The same person continued, "Who was most angry at this were the merchants of Cantabal. They viewed this as unfair competition, because he did not have to pay for the merchandise or pay taxes. That is why they did not like him, and that is why so often he was denounced."

Tiziano was a talented photographer and was obsessed with the female body, especially the upper part of the body. He carried his camera everywhere, and there was not a mother breast-feeding her baby whom Tiziano did not photograph, often showing large exposed breasts. He then enlarged the colorful photographs and decorated the walls of the parish house.

Rumors floated through the Ixcán about everything and everyone, especially about the few outsiders. In this nest of intrigue and rumors, gossip and jokes about Tiziano were at the very top of the list. In the bipolar world of the cold war, and in the midst of the counterinsurgency campaign and tight military controls, everyone wanted to know which side you were on. So there were those who claimed to be sure that Tiziano was with the military. Clearly a spy and "*oreja*," a friend of the military, a supporter of the counterinsurgency; in fact, part of the military project. How else could one explain that he was there? That the military would allow him—a priest of the religion denounced as "communist" — to work there? The same military that had sponsored thousands of Evangelicals to settle lands left by Catholic refugees now tolerated this priest? He did not do much to dispel the rumors. Instead he boasted that before coming to the Ixcán he had been a parish priest in all the hot spots of the planet: Iran, the Philippines, Ecuador, and within those countries always in the politically hottest places.

One time I asked Father Tiziano if he had run into the guerrillas in his rounds to visit isolated villages in the jungle. "Oh, yes," he said. "They stopped my sacristan and the people that were carrying the instruments and other loads. When I caught up they said, 'Stop!' So I said—knowing full well who they were—'Who do you think you are? Don't you know who I am?' They said, 'Oh yes, we know. You are Father Tiziano.' " He was delighted to be able to tell this story, especially the part that indicated he was so well known. The guerrillas told him they knew of him and his reputation, as did many others. Tiziano would not acknowledge their authority to stop him, but stop he did, turning the encounter into his questioning of them rather than the other way around. He did not like to recognize anyone else's authority over him. He said to them, "So you want a revolution? Let's engage in a philosophical discussion, shall we?" As he told the story he informed me that these were ignorant, uneducated peasants who knew nothing of European philosophy. His universal contempt for the locals—peasants, guerrillas, soldiers, generals, merchants, prostitutes, Evangelicals—was so overt I often wondered, given the violence in the Ixcán, if they would not all for once put their differences aside and just go after him as an act of unity and good will toward one another. Had he been hurt this would have been the only case where the culprit could have been any of a dozen competing entities on all sides of the highly charged political world of the Ixcán. One villager said in 1999, "He didn't get along with anyone in Cantabal. Well, maybe there were five or six families who agreed with him. The rest hated him. They all spoke very badly of him; they criticized him and would denounce him to the authorities. The people of Cantabal also denounced him to the bishop so he would get rid of him."

In 1987, when I went to the Ixcán with Myrna Mack and Liz Oglesby, we stayed at Tiziano's because there were no *pensiones* in those years. We drove in the back of his vehicle to nearby villages where large baptisms were to take place. At the baptism he was, not surprisingly, demanding. He wanted every child to have a particular type of white clothing, which would then be taken off and replaced by a new dress after the child was christened. He yelled at parents who did not do as he had demanded. Disobedience indicated, in his view, total irresponsibility and irreverence toward him, the church, and the holy sacrament he was performing. He did not want to hear about the extreme poverty and desperation of these families. To him, there were simply no excuses to justify that disregard. He demanded certain order, such as how people were supposed to line up. The three of us became exhausted just watching him carry out the never ending ceremony according to his dictates.

When we returned to Cantabal late one evening, after several more stops, Tiziano saw a fire coming from the direction of the church. He became hysterical and jumped out of the pickup truck, not even putting it in park or turning the motor off, nearly killing those of us in the back as the truck lurched down the side of the road. He ran with his hands up screaming like a lunatic, "They are burning my church." Myrna, Liz, and I felt little surprise, but this fire turned out to be a false alarm. People were burning some garbage, and his paranoia had gotten the better of him.

Don Tono, a tall Afro-Caribbean carpenter from El Petén, was the only local person Tiziano respected. His carpentry talents were extraordinary. He was also my confidant when it came to discussing Tiziano and the conditions in the Ixcán. In one of my trips in 1987, he told me about the increase in guerrilla activity. His analysis of events was always thoughtful and based on considerable local information. He was an astute observer. He told me also that Tiziano had a new dog named Kaibil, the same name as the fiercest counterinsurgency military unit. (Rumor had it that in reprisal the military had a dog at the base named Tiziano!)

Kaibil quickly became legendary. One villager in Santa María Tzejá told me about a particular incident with the dog. "One time we were accompanying Padre Tiziano," he commented. "On the road from San Lucas to Xalbal, before the bridge, two soldiers stopped us and asked for our documents. Tiziano told them that the whole world knew him in the Ixcán, and he refused to show them his documents. The rest of us had our papers, except for Casimiro, and because of that they wanted to detain him." So far nothing seemed unusual. Then the villager continued, "Tiziano, without the soldiers noticing, gave a signal to the dog and he jumped to the throat of the soldier that was holding Casimiro, throwing the soldier violently to the ground, his rifle flying about two meters away." If this were not enough, "When the second soldier came up to the dog, the dog did the same with this one. Now, with both soldiers on the ground, Tiziano called the dog and pretended to be scolding him, saying, "Calm down Kaibil, calm down! How could it be that you are going to harm your brothers, the Kaibiles! The dog stayed calm and the soldiers did not try anything else against us and let us go."

While this tale of the dog seems exaggerated, stories of the dog and Tiziano tended to take on surreal proportions. It was never quite clear where truth ended and imagination began. Tiziano went everywhere with him. I even saw him place the dog on a little wagon pulled by his motorcycle. Kaibil was no ordinary, impoverished mutt. One villager described him to me: "Kaibil was a big dog, from a fine race, and very well trained, he could comprehend better than even some people. He was a very obedient dog and loyal to Tiziano. He was dark brown, Kaibil's skin was soft and shiny and his hair was short, or perhaps he had no hair."

I often found Tiziano and the military at war. One commander might pay visits to Tiziano and have a drink; the next might not. And that lack of engagement used to annoy him. He was unaccustomed to being slighted. "The general is no longer coming to visit," Don Tono told me with some apprehension. "There is a confrontation going on." Tiziano complained about the insolent and ignorant new commander who quite obviously was not putting up with him or even paying him pro forma respect. Tiziano also said his fine Venetian tea set had been stolen and suspected the corrupt military as the culprits. Previously, Tiziano had been honored with space in the air-force planes. All of a sudden he was told there was no space.

Tensions among Evangelicals, Catholics, and the military were frequent. In the late 1980s there was a proposal by a developmental agency to build a road in Santa María Tzejá, which would pass near the village's Catholic church. The Catholics were told by Tiziano to run barbed wire around the area covering the property of the church. The Evangelicals went to the military base and accused about a dozen Catholics of being obstructionists and collaborators of the guerrillas. Everyone in the village at the time remembers this incident, and it has become part of the village's folklore. This is how one villager tells the story: "Tiziano told us not to allow the road to go near the property of the church," he recounted. "He told us to surround the area to prevent anyone even walking within its limits. We did that, and so the *nuevos* went to accuse us to the base. They said we are 'delinquents terrorists,' for impeding the path of the road, that we did not want means of communication here, because we are used to living in the jungle, and a whole bunch of stuff they wrote in their official complaint that they took to the base." Charges like this could be serious, and sure enough the base "had a list with about twelve names and ordered us to make ourselves present at the base the next day," the villager continued. "So we went. We stopped at Father Tiziano's first and told him where we were going and why. He said, 'And at what time are you going there?' 'At such and such a time,' we answered. 'Ah, good, don't worry,' he said, 'there is still time. Work awhile here first and then at ten I'll take you there in my vehicle.'" Despite the tension of the moment, Tiziano never saw an idle peasant he could not use. "We worked for a while and at ten he took us to the zone," the villager elaborated. "We hardly spoke. He spoke for us. And did he ever treat the lieutenant colonel of the G2 [intelligence unit] badly!" The villager then elaborated, "Oh God. He told the lieutenant colonel that the military has absolutely nothing to do with the people. They wired the perimeter of the church because that is the Catholic Church's right. That is the property of the church. You should not go around bothering people! Then the lieutenant colonel said to us, 'When you want to do something come here with me, talk with me. Ask for advice here with me. Come to me so you will not have problems.'"

If the villagers thought that was the end of the conversation, they were mistaken. "Then Father Tiziano said. 'You have no reason to go around advising the civilian population. You advise your soldiers! And least of all the Catholic people! You are used to having the poor people under your shoes. But the time has passed to do that! Cobbler to your shoes," the villager recalled in amazement. "That is how Father Tiziano spoke! He was angry, fierce. He would stand right up to the lieutenant colonel. The lieutenant colonel said nothing more. Father Tiziano would hit the table with his fist. Oh, he was angry, very angry. And at the base they did not like him at all. He would stand up, right up to the lieutenant colonel" (and Tiziano was over six feet tall). The people were very impressed! Several people told me about this encounter, and the details never varied, especially the saying "Zapatero a tus zapatos!" (his way of saying the military should stick to what it knows best). The villagers did not understand what that expression meant.

Despite his pronounced idiosyncrasies, Tiziano may have been the right priest for that period. His combative spirit and willingness to test it gave the people some confidence, opening the possibility to reject certain obligations, such as the military commissioner's position, or the military-mandated civil patrol sweeps. Tiziano made it clear to the officers that he had no problems with the military ordering soldiers, but civilians fell under his purview. He was eccentric enough to throw the military off balance. They were not quite sure how to respond. And he kept the military off balance until 1992, when he was transferred out of Guatemala.

Tiziano's stay in the Ixcán led to speculation about his past, particularly about his ideology and political affinities. The explanation for his assignment may be simple. Tiziano could only have been assigned to the Ixcán with the consent of the military at the highest levels, and the Catholic Church needed to have a parish priest in that area of the country after years of abandonment. Tiziano may have been allowed to establish a parish in Cantabal because of his personal background. He had not been to Guatemala before, had not been embroiled in the mobilization period, and was a member of the Salesian order—known for its theological and social conservatism—and the acting bishop of El Quiché diocese at the time, Monsignor Urízar, had recommended him. This bishop was quite removed from, if not hostile to, the liberation theology movement, and during the difficult years of violence he felt that his mission was purely ecclesiastical. If the military checked Tiziano's past, they likely heard more about his eccentric personality than any undesirable political bent.

The decade during the village's militarized period (1983–1994), especially in the early years, was the only time fault lines split the original settlers in Santa María Tzejá. Not even in the various refugee camps did villagers become so atomized, lost, and vulnerable—each family looking after themselves without social institutions to resolve conflicts or coordinate village endeavors. There were no independent civil authorities, no independent leaders, no organizations other than the military-dominated civil patrols. Consequently, conflicts had no outlet and no institutions to mediate them.

In those years I would often arrive at the village exhausted from the hot and muddy hike only to find within minutes a long line forming wherever I had dumped my backpack. I realized the villagers had a need to be heard, to have someone help them in mediating a dispute, or to clear their conscience. On one occasion a man who was first in line told me that "perhaps you have already been told," and proceeded to tell me about an incident between him and another villager. I eventually heard the accusation from someone further back in the line. With time, other villagers among the *antiguos* helped in settling disputes. Xan, who received the worst tortures at the military base, got into an argument with Manuel Saquic, a fellow villager and one of the few *antiguos* who seemed not to mind the military presence, having enriched himself with the cattle he rounded up after the destruction. Manuel publicly yelled at one point that Xan was a *guerrillero*. He had bullied Xan and others before, but this time Xan had had it. Rather than the customary rapid withdrawal in the face of such a dangerous accusation, Xan yelled back at him, "Yes, I am, I am. And what about it? Go tell whoever you want, go accuse me." He then got closer to him and said pointedly, "But I shall see you on judgment day. I don't care any more what will happen to me, but you will have to face God and respond to Him."

Xan told me he had gotten so angry he thought he could have killed this man with a knife. But then he mentioned with some gratification not only that this was the last time he had to hear from Manuel or anyone else on this score, but also that Manuel went looking for a go-between to ask for his pardon. The thought of facing God on judgment day with the blood of Xan on his hands frightened him enough. Thus, Pablo Pérez, the go-between, wound up bringing the two together. Manuel said he was sorry, asked for forgiveness, and explained that he could not let this go without Xan pardoning him. Xan decided to be magnanimous and told him, "I forgive you, and now you don't have to carry that weight on your conscience." Problem solved.

While villagers were surviving the best they could in the militarized "model village," Father Luis was working with the communities of population in resistance (CPR) only fifty or so miles from Santa María Tzejá, but a world apart in most ways. Luis, who had been so pivotal to the formation of the village, was playing an equally central role under the harshest of circumstances with the survivors who were holding out in the rain forest. After a serious bout with malaria in the late 1980s, he reluctantly left the Guatemalan CPR, crossed the border, and went to work in the Quintana Roo refugee camps in Mexico.

The military had succeeded in flattening the village physically, shattering its social relations, displacing its people, and dominating its present. Yet, the story of Santa María Tzejá was far from over. The village had experienced a remarkable birth and a tragic destruction. The resilience of its people and the spirit they had forged offered a glimmer of hope for the future in a very dark present.

chapter 6

Reunification

After the living hell the village endured, survival would have been a victory in itself. And the village did survive. Villagers built homes on the ashes of the wreckage, worked their land parcels in the unforgiving sun, and once again harvested corn as they always had. The shootings, the torture, and the viselike military control wounded the survivors but failed to extinguish totally the idealism and hope that had inspired them in the first place. As the village was rebuilt from the ruins in 1983, the fate of three groups of peasants—*antiguos, nuevos,* and refugees—was increasingly intertwined, although the groups themselves were separated by mistrust and at times pulled apart by hatred. The *antiguos* and the *nuevos* were living side by side but were torn by differences and conflicts. The third group—refugees in Mexico—felt betrayed by their former neighbors and despised the newcomers as usurpers. Despite their geographic distance, the refugees cast a long shadow over what was happening in Santa María Tzejá. The army did whatever it could to nurture the mistrust and deepen the divides because a fractured village was far easier to control. Bridging these divides, however, was the central challenge to ensure a more promising future for the village.

In the mid-1980s, Vinicio Cerezo, the newly elected civilian president, was eager for political reasons to return the refugees to Guatemala. Cerezo felt the repatriation would symbolize the return of democracy and burnish the country's image internationally, despite the unbridled power the military continued to exercise. To hasten the return, the government created an agency in September 1986, the Special Commission to Aid Repatriates, and set up a place near the Mexican border called Chacaj to receive and settle the refugees.[1]

The Cerezo administration, sensing hesitancy on the part of the refugees to return, decided to give an ultimatum: come now and get your land back or you lose the land forever. First Lady Raquel Blandón traveled to Mexico to meet with the refugees. The government was staking its case on Article 114, a law regarding settlement on national lands, which stipulated that settlers would lose the rights to that land if it was abandoned for a year. The Catholic Church, especially the diocese of Huehuetenango, challenged this move, correctly pointing out that the refugees had hardly abandoned the land "voluntarily." On the contrary, an army onslaught forced people to flee the country and desert their land and homes. While the government ultimately hesitated to implement the law, the very suggestion unsettled the refugees and intensified the pressure on them to return. Some refugee families did in fact drift back to Guatemala in small groups with the government's program, but the majority decided it was best to negotiate an "organized and collective return."

The refugees formed a broad organization called the Permanent Commissions (Comisiones Permanentes, or CCPP) in 1987 to negotiate the terms of their homecoming. The umbrella insurgent organization, Unidad Revolucionaria Nacional Guatemalteca (URNG, or Guatemala National Revolutionary Unity), promoted the refugee organization and exercised considerable influence on the refugee leaders.[2] The CCPP sought to unite the tens of thousands of Guatemalan refugees located in Chiapas, Campeche, and Quintana Roo. Miguel Reyes emerged as one of the top leaders, and many others from the village took on active roles. Surveying the political and military quagmire on the ground, the refugees from Santa María Tzejá were determined to proceed carefully but forcefully. Despite their desire to return, they focused on first achieving their key demands: removal of those now occupying their land, the dismantling and disarming of the civil patrols, and the right to political participation.

The process of reunification in Santa María Tzejá did not begin smoothly in either the village or the camps. When I first spoke with the *antiguos*, most did not want to know much about a possible return of the refugees; the *nuevos* were yet more hostile, not even wanting to raise the subject of the return. Some *nuevos* became very agitated and threatened to fight to the death over their land. "We will wait for them with machetes and guns," one of them said to me defiantly in 1990.[3] Making matters worse, the *nuevos* were understandably suspicious of me, knowing of my prior relationship with the village and that I was shuttling between the refugee camps and Santa María Tzejá. The refugees for their part were initially as uncompromising and took an especially dim view of the *nuevos*. They felt the newcomers were illegal occupiers who were either "with the enemy" or more directly "were the enemy." The refugees were tough, demanding, and at times unrealistic, but their intransigence also reflected what had always been so positive about them, their boldness and determination. In light of the hostility and division, I pointed out, especially to the refugees, what the three groups had in common: all were poor and insecure peasants in search of land.

Miguel Reyes summoned me to his house in the Maya Tecún refugee camp in 1988. In a tense conversation he said that he did not appreciate my interference—bringing personal news, letters, photographs, and tape-recorded messages, among other things, from Santa María Tzejá. These photos included the *nuevos,* so that each refugee could see and learn something about the families who were occupying their land. He wondered about my political purpose in a tone that indicated it couldn't be very good and implied I wanted to promote the return by skirting the refugee organization. He may have also thought that I was assisting, perhaps even spying for, the Guatemalan military.[4] Ultimately, Miguel may have been persuaded to forge new bonds with the villagers—*antiguos* and *nuevos*—by him realizing the answer to a simple question: Who would benefit most from division and intransigence? The inescapable answer: the army. The leaders of the refugees, such as Miguel, also began to feel the pressures and needs expressed by the refugees themselves. The refugees were looking toward home.

In the end, good will proved to be the most pragmatic approach, laying the basis for the return. Good will, however, did not emerge out of thin air. It was slowly developed through personal contact and aided by the political savvy of those in the Mexican camps. The refugees and the *antiguos* began exchanging letters, photos, and news in the late 1980s, slowly restoring bonds of family and friendship. Later, some refugees visited the village, and some villagers went to the camps, bringing the quasi antagonists face-to-face. When they saw each other, anger and recrimination began to fade. The powerful emotions that had united them in the first place proved stronger than the barriers dividing them. Moreover, the *antiguos* renewed the cooperative in the village, further underscoring their common heritage.

The refugees' political skills proved important. I interviewed Miguel several times in the camps and later back in the village. "I think we were able to accomplish the return," he observed in 1999, "because from the very start we linked the plan to come back with the removal of the peasants occupying the land parcels." While some thought the approach unrealistic at the time, this linkage proved important later on. Once the refugees talked over the specifics of their demands with the *antiguos,* the two groups realized they were working toward the same goal: a unified and prosperous village. "There was agreement with the members of the cooperative who were in Santa María Tzejá," Miguel maintained, which in turn strengthened the work the refugees were carrying out in Mexico. The refugee negotiating team ultimately reached an official agreement between the refugees and the *antiguos* concerning the conditions of the return. Thus, when refugee commission leaders met with officials of the Instituto de Transformación Agraria (INTA), or National Institute for Agrarian Transformation, they "pulled the document" at the first sign of government roadblocks to resettlement. In contrast, as Miguel pointed out, "the refugee leaders from other communities had nothing" and therefore were much more likely to fall victim to manipulation and foot dragging. Miguel says that the refugee representatives of Santa María Dolores, for example, mentioned that "they were just coming to put forward the idea of vacating the lands but that the refugees were not yet thinking of returning." The ones from San Juan Ixcán said that if they see the occupiers leave, only then would they consider returning. INTA functionaries were adept at seizing on these attitudes and slowing, if not derailing, the return. While the government and the army wanted the refugees back in the country, they would just as soon see them locate in new areas, particularly if there were army-recruited settlers in the old places. INTA picked up these cues.

Once the people from Santa María Tzejá—refugees and *antiguos*—agreed that reunification was the best course, they covered all their bases. Roselia Hernández and her husband Salvador Castro, two outstanding refugee leaders from the village, moved from the camps to an area in the Ixcán called Victoria 20 de Enero, where they planned to monitor the situation. Roselia was a leader of the women's organization Mamá Maquín, and Salvador was a leader of the refugee commission. I went to visit them in 1993.[5] For reunification to work, the *nuevos* would need something that secured their interest; the eventual agreement offered a plan that would allow them to leave the village with dignity and hope for building a new life: financial restitution for their work in the parcels and funds for purchasing land elsewhere or to set up a business. The United Nations was key in this process. Several European embassies also were involved for many years, and in practical terms the funds they provided through FONAPAZ (Fondo Nacional para la Paz, or National Fund for Peace) were crucial in resettling the *nuevos.*

Pedro Canil emphasized the importance of solidarity in the return. "We were united and we had made up our minds to return," he emphasized. It wasn't easy. The process was plagued with long, frustrating setbacks and delays. In the midst of this morass, some lost hope and were willing to take any offer from the government, while others wanted to slip back on their own. The leaders, on the other hand, realized that strength required unity, and they were determined to keep everyone together—no small task under these circumstances. The Santa María Tzejá refugees were initially scattered in camps along the Chiapas border, their location determined by the date they fled. When the Mexican government forced the relocation of the camps away from the border to the states of Campeche and Quintana Roo, the villagers sought to be relocated together. Most ended up in Campeche in the huge Maya Tecún camp; not only were they in the same camp, but they were in módulo 2, that is, in the same section of the camp.[6] All along they had kept in touch, but their close proximity now facilitated their coordination, communication, and unity.

Pedro Tum stresses that paradoxically friction between the old and new villagers lessened tensions between the old villagers and the refugees, facilitating reunification.[7] The *antiguos* may have thought that a devil you know (the refugees) is preferable to a devil you are just beginning to know (the *nuevos*). "Better they return from Mexico," said one *antiguo,* summarizing the feeling of others about the refugees. "Perhaps we will understand each other better, even if they are with the guerrillas. We will see their faces, they must ask forgiveness." It was not exactly clear why the refugees should ask for forgiveness, since they could as easily have demanded an apology from the *antiguos.* After all, the *antiguos* often divulged the locations of hidden camps, leading to the starvation and traumas that followed. Over time these demands for contrition on both sides slowly melted away, and constructive joint demands took their place. When the option of reunification became a real possibility by the early 1990s, the *antiguos* became more optimistic about their long-term future. They remembered their accomplishments together with the refugees in the dense jungle in the early 1970s, inspiring confidence to move forward. Nonetheless, the animosities didn't evaporate overnight. Angry words and painful charges would erupt even a few years into the reunification. The *antiguos* would echo what they had heard so often from the military—that the refugees had been with the guerrillas and therefore were blamed for all the suffering. The refugees, in turn, would look down on those who had stayed. Complicating the situation, the refugees brought with them strange, Mexican colloquial expressions, dressed and behaved differently, had more education, wider experience, and at times threw their weight around with superior-sounding pronouncements. But eventually everyone settled down to the daily routines of cooperation, each shouldering the heavy commitment of rebuilding. When all was said and done, the cooperative spirit painstakingly forged in the highlands of Guatemala and tempered in the rain forest proved invaluable in the reunification. "[In Santa María Tzejá] the people were better organized from the beginning, they were sharper from the very beginning," Paulino commented. He had fled for Mexico as a youngster and later obtained land in El Petén. "The people who went to Mexico remembered those who stayed behind. They knew they were suffering." Despite the mistrust and anger, their history as a community had not been erased, although it had been tested severely. "When we had the opportunity to return, we communicated with the village, we knew who was here," Paulino continued. "That helped us to maintain the relations. When we actually returned, we felt great happiness to be reunited again. More than anything, it was the understanding we had among us, the consciousness of the community."

This "consciousness of the community" is itself a remarkable phenomenon. The refugees had been living together for little more than a decade in the Ixcán and were not from a common ancestral highland *municipio* with ancient kinship ties. Nonetheless, the experience of building the village had been so powerful that the villagers viewed themselves as a community in Mexico, often in the face of considerable obstacles. Those who were "separated in Quintana Roo would respect the voice of those in Maya Tecún, because they respected and adapted to the voice of the majority," Paulino said. "Thus when we made the decision to return to Santa María Tzejá and we came up with the conditions for the return, they adapted to it." He said dispersed refugees from other villages remained fragmented and unable to reach consensus about the future. "The various opinions among the others were never able to unite," he observed. Several refugees from other communities confirmed their isolation in the camps and, lacking intermediaries to link them to Guatemala, lost contact with their villages. Refugees from Santa María Dolores, for example, were impatient, divided, and lacked a coherent strategy concerning their return. Therefore, they were not allowed back in their village.

Although their time in Mexico was difficult, most of the refugees felt it provided them with important advantages. "In Mexico we had freedom, we could think, analyze," Gaspar said. "We heard the radio, read newspapers, we learned what things were like back in Guatemala, and

through that we were able to analyze what may be the best ways to organize men and women for the return." As a result of this greater openness, refugees developed stronger leadership and organizational skills.
"We thought we should take to Guatemala a solid organization and be
able to unite with the other organizations that were already operating
inside Guatemala," Gaspar added.

Visits and news also helped the process of return. "With that we saw
that the families in the village were alive, as well as the suffering they were
enduring," Paulino recalled. "Your visits opened the path between us more
and more. Your visits helped a lot. Then the situation calmed down a bit
and that allowed for visits among us. We found out that the people in the
village had their arms open, and they, in turn, found out that we had no
conflicts with those who stayed." Ironically, when the refugees were close
to the border, they had no news about their home. "In Chiapas we had
no information," Paulino states. The refugees were surprised to hear from
me that Nicolás had emerged as a leader, since he had never revealed leadership qualities before. Since the most experienced leaders had fled to Mexico, a leadership vacuum had emerged in the village, and Nicolás filled it.
I pointed out that the refugees could think what they wanted about him,
but they had to face this new reality. Any accommodation and negotia-
tion would have to begin with Nicolás.

The *nuevos* became unwitting accomplices of the political manipulation of INTA and the army. Officials would continue to raise the fact that
the land parcels belonged to the *nuevos* because the refugees in Mexico
had been away for more than one year. Moreover, these declarations
would be followed by concrete action such as taking a census and even
accepting payments from the *nuevos* for the land. At other times, another
local INTA official would tell them that everything was up in the air, and
no more payments would be taken. I became alarmed when I heard that
INTA was accepting payments and promising titles, knowing that additional commitments would make it all the more difficult for the refugees
to regain their land. I raised the idea with the *antiguos* of reactivating the
cooperative, which they did. Modest funds were left in the village to hire
a lawyer to investigate how to do this and also how to recover the cooperative house in Santa Cruz del Quiché in order to sell it to obtain further resources.[8] The reactivation of the cooperative proved critical in staking out the land and claims of those still in Mexico.

On one trip to the village in 1988 I ran into INTA personnel regis-
tering *nuevos* and documenting their land parcels. I spoke with them pri-
vately to inform them that the refugees had every intention of returning

and that their registration of *nuevos* and collection of payments for land titles were not national government policy. Any interference at the local level could only be meant to sabotage the negotiations and the possible return of the refugees. I told them I intended to report these local developments to INTA headquarters in Guatemala City, on my way out of the country (which I did, as well as to other government ministries, the Catholic Church, and some European embassies). INTA's behavior in Santa María Tzejá was needlessly complicating and inflaming matters. They stopped the registration midway through the process. At the same time, the *antiguos* wrote an *acta,* an official document, stating that the cooperative had been reactivated and therefore the original cooperative members were part of it, including the refugees. This *acta* was then presented to the INTA representatives who were in the village.

Another important factor fueling reunification was the *antiguos'* sense of tremors of the global tectonic shifts underway. With the collapse of the Berlin Wall at the end of 1989, followed by the even more consequential collapse of the Soviet Union, Nicolás and others realized that peace negotiations in Guatemala were more likely to take place and that the military's interest in the Ixcán might recede. The end of the cold war would also mean less U.S. interest in aiding the Guatemalan military and more pressures on the guerrillas to seek peace. In July 1991, I attended a meeting under the auspices of the U.N. secretary general in Sigtuna, Sweden—one of the first between representatives of the Guatemalan government and the URNG. National and international changes were enhancing the possibilities of a peaceful solution.

The changes taking place in Central America were also making the refugees more eager to return. In 1987 Costa Rican president Oscar Arias had been awarded the Nobel Peace Prize for his efforts to bring peace to the region; by 1990, the Sandinista government in Nicaragua had been ousted at the polls; and in 1992 peace accords were reached between the military and the insurgents in El Salvador. By 1993 the refugees were also scaling down the demands for their return from, at times, unrealistic positions. Miguel Reyes quite confidently told me in 1990 at the Maya Tecún refugee camp, for example, what they wanted before their return, a long list that included the military withdrawal from the Ixcán region. I asked him sarcastically, How far did they want the army to go? Would the other side of the Chixoy River be acceptable? Missing my sarcasm, he responded that those details had not been discussed yet.

Many factors went into favoring the reunification of Santa María Tzejá. I myself feel satisfied to have played a positive, though minor, role in this outcome. Nicolás has tried to take the credit away from the refugees—especially from Miguel Reyes, whom he dislikes—by crediting me with more of a role than is merited. Nicolás also mentions that the guerrillas were a source of information when they came to visit relatives and people they trusted in the village. "The guerrillas would also come here. They came up to a year before the return." I was actually cautious with Nicolás, especially in the early years when the village was militarized, knowing that he had been an informer. I was concerned he might mention to the army, even in passing, my conversations among the refugees, the *antiguos,* and the *nuevos*—something the army would have clearly viewed as unwelcome political interference. Yet Nicolás insisted that he relied on me for advice on strategies for reunification.[9]

The return began slowly and cautiously. Only seven families went back to Santa María Tzejá in the first repatriation in 1988. The rest would come back in the mid-1990s after the refugee organization had negotiated the terms of the return: principally, resettlement for those occupying their land and the dismantling of the civil patrols. As I mentioned, the United Nations and nongovernmental organizations (NGOs) were critical to the success of this complex, contentious process, dragging a reluctant INTA along. The Fund for Peace did come through, reimbursing the *nuevos* for the improvements they had made to the parcels and providing funding so they could buy land elsewhere. Some *nuevos* acquired land in La Trinitaria, the ill-fated USAID project where the army had massacred the villagers. Others settled in Cantabal and opened a store or, in the case of Desiderio Caal Ja, an evangelical church. La Trinitaria now has a school in an elevated area in the village center. People from neighboring villages claim that the school was built over the site of the mass grave of villagers who were murdered in February 1982. The houses of the *nuevos* are visible from the school site.

The official return to Santa María Tzejá finally occurred on May 13, 1994, bringing to an end twelve hard years in the Mexican camps, a lost decade of separation infused with despair.[10] They were flown from Campeche directly to Playa Grande. Crucial, at least psychologically, has been the presence of international *acompañantes* (witnesses or companions) from the very beginning of the return. This has given the returned villagers more courage and boldness. Within several years of the official return, the village had regained a semblance of its original community spirit, a remarkable achievement given the conflagration through which it had passed. The stay of the *nuevos* certainly left its mark. They too had lived, dreamed, and hoped to stay in one stable and peaceful place.

Figure 14. A *nuevo,* Pocomchi'-speaker and Evangelical pastor Desiderio Caal Ja with his wife, Carolina Ak Catún, to his right, by the altar of his church in zone 3 of Cantabal. He is proudly holding his platinum-colored plastic ID card, with his name and photo, which officially identifies him as a pastor of the Misión Cristiana Evangélica "Lluvia de Gracia." He said, "I first arrived in Santa María Tzejá looking for land on May 1, 1984, and I left also on May 1, 1994, exactly ten years later. Now here I am in 2003 without land but with a church." Photo by Beatriz Manz.

But ultimately they had to face the unity and determination of the refugees and rebuild their lives elsewhere. With their peaceful departure, the village had made history. It was and still is the only village in which the original inhabitants were reunited and the peasants who had occupied land departed quietly—resigned to the inevitable.

The return, as important as it was, made a successful future possible, not inevitable. In fact, the reunification might have simply been a fascinating historical footnote had the village stagnated or failed. Instead, some of Santa María Tzejá's most important achievements lay ahead. Villagers reestablished a vibrant cooperative and developed a strong reputation with international funding agencies and NGOs. They constructed buildings, roads, and bridges, and Santa María Tzejá emerged as a strong regional center. The villagers did not simply rebuild, they became an ex-

Figure 15. Antiguos welcome the refugees back to their land and their homes. Photo courtesy Randall Shea.

ample, deploying new technologies and new approaches. They installed solar panels to generate electricity for a new school, a few houses, and even a cellular telephone. A Canadian NGO provided a Mazda truck, individual donors from the San Francisco Bay Area donated a Toyota Landcruiser, and one villager obtained a pick-up truck with savings earned in the United States, all by 1997. In the fields, peasants began experimenting with organic agriculture, simple alternative technologies to protect grains, a reforestation effort, and new links for direct organic cardamom exports.

The aspirations of the village flowed through its school, which the villagers rebuilt with long-lasting cement and considerable care, investing their dreams in the project. The school began with primary grades but expanded to include high school as well. The secondary school principal, a North American named Randall Shea, who had worked as a teacher in the refugee camps in Mexico, played, and continues to play, a key role. He had a solid dedication and unswerving commitment to both teaching and the village. By 1998 all the teachers came from the village itself, an unprecedented achievement. These teachers eliminated the Ministry of Education's policy of offering ten days off for each twenty days of work, a practice meant to attract people to "remote, harsh" zones. For these teachers, the village was neither remote nor harsh; it was home.

The villagers, many of the elders themselves illiterate, have developed a deep reverence for learning in general and a dedication to the school in particular.[11] They view it as the village's finest achievement and therefore hold accountable everyone associated with it—teachers, students, and themselves. The school offers hope for an escape from the "iron law of division" facing peasants: If their children lacked alternatives, they would have to subdivide the land and face sinking living standards. The villagers feel that the school opens up possibilities based on their own children's efforts and merits, not chimera based on vague promises by politicians or anyone else. The parents are still awed to see students, notebooks in hand, walking down paths toward the village center to attend classes. When a teenager is selected to attend the university or a professional school in Guatemala City, there is deep pride and celebration. The school has been so successful that now one hundred students are studying on scholarship at the University of San Carlos in Guatemala City, in Quetzaltenango, in Antigua, and other places. One student received a scholarship to study agronomy in Honduras at one of the best agricultural schools in Central America and another to study medicine in Cuba.

"In the future these students, these sons and daughters of illiterate peasants," Luis commented, "will become their lawyers, their defenders, they will give advice to the community so no one can just walk all over them. That is a tremendous advantage not only for Santa María Tzejá but for all of the Ixcán." Luis recalled that often professionals from the capital "get frightened away the minute they step on the mud"; they can't tolerate the heat, the bugs, the humidity. "That will not occur when Santa María Tzejá has its own agronomist because they are the sons and daughters of the village." Moreover, local professionals are passionately committed to the village. The students give one-year service to the village and pledge a percentage of their income to future scholarships. Aware that Santa María Tzejá can't absorb all the graduating professionals, they realize that they "will have to extend the radius of action to other communities of the Ixcán," Luis said. This extension will no doubt contribute to good relations throughout the region and further heal the lacerations of the war. For example, the municipality of Ixcán hired two young women from Santa María Tzejá. One received her degree in forestry conservation and the other in accounting. Marcos Ramírez, the mayor, told

Figure 16. Edwin Canil, the six-year-old survivor of the February 1982 massacre, at age twenty-six had become an activist and a serious law student at the University of San Carlos in Guatemala City. Photo by Beatriz Manz.

me in February 2003, "This is the first time that our financial books are in order and that we are getting a handle on the deforestation problem." He added, "These two women are exceptional. I don't know what I would do if they were to leave."

In the beginning, reunification was difficult and called for major, at times painful, adjustments on everyone's part. "When we first returned, the people who stayed here did not trust us," Jerónimo remembered. "They thought we were still the guerrillas." He maintained that the *antiguos* sought to frighten the refugees psychologically and politically by implying that the violence was going to resume. "Afterward we began to notice that there was nothing going on," he said. "Of course we were a little concerned [at first]. Now with the peace accords we feel a little better." Paulino remembered the initial tensions. "When we first returned," he said, "those who stayed would always taunt us with comments, and some among us could not resist and would respond." Nonetheless, most refugees were conscious from the beginning that unity was both fragile and essential. "There was an effort to convince ourselves that it was better to wait, not to give it any importance—any meaning—as if what they were saying was nothing," Paulino maintained.

In 1994, leadership of the cooperative included both former refugees and some who had stayed. "We had the idea that there should be a mix," Paulino said. "If [the refugees] had taken all the responsibilities of the board of directors of the cooperative," he continued, "[the *antiguos*] would have felt dominated, that we did not respect their opinions. To avoid that we agreed that it should be mixed." The election of a mixed board allowed a healthy, valuable exchange of experiences, but it made little sense in terms of efficiency. Often the president would be an *antiguo* who was not only illiterate but monolingual in a Mayan language. The secretary or vice president, always in consultation with the president and providing advice (requested or not), would fill in the technical details or recording data on whatever project they were engaged in.

Jerónimo remembered the give and take that characterized the years following the return to the village. "This is the situation: we left; they stayed," he bluntly put it. "Because they stayed they became politicized by the army. Their attitude became 'We don't want you,' and when journalists would come they told them that the guerrillas took their cattle, took their chickens, their corn." The situation became black or white; you are with me or against me. If the *antiguos* didn't do what the army ordered, they had every reason to fear being branded allies of the guerrillas. The returnees, in contrast, thought they had the right to speak out and make demands. They were aggressive in demanding and enforcing government commitments. Those who stayed felt this assertiveness showed a lack of respect for the authorities and could prove dangerous. "We always observed the Mexicans, how they expressed themselves, what they demanded of the government," Jerónimo stated. "We observed and realized that they were right, and that was the way we should act. We are humans. We have rights. We have the right to speak, and we should not allow people to walk all over us."

In the refugee camps they could and did organize. "And we brought all of this with us in our minds," Jerónimo explained, referring to the experience gained in Mexico. "That is why when we got here some said, 'They are guerrillas, because they have that idea of not bowing, whereas we acquiesce. The refugees do not respect the authorities,' and for that they would chide us." I asked him to give me an example, and he readily complied. "On one occasion the army entered the community, and we, the returnees, said that the army had no business coming in here," he related. "The ones who stayed said that we should not say anything against the army, because otherwise the persecution and assassination will start all over again. They were quite frightened. On the other hand we, the returnees, knew a little more how to defend ourselves. We knew about our rights, we did not want to remain silent and hide reality." And what happened? "Nothing," he said with some satisfaction. The returnees were often frustrated by the meekness of those who stayed. "The ones who stayed go along with the authorities and the army imposing things on them," he maintained. "The returnees do not go along with that. We can decide ourselves. They scold us that we don't let others order us around, and therefore we must still be *guerrilleros.*"

The atmosphere in the Mexican camps was far more open than in Guatemala. "The Jesuits would come and give us workshops about human rights, about the Guatemalan constitution," Jerónimo recalled. "Sometimes these seminars would last three days. We learned about citizens' rights and obligations and about the political constitution, what it all means. Those who remained [in Guatemala] were given speeches and training in counterinsurgency to obey the orders of the military." The Jesuits encouraged active participation in learning so that the process mirrored the democratic nature of the content. The army, in contrast, combined an authoritarian message with an equally authoritarian teaching style: lectures in front of large groups and rote learning. No questioning, no participation.

Disputes between the refugees and the *antiguos* revealed the profound divergence in their experiences during the preceding decade. The *antiguos* would rarely take their arguments much further than accusing the refugees of being guerrillas; the refugees, in contrast, drew on new analytical skills as well as on the specifics of what they had learned. "In the first years the ones who stayed were afraid to do anything," Jerónimo observed six years after the return, "but now all of that is out of their minds." He continued, "We came with the idea of rebuilding the community, and we convinced them, and now we are all working together. The way of talking has also changed. I think this is also how it's going to be in the whole country." He said philosophically, "He who wants to walk looking backward is going to fall."

The memories of events in the 1970s diverged sharply between the refugees and those who had lived in the militarized Santa María Tzejá. Consider two individuals who offered differing recollections: Gaspar, who was in Mexico from 1983 to 1994, and Nicolás, who spent these years in the militarized settlement. Prior to the destruction of the village in 1982, Gaspar and Nicolás both supported the insurgency. Gaspar is a Maya, Nicolás a Ladino. I asked Gaspar in 1997 to tell me how many people had collaborated with the guerrillas in the village and to define their involvement. "At the end everyone collaborated in various ways," he readily answered. "The least [involvement] would be helping to give information or to keep the secret [of the involvement of the others]. In either case there was the belief that there would be a victory soon, due to the explanations [the guerrillas] gave us." He clarified, "It also had to do with the attitude of the army. We hated the army. People understood quickly what the guerrillas said because they explained the situation well and the objectives that they were seeking."

Between 1979 and 1981, Nicolás had been among the most enthusiastic members of the Local Irregular Forces, or Fuerzas Irregulares Locales (FIL), the basic unit of the insurgents. "You should have seen him," a villager recalled. "He marched with gusto during training drills, he carried an old weapon, he was committed, he liked being in the FIL." Moreover, Nicolás's brother Sabas had been the first person in the village to join the insurgency. Asked in 1987 why people joined the guerrillas, Nicolás responded quite differently than Gaspar: "People joined because the guerrillas manipulated the people and said they had to go with them.... The army became angry and had to do what they did [destroy the village]. The people joined because in those days we did not know anything about politics, from one group or the other." He said, "So [the guerrillas] took advantage of us by talking with one and then another without people realizing what was going on. Then when we all became aware, everyone was involved."

Gaspar and Nicolás reflect a broader divide in the village. As Víctor Montejo found, "The refugees have chosen exile as a form of resisting and avoiding military repression in Guatemala."[12] In the process, "The refugees have become politicized as they have questioned their social relations in Guatemala."[13] In the case of Santa María Tzejá, those who fled to Mexico were the most experienced, the most involved politically, the ones with the most education. Former combatants can often be very critical of what took place and the mistakes that were made, but they are more inclined to view their participation as necessary and worthwhile. They will say, "It was worth it," or they will affirm their contribution by saying, "I gave my grain of sand." Some even feel defensive, if not offended, by the idea that they were deceived.

The army and its related institutions sought to redefine the past in order to buttress political dominance of the present. The army went beyond separating the villagers from the guerrillas; it sought to dissolve the social bonds among the villagers themselves. Those who stayed avoided speaking about what happened even among themselves. The military for many years became the only authority and *patrón* for those who remained. It relentlessly promoted the view that the guerrillas stood for violence, destruction, chaos, deceit, and lawlessness, while the army represented peace, happiness, development, and truth. This message, however, collided with the inescapable reality about the army's actual role. Nonetheless, since the army dominated the present, some villagers came to believe that they had been manipulated by the insurgents rather than recruited voluntarily to the cause of the guerillas.

Consider the nature of the civil patrols. In 1997, after the civil patrols had been dissolved in the wake of the peace agreements, I asked Nicolás if they had been voluntary or obligatory. "Voluntary," he answered without hesitation, despite the fact that the obligatory nature of the civil patrols had been widely recognized in the country by then. Upon hearing this, I reflected on the impact of his incarceration at the military base in 1982 and the subsequent years of living under military rule. What else has made him so bitter and cynical? What role might guilt play for his alleged collaboration with the military? Personal circumstances shape changing attitudes, and in Nicolás's case, pride, guilt, and stubbornness may have played a part in his insistence on the voluntary nature of the patrols.

In April 1999 I again asked Nicolás if the civil patrols had been voluntary or obligatory, and the answer this time was more nuanced. "They were forced and voluntary," he responded. Could he explain this paradox, if not contradiction, that they were both "forced and voluntary"? He said they were voluntary in the sense that the guerrillas once fired at the center of the village and people wanted to protect themselves. I asked why the guerrillas did that. "Because the army was here," he replied. He then said the villagers did not want the guerrillas to come into the center of the village, although "it was OK for them to be in the outskirts of the village." Then I said, "So that is the 'voluntary' part. What is the forced part?" Nicolás answered, "The forced part is that if one did not do the patrol service, the army would punish you." He then elaborated, "Let's say they would make us work a day at the army base."

Nicolás went on to give many examples of army control, and with each he said it was because the army did not trust the population. Some of his answers were not too different from those he had given years before. Why wouldn't the army let the villagers work in their fields in 1983, the first year after he returned to the village? "Because those from the mountains [the guerrillas] could grab us, so it was preferable that we not go there." I asked him why the guerillas would grab them. "To take you, that is what [the soldiers] said." I then asked, "Tell me why do *you* think the army would not let you go work in your parcels?" "Ah, because [the army] did not trust us. They thought we would go talk to [the guerrillas]." As a result, the army would let them work only in groups of ten or twenty men, and only in the fields closest to the village center. He repeated that the army would check the number of tortillas that peasants took to the parcels. "They suspected we were taking food to the guerrillas," he said with a grin. Moving to another subject, I asked why the village was burned. "It was burned so we wouldn't have anything, no place to return," he replied. "So we wouldn't have a house, nothing." Regarding the massacre of women and children, he said: "Well, [the army] was not just looking for those who were armed, but whoever they found. The orders were to kill anyone they found. It didn't matter."

I asked him once more about his views of the guerrillas. "The army said that we should not let ourselves be deceived by the guerrillas again," he responded. "They only bring problems to the people; they are terrorists."

I forced the issue, "When you heard that, what did you think?" I followed the question by probing more personally, "Given your past collaboration with the guerrillas and that your brother Sabas was the first in the village to become a combatant, was the army describing your brother when they talked about terrorists?"

After a long pause, he said, "Well, when they would say that, one would know what they were doing, that it was a lie, of course, that they were saying that only to deceive the people themselves."

I asked for clarification. "Who used to say that?"

"The army," he said. "They would say [the guerrillas] were terrorists, but the truth is that the whole world knew that was not so."

Ultimately the divergent collective memories of the 1970s began to come closer together. The realization that division would breed failure proved to be a significant motivator to bridge divides. Nowhere was the complexity and importance of finding common ground more evident than among the women in the village. Roselia Hernández was a founding member of the women's refugee organization Mamá Maquín in Mexico and the wife of Salvador Castro, a leader of the Permanent Commissions. "At the time of the return, the most active women were organized in Mamá Maquín," Luis observed. After Roselia returned to the village, however, she realized that her organization was not popular with the local women's group. A local group, Progreso, had been organized when the village was under military control and reflected these roots. "These women were totally and radically opposed to Mamá Maquín in the village, accusing its members of being communists, guerrillas, and troublemakers," Luis remembered. Despite the hostility, Roselia was initially reluctant to abandon her group. She felt that Mamá Maquín was a broader and more sophisticated organization and that the local women were opposed to it out of fear of the military.

The struggle between the two groups began right away. The divisions were serious and deeper than the differences among the men's organizations, since the men decided to join the cooperative. "We in Mamá Maquín looked for funding for our projects, and they in Progreso did too," Roselia recalled. "They pulled and we pulled. So we thought we should call a general assembly." The women called a meeting with representatives from several international NGOs. "The arguing began," she related. "I saw that this was no good. Neither one of the two groups is going to get funding with these divisions." The NGOs also realized that funding one group instead of another would exacerbate the split. Roselia became concerned that the bickering could jeopardize aid for everyone. To make matters worse, while women in the village accused her of being a guerrilla, national leaders of Mamá Maquín charged that she was now allied with the army because of her willingness to compromise locally. Roselia said that some of the women who had stayed in the militarized Santa María Tzejá "would say that the coordinators [of Mamá Maquín] were guerrillas, and I was particularly singled out because I was the one coordinating the organization."

The national organization of Mamá Maquín kept on insisting that Roselia not give in. On one of her trips to Guatemala City, she recalled going to the office on Fourth Avenue in the capital. While there she said, "We saw the problems they are having elsewhere in the Ixcán, and we saw that it is not worth it to create problems." Roselia continued, "So the women of Santa María Tzejá formed a new association and we gave it a name [Unión de Mujeres]." Roselia insisted that "the name has changed but it is the same objective," but the national organization was not happy. Removed from the local realities and often unaware of local histories, it was easier to develop political agendas and development projects that ignored local practical consequences. Roselia knew the women in the village, and she had to live with them. Persisting on meeting and finding common ground, the women in the village reached a sensible agreement. "What we did was agree to put aside both Progreso and Mamá Maquín," Roselia said. "There was general understanding, and

Figure 17. Roselia Hernández, center, a leader in the refugee camps and of the women's organization Mamá Maquín, back in Santa María Tzejá in 1996, running a villagewide meeting of the Unión de Mujeres. Photo by Beatriz Manz.

that is how we formed one group—a new group. That was the end of Mamá Maquín and the end of Progreso, and those projects stopped there. From here on Unión [de Mujeres] became the new women's group. We changed the name. This means that union is now what we women understand."

Still, for Roselia, who was determined and tireless in her efforts and bore the brunt of the criticisms, the conflict "was very unpleasant, very sad." It was particularly difficult when she was attacked both in the village and by Mamá Maquín at the national level. Despite the national group's protestations, Roselia explained that forming a single organization was a logical step forward. "With that we were able to turn down the fire a bit in this community," she said two years after a 1994 impasse. Unity among the women also contributed to calming the tempers among the men. "Otherwise there would have been a huge problem here. I saw that things were not going well. It was important to calm things down. Now things are quiet."

Roselia's determination and strength were impressive. Despite the bitter words, she faced the accusations against her with aplomb because she felt she was right. I asked her how she faced her critics and maintained her optimism. "I just listened. I didn't pay much attention," she said. "I thought it is better to respect the wishes of the community." She was convinced unity was essential. "We better find a solution," she had warned the women in the village. "The community should decide and that is it. There were some who were capricious [among those who stayed], but that was no problem." To her, this compromise was democracy in action, and there was no sidestepping it. Her spirit and her actions reflected what she had learned from the workshops in Mexico.

Roselia was also quite unusual in both her independence and the support and respect she had from her husband, Salvador. They believed in the need for women to be organized and participate politically and economically to achieve development. She was also a firm and outspoken advocate for birth control. She had two children, making it clear to me that she had exercised her choice. She was critical and concerned about women having as many children as they could bear, and she was especially critical of unsympathetic or even antagonistic husbands who wanted women to have unlimited numbers of children. Some women in the village have given over a dozen births. She realized that education was essential and that women should be aware of options and choices. She always linked economic and social development to the number of children per family, but confronting machismo was an uphill battle. "The women remain subject to their husbands," she remarked. "There are many men who watch and control women, the women cannot participate because the men scold them. They will not let them leave home and attend meetings." The problem affects the leadership as well as the rank and file. "I need to do what is convenient to me," Roselia emphasized. "I do not do bad things—I go to classes, I attend workshops, and I go where they ask for me." At times, this leadership role confronted stereotypes and stirred gossip and hostility. "People are always speaking badly of me," Roselia once complained. "They say I am going around looking for men. That is their great mentality. I speak a lot. I speak to everyone, I don't care if it's a man, a woman, a youth. Then sometimes I go to a workshop, and you get to meet all kinds of people. So, when I run into them we greet each other and so on. A lot of people greet me, and therefore some of the people here start with the gossip. But I stand firm, because that is not what is on my mind."

Salvador was supportive throughout the impasse, remembering that the two groups collided almost immediately. Roselia's mother-in-law was also understanding and a great help. Every time I went to Roselia's house, her mother-in-law was attending to the household chores. Salvador admired his wife's political skills. He reflected, "Since Roselia was the leader of Mamá Maquín, she thought, 'We better change the name. We should come up with a name that does not affect one group or the other.'" He was clearly proud of his wife's leadership abilities.[14] I attended meetings of the Unión de Mujeres. The discrepancies in skills among the two groups of women was noticeable. The former refugee women were better able to take minutes, keep records, run meetings, or go to Guatemala City to report on the local meeting. When Roselia, a most exceptional and independent leader, died in 1998 at the age of thirty-six—most likely from cancer—the loss was felt immediately. "Her death was very painful," Salvador said, choked up with emotion and crying. "It was painful for me, for our children, and for the women's group." He was hopeful, however, that the women's group would overcome her loss. "The seed is there! What is needed is that it grow and develop." Women speculated if Roselia had acquired cancer by taking birth-control pills.

Despite the successes of the village and the optimism many villagers expressed, some remained skeptical and critical. Tencho, a combatant since 1979, no longer lived in the village. He was not impressed with the development and did not think people were better off. "The situation in which people live is very difficult," he stated. "There is land but there is no money to invest in it." The lack of funds and markets meant, in his view, that the peasants could only plant enough to eat and cover their basic expenses. "It's not even enough for that," he charged, "let alone to sell products. Instead of selling, we must buy things for our needs. This doesn't mean that we are lazy. We work every day." He continued, "The government's response has been negative in the face of the necessities of the people. What I'm trying to say is that the lands in Ixcán are of good quality, but no matter how good it is, the land doesn't produce all by itself, if there's nothing with which to start and develop." Several others also emphasized the larger economic issues, the problem with finding markets and the low prices for the peasant's production. Tencho somewhat reluctantly recognized the improvements in Santa María Tzejá, admitting small changes in villagers' lives. There was a note of wistfulness as he said he was glad it was now possible to go visit the village. "The living conditions have improved a little because they no longer have to go to work on the plantations on the coast," he admitted. "But the poverty remains the same, that has not changed. People continue to live in harsh conditions. It's only because they already live that way, that they have gotten used to it. They don't go beyond eating corn and beans." He felt that the people of Santa María Tzejá "have learned to suffer."

The pressures on the people of the Ixcán are exacerbated by serious environmental problems associated with deforestation, inappropriate agricultural practices, soil depletion, cattle raising, contamination, and overcrowding. Hurricanes cause tremendous problems and push people further into desperate conditions because they lack a safety net. Access to potable water is practically nonexistent. Rivers and streams contain residues of insecticide and chemical fertilizer, laundry detergents, soap from human bathing, as well as human feces, creating contamination and health risks. The area is seriously affected by mosquito-transmitted diseases such as malaria, dengue fever, and many others. Lack of proper hygiene and prevention also have negative health effects, as indicated by poor latrine systems and improper use of open fires for cooking. Malnutrition is also severe. As a headline in the *New York Times* reported recently, "Malnourished to Get Help in Guatemala."[15] Ixcán is one of the most severely affected regions in the country.

The human population is competing with the natural fauna for space and food. Large hordes of wild boars commonly overrun cornfields, devastating the harvests. The peasants of Santa María Tzejá have to guard their cornfields against these "invasions." As of 2003, the population in the Ixcán may have increased 100 percent since 1982, and in the next few years it will likely reach one hundred thousand people; half of that population is under the age of fifteen.[16] According to local health and development sources, women have an average of seven children, and the annual rate of population increase in the Ixcán is about 3.5 percent; infant mortality is 54 per 1,000 live births, and 78 percent of the population is illiterate.[17] While local census data are unreliable, the growing population density and severe environmental degradation are obvious.

Villagers say that the mahogany was depleted during the years after the scorched earth counterinsurgency campaigns. The land is less productive now. Peasants maintain that the fields used to be greener, the corn yields better. Prior to 1982, palms (*pamaca* and posh) existed in abundance and were used for roofing. "The palms were all depleted" by the people during the militarized phase of the villages in the Ixcán, explained one villager. The ecological devastation during that period was profound and continues at an alarming rate. The mass influx of starving peasants, military corruption, and business speculators all contributed to the uncontrolled harvesting of the precious wood and the resultant deforestation that has now caused severe erosion.

Despite frictions and continuing challenges, the divisions of the past have begun to recede. Returnees are more sympathetic with those who stayed and direct their attention to reconciliation. The *antiguos* criticized the guerrillas because "they had to," Jerónimo, a returnee, now believed, "otherwise they would have been killed. So, to save their lives they had to say that." If some continued talking that way it was because they were still afraid and wanted to ensure, in his view, "that nothing will happen to them." While everyone is acutely aware of their disparate experiences— living in an army-controlled village versus fleeing to Mexico—they no longer wanted to be known as "returnees" or "those who stayed." "Ahora somos todos iguales [now we are all the same]," they insisted. They want to focus on the future, or as Jerónimo would say, they have to walk looking forward. "All is calm now," a number of people commented in 2000, although "calm" has a relative meaning in Guatemala.[18]

The emergence of a more common vision in the village was evident in the last municipal elections. The village invited all candidates to a forum in 1999; the villagers took note of their promises and after the meeting asked each to sign a list of their promises (only one candidate complied). On election day they organized the cooperative vehicles to make several trips to the polls in Cantabal. The village's choice, Marcos Ramírez, the left-wing mayoral candidate, won.

The cooperative remains a pivotal institution, the economic frame supporting the village. Although membership had been a condition for settlement in the village in the past, only about 60 percent of the villagers belonged to the cooperative in 2002. Juan Reyes, who remained in the village, was one of the holdouts. Ironically he is the brother of Miguel Reyes, the former refugee leader and president of the cooperative in 1994–95. "I now have found a way to live individually," Juan said in 1997. "I have my family. It's better to make my cooperative at home. Look, we are four, we work together, we harvest, we sell and we divide the money. Some people think that only with the cooperative one can work. True, they obtain aid and all that, but then there are chores they have to do." He returned to the issue of past efforts. "Now the cooperative members do not suffer as before. But those who suffered more than enough before, know that working in the cooperative is not easy, it is always a bit exhausting." His brother Miguel sat near him with his arms folded, his shoulders slightly arched, and a mischievous grin on his face. He didn't respond, offering a silent "no comment" with his head. The

Figure 18. The vivacious and extraordinary refugee leader Miguel Reyes, left, with his brother Juan Reyes, in Santa María Tzejá in 1997. Miguel returned to the village in 1994. Photo by Beatriz Manz.

reaction of the other cooperative members has also been measured and pragmatic: pretend the dissidents don't exist and do not waste energy in arguments. I once asked if nonmembers were allowed to use the vehicles donated to the cooperative. Villagers responded that everyone has access to all the improvements, including the Toyota, the public telephone, and the cooperative store, and that was fine.

A dirt road, constructed with international funds earmarked for the refugee return, now links the village to Cantabal, the municipal capital, and from there to the rest of Guatemala. In the village center, neither the church nor Luis's house have been rebuilt, but other buildings are functioning again and new ones have appeared. When a project needs to be undertaken between two villages (such as the new bridge to San José la 20), labor is donated from both places. The people supply free labor on rotation; the government agencies provide the material and machinery. While the major projects—such as roads, bridges, communal buildings, development aid, solar panels, a communal phone—were originally obtained as part of the international relief in support of refugee return, the aid also benefited those who had stayed. Donations or grants received by the village, for example, a vehicle or schooling material, are shared with everyone, highlighting the fact that the return has benefited all.

The visible success of Santa María Tzejá raises a critical question: Why was this village able to succeed when so many others have stagnated or failed? Underlying the success was the strong sense of cooperation and community that Father Luis and the villagers forged in the highlands and tempered in the early years in the village. This "consciousness of community," to use Paulino's term, was infused with liberation theology, which provided a moral center that even the onslaught of the military could not break. This spirit survived and was able to provide the energy and framework for the reconstruction.

A number of factors explain why the refugee return succeeded in Santa María Tzejá and not elsewhere. Paula Worby, who worked for the UNHCR in Guatemala and followed the Santa María Tzejá case with particular interest, laid out eight reasons for the village's success, reflecting a combination of solid strategy and good luck. The first three reasons reflect the villagers' political savvy and organizational skills. One clear advantage Santa María Tzejá had, according to Worby, was in great part "due to the presence of Miguel Reyes in the leadership of the CCPP; no other *parcelamiento* had a well-placed representative."[19] The villagers were fortunate to have an effective leader but also understood strategically the importance of playing a broader leadership role in the Mexican camps. Second, "geographic cohesion" played a role, "that is, all the refugees from Santa María Tzejá were practically in the same refugee camp" while refugees from other villages in the Ixcán "were dispersed among several camps and [Mexican] states." The refugees worked hard to ensure their placement in the same camp and kept up good communication with those who wound up elsewhere. Third, the *antiguos* had reestablished the cooperative, which included the original members in the refugee camps, important for maintaining critical linkages as well as for claiming rights.

A number of other factors were important for the success as well. The fourth reason was the presence of sufficient original settlers in Santa María Tzejá, half of the population and therefore a critical mass. In other neighboring villages the number of original settlers was usually very small and as a result did not have the critical mass to support a return migration. Fifth, "arriving en masse inadvertently became the psychological pressure that may have set the *nuevos* thinking they should leave." Sixth, the number of repatriates in 1988 was small, only eight families, thus the local reaction—in Santa María Tzejá and the Ixcán—was subdued. Seventh, INTA had never given land titles to the *nuevos* in Santa María Tzejá, even though it had accepted payments, while in other villages titles were issued to the occupiers. Finally, "Santa María Tzejá was the first among the *parcelamientos* to have negotiated the return," and according to Worby, "one interpretation is that this closed the way for the rest based on the economic and political cost of relocating the *nuevos.*"[20]

Worby wrestles with the importance of circumstance in the village's success. "Whether Santa María Tzejá emerged as the priority case because it had the best case scenario or whether it was a product of favoritism—the only *parcelamiento* to have someone in a position of power among the CCPP—it is hard to tell."[21] She points out that "theoretically, Santa María Tzejá success should have opened the way for other groups by setting precedent. Instead it made those in opposition to the return close ranks, whether the determination to resist came from the campesinos appealing to the army, or the army deciding that at all costs returnees should not establish too much of a beachhead in Ixcán." She elaborates, "How could we know for sure? Certainly there was a moment when the *nuevos* in Santa María Tzejá went from all out resistance to acceptance that they could relocate if several conditions were met. This turning point was critical and palpable." By January 1994, the *nuevos* presented a buy-out plan to FONAPAZ. What role the army played in other settlements to oppose the reunification of the refugees back in their villages is an open question.

The presence of well-organized international accompaniers *(acompañantes)*, dedicated foreigners willing to be witnesses and offer at least symbolic protection, also played an instrumental role in the success of the reunification. Randall Shea, in addition, has provided crucial technical skills as well as long term commitment to the village.

Years after the first successful reunification in Guatemala I asked villagers about the reasons for their success. Usually the question took them by surprise. They tended not to see themselves as a "model" or as special in any way. After some reflection villagers repeatedly pointed to their commitment to reunification as laying the basis for their success. Other villages "remain frightened and sick in the head" as a result of the war, according to Jerónimo. "They think it is a waste to get involved in projects when another war will come and will eliminate everything again." These other villagers remain traumatized to the point of immobility, fearful they might attract the unfavorable notice of the army. "They got in their heads that to join the cooperatives is to join the guerrillas," Jerónimo continued. "They are afraid, so they do not want to get themselves involved in anything. They have their local committee, authorized by the government, and with that they are satisfied." People from neighboring villages cautioned Santa María Tzejá that their boldness will sooner or later provoke reprisals against them. Nonetheless, the village has been bold. Villagers have invited people from the United Nations to give classes on human rights, they are active politically, they have received funding from various international organizations, the women have organized projects, and the school is turning out first-rate graduates.

In other villages of Western Ixcán that have cooperatives, the organization was languishing, according to Jerónimo. He charged that these people were more concerned with getting things out of the cooperative than with putting things into it. People are more eager "to be president of the cooperative than they are to step down at the end of their term," he commented. Other problems contribute to the division and lack of progress. Some neighboring villages either refused or failed to get involved in projects promoted by foreign funding. In other cases, new settlers have successfully blocked repatriation efforts. Santa María Tzejá became the exception. When other villages heard about the departure of the new settlers from Santa María Tzejá, occupants of refugee lands dug in, refusing to leave. The government did not have the will and claimed not to have the resources to find a similar solution.

In Kaibil Balam, a village bordering Santa María Tzejá to the west, strong promilitary leadership sabotaged the return of refugees. An infamous leader named Raúl Martínez, a fundamentalist evangelical Jehovah Witness pastor, had been fostering fear throughout the Ixcán. Virulently opposed to the return of the "communist" refugees, he organized the Association of Patrollers of the Ixcán, likely with military support. When refugees sought to return to nearby San Antonio Tzejá in 1995, he was determined to prevent it. Given his fearsome reputation, a number of people accompanied the refugees to protect them, including representatives from the United Nations and the government's office for repatriation, as well as foreign religious leaders. This high-profile group did not particularly faze Raúl Martínez. He held captive the refugees along with their governmental and international protectors, keeping everyone in detention for two days. Only the intervention of the army and the government at a higher level, sensing an international public relations disaster at the least, made him release his hostages.

Perceptions of Santa María Tzejá have changed radically throughout the Ixcán in the wake of its success. Initially, neighboring villages did not want any association with Santa María Tzejá out of fear of what the army might do. By 2000, however, many looked at the Santa María Tzejá experiment as a model. The secondary school is considered the best in the Ixcán. As other villages saw these opportunities, they began overcoming their fear and sending their own children, who were able to stay in boarding quarters built for them. Other Ixcán villages may even seek to follow Santa María Tzejá's lead in reestablishing cooperatives, sending children to school, strengthening civil society, participating politically, and feeling more confident again.

By the mid-1990s most of the original settlers were back in Santa María Tzejá. A few obtained land in La Esmeralda, El Petén; some remained in Mexico, and some former combatants settled in Guatemala City. Rosa, the widow of Santos Vicente Sarat, kidnapped and disappeared by the military, came back to the village with the refugees' return. She still has the weathered, faded photograph and the crystal-clear memories of Santos and the night the military forcefully took him from their home. Rosario, widow of Andrés Ixcoy, who was killed by the guerrillas, is also back and looking quite frail. Father Luis, nearly seventy years old, returned to the country in 1994, lives in Guatemala City, and is still energetically engaged in village development projects. He raises substantial funds in Spain and still conducts cooperative training workshops. In the mid-1990s Nicolás still had a pessimistic attitude. While he detects some progress around him, his own two boys did not get beyond elementary school, and one of them spent time in prison for "delinquency."[22] Valentín, whose family was the first to settle Santa María Tzejá, is now the effective principal of the secondary school, and his wife, Magdalena, the best student at the Chichicastenango boarding school in the 1970s, is a certified teacher in the village's school. Jesús, father of five children living in Kesté, Mexico, in the mid-1990s, was considering migrating to El Norte and was looking for a *coyote*, as these years draw to a close.

Looking Back on the War

The signing of the peace accords at the end of 1996 brought a formal end to the bloody fighting between the Guatemalan military and the insurgents. Santa María Tzejá was at the vortex of this conflict from the very beginning. About fifty men and women from the village were actively involved with the insurgents. Many others were political organizers, secured food supplies, acted as couriers, and supported the rebels in other ways. Four combatants died in the war. After the signing of the peace accords and the subsequent demobilization, I spoke with several former combatants (some of whom had been interviewed years earlier) to gather a sense of their own reflections of their years in the insurgency, how they viewed the peace accords, and how they view the future. Their thoughts not only provide a fascinating glimpse into how they see the past but also offer insight into what the future might hold. The views of several seasoned former combatants highlight their extensive experience during the height of the conflict and the demanding nature of their reintegration into civilian life.

A large literature, much of it written over the last four decades in the wake of outbreaks of insurgencies from Vietnam to Nicaragua, seeks to analyze the role of peasants in Third World revolutionary movements. "Frontiers of research move with history," Goodwin and Skocpol observe, "although often with a lag."[23] The research on peasant rebellion that emerged from the 1960s is riven with deep intellectual divides: The Wolf-Paige debate seeks to define the type of peasant drawn to insurgency; the Scott-Popkin debate focuses on the context and psychological motivation of peasant rebellion; and the Paige-Scott debate questions the "moral economy" argument. Goodwin and Skocpol point out that "two myths have long colored popular views about revolutions in the Third World: that destitution, professional revolutionaries, or perhaps both are sufficient to precipitate revolutions; and that local events in Third World countries are easily manipulated by imperialist Great Powers."[24] They then quote Goldfrank, who argues that theories of peasant insurgency limited to poverty and professional revolutionaries as explanations "are not wholly illusory, but as theory they do not take us very far. Both widespread oppression and inflammatory agitation occur with far greater frequency than revolution, or even rebellion."[25]

As demonstrated in Santa María Tzejá, peasants became involved in the revolutionary movement because of a vision of a radically different future. That vision of a better society was rooted in a political consciousness shaped by liberation theology and the cooperative movement, as well as the hope of being able to have a better and fruitful life in the "promised land." Unlike most peasants, those in Santa María Tzejá had sufficient land; they did not work in plantations, they had no *patrón,* and they were not sharecroppers. Nonetheless, they felt insecure about keeping their land, and their efforts to improve their lives were choked by military repression and authoritarian rule.

After years in the trenches, how did the former combatants view their participation after the fighting had stopped? Given their depth of commitment to the insurgency, I was particularly interested in hearing their assessment of the long war and the future prospects for peace. Most former combatants felt positive, though not necessarily optimistic, about the peace accords. "Everything the URNG wanted was signed, and this will lead to democracy," Jerónimo, a former combatant for a few years and then a refugee in Mexico, stated. "So the URNG won." He then reflected for a moment and added, "Now if these accords are not implemented as they should be, then it's no good." Almost everyone I spoke with in the village, from former combatants to critics of the guerrillas, felt the insurgents represented their interests in one fashion or another at the negotiating table. There is a general consensus that the guerrillas won politically, but lost militarily.

In fact, despite the traumas they had endured, some former combatants would have preferred an out-and-out guerrilla victory, something that in retrospect sounds quite implausible. "When the war got bigger, when it had strength, it seemed as if the guerrillas were going to win," Tencho said. "But the strength of the government kept getting bigger, with support from the United States, so how could the guerrillas win? There was nothing left to do but to retreat. . . . The truth is that we didn't achieve what we had hoped." Yet, he also agreed with many that while militarily the guerrillas may have lost, politically they achieved something. "I think that peace was negotiated," Tencho continued, "because neither side, the army nor the guerrillas, wanted to continue the war. That is, the URNG thought that they would never take power with weapons, and that it was better to try through political means. . . . Peace was reached because the military force was used up on both sides. Also, the URNG was tired in the jungle and realized they were beaten."

Those who joined the insurgency were for the most part fighting for broad ideals as well as immediate, tangible gains, such as bringing an end to military oppression. Fundamentally they wanted better social, political, and economic conditions in Guatemala. Despite their physical isolation, many combatants had an awareness of international issues—particularly the fate of other revolutions, such as those in Cuba and Nicaragua. Moreover, much of the fighting took place at the height of the cold war and the combatants were well aware of U.S. support for the Guatemalan military. They were also aware, in general terms, of the competition between the United States and the Soviet Union. As a result, some adopted the attitude that the enemy of my enemy might be a friend, although overwhelmingly the conflict was driven by local, regional, and national issues. They were caught in the global cold war, but in their view they were not participants in it; they viewed the conflict as local.

María, a vivacious K'iche' woman who joined the EGP as a combatant at the age of eleven, stated, "Victory wasn't achieved because, given the international situation of the socialist camp and what was happening in Nicaragua and El Salvador, there was demoralization in the EGP. There were internal problems among the leaders as well as personnel changes. What was left was just negative." The combatants from Santa María Tzejá followed international news keenly. "The Sandinista victory [in 1979] had a great impact because it was a revolutionary victory," Tencho stated. "But unfortunately it only lasted ten years." Güicho also felt that the Guatemalan struggle could not be divorced from changes in the international scene. "At first, yes, I thought that the guerrillas would accomplish the objectives that were foreseen: to beat the army, to take power and start a revolution. But then the international situation got more and more complicated...From that point on the guerrillas [in Guatemala] had to consider a dialogue with the government and the army."

Ultimately most former combatants from Santa María Tzejá blamed Guatemalans themselves for not achieving the goals of the insurgency, expressing the view that perhaps, unlike the Vietnamese, they did not have the patience or willingness to sacrifice. "The Vietnamese had nationalist views. The U.S. direct presence there contributed to that," Jesús, the political organizer in the Local Clandestine Committee (Comité Clandestino Local, or CCL), says. He observed that "in Guatemala, the United States was also involved, but behind the scenes." He added, "Also, the Vietnamese had a lot of help from outside, such as from the former Soviet Union," which the Guatemalan insurgents did not have. For Braulio, the United States' economic and military might was critical: "Capitalism had too much force. Nicaragua triumphed but then they lost it. So the solution was the peace accords, which we achieved in Guatemala."

While Tencho viewed the end of the war as inevitable, he felt that social conditions in the country have not changed much since the conflict began in the 1970s. His concern over the deplorable economic and social conditions are not without merit, given either the lack of improvement or deterioration indicated by the social statistics of the country. "Regarding the peace accords," Tencho said, "it's true that the peace was signed on December 29, 1996. But I think that this peace only served to maintain the rich landowners in their positions of power, so they can keep exploiting people. This peace wasn't good for the poor at all, because it didn't resolve any of the needs of the peasants. On the contrary the peasants continue to live in poverty as before." He then added, "Those who came out winning were the wealthy, the landowners, because they didn't have to spend any more. They got what they wanted. For the peasants there is no peace. There is no freedom. Maybe oppression and discrimination diminished some, but they continue in other forms. They simply put candy in the mouths of the poor so they won't cry, as if they were small children."

Several Mayas from the village doubted whether the professionals graduating from universities will in fact be able to obtain positions and salaries commensurate with their degrees. The fact that a professional in Guatemala has a certain physical and cultural profile may hinder those from the village in obtaining well-deserved jobs, in their view. Since social networks are essential in placement and advancement, a professional from Santa María Tzejá will likely have to fight an uphill battle to compensate for these shortcomings.

One also hears frequently that the low-ranked, indigenous fighters were abandoned after the peace accords were signed, without land or training opportunities, and were left to fend for themselves. The Ladinos in the insurgency "don't have those worries, because they were able to adapt, they even have cars, their children are in school," Tencho insisted.

Martín, who returned to the village and worked alongside his father in the parcel, recalled the day of the demobilization. "After turning in my weapon, I was a little sad because I was not sure if the government was going to carry out the peace accords. But the war lasted thirty-six years, it had to end finally. However, the fight still continues. Our way of fighting is through politics to achieve democracy in this country." "We have to fight with our mouth now, not with weapons," is how Jerónimo put it. But, he added that "fighting in the mountains against a clearly defined enemy is easier than changing people's ideas. To combat ideas is the most difficult thing there is."

María reflected on failures within the guerrilla organization in the mid-1980s. "At first I believed the guerrillas would achieve their objectives; in fact I even repeated this because it was my job to organize the population, but the times change, everything changes, and you start noticing the achievements and failures. I remember the first big blow, which was when a group we called the Factionalists split off [in 1984] from the organization and turned against it," she recalled. "Now, after everything, you can see that they were right in some respects—there were things that they realized were going badly. For example, at first the organization thought that all the people would be participating, but it didn't turn out that way. Because there was no shortage of people who opposed the guerrillas and supported the army." She agreed with the objectives of the guerrillas and wanted to believe they were obtainable. "Well, I think that the guerrillas also exaggerated because I remember they said that when we obtain power, all of the peasants were going to live well. Everything would be evenly split between men and women, to tell you the truth it sounded very nice." I asked her if it had been worth spending more than fifteen years of her youthful life in the insurgency. Her response turned personal as she reflected on the changes she went through while she was in the insurgency. "On the one hand, yes, because the way the situation was, if I had stayed with my parents I wouldn't be the kind of woman I am today. I would have lived a normal civilian life with a lot of children. My vision or my world would have been limited to what surrounds me." In contrast, she maintained, "Now I value myself, I even feel that I am ready for any job that they give me, in any area of, say, education or health." Nonetheless, she paid a price for her participation, "I feel that my involvement in the armed struggle left me traumatized, because I get very depressed about everything I saw, everything I suffered. I always dream of the soldiers in the jungle, that they are following us and killing my *compañero* and my children." María, who lived on the outskirts of Guatemala City at the time of our interview, said she has at times questioned herself about the path she chose: "Sometimes I regret it, when I see that we have no money." She said the first time she wondered about her involvement was during the big army offensives in the late 1980s when the guerrilla could not stand up to the army. "That is when I opened my eyes and we talked with other *compañeros,* and we realized the army was grinding us. And you begin to feel insecure about what you are doing. And then you begin to question things."

Several former combatants found challenges in adjusting to civilian life and complained of having difficulty in making friends and communicating—even the vocabulary seemed different. This is compounded by the fact that many who did not return to the village—about a dozen people—are performing marginal, menial, low-paying, and insecure jobs. "At first when I reentered civilian life, legal life," Domingo said, "to tell you the truth I couldn't get used to it." The problem was not simply in adapting to new social settings and daily routines but also in the difficulties of making a living. Only a few former combatants from Santa María Tzejá who requested land or training received a positive response. They are now settled in El Petén with other former combatants. Most are left to find their way on their own. "Those of us who were in the war are now the ones who are most at a loss in finding a way to live," Domingo continued. "My idea now is to find work, earn a living to support my family, find a place to live, some land, a house for my children, give them the education that I did not get." The only training Domingo has had, including six months in Cuba, has been war related. "I am trying to find ways to learn a skill that would allow me to earn a living." He did not have a stable job in Guatemala City, although he kept active with the political organization formed by the URNG. In contrast, Sabas, one of those who chose to settle in El Petén, even though he had a land parcel in Santa María Tzejá, did not find the adjustment to peasant life complex and was optimistic about the future. "No," he said, "it was not difficult to go back to that work." And surprisingly, despite the fact that he grew up in a household that was unusually distant from the K'iche', and he himself is light skinned and could pass as a Ladino, he regarded himself as indigenous. In fact he has become a member of a Mayan national organization, although he did not know how to speak K'iche' or any other Mayan language.

Many feel they had emerged from the insurgency as different people and therefore found little in common with their peacetime social environment. The personal once again blends with the political. Among many complaints, María expressed one type of annoyance: "There have been the problems we face in our jobs, because we were taught [in the insurgency] to be very exact in our actions, dedicated, very punctual. And if I commit myself to something, I want it all to come out well. It bothers me when other people don't do their part, when they are only interested in getting their paychecks. It's hard for me to accept that attitude. Sometimes I feel as if I can't tolerate it." María, in her early thirties at the time of my interview, felt that she learned much in the insurgency, where she spent most of her formative years. As a woman, she came out of the organization with a very different attitude and became a vocal advocate for women's rights. She noticed that several men went back to the domestic violence so prevalent in their parents' lives. The women no longer have the recourse of the organization to bring up these issues.

Tencho, among others, recognized serious crimes and injustices committed by people in their own ranks. "There were times when the URNG committed grave mistakes," he admitted. "For example, executions of the civilian population, those who were called *orejas* [spies] for the army. Some people they executed hadn't committed crimes; others really were spies for the army. But there were cases where simply because of envy, hate, or anger between people one accused the other. And they were shot unfairly. This left people with resentments."

Overall most of the former combatants did not regret their decision to join the rebels. "I think that giving my grain of sand in the struggle was not just for nothing," Jerónimo expressed. "It was through this struggle that the peace accords were signed, and they contained what the revolutionaries wanted. The foundations for a new era for Guatemala were thus set, though we know it is a long-term process. Now we have to make sure these accords get implemented. That task now is not with arms but with politics." Because he left the ranks many years before the demobilization, he held grudges against the URNG. "It really bothers me a lot that they don't consider me a revolutionary. They have not taken me into account in the demobilization nor in the courses that are now available." I asked Jerónimo if his wife and children know of his revolutionary past. "My oldest son knows. He has admiration. He feels very proud. My wife says, 'I feel proud to be with a man who struggled, was truly in the battlefield and nothing happened to him,'" he said with a pleased smile. I asked him what he felt was the legacy of the war. "It would be worse if there had been no war, because then no one would have taught them [the rich, the army] to respect us. Instead, now they are afraid. Now they know people will not just go along, that people know how to defend themselves with arms and form a large organization. Also I personally would not have had the ideas I now have." He paused as he reflected on what he wanted to say. "All of this is a door that is open, and each day it opens more widely for the future benefit of humanity. To know their rights and obligations as citizens."

Over and over former combatants as well as other villagers emphasized that their parents had never heard the term "rights," let alone "universal human rights." And they proudly stated that they now have legal rights, even if they are not always able to exercise them. Emiliano as usual was direct and quick in his answer to the question if the struggle had been worth it. "If it had not been for the ideas of the sixties, when we got to the nineties we would still be in a darkened thick fog [*tinieblas*]. We would still not be able to see beyond what the eye can see. In general we are better off, but at the individual level perhaps we are the same as before." Asked if he had doubts, he answered quickly, "No, doubts I did not have. Because even if victory was not achieved I still had the vision that something had to be gained. That is why I felt that to surrender was cowardly."

Paulino, a noncombatant who collaborated with the insurgency and is now critical of the guerrillas, said, "What is positive about the struggle is that it opened minds. It left big lessons." He felt people like himself are more astute about social and political matters now as a result and, like so many in the village, he pointed to the awareness of human and civil rights. "Before, whatever the government said or did, that was the law." He, like so many others, also mentioned that his parents, and surely his grandparents, never knew about human rights. "My grandfather never knew that there were laws that protected his rights. He depended on what the authorities told him. He never realized he had rights, nor could he speak Spanish or write even one letter. I can read a little, can speak a little Spanish, and more or less know that there are laws that protect us." He, unlike his grandfather, understood that all citizens are equal under the law. "Yes, now I understand that. But my grandfather never got to understand that. He used to say that being rich was a power that God gave that person, because he has that money." Some villagers related similar stories that their fathers or grandfathers felt that being rich was God given. By implication the rich had to be respected and thanked for providing food for the peasants.

A veteran combatant such as Sabas felt that all in all, "For the poor, what the war left them was even more poverty." Yet, when I asked him if he had regrets, if he was sorry he was the first in the village to join the insurgency and had stayed for sixteen years, he said, "I did not waste my time. I am not sorry. I learned a lot and gained a lot." When asked about what he had learned, his answer appeared to lie between the mundane and the surreal. He said he learned to type, and then he continued, "I got to see many places and meet many people. Now it feels like a movie, but a real film." He then elaborated on the difficult days in the guerrillas, the hunger, the exhaustion, but he said it was all an experience that serves him well today. He ended by saying rather philosophically, "One thing is to see; the other is to live it." Would he join the struggle again? "It is very difficult to say." But after thinking for a while he added, "However, with a different approach I would dare again, even if we had to use the same means." In evaluating the war overall, he restated, "The war left the poor in further poverty, more abandoned and with more debts. The war left us with more difficulties. . . . We had a good ideal. We didn't achieve it for many reasons."

Martín had hidden with his family in the jungle in 1982 and ran as the army approached and fired, narrowly escaping with his life. He subsequently became separated from his parents for fourteen years. He joined the insurgency as a teenager in 1986, while in the refugee camp in Quintana Roo, and remained in the ranks until the demobilization in 1996. "I feel proud to have been in the war for ten years, struggling to achieve [*lograr*] democracy in Guatemala," he reflected in 2000, and then added, "It was never my idea to struggle for six months and then go home. No,

I wanted to achieve something. I was thinking of everyone." He elaborated, "I was in the guerrilla ranks, gaining experience and learning something better. We hope from now on the peace process goes forward. That is to be seen." He reflected, "I'm not saying whether it's going to happen or not. It's a process. There are always difficulties. The army will do political work. They'll try to screw us over. We are conscious that we have to face difficulties along the way of the peace process. In my case, my feeling was that if I die, there was nothing I could do, but I know that I fought for a whole people, and not for nothing." He continued, "Our aspiration was to achieve life with dignity for every village and town in the country, and to have our rights and identities as indigenous people respected, as well as accords regarding the role of the military in civil society. Now I hope the peace process will go forward."

When Domingo was asked the same question—if it had been worth it—he paused for a very long time, thinking of his response. "Yes, I think so," he said finally, "despite the fact that there were errors. But personally I think it was worth it. I learned how to read and write. And I also feel proud that I struggled, I worked so many years for the benefit of the people." Despite the wounds and suffering, he said that had there been no war, "We would be even worse off." He mentioned the political space and participation that was created as part of the gains. "The government on its own would not do anything. They do it now because they are pressured, though the aid is coming from abroad, but all of that is a product of the war and the peace accords." Braulio also agreed, "It was worth it. The accords that were signed are the basis for a new life that will start in Guatemala. It was worth it, though it cost blood, it cost lives, but yes, it was worth it."

Jerónimo felt that what he learned in the guerrillas has been of use as he carries on his life as a husband and father, a peasant, and a member of the cooperative in Santa María Tzejá today. Juan stated simply, "I am glad I participated," adding that the foundations have been laid, and "what is needed now is for the people to demand their rights. The rights are there. But if we don't demand them, then they are worth nothing." Güicho expressed concern that political leaders (formerly with the URNG) may stray from a path that would bring the much needed changes through the political process. "I think this is a very important question because I have heard a lot of *compañeros* saying—even when we were in the organization—that perhaps it's not worth it to be fighting, that perhaps afterward, our leaders will become reactionaries or will take some path that may betray the people. We talked that perhaps many former combatants, like us, won't be taken into account and will be left without jobs, just as in fact is happening now after the signing of the peace accords. Many people are unhappy. For example, some have managed to get jobs and are doing well while many others don't know what to do, how they will eat." He supports the fact that "some of our leaders are now working to form a legal party for the people. I hope that they don't stray from this path, as other former leaders have done. Of course it wouldn't have been worth it to fight for so many years if afterward the leaders choose another way, with reactionary ideas, and leave the people stranded by the wayside." He concluded by saying, "Without a doubt the guerrilla movement, historically, will be viewed as having aimed for something positive, it was an experience, it has a history that cannot be forgotten. An effort was made to achieve something of benefit for the people."

Pedro Tol responded in a similar way. "It was worth spending nearly twenty years in the organization, to struggle against the injustices. I did not waste my time. I worked for the organization and I took advantage of the time to learn." Braulio, who was back in Santa María Tzejá, felt it was worth the struggle even if little was accomplished concretely or immediately. "If we had not struggled we would even be worse off than before," he maintained. "The war woke us up, we realized and learned many things, such as how to organize, to be united, we were forced to struggle out of need." He pointed out that the rich had become organized. "The rich wanted to keep us down, expecting that none of us would rise up, that we should be conformists and continue living as we have been doing. Because of the war, we consider that we changed a lot, our mentality, how we work, how we organize." He then went on at length to explain that the war occurred because of the desperate conditions in the country. "It did not arise because we felt like [fighting] it."

Pedro Tol said he thought there would indeed be a victory, at least he was convinced that there was a need for change in Guatemala. Yet, he realized that victory would not have been without difficulties, because an insurgency does not end with the taking of power. "After victory then comes another difficult period, because a revolution depends on the international *coyuntura* [juncture], because without economic and moral support, and if the internal situation is not resolved, then the revolution drowns." For him it was difficult to deal with a new strategy of negotiations and accept a new, very limited dream after struggling for so long. "When the strategy changed I suffered internal frustration and so many things I found no answers or explanations for." He felt that at least the insurgency managed to "slacken [*aflojar*] a bit the political power of the [army and the elites], but that small change came at a very high cost for the poor people in general, a very high price in lives, destruction, dislocation."

Perceptions of the future tended to tread between apprehension and hope, a wait-and-see attitude. The most pessimistic view was expressed by Tencho, a K'iche' Maya, born in the highlands of Joyabaj. He joined the insurgents at the age of twenty-five and remained in the ranks sixteen years. Forty-six years old in 2000 and a father of eight, he lived in southern Mexico. "We will end our lives as we are; there is no hope for a better life because there won't be any. We will just make use of what is in our reach, and what is not, well." As a result, horizons have become more limited, he said. "We also don't have dreams like the one we had before. We'll struggle for our lives, for the family, as much as possible. For my part, I no longer want to fight for the people, to be thinking the way I did before. I believed that everything was going to be accomplished easily." He looked back to the time of the Mayas. "The land was theirs, there were no lines, boundaries, or *ixcos*. The Mayas lived through difficult times, but they didn't live away from their land. They learned to cultivate and make use of the most fertile land, while today there is nothing." There was a renewed interest among villagers in Santa María Tzejá in examining their Mayan ancestry. This is encouraged in the village's school as well as through the adult participation in Mayan historical and cultural workshops and in researching and producing a book on Mayan culture based on local knowledge.[26] Emiliano puts his faith in God. "Given the hardships I am going through I wish in ten years I will have money to buy at least the very basic necessities for my family. Now I am very poor. I have no cash. But I ask God that this situation change sooner than in ten years, because who knows if I will still be alive then."

The sentiments, memories, and reflections of the former combatants are complex, nuanced, and at times contradictory. No doubt their responses were often deeply personal and evolved over time, as they examined and reexamined their situation and prospects for the future. The reflections among former combatants are likely to be more critical of the insurgency. On the other hand, in the village, where others blame them for their role in dragging the village into conflict, former combatants may feel the necessity to reassert the values of the insurgency. To an outsider they are likewise more likely to give a positive interpretation: it is an opportunity to validate their struggle. One also detects conflicting views about their struggle—remorse at the suffering, regret for time lost, and humiliation for the lack of victory—yet they possess a continued belief, given the poverty and marginalization, that more fundamental change is needed.

Unlike the former combatants, many of the *antiguos* tend to be far more critical of the war years. In simple terms they view this period as a net loss and thus in retrospect wish it had never happened. Their experience, their stake, their psychological engagement are profoundly different. The *antiguos*' participation tended to be for a shorter term and more likely as irregular forces (FILs). A few families that were against the village's involvement with the insurgents (but went along), have in the aftermath taken a self-serving stance, as if saying, "I told you so."

chapter 7

Treading between
Fear and Hope

I t took more than a decade after the worst of the violence, but eventually the Catholic Church, the United Nations, and the president of the United States rendered a verdict about the horrors suffered by villagers in Santa María Tzejá and the rest of Guatemala. The verdict appeared in two forceful reports—cited extensively throughout this book—and an unexpected, historic apology. The Recovery of Historical Memory Project, or Recuperación de la Memoria Histórica (REMHI), issued a scathing study in 1998 entitled *Guatemala Nunca Más!* (Guatemala Never Again!); the U.N. Commission for Historical Clarification, or Comisión para el Esclarecimiento Histórico (CEH), produced a twelve-volume report a year later entitled *Guatemala Memoria del Silencio* (Memory of Silence); and President Bill Clinton visited Guatemala in March 1999 and apologized for the role of the United States in that country's bloody past. "For the United States it is important that I state clearly," he said, "that support for military forces and intelligence units which engaged in violence and widespread repression was wrong, and the United States must not repeat that mistake."[1]

Bishop Juan Gerardi was the guiding light behind the Catholic Church's report. He knew firsthand the extent and viciousness of the violence—he had been the bishop who shut down the diocese in the province of El Quiché in 1980. He released the report to a somber, attentive audience that packed the cathedral in Guatemala City on April 24, 1998. Two days later he was bludgeoned to death in his garage, underscoring the contemporary relevance of the horrors documented in the report.

The CEH (U.N.) report charged the Guatemalan military with genocide in a stunning judgment that sent tremors through Guatemalan society. The CEH did not equivocate: No other country in the hemisphere has been charged with genocide. The findings are worth citing at length. "After studying four selected geographical regions," the report declares,

> the CEH is able to confirm that between 1981 and 1983 the Army identified groups of the Mayan population as the internal enemy, considering them to be an actual or potential support base for the guerrillas, with respect to material sustenance, a source of recruits and a place to hide their members. In this way, the Army, inspired by the National Security Doctrine, defined a concept of internal enemy that went beyond guerrilla sympathisers *[sic]*, combatants or militants to include civilians from specific ethnic groups.[2]

The report continues,

> The CEH concludes that the reiteration of destructive acts, directed systematically against groups of the Mayan population, within which can be mentioned the elimination of leaders and criminal acts against minors who could not possibly have been military targets, demonstrates that the only common denominator for all the victims was the fact that they belonged to a specific ethnic group and makes it evident that these acts were committed "with the intent to destroy, in whole or in part" these groups [Article II, first paragraph of the convention].[3]

Therefore, in a finding that shocked many, "The CEH concludes that agents of the State of Guatemala, within the framework of counterinsurgency operations carried out between 1981 and 1983, committed acts of genocide against groups of Mayan people."[4]

This judgment was of great moral importance to the people of Santa María Tzejá and so many others like them who had suffered grievously at the hands of the military. No longer feeling alone, on the contrary feeling vindicated, the village has sought to pursue justice. The Association of Family Members, victims of the massacre of February 15, 1982, brought charges of genocide against the army in July 2001, an act of enormous courage. Filing their case with the Department of Public Prosecution, they specifically charged three generals, including the head of state at the time, General Lucas García. This precedent-setting move, carried out together with three other villages, made front-page news in Guatemala, placing Santa María Tzejá in the eye of the storm once again.

The villagers have journeyed through the most punishing of storms and, despite the fact that the dark clouds have yet to lift, have sought to rebuild their lives. They cultivate their parcels; harvest corn, beans, rice, and cardamom; repair their homes; and tend to their daily lives—cooking, washing, mending, caring for their children. They have a well-run cooperative, regular meetings, women's organizations, and many projects to improve the village. An undercurrent of apprehension nonetheless haunts their lives—a sense that individuals cannot let their guard down, a fear of new violence, and a knowledge that the peace accords are fragile.[5] "This peace process is not irreversible," the deputy director of Guatemala's U.N. mission affirmed. "If Guatemala doesn't have a period of social peace so that these changes can take hold, things could begin to fall apart. There is still the danger of a return to the past."[6] On the sixth anniversary of the peace accords, the United Nation's Mission in Guatemala issued a press release listing some still unmet commitments:

> It is impossible to ignore that discrimination and poverty, principal causes of the internal armed conflict, still have not been eradicated.... It is impossible to ignore the persistent high levels of impunity, and that the defenders of human rights and labor and social leaders have to continue operating in the current climate of threats and intimidation. It is impossible to ignore that the population in general has to continue suffering the effects of violence and of a constant insecurity.[7]

The shadow of that tormented past falls over the village. Occasional lynching and lawlessness in the countryside remain a frightening reality in Santa María Tzejá.[8] The slow pace of social, economic, and political change continues to breed disappointment and frustration. Fear became reality on May 14, 2000, at 2:10 A.M., when the cooperative store in Santa María Tzejá was torched. Everything was incinerated: merchandise, accounting books, records, and office equipment. Villagers estimated the loss at fifty-two thousand dollars, a colossal amount. There had been several other attacks before, such as holdups of the cooperative vehicle and the robbing of everyone on board. These attacks are "not mere chance," according to the cooperative's board, but rather "follow a premeditated plan to destabilize the regular operations of our cooperative." In fact, the fire had been set ten days after relatives of those massacred brought formal charges of genocide against the generals, and on the very day the village was celebrating the sixth anniversary of the return of the refugees. The villagers call May 13 the "Holiday of Reconciliation and Initiation of the Reconstruction of the Community," a feat no other village has been able to achieve. After the burning, to the surprise of neighboring villages, the villagers made a unified, bold, and determined response to rebuild. The people of Santa María Tzejá secured funds—much of it raised internationally—to construct a new cooperative, and they now have a more effective security system. The attack, however, is an ominous sign that the village is in someone's sights. Many believe the

Figure 19. Seventy-year-old Petronila de la Cruz in 2003, back in the village, washing clothes in the Yarkon River, named for a river in Tel Aviv. Photo by Beatriz Manz.

military and its allies—disbanded civil patrollers well practiced in bullying, violence, and acting with impunity—were responsible for the attack on the cooperative.

Most alarming was the murder of Domingo Us Quixán, a returned refugee and a strong, outspoken community leader. He was shot to death while working in his parcel on June 28, 2001, an attack that underscores everyone's vulnerability.[9] Now the simple act of cultivating distant fields surrounded by a thick forest—something that almost all family members practice—is cause for anxiety. While the village responds to these traumas courageously, the repression and fear take their toll, creating a state of mind someone has termed an "emotional coma."[10] The villager most severely tortured at the military base in 1982, who remained physically and psychologically impaired, recently recognized one of his torturers in Cantabal. This encounter was devastating.

As I stated in the introduction, there are no "typical" villages in Guatemala.[11] Santa María Tzejá is especially unique given its particular genesis and trajectory. The overall issues affecting this village, however, are all too familiar: racism against Mayan populations, impoverished peasant conditions, economic exploitation and insecurity, human rights abuses, and military control. When all is said and done, this village tells a story of the collision of hope and fear, courage and death, roadblocks and optimism, grieving and determination.

Research in settings of pervasive violence such as Santa María Tzejá is not easy, as I have surely come to understand over the years. The fear and psychological scars make talking to people about the past particularly complicated. Remembering can be painful and at times traumatic, and the risks of confronting the past are real. Powerful forces interfere by attempting to define how events are recalled, to shape a past that mirrors the present they would like to see.

The unprecedented charges of genocide against the army finally brought national and international attention to the abuses endured by Santa María Tzejá and countless other villages in Guatemala. The respected German jurist Christian Tomuschat, who was appointed head of the CEH, stated that though knowledgeable about events in Guatemala, "not one of us could have imagined the dimensions of this tragedy, not even the Guatemalan commissioners who had lived through the experience directly."[12] He also placed Guatemala in the U.S. orbit: "Until the mid-1980s, the U.S. government and U.S. private companies exercised pressure to maintain the country's archaic and unjust socioeconomic structure."[13] As Guatemala comes to terms with the past, a desirable outcome for the future would be for the international community, and more importantly for Guatemala itself, to address the racism and historical contempt of the Mayans as well as the structural and social problems that marginalize so many in the society. For the United States, however, Guatemala has vanished from the political radar as if the country and its problems have disappeared along with the cold war. Yet, the destruction, poverty, lawlessness, violence, and impunity that grew to such alarming proportions, fed by the cold war, remain a malignant legacy.

Within Guatemala, a broader discussion is difficult since it "is a country whose rulers have for half a century suppressed historical memory as if it were a poison," writes Stephen Kinzer in the *New York Review of Books*. "Now, for the first time, there are serious demands to examine the past."[14] In this context, the collective memory of Santa María Tzejá is in transition, fashioned not only by the legacy of military action but also by the return of the refugees and a more open national dialogue. Refugees became more politicized, and many returned with a deeper awareness of their rights. National dialogue came in the wake of negotiations between the military, the government, and the Guatemalan National Revolutionary Unity, or Unidad Revolucionaria Nacional Guatemalteca (URNG), the insurgent umbrella group. These negotiations led to the December 1996 peace accords, an amnesty, and this broader national desire, at times hesitant and still fearful, to come to terms with the past.

Memory

The role of memory played a critical part in writing this book. When accounts diverged at critical points, I had an important resource to draw upon: my own recollections and, as important, my personal judgment that matured over three decades of visiting the village. I had the advantage of perspective developed over time and tempered by history. I had participated in important moments of the village's life, spoken to people as critical events unfolded or soon after they happened, and remembered the roles that villagers played. Moreover, I had written field notes. I may have had a record of what a villager told me in 1985 that I could compare to what he or she said in 1997. Sometimes stories blurred; other times they shifted—thus the importance of looking at the role of memory.

Memory is central in defining the ways in which individuals in Santa María Tzejá interpret the past, view the present, and think about the future.[15] Memory affects an individual's assessment of others and his or her willingness to engage in collective activities. The role of memory is also important to a researcher in reconstructing the past and interpreting the present. Scholars have noted the importance of understanding memory by documenting the interpretations and recollections of individuals and groups, during and after violence.[16] Guatemalanist ethnographers have also recently emphasized the effort to recover memory and interpret the Mayans' situation in the war.[17] "*La violencia* gives a shape to memories and to later experiences of repression," Warren observes.[18] Zur notes, "The entire history of *la violencia* can be read as a war against memory, an Orwellian falsification of memory, a falsification of reality."[19] Falla, Montejo, the Equipo de Antropología Forense, and others have produced detailed, moving accounts of the experiences of villages during the terror in the 1980s, to recapture what took place.[20]

This village does not speak in a single voice. While practically everyone collaborated with the guerrillas, vast differences exist among the participants concerning the degree of their participation, the reasons why they became involved, and more generally the ways in which they remember the past. In the mid- and late 1980s, when asked to recall the violence, those who remained in the militarized village remembered certain "fixed events" without disagreement, such as when the army entered the village, the number of people killed, dates and time, and the army's culpability. What became contested were the interpretations and recollections of degrees of participation and individual motivations. When respondents make statements recalling the past, several considerations shape the dynamics at play: the role of memory, personal background, experience since the event, apprehensions about speaking frankly, and outside forces influencing the discussion.

On one level, memory reflects the struggle of an individual to deal with the past. The villagers' more conditional answers are rooted in the fact that, as Primo Levi stated, "human memory is a marvelous but fallacious instrument," often shifting or obfuscating its outlines. "The memories which lie within us are not carved in stone; not only do they tend to become erased as the years go by, but often they change, or even grow, by incorporating extraneous features."[21] In the aftermath of major social and political upheaval, events are reorganized even more rapidly. Those who lived in militarized villages, such as Santa María Tzejá, may not have distorted the past in their minds, but history is a remarkably heavy burden to come to terms with. Some "lie consciously, coldly falsifying reality itself," Levi observed, "but more numerous are those who weigh anchor, move off, momentarily or forever, from genuine memories, and fabricate for themselves a convenient reality. The past is a burden to them; they feel repugnance for things done or suffered and tend to replace them with others."[22] Over time, if not challenged, the distinction between the early and the later remembrance "progressively loses its contours."[23] It does not take much to reshape a suggested image: small omissions here and a bit of embellishing there until a new picture emerges that embraces the current context and, over time, barely resembles the original.

On another level, memory is both collective and socially formed. "Collective memory is biased towards forgetting that which is negative," Maurice Halbwachs suggests, and painful or shameful events are even more difficult to handle.[24] Halbwachs's main contribution to understanding the molding of collective memory is in formulating its shifting and fluid nature, the collective interest of a group to recall their common past in a selective, acceptable, and partial manner. Collective memory is clearly a social product, but individual memory also flows from social context. Individuals tap their own recollections, draw on discussions with each other, and filter these perceptions of the past not only through their own interim experiences, but also through the social arena in which society as a whole interprets these events.

One way of legitimizing the present is by reshaping the past or, if faced with factual truths, by rationalizing the terror that took place. A career Guatemalan military officer somewhat surprisingly delved into the French social theorist Michel Foucault in his book *Historia moderna de la etnicidad en Guatemala* (1998). Cifuentes claims to draw on Foucault to interpret recent historic events. He writes that there could be various interpretations of events, inferring that "there is a historic truth in Guatemala, which is a truth from the perspective of power and that is the one that we know and accept."[25] Nonetheless, as Hannah Arendt puts it, facts possess "a strength of [their] own: whatever those in power may contrive, they are unable to discover or invent a viable substitute for [them]."[26] Unfortunately for those who seek to deny or reshape an uncomfortable past, "facts assert themselves by being stubborn" and are, ultimately, "beyond agreement, dispute, opinion, or consent."[27] This tension between interpretation and reality is the terrain on which memory is constituted.

The relationship between the researcher and an individual or a community is at the heart of the process of documentation and interpretation. A respondent's perception of the researcher may influence, even determine, what is said. Jesús, for example, became confused at my persistent questions during an interview in 1997. At one point, he blurted out: "You mean, you don't care what my position is, what I think, you don't care if I am for the army or the guerrillas, it doesn't matter to you? You want to hear what I really think?" At first, he assumed that my purpose for writing about the village was to buttress my point of view, and he wanted to show his consideration by telling me what he assumed I wanted to hear. I inquired further about this attitude. "When someone we don't know asks a direct question, the first thing we think about is, who is he?" he confided. "Why is he asking this question? What is behind the question? What are the consequences of my answer? We try not to give a direct answer until we figure out where the question is coming from. Then we respond accordingly. For example, if I know you are Catholic I give one type of answer, if I know you are Evangelical, then another. The same, and even more so, politically." I looked at him and smiled. "Hmm, same here," I said, "I also try to find out where a person is coming from before I interpret what I am being told." He laughed heartily.

Trust is central to ethnography. Participant observation requires a level of confidence that grows unevenly and deepens over time. Often this confidence develops in personal interactions, sharing the jokes and gossip of everyday life; at other times it is reflected in insights about sensitive matters where a chance comment could have catastrophic consequences; on occasion it is tested in trying times and reinforced in the aftermath of crisis. Researchers need to be trusted, but also the researcher needs the ability to assess the informant. Trust increases with patience, often requires restraint from overt judgments, and can grow when one is repeatedly called on to be a mediator. Year after year these villagers afforded me hospitality and exceptional confidence. At the height of the militarization and violence during the early and mid-1980s, they confided their collaboration with the insurgents and divulged details of what took place. I often feared for them as well as for myself for knowing about their activities, such as relatives in the guerrilla forces coming to visit them secretly in the village. Confidences, familiarity, arguments, and disagreements over many years laid the basis for discussions that could be open, at times painful.

Given the apprehension peasants feel, the challenge for a researcher is to discover what people thought as the events were unfolding, and to understand what factors have molded their current memory and point of view. In many Guatemalan villages, diverse, often contradictory, memories coexist uneasily concerning relations with the insurgent forces, and Santa María Tzejá is no exception. As we have seen, while the entire village provided at least tacit support to the guerrillas, people recall that collaboration differently. Some remember their involvement with the guerrillas as a conscious decision, fully voluntary, and are proud of their actions, even in the wake of the devastation that rained down on them. They blame the army for the massacres, terror, and destruction. Others admit to having provided support but in retrospect feel they were deceived. A few remain very resentful and fault the guerrillas for provoking the massacres and destruction. Thus after twelve years of separation the villagers shaped different collective memories of the events. Once the village became reunited, the former refugees began to dominate the discussion. Their version of events was buttressed by the peace accords; the U.N. Commission for Historical Clarification and its report, *Memory of Silence;* and the archdiocese report *Guatemala Nunca Más!*

Coping with the Past, Defining the Future

In Santa María Tzejá, villagers have taken various paths to address the past, including human rights workshops; providing testimonies to commissions of inquiry, particularly from the United Nations and the Catholic Church; writing and performing local theater productions; insisting on exhumations; publicly denouncing the crimes in national and international forums; erecting a monument to the memory of those killed; and bringing legal charges against the military in court.

Their devastating experiences—painful to recall and even more difficult to come to terms with—were engaged in an extraordinary play called *There Is Nothing Hidden That Will Not Be Uncovered (No Hay Cosa Oculta que no Venga a Descubrirse),* written by young people and teachers, particularly Randall Shea, in the village. It narrates the story of the violence of 1982. After initial angst, disagreements, and fears of reigniting reprisals by the army, the play was performed in the village itself for the first time in the mid-1990s. The performance spurred intense discussions and caused heartbreak, tears, and trauma, but also, most important, accelerated the process of coping with what took place. The play was so powerful that the theater group took it on a national tour, and it is now generally viewed as a proud accomplishment.

Few activities at the secondary school have so energized the students as theater productions. The day of a performance produces great expectation as well as preperformance jitters, and the entire village gathers. International visitors have come to see *No Hay Cosa Oculta que no Venga a Descubrirse,* the first and most dramatic of the plays. The BBC has taped the performance and has included it in a documentary under the title *No es tan Fácil Olvidar* (It's Not So Easy to Forget). Another play examines racism and discrimination against the Mayans and the working conditions in the *fincas,* portraying submissive Indians being abused on the plantations. Watching the audience is as fascinating as watching the play. They roar and laugh most heartily when the Indians are portrayed as humble, deferential, and subjugated; the actors lower their heads, not daring to look at the *patrón*—they bow, they thank, they trot willingly at every shouted command. The play, written and directed by the students organized as the "Teatro Maya," has provoked serious discussions about social issues throughout the community. This play was called *This Is How Our Mayan Fathers and Mothers Suffered (Así Sufrieron Nuestros Padres y Madres Mayas).* The most recent play, *A*

New Fire Lights Our Way (Un Nuevo Fuego Nos Alumbra), had its debut performance in February 2003. It was directed by a Santa María Tzejá advanced art student, Leonel Bolaños. With the music of Ravel in the background, the play is a very hard-hitting exposure of domestic violence and other gender issues. As with the first play, which provoked political anxiety, this play will no doubt be controversial and will have some older male critics.

The young people in the village show the greatest promise for the future, especially those who had been in Mexican refugee camps. Many were born and educated in Mexico, became used to a more open setting, and returned with a confidence seldom seen in rural Guatemala. In contrast, their counterparts came of age in a tightly controlled village where military authority and fear prevailed, education was not emphasized, and teenage males were forced to join armed civil defense patrols.

The success of the village since the return has drawn on a few key institutions: the school, the cooperative, and villagewide committees.[28] Santa María Tzejá has established an elementary and secondary school staffed by dedicated teachers from the village who are accountable to an elected parents' committee. These teachers have made a difference. More than one hundred students are pursuing professional degrees elsewhere in Guatemala and even abroad, and many more have engaged a solid basic education. This achievement has created a spirit of hope: Sons and daughters of peasants can aspire to what was unthinkable for their parents.

This impressive educational achievement has a down side as well. A sharpened inequality exists between those who attain professional degrees and those who till the soil, or are unemployed and marginalized. The optimism and self-confidence of educated villagers stands out even to a first-time visitor to Santa María Tzejá; the resentment and despair of those faced with far fewer alternatives has already created problems in this and nearby villages, inflamed by the general lawlessness in the country. A third alternative to enterprising and energetic individuals from both groups is to migrate north. For uneducated youth, migration to the United States provides an alternative to the lack of jobs and land in their own country. For those with professional degrees, migration could become an alternative to not finding a job in their own chosen career. The possibility of working as a construction worker in the United States may look better than being unemployed or underemployed with an accounting degree in Guatemala.

The cooperative is less central to the life of the village than it was in the early years, but it still binds people together and creates economic opportunities. Although membership is not mandatory today—nearly half of the villagers have not joined—most of the development projects are channeled through it. Interestingly, Miguel Reyes, the key leader in the refugee camps in Mexico and president of the cooperative in Santa María Tzejá when he returned to the village, is no longer a member. Salvador Castro (widower of Roselia Hernández), another refugee leader and an important leader in the village, also resigned from the cooperative. Nicolás, on the other hand, is an active member and the veterinarian—a critical position. He is also the president of the cattle-raising committee. He is performing these tasks admirably. In 2003, María Hernández, a thirty-three-year-old K'iche', became the first woman president of the cooperative. One of the recent projects of the cooperative is the attempt to commercialize hearts of palm *(palmito pejibaye)*. The women's organization is packaging fruit juice for sale.

An increasingly serious problem throughout Guatemala is a more general lawlessness, fueled by decades of violence and disregard for human life and the law, as well as continued economic hardship and exclusion. Rural gangs have emerged in what previously were villages largely free of violent crime. The result has been imprisonment for some and even the killing of a Santa María Tzejá youth.[29] Getting drunk, taking drugs, stealing, burglaries, raping, and taunting fellow villagers have become more frequent. While Santa María Tzejá may have fewer social problems than other nearby villages, it nevertheless confronts tough, at times shattering, issues; alcoholism has been and continues to be one of the most serious social problems in the village, which exacerbates other social dysfunctional behaviors, such as domestic violence, incest, rape, drug abuse, depression, murder, and suicide.

A New Path Heading North: Jesús Meets "La Migra"

A significant new trend emerged in Guatemala in the mid-1980s: migrations by rural Guatemalans to the United States in large numbers.[30] Evidence of this trend is visible throughout the countryside. Small offices of King Express, a courier that specializes in U.S.-Guatemala service, dot rural areas throughout the country, and a successful new business is charging for calls on solar-powered cell phones that connect people to their relatives in the United States. In Santa María Tzejá, those individuals who have access to dollars have set up stores, purchased land, acquired pickup trucks, and bought cattle. Those with links to the North

(El Norte) are able to set up a small business that generates modest additional income to farming. Probably about fifty individuals from Santa María Tzejá and from the refugee camps in Mexico have sought safety or opportunities in the United States since the mid-1980s, and the money they have sent has been important to the village and has created new divides.

Jesús, one of the most promising students in the Chichicastenango boarding school in the 1970s, who dreamt of becoming a teacher, went ahead with his plans to reach El Norte in 1996. He had decided to stay in Mexico after the collective return of fellow refugees because he was fearful of going back. Yet, he knew there were no opportunities for advancement in Mexico, and the possibilities in the North finally proved irresistible. He saw that those who had relatives or had themselves gone to the United States were able to improve their houses or start a small business. A better life for his family beckoned. He said to himself, "If people who never amounted to anything, and who had less education than I had, made it in the United States, why couldn't I?"

He had walked with his father down the demanding trail from the highlands to the rain forest over twenty-five years earlier, and now he made the tough journey north across all of Mexico to the United States border. With several others, he found a *coyote*—a guide to help them cross and lead him to safety on the other side—whose charge was more than one thousand dollars per person. Instead of leading them to safety, however, the *coyote* abandoned Jesús and his companions in the Arizona desert, a frequent occurrence when conditions become too hazardous or the *coyote* simply doesn't care. The others with him, buckling under the fierce heat of the desert in the day, the chilling cold at night, the gnawing hunger, and, most of all, the desperate thirst, headed south back to Mexico. Not Jesús, he refused to give up; he was too close to his dream— providing a better future for his family. On the third fatigued day, laying in a ditch in the desert in the punishing heat, he tried desperately to squeeze fluid out of an avocado, frantic and near death.[31] He asked God what he had done to deserve this suffering. A Native American woman who spotted him turned him in to the border patrol and that, as it turned out, saved his life.

With the sun burning into his soul, Jesús met "La Migra" (the Immigration and Naturalization Border Patrol) in the Arizona desert. He was given water and food—unlike hundreds who have died of heat exposure—and then put in an INS detention center.[32] Jesús had memorized my phone number from six years earlier when I had stayed with him and his family in a refugee camp in Mexico. When he phoned, I was surprised—actually I was shocked—and immediately arranged legal aid for him. After a few months in detention he was released to Berkeley pending a court decision and ultimately obtained political asylum a few years later. Now forty-four years old, Jesús lives with several Guatemalans in an East Oakland apartment, works as a gardener, and has since been joined by his elder daughter and son. Earphones in place while he works, he listens to popular national Spanish-language talk radio Única AM 1010; in the evenings he watches Univisión TV. His wife and three smaller children remain in Kesté, Mexico. His remittances have built a solid concrete house. He is resentful and cynical about the insurgents now and still despises the military. He is focused on himself and his family, saves as much money as possible, and attends English classes at the Berkeley Adult School, a support group, and religious retreats. Jesús has remained deeply religious since his days in Shalom Alehem. Given that his own education was interrupted because of the violence, his goal is to have each of his five children become professionals. No sacrifice is too great to achieve that aim. There are some similarities, he mentioned with a wry smile, between his trek down from the mountains to the rain forest in Guatemala and his crossing the border into Arizona: in both cases he was hoping for a better life, did not know the way, and was opening the path with his hands. In Guatemala it was the thick, green forest; in Arizona it was finding his way with his hands at night while avoiding the dry, prickly brush of the desert.

Magdalena Ixcoy, the niece of Andrés Ixcoy, left the village in 1987, one of the first to leave for the United States from Santa María Tzejá. She was sixteen years old at the time and was able to find work as a live-in maid in Rancho Santa Fe, one of the wealthiest "villages" in Southern California. She earned four hundred dollars a month. Her daily work routine began at 6:30 in the morning and usually ended around 8:00 in the evening. She worked six days a week. Sundays she was off.

While villagers view migrations north as worthwhile, those who have gone to the United States have encountered abuses, and a surprising number have returned to the village voluntarily. Homesickness, loneliness, nostalgia, culture shock, and the reality of a hard and alienating life in the North have made many think twice about living away from their familiar though impoverished village. Some migrants were repeatedly cheated of their wages, subjected to urban violence, or defrauded by the courier companies. "What is the point of sacrificing in the United States?" one person now back in the village stated. "I worked hard, there was no job I would not do, they always gave us the leftover jobs, the heaviest, the hardest. I was honest, responsible, and then when I sent my little savings to my family, I was deceived, I was robbed. There was nothing I could do. I lost more than two thousand dollars once." Jesús echoed the same refrain. "We get the leftover jobs, the dirtiest, the heaviest, and get the lowest wages." Villagers from Santa María Tzejá work in construction, factories, landscape and gardening, and house painting. Young women work in housecleaning, babysitting, nursing homes caring for the elderly, and meatpacking plants.

I heard disheartening accounts of mistreatment. Francisco, from Santa María Tzejá, working without documents in 1997 as he crossed the United States from one job to another, would pick up a phone card at a 7-Eleven and call me once a week—just to talk, often not sure where he was. On one call, he told me that he had sent almost three thousand dollars from Florida to his wife in Santa María Tzejá, but the money never got there. When he told me his bad news he was already far from Florida, ironically building a roof for a prison near Washington, D.C. Although very upset, he seemed resigned to accepting the loss, not seeing much of an alternative. While Francisco had little information about the agency in Florida, I was able nonetheless to track down the business. I gave the manager one week to deliver the money, and mysteriously, the money arrived into the hands of the needy family in Santa María Tzejá in time. Francisco himself is now back living in Guatemala.

Rural Guatemalan Mayans are especially vulnerable in urban settings in the United States. They tend to live in the most depressed areas where violent crime, racial hostility, and drug use are common.[33] The poverty and social decay of the inner city often places new arrivals side by side with the poorest, most neglected and discriminated-against Americans. Living in extremely crowded dwellings in an effort to save as much money as possible to send home, Mayan immigrants often venture out in groups for protection when going to the Laundromat or store. They sleep on the floor, as many as two dozen in a three-bedroom house. Unprovoked attacks and taunts are common against these defenseless, often diminutive migrants. Jesús called me nervously once to say he had just been violently robbed of all his money. When I told him I would call the police and wanted to know if he could recognize his assailant, he pleaded with me not to inform the authorities. "Yes, I know him. He is always on drugs, he hangs out by the Fruitvale BART station or the liquor store. He will harm me even more next time if you call the police." A few days later, as I copied all of his documents for safekeeping in case of another rob-

Figure 20. Felipe Panjoj gave up earning dollars in the United States and returned to the more comforting, though poorer, life in Santa María Tzejá. This photo shows him at home in the village with his wife, Estela Larios, and three of their children. Estela was orphaned in 1982 when her father, Diego Larios, was killed by the military. Photo by Beatriz Manz.

bery, a depressed Jesús sadly reflected that all in all, the situation never changes fundamentally for Guatemalans; for him the rain forest and what he calls the "cement forest" or the "gold cage" have unfortunate similarities. In the face of countless obstacles, the familiarity of the village beckons some. "I am content with a tortilla," said Felipe Panjoj, who spent several years in Los Angeles and Florida. "At least now I am home."

In another incident, two Guatemalans waited in the parking lot of Walgreens drugstore in East Oakland before being picked up for work. The job was to clean an abandoned house and yard in the Berkeley Hills. The yard contained a dead dog, full of worms and a horrendous stench. At the end of the day they waited for the *patrón* to pick them up and pay them for their ten hours of work. He never showed. Racial and ethnic stereotypes easily emerge out of incidents of abuse and exploitation — unfairly targeting entire groups out of the actions of a few. According to the Guatemalans, even if desperate for food, they would no longer work for "los Tongas," immigrants to California from the Pacific Island king-

Figure 21. Dollars he earned in the United States helped Víctor Tebalán set up his store in Santa María Tzejá, which in 2001 was adorned with a poster of pop singer Shakira. Photo by Beatriz Manz.

dom of Tonga. In one instance a crew worked for "un Tonga" contractor for a week. The boss said on Friday he would go to the bank to get the cash to pay everyone. They waited and waited until nightfall. He never showed up. With no public transportation available, it took them several hours to find their way back to East Oakland. On another occasion "un Tonga" apparently threatened a Guatemalan with a machete.

Although migrants tend to focus their attention on returning home, the overwhelming majority of Guatemalan migrants stay in the United States, especially now that crossing the border has become more difficult, dangerous, and expensive. They continue to make contributions to the economy in the United States—toiling in some of the most arduous and least desirable jobs—as well as providing substantial aid to their home communities. Remittances are becoming increasingly important economically to Guatemala, totaling close to $1.7 billion in 2002, as they are throughout the Americas.[34] While the United States sent large amounts in military and economic aid to military regimes during the cold war, the aid to Guatemala, which includes Peace Corps funding, amounted to $67 million in 2002.[35] The amount sent in remittances by July 2002 ($781.4 million) had already surpassed revenues obtained from coffee, sugar, bananas, and cardamom combined ($631.15 million).[36] Estimates of the number of Guatemalans in the United States, mostly from rural areas, range from 250,000 to a million (Guatemala's population is eleven million). About two-thirds are in California. Remittances from these displaced individuals surpass U.S. economic aid to Guatemala.

Reflections

The success of Santa María Tzejá against tough odds highlights a troubling paradox: The village's accomplishments—impressive as they are—underscore the limits to achieving development on the village level alone. Despite its impressive achievements, international funding and aid sustains the village today. It remains to be seen how long this international support will continue, or be essential. Young people now attend professional schools, yet those who remain do not have potable water and are vulnerable to tropical diseases. Professional degrees, moreover, may not guarantee a professional job. Migrants return from the United States with enough money saved to buy pickup trucks, yet often do not earn enough to repair or replace the vehicle. Nutrition, health care, housing, and earnings have not changed much since the early 1970s. The larger social and economic context creates a wall of indifference. The cooperative is active, yet access to state-level resources and infrastructure is almost nonexistent, choking the possibilities for change. The Guatemalan government lacks an effective development strategy, and few resources are available from the international community, particularly the United States. Writing about Chiapas, Mexico, in the *New York Times,* Ginger Thompson might have been describing the Ixcán as "the deepest corners of a region so cut off from the world by poverty, racism and impenetrable geography that many of the people live without electricity, health care or paved roads."[37] Moreover, unbridled corruption—often at the highest levels of the government and the military—is fueled by Guatemala's emergence as a major trans-shipment route for drugs from South America to the United States. The legacy of violence, impunity, and a dysfunctional legal system makes the mixture of drugs and corruption even more lethal and further plunges the country into poverty.

I came face-to-face with this sad reality on a trip to the village in December 2001. I encountered a young child while walking down a path. He was shy and barefoot and wore torn homemade pants and a faded, ripped shirt that revealed his overblown belly. Both his eyes were infected. I took a photo as he stared at me expressionless. Looking at him through my lens I recalled a similar photo I had taken in 1973. I watched him for a while realizing how little in fact some things had changed. I made a mental note to remember to date this photo so I would not confuse it with the one that was thirty years old.

Several factors stand out in the short history of this village. The families that migrated from the cool highlands to a tropical rain forest were bound by a cooperative and brought to bear tremendous inner resources on the tasks before them. They were not saints—that makes their story all the more impressive—but determination drove their abilities to unexpected heights. The very isolation of the region compelled them to work together, and in the process, a strong sense of community developed. They faced harsh and seemingly endless challenges together. Father Luis, the priest who inspired the cooperative and inaugurated the village settlement itself, was crucial to the success of the project. He was an authority people trusted and admired; though demanding and impatient at times, he embodied remarkable dedication and selflessness and had an unbending determination. He had broad links throughout Guatemala and to the outside world—without this aid the village would have found it much more difficult to succeed then or now.

Military repression combined with insecurity over land titles fostered deep anxiety and anger. As a result, villagers were more open to the message of the guerrillas. While some families were skeptical or fearful about any relation with the insurgents, others were vocal and enthusiastic. Despite their differences, the villagers presented a united front to the outside world, especially to the army. Unlike with other villages, where the military was able to find informers, the army had far less success in Santa María Tzejá. The fate of each was linked to the fate of all. The nature

Figure 22. Father Luis Gurriarán (right) has been a promoter of cooperatives and a long-term companion of Santa María Tzejá. He sits with Gaspar Quino at a meeting of the cooperative directorate in 2001. Photo by Beatriz Manz.

of military repression changed over time. The villagers had endured the arrogance and brutality of the army both in the highlands and in their new home in the rain forest; fear and humiliation at the hands of soldiers was not a new story. The appearance of the insurgents caused the brutality to become widespread terror, and once unleashed in a society in which impunity ran rampant, the terror exploded into massacre and despoilment.

When the military finally made its move, destroying the village and murdering everyone in its path, it uncovered fissures and resentments that fractured the community and would keep it divided for years to come. In the wake of the tragedy, some families decided to place their fate in the hands of the military; others were trapped by the soldiers. With the guerrillas on the run, those who had turned themselves over to the army—they tended to be the least politically involved—remembered the assertive, arrogant, and to some, overbearing political pronouncements of the guerrillas and their sympathizers. With the army in firm control of the village, compliant villagers were not hard to find.

Among those who fled to Mexico were the activists, the leaders, and the most educated. Their exodus was a sign of defiance as well as a bid for survival. In the refugee camps they regrouped and again made the decision that working together would bring the best results. The solidarity that had developed over a decade of building the village now held them together in a new, uncertain place and allowed them to negotiate their return effectively. In contrast, the village was fragmented in Guatemala; the new settlers, recruited by the army, added anger and mistrust to the mix. For the military the divisions and tensions kept villagers divided, but in the end it was to be the army's Achilles' heel. The reunification of the settlers who had remained and those who had fled to Mexico succeeded because many of the original settlers, or *antiguos,* tired of the frictions—ethnic, religious, political—and disunity with their new imposed neighbors. The timing of the refugee return was well planned and had the support of the *antiguos.*

I have argued that a "consciousness of community" is central to the understanding of this village. Recent anthropological theory delivers sharp critiques of the very notion of community, challenging it as a concept that is reified, romanticized, and homogenizing. In Santa María Tzejá several factors underscore the formation of community, principally that diverse individuals had a new exposure to the values of liberation theology coupled with a new understanding of rights. These perceptions were cemented by the cooperative to which they all had to belong. They realized the importance and benefits of unity and consensus and that only through active participation could improvements come about. In addition, the isolation created a further sense of common purpose. The fate of each villager was intertwined with the fate of the community. Reciprocity became the norm, and the sense of commitment to each other grew. This sense of community is not an imagined subaltern solidarity. I am aware that in many rural localities the realities of conflict and divisions overwhelm common bonds, but in this case, the villagers formed a community by choice rather than as a byproduct of geography or ancestry.

Santa María Tzejá has revived, but at a cost; it is no longer the community it used to be. The social erosion, brought on by the destruction of the village in 1982, is a continuing challenge. Moreover, the village now exists in a new national and international context. Villagers are more individualistic; families are more prone to look after themselves. When the old generation of settlers is gone, the next generation will have a different perspective—a different trajectory—and will live in a different

Figure 23. The remains of Vicenta Mendoza, whose tombstone inscription was written by her nephew Edwin Canil. It reads: "Vicenta Mendoza 1950–1982. Civilian woman viciously assassinated in February 1982 by the Armed Forces of the Guatemalan State, during the military regime of Fernando R. Lucas García. Exhumed in August 2000, 18 years after her death, and given a Christian burial on July 30, 2001. With assassin's bullets they have taken your life, but your spirit remains alive in the memory of those who knew you, in the hopes of those who demand justice and reconciliation, and in the tasks of those who work for peace. May you rest in peace." Photo by Beatriz Manz.

world. Hundreds of children were raised in Mexico with their own set of experiences and expectations. The geographical isolation has diminished with new roads, and migration to the United States has become a realistic alternative and dream for many. Individual remittances from the United States may replace the cooperative as the engine of the village's economy. Moreover, throughout the Ixcán and Guatemala more generally, environmental degradation is accelerating, and the economic, social, and political situation remains a quagmire.

Memories are still fresh. The peace accords granted amnesties, but amnesia has not taken root in villages such as Santa María Tzejá. Individuals carry on daily activities under the shadow of past violence and an uncertain future; insecurity hangs over the heart and mind. The psychological imprint of violence is not easily annulled—it may be transformed, reshaped, at times repressed, but it stays with those traumatized by the experience. People live with the everlasting burden imposed by arbitrary, ghastly, and impudent terror as well as rigid, unchanging social structures. Crime, impunity, and general lawlessness have not dissipated.

The original villagers, most back in Santa María Tzejá, others scattered throughout Guatemala, Mexico, and the United States, could not have imagined this outcome in January 1970 when they began their journey to the promised land. They have walked down a path over three decades long in which joy, pride, and accomplishment mingle with sorrow and loss. With all they have endured, their efforts are far from over, their spirit not extinguished. A new generation has their own challenges, their own hopes and dreams in an uncertain future. The village has survived against tough odds; only time will tell if it will prevail.

Notes

1. All translations from the Spanish are by the author. The real names of all the individuals who are dead are given in the book, as well as those who are publicly known, for example, the Canil family. I always intended to use pseudonyms to protect the sources. However, on my last trip to the village, in February 2003, several villagers asked if I would identify them by name. When I said I would not use their real names, to my utter surprise, they expressed deep dissatisfaction with that approach. This became an immediate dilemma for me. I was afraid to honor their request, and that made me realize that I had opted for pseudonyms as much to put my own mind at ease as for them. Given that the book was in production at this point, the logistics of locating each individual to find out what he or she preferred became a potential nightmare. In each case, except in a few instances, the individuals said they wanted their real name used.

These are some of the responses individuals gave me: "I would prefer if my real name was used," Jerónimo said. "I am proud of what I did, and I want my children and my grandchildren to know that is me [being quoted]." María noted, "I did not struggle and risk my life for more than ten years to be now reduced to a pseudonym," adding, "It is not often that we are asked our opinions and that we get a chance to explain what we did and why. Yes, I do want my real name used." Francisca, also a former combatant asked, "Do you know my last name?" When I responded that of course I knew it, she added, "but my second (maternal) last name too? I want to make sure you give both." Domingo stated, "I want my name used, and I will go buy the book as soon as it comes out." Emiliano was characteristically to the point, "Why would I not want my name used? Everything I said is true."

The final decision I made may not satisfy everyone: I use a combination of full names, first names only, and pseudonyms. Individuals will be able to identify themselves in these pages, yet there is enough ambiguity or anonymity for protection. If a person is only quoted once I do not use a name and provide instead a description such as "an elderly man" or "a K'iche' woman."

2. Amnesty International 2002: 5–6.

3. Bounds 2000: 5.

4. CEH 1999a: 18, 20. See also Oficina de Derechos Humanos del Arzobispado de Guatemala 1998a, 1998b, 1998c. The CEH was the United Nations truth commission formed as a result of the accords reached on June 23, 1994, in Oslo, Norway, ending the Guatemalan civil war. Its objective was to "clarify with objectivity, equity and impartiality, the human rights violations and acts of violence." As stated in the prologue of the report, the CEH "was not established to judge—that is the function of the courts—but rather to clarify the history of events of more than three decades of fratricidal war" (CEH 1999a: 11).

5. CEH 1999b: 256–59. According to the CEH, between 1962 and 1996, 669 massacres were perpetrated by all responsible forces, 334 in El Quiché: "626 are attributed to the Guatemalan military, security forces or paramilitary structures such as the Civil Defense Patrols and Military Commissioners. This includes five massacres committed in refugee camps in Mexican territory in 1982 and 1983" (CEH 1999b: 256).

6. CEH 1999a: 30.

7. Ibid.: 23.

8. Kinzer 2001: 61.

9. The field research for this book began in 1973 and continued through December 2001. In February 2003 I went to the twenty-first anniversary of the village's destruction and while there took new photographs and discussed the names to be used in the book. From 1982 to 1990 I went to the refugee camps frequently and was able to take notes and tape-record interviews. The Mexican government prevented me from going to the camps on several occasions, but in general the research in the camps was uneventful. From 1985 to 2001 I went to the village of Santa María Tzejá either every year or every other year.

Because of the vast number of interviews extending over decades, I only mention the year of the interview when it is significant. For example, if a villager's perceptions on the guerrillas or the army were expressed during the militarization period, that year is noted because the context is significant. If the remark is made after the peace accords were signed, that is noted as well. Otherwise, if I felt that the specific year was not essential, I simply note in general when the bulk of the interviews were done in a particular chapter, omitting the particular year to preserve the narrative flow.

Initially I did not take notes in the village for security reasons. I waited until my return plane would take off from Guatemala City and then I would write my impressions and recollections and continue when I got back to the United States. At other times I would write in codes, in several different notebooks, which often became nearly impossible to decipher when I returned to the safety of the United States. In 1983 Guatemalan military security forces took me to a military base where my belongings, including my notebooks, were searched. Given that experience and the sensitive nature of my research, it was not until the mid-1990s that many villagers were interviewed again, and this time the interviews were tape-recorded. I wanted to capture their articulate voices, insights, and reflections. The bulk of these interviews were then transcribed and resulted in more than one thousand pages of transcriptions. Extensive excerpts are included in the book.

10. About half of Guatemala's eleven million people are Mayan. Twenty-two ethnolinguistic groups exist. Some are small in number. The largest of the Mayan groups is the K'iche', who live primarily in El Quiché, the province most targeted by the military. Thus they suffered a disproportionate number of deaths during the civil war and more than half of the massacres. The majority of the inhabitants of Santa María Tzejá are Maya K'iche'.

11. Scheper-Hughes 1995: 415–16.

12. Those anthropologists who feel that in taking an active interest, they would risk closing off "various avenues of information and cloud[ing] judgment" pose the issue as objective distance versus activism, with nothing in between. "Whatever its moral justification, activism does not generally go hand-in-hand with good research," says one anthropologist, Adam Kuper, although no evidence is provided that an aloof anthropology has illuminated the human condition or provided predictable findings any better than an engaged ethnography. He concludes, "If there is a trade-off between ethnographic enquiry and political activism, should we always—usually? ever?—choose activism? There are often many local activists and rather few ethnographers" (Kuper 1995: 425).

Another misrepresentation is that an engaged and committed anthropologist will be too impulsive once exposed to wrongdoings and thereby will compromise the research. "As a pragmatic matter, becoming an emotional or political participant in the lives of the people we study may sometimes open new doors and help reveal new insights to us," but other doors, and this is viewed as more alarming, "may then be closed to us." Therefore, the advice is to be sensible: "[I]f the goal is to help the downtrodden of the earth, it is a pragmatic as well as a moral question whether we should become street partisans—knowing that the internal workings of the power elite will then be hidden from our view forever" (O'Meara 1995: 428).

Here we see a possible social commitment of ethnographers being equated not just with activism, but with street partisanship, shutting out the serious anthropological research. The assumption may be that the marginal have no power and no voice to agree to, or reject, our fieldwork. Indeed, in conducting anthropological research, choices need to be made. The military's rejection of research should not deter research among those oppressed by the military. It appears that some feel pulled to extremes in the field, or that the choices are to take "an objective model of the world," or a "moral model of the world" (D'Andrade 1995: 399). But these two models, the objective and the moral, are not necessarily counterposed. In fact, it may be misleading to presume "that scientific inquiry should be (or can be) conducted in a political-moral vacuum," Marvin Harris observes. "First of all, there is strong empirical support for the position that morality in the form of culturally constructed values and preferences influences the definition and selection of researchable projects. What we choose to study or not to study in the name of anthropology is a politico-moral decision" (1995: 423). Indeed, there is not such a thing as a moral vacuum or political neutrality.

13. On May 23, 1981, eight individuals (most of them anthropologists) concerned about human rights violations in Guatemala met at the Deep Run Farm, near York, Pennsylvania. At the meeting were Margarita Melville, Shelton Davis, Chris Krueger, Phil Berryman, Angie Berryman, Rarihokwats, Marilyn Moors, and me. The purpose of our gathering was to organize a national teach-in on October 20 of that year, the thirty-seventh anniversary of the 1944 revolution, which brought to power a democratic government. The teach-ins were successfully launched that fall, and the Guatemala Scholars Network (GSN) was born a year later. Since the mid-1980s the mainstay at the GSN has been Marilyn Moors, whose dedication and concern for human rights and justice in Guatemala have been truly remarkable.

14. Glueck 1984. A second article, "Mayan Specialists Hail a 'Fancy Discovery' at Río Azul Site," covered an entire page of the paper that same day (Wilford 1984a). The following day a third article appeared about the archaeological find: "Professor's Path to Mayan Discovery: The Delight in Finding Time 'Frozen' " (Wilford 1984b).

15. Manz 1984.

16. Responding to an article I published in *Cultural Survival* in 1981 about Guatemalan refugees entering Mexico from El Petén, archaeologist Ian Graham, from Harvard's Peabody Museum and a recipient of one of the first MacArthur (genius) awards, wrote to the editor questioning my accusations that the army was repressing peasant cooperatives in Western El Petén: He wrote that "it is far more likely that a guerrilla group excited the cooperative farmers over the possibility that the Government may agree to the Mexican plan to build a dam." Graham questioned: "Is this a matter for Cultural Survival? For Amnesty International, yes....My doubts stem from the fact that the co-operative farmers, referred to as 'Indians' in the article, are not properly so called, in two of the three senses of the word. Racially yes: They are indigenous people, of largely Mayan descent. But culturally and linguistically they are not. Rather they are Ladinos—people who have turned their backs on their traditional culture, or whose fathers or grandfathers did. These farmers speak Spanish, have in large part embraced evangelistic Protestantism in further rejections of their cultural origins, and seem happy to become undifferentiated Peteneros." (1981: 15).

In my response I took issue with Graham's "implication that those cultures whose survival is threatened must conform to some vulgar stereotype of what 'real Indians' are like and those people whom Graham scolds for having been forced to become 'undifferentiated Peteneros' are no longer eligible for the attention and concern of *Cultural Survival*. All anthropology is built on the root assumption that every human group is culture-bearing, that each culture is equally precious, creative, and therefore worthy of serious attention and, where its survival is threatened, of public debate and opposition" (Manz 1981: 15–16).

17. Ehlers 1990a: 141–42.

18. Only a few academics approached human rights organizations, the media, or the U.S. Congress or spoke out publicly against the abuses in Guatemala. Human rights organizations such as the Washington Office on

Latin America, Americas Watch, and Amnesty International played an exemplary role, as did a number of other groups, such as the Anthropology Research Center, CAMINO (Central American Information Office), the GSN, Cultural Survival, and Survival International. In 1985 I testified before the U.S. House of Representatives (Manz 1985a). I also wrote an op-ed for the *New York Times,* "Dollars That Forge Guatemalan Chains" (Manz 1985b) and contributed pieces to *Cultural Survival,* the *National Catholic Reporter, Americas Watch,* and the *Boston Globe.*

19. Colby 1983: 211.

20. Colby 1988: 991.

21. Stoll 1999a: 273.

22. Stoll 1999b: 75.

23. Ibid.

24. Ibid.: 72.

25. Ibid.

26. Cifuentes 1982a: 27.

27. Stoll 1999a: 214–15.

28. This is not the place for a lengthy discussion of the many complex issues raised by Stoll's work. See Burgos-Debray (1984), Menchú (1998), Hale (1997a), Stoll (1999a, 1999b), Arias (2001), Nelson (1999b), Lowell and Lutz (2001), and the November 1999 issue of *Latin American Perspectives.*

29. Starn 1991: 64.

30. Montejo 2001: 381.

31. Warren 1998: 79–80.

32. Ibid.: 82.

33. Quoted in Belpoliti and Gordon 2001: 251.

34. In February 1993 Noel de Jesús Beteta, the former sergeant of the Presidential High Command (Estado Mayor Presidencial, or EMP), was sentenced to twenty-five years in prison for murdering Myrna Mack. Helen Mack, Myrna Mack's sister, was not satisfied with the conviction of the material author of the crime, insisting that it was essential to prosecute the intellectual authors of her sister's murder as well. In 1994 the courts opened legal proceedings against three high-ranking military officials (two colonels and one general), who were detained and released on bail after being accused of ordering and planning her death. The investigation into the murder was marked by irregularities, controversy, and violent attacks. The chief investigator of the case was murdered, others involved faced harassment by government officials, and routine forensic procedures were ignored. The Misión de Verificación de las Naciones Unidas en Guatemala (MINUGUA, or United Nations Verification Mission in Guatemala) confirmed in August 1996 that the case was "heard in a climate of insecurity" and that "some of those involved continued to be followed by unknown individuals." In light of the contempt shown by the Guatemalan military for due process, the Inter-American Commission for Human Rights determined in 1996 that the case would be admissible in the Inter-American court. After many setbacks, in January 1999, once the U.S. State Department issued a public statement raising the possibility of involvement of the three officers, a Guatemalan judge ordered General Augusto Godoy Gaitán, Colonel Juan Valencia Osorio,

and Colonel Juan Guillermo Oliva Carrera to stand trial on charges of orchestrating the murder. After further appeals *(amparos)* and procedural delays, the case against the intellectual authors was finally heard beginning September 3, 2002, twelve years almost to the day after Myrna Mack's brutal assassination. Colonel Juan Valencia Osorio, the head of *"el Archivo"* —the secret branch of the EMP—was found guilty on October 3, 2002, and sentenced to thirty years in prison, although his direct superior and head of the EMP, General Augusto Godoy Gaitán, and Colonel Juan Guillermo Oliva Carrera were acquitted. Two weeks later, the Guatemalan Supreme Court accepted a military appeal. Although it was rejected on December 5, 2002, the appeal was heard in May 2003. Helen Mack appealed the two acquittals. On May 7, 2003, Guatemala's appeals court (Sala Cuarta de Apelaciones) reversed the conviction of Colonel Juan Valencia Osorio. The appeals court also upheld the acquittals of General Edgar Augusto Godoy Gaitán and Lieutenant Colonel Juan Guillermo Oliva Carrera. The three officers are free. Helen Mack intends further appeals before the Guatemalan Supreme Court. Despite these setbacks for the Mack family, the trial of the intellectual authors of the crime has been a unique case not only for Guatemala but also internationally. Particularly since the arrest of Chile's General Pinochet in London in October 1998, human rights activists have been willing to cross geographical boundaries in pursuit of justice and accountability. Helen Mack also brought the case against the Guatemalan government before the Inter-American Court in San José, Costa Rica, for its failure to properly investigate and prosecute the military officers. The court has heard the case, but a decision has not been rendered.

In 1992 Helen Mack received the Right Livelihood Award from the Swedish Parliament for her personal courage and perseverance in seeking justice, her human rights efforts, and for challenging impunity on behalf of her sister and other Guatemalans killed by the military. The award is presented in Stockholm on the day before the Nobel Peace Prize and has become known as the "alternative Nobel Prize."

35. Manz in Falla 1994: xiii.

36. People tended to use indirect language or codes to refer to sensitive or dangerous political issues. *Envueltos* were the subversives, those that were "involved." The very term "guerrillas" was avoided even if speaking against them. It was as if to use the term compromised them. Counter-insurgency became *la situación,* or *la violencia. Aquellos* (them) were the guerrillas.

37. Quoted in Oglesby 1995: 256–58. A week after Myrna Mack's assassination there was a memorial service at the University of California, Berkeley. High level campus officials, members of FACHRES (Faculty for Human Rights in El Salvador)—which became Faculty for Human Rights in Central America—and Myrna's only child, sixteen-year-old Lucrecia, spoke movingly at the service. Myrna's sister, Helen Mack, was also in attendance. The campus paper, the *Daily Californian,* had a cover story with the headline, "Memorial to Honor Slain Anthropologist" (Quigg 1990). The academic community in the United States committed to human rights responded quickly. Close to eight hundred signatures were gathered (before the advent of email). Those names were placed in newspaper ads in Guatemala as well as in the *New York Times.* United States

ambassador Thomas Stroock wrote to the joint Berkeley-Stanford Center for Latin American Studies in response to an earlier ad placed in a Guatemalan paper soon after the murder. He stated that the "murder was criminal in nature," adding that this conclusion had been reached by the National Police because of the "multiple stab wounds and that her purse and credit cards were stolen" (letter, Guatemala, September 25, 1990). I wrote an op-ed in the *New York Times* about her murder, "In Guatemala, No One Is Safe…Why Was Myrna Mack Killed?" (Manz 1990). On the tenth anniversary of her death there was a memorial in Guatemala, which included a beautifully produced publication about Myrna's life and recollections of friends and colleagues.

38. I borrow the phrase from Carolyn Nordstrom and Antonious C.G.M. Robben, eds.: 1995.

39. *Confianza* translated as "trust" is not quite suitable. *Confianza* connotes confidence, commitment, security, compromise, reliance, and caring. It means being "on the same page," sympathetic, understanding, able to guard a secret, shield, protect. There are individuals that are "de confianza" and those that are not: "no es de confianza." If one breaches *confianza,* one can move to "ya no es de confianza." *Confianza* as used in Guatemala is more personal, political, and social. It says a lot about the character of the person. Whoever presents a person as being "de confianza" also places his/her reputation on the line.

40. Geertz 2000: 33.

41. Then and now, it is also possible to take a small, single-engine plane from Guatemala City or Cobán to the airfield in the Playa Grande military base, thirty miles away, and arrive in half a day.

42. According to the Inter-American Development Bank, thirty-two billion dollars a year in remittances were sent to Latin America and the Caribbean from migrants in the United States in 2002. El Salvador alone received some $2.2 billion, Guatemala almost $1.7 billion. Mexico receives about $10.5 billion in remittances (MIF/IDB 2003: 4). About 64 percent of the Guatemalan immigrants are in the state of California; 12 percent in New York, 7 percent in Illinois, 5 percent in Florida, 4 percent in Texas, 3 percent in Georgia, 2 percent in Oregon, and 3 percent in other states (Sistema de Naciones Unidas en Guatemala 2000: 171). The Guatemalan population in the United States ranges from 372,487, as of the year 2000 according to the U.S. Bureau of the Census (2001), to estimates of more than one million (out of a Guatemalan population of eleven million).

43. Geertz 1988: 132.

44. CEH 1999c: 83.

45. Gobierno de la República 2001: 27. See also Sandoval 1987.

46. CEH 1999c: 156. According to the Guatemalan government, the proportion of agricultural households without access to land stands at 37 percent nationally with certain regions having much higher landless concentrations. The concentration of land ownership—and the best land—in the hands of a few wealthy families has remained constant over the decades.

47. Episcopado Guatemalteco 1988: 1.

48. Ibid.

49. Gobierno de la República 2001: 10.

50. Ibid.: 13–14.

51. Kinzer 2001: 63.

52. International Institute for Democracy and Electoral Assistance 1998: 27, 33.

53. Gobierno de la República 2001: 29.

54. Quoted in ibid.: 30. See also Conferencia Episcopal de Guatemala 1995. "Urge la verdadera paz," in www.riial.org/guatemala/alfabe.htm (as of Nov. 2002).

55. Cited in Gobierno de la República 2001: 27.

56. Ibid.: 36.

57. USAID became a prime funder of land colonization in the eastern sector of the Ixcán by the mid- and late 1970s.

58. CEH 1999c: 86.

59. Kita 2000: 51.

60. Ibid.: 54.

61. CEH 1999d: 112.

62. Ibid.

63. Quoted in CEH 1999d: 112.

64. See Gleijeses 1991; Immerman 1982; Schlesinger and Kinzer 1982.

65. Since the CIA-backed military coup in 1954, the United States has supplied the Guatemalan military with direct military aid, covert aid, training, and economic assistance. Only during the presidency of Jimmy Carter was military aid made conditional on the military's improvement on human rights, although the government permitted pipeline aid to continue. The Guatemalan military rejected the conditions and looked for military hardware and training elsewhere. With the Reagan administration, congressionally approved aid was resumed.

66. Mr. Vaky to Mr. Oliver, Secret Memorandum, Department of State, Policy Planning Council, Washington, D.C., March 29, 1968. In http://www.gwu.edu/~nsarchiv/NSAEBB/NSAEBB11/docs/05-01.htm (as of April 1, 2002).

67. Ibid.

68. Ibid.

69. Department of State quoted in Schoultz 1983: 197 (emphasis added).

70. Quoted in Schoultz 1983: 197.

71. Robert L. Jacobs to Mr. Einaudi, Secret Memorandum, Department of State, Washington, D.C., October 5, 1981. In http://www.gwu.edu/~nsarchiv/NSAEBB/NSAEBB11/docs/13-01.htm (as of March 7, 2002).

72. The U.S. government found ways to circumvent congressional restrictions in their zeal to bolster the Guatemalan military. All sorts of equipment, such as helicopters, trucks, and jeeps, went to Guatemala through reclassification for civilian, rather than military, use. "On April 5, 1981, the Reagan administration had bypassed legislative restrictions on sales of military and crime control equipment to Guatemala by simply changing the rules regulating such sales," McClintock observed. "The export of 50 two-and-a-half ton trucks and 100 army jeeps was made possible by removing both items from the 'Crime Control and Detection List' and reclassifying them as goods for 'Regional Stability Controls'; the sale went ahead in June 1981." (McClintock 1985: 189).

A *Washington Post/International Herald Tribune* headline speaks for itself: "Guatemala Gets Arms From U.S. Despite Ban" (Dickey 1982).

73. Americas Watch 1984a: 135.

74. Amnesty International 1982.

75. Department of State 1983: 517 (emphasis added).

76. Ibid.: 518.

77. Riding 1982.

78. See Falla 1983a, 1983b, 1992, 1994; Amnesty International 1981; Americas Watch 1982, 1983, 1984a; Davis and Hodson 1982.

79. Americas Watch 1982, 1983, 1984a.

80. Central Intelligence Agency, February 1982.

81. Ibid.

82. Department of State ca. late 1982. Interestingly the document warns about the Ríos Montt government's program of arming the entire Indian population, "which could boomerang should they turn against the government in the future."

83. Copy of Diary. Personal archive. Emphasis added.

84. Dennis, Elbow, and Heller. January 1984.

85. United States Agency for International Development. January 1984. See also United States Agency for International Development. March 31, 1982.

86. Following are some additional examples of the type of editing by USAID: "military action" became "the political problem," and in its entirety the following was deleted:

> "People were killed selectively in some communities, and others fled to Mexico to escape the army. Three entire settlements were also completely exterminated: Trinitaria, Santa Clara, and El Quetzal. It is estimated that army action in 1982 accounted for 1,000–1,500 settler deaths."

A few pages later the following sentence was deleted:

> "It may well be this reputation that led the Guatemalan military to kill everyone in the ill-fated settlement in March 1982." (Actually the massacres occurred in February.)

> Original: "An estimated 220 colonists' families were killed by the military in early 1982."

> USAID's edited version: "A number of families were killed by conflict in early 1982."

> Original: "...Several hundred families fled the project area when the killing began."

> USAID's edited version: "...Several hundred families fled the project area due to the political violence."

> Original: "Some of these families have returned."

> USAID's edited version: "Many of these families have returned."

Discussing the construction of a road, the sentence "They also allow quick troop movement by the military" was omitted. The following mention is no doubt in reference to Santa María Tzejá:

> Original: "At least one other aldea also had a prosperous co-op. However, during the conflicts of 1982 the military stole a truckload of 800 quintales of coop supplies coming from Guatemala, in addition to murdering a number of families. Since then the cooperative members commented that 'they have not had the heart' to organize another coop."

> USAID's edited version: "At least one other settlement also had a prosperous cooperative. However, during the conflicts of 1982 a truckload of 800 quintales of coop supplies coming from Guatemala was stolen. Since then the cooperative members commented that 'they have not had the heart' to organize another cooperative."

87. United States Agency for International Development, March 31, 1982.

88. One U.S. Congressional committee allocated funds to settle peasants, and another committee provided funds for weapons that were killing those same peasants.

89. LaFeber 1984a: 260–61.

90. LaFeber 1984b: 7.

91. Manz 1986.

92. Mr. Abrams, whom the *New York Times* calls a "pugnacious conservative" (Weisman 2002), pleaded guilty to lying to Congress in 1987 about the illegal funneling of money to the Nicaraguan Contras. He was convicted in 1991, and then pardoned by President George H. W. Bush in 1992. Among other activities, Abrams traveled to London in disguise to solicit a ten-million-dollar donation from the Sultan of Brunei, despite Congress having barred all such activities. For more information, see Doyle and Isacson 2001. Abrams, the hard-line, controversial political figure, is back again in government service. President George W. Bush has named him senior director for Near East and North African Affairs at the National Security Council.

Chapter 1. The Highland Homeland

1. Coates 1997: 86–87.

2. Williams 1986: 13.

3. See Carmack 1981, 1995.

4. Ibid.

5. Carmack 1981: 87.

6. See Carmack 1979, 1981; Sharer 1994; Coe 1999. The K'iche' population in 1520 is estimated to have been 823,000 (Carmack 1968: 77 and Veblen 1977: 497). The K'iche' had by far the largest population, followed by the Kaqchikel's 250,000. The total Maya population at the time of the European arrival is calculated to have been two million in Guatemala (not including the Mayas in southern Mexico). As in Mexico there was a devastating population decline in Guatemala after the Spanish conquest. From a population of two million in 1520, it is estimated that by 1550 there were 427,850; by 1575 the pop-

ulation had been reduced to 236,540, and by 1625 to 128,000. See Lovell and Lutz 1996: 398–407; and Lovell and Lutz 1995. The current Maya population, according to the Guatemalan census, is around five million, representing about 50 percent of the total population.

7. Carmack 1981: 82.

8. Carmack 1995: 28.

9. Mayas, especially the elders, often refer to themselves as *naturales*.

10. Orlove 2002: 67. For further readings on identity in Guatemala, see Smith 1990b; Warren 1998; Nelson 1999a; Grandin 2000. A good discussion of ethnic identity in Brazil can be found in Warren 2001.

11. Oglesby 2002:111–13.

12. Lewis 1958: 409.

13. Cambranes 1985.

14. Williams 1986: 64.

15. Ibid.

16. For a recent study of the sugar plantation sector, see Oglesby 2002.

17. I visited them again from late 1975 through early 1976. My last and most troubling trip was in 1983, on occasion of the pope's visit to Guatemala. I thought that the pope's visit would be a good time to travel to Guatemala and get a sense of what was happening in the highlands. (I covered the pope's trip for the *National Catholic Reporter*.) After the pope left I stayed in the country. I decided I would first go to the plantation region. I had heard that many highland Mayas escaping from the terror in the highlands were descending to the south coast to look for work and gain a little anonymity. It is estimated that 1.5 million people became displaced out of a population of eight million.

This trip to Guatemala would prove to be especially difficult. My visit to the *finca* was very unpleasant not only because of the number and conditions of highland peasants there, but also because the *finquero* was particularly apprehensive and hostile. During the ride to the *finca,* he questioned me about the purpose of my trip to Guatemala and made constant unnerving comments. He mentioned that his wife no longer went to the plantation because of the danger, adding, "But you are brave, aren't you? You must be brave to be coming here, or are you afraid?" My room at the plantation had several guns up against the wall, and the whole house was surrounded by sandbags. He made some comment that this time I would not be able to "look out" as well. I was not sure if this comment meant that on previous trips I had "looked" too much.

That first day, while I was sitting on the open veranda, he walked toward me and pointed a gun, stating: "Now let's talk seriously. That's it, this is the only way to make people talk." It was a joke. He also insisted I should accompany him and several office workers to the bank in Santa Lucía Cotzumalguapa to withdraw money for payday. The people in the back of the vehicle were heavily armed, their weapons pointing out and ready to fire. He said all his neighbors had been robbed or killed and that guerillas hold up banks and vehicles after customers make large withdrawals from the bank. Therefore, for some unexplained reason, I could be of use on this journey to the bank. I cut my trip short and have never seen them again.

Later that year I went by bus to Santa Cruz del Quiché. After three days there I was apprehended by two individuals from G2 (military intelligence) and taken for interrogation to the military base.

18. James 1989: 10–11.

19. These lands were given to Ladino militias many years before. It was a common practice for military generals to reward soldiers with lands.

20. Bourdieu and Wacquant 1992: 162–73, 200–205.

21. Huxley 1934:145–46.

22. See Martínez Peláez 1998. A recent publication on the historical views of Kaqchikels from Chimaltenango treats the Ubico period; see Carey 2001.

23. While at one plantation in 1973, the *finquero* showed me a banana plant that shaded the coffee trees. He pointed to where a stem of bananas had obviously been cut as proof that "Indians are thieves." They could never be trusted, he charged; lying and stealing came in their blood. Pointing to his gun he said, "That is why I have this, I am the law here in this *finca,* I could kill the person for taking my property but I am not going to bother and yet they say we are harsh. I will let it go." He implied that if he wanted to get rid of a trouble-maker, say a union organizer, he would not be as lenient. When I pointed out that the bananas were not harvested but would simply rot in any case, he be-came incensed, stating that it was his property and he could do as he wished.

24. CEH 1999a: 17.

25. Bourgois 2001: 3.

26. CEH 1999a: 18.

27. Ibid.: 19.

28. Ibid.: 22.

29. See Lernoux 1980; Melville and Melville 1970, 1971.

30. Iglesia Guatemalteca en el Exilio, n.d.

31. The best background on the Catholic Church in El Quiché is Diócesis del Quiché 1994. See also Iglesia Guatemalteca en el Exilio, n.d.

32. In Guatemala, several foreign priests and nuns became deeply radical-ized. By the end of 1967, two American priests and one American nun had been expelled from the country. While Father Luis had been an admirer of General Franco of Spain, one of the expelled American priests, Thomas Melville, had been an ardent anticommunist. He wrote, "Senator [Joseph] McCarthy became a big hero to most of us for his anti-Communist crusades, as did Bishop Sheen for his philosophical dissection of Communism" (Melville and Melville 1970: 14). Interestingly, in their book, Thomas and Marjorie Melville mention Luis Gurriarán's participation in the meetings to discuss actions the Catholic clergy could undertake given the social conditions of the rural indigenous population. They had come to the conclusion that taking up arms was the right course of ac-tion. Their plans were discovered, according to the Melvilles, because Luis Gur-riarán talked to church officials, which led to the Melvilles' expulsion and an explosive scandal in the country. At the time, they felt betrayed by Luis. The Maryknoll order became synonymous with "communist priests and nuns" in Guatemala, though historically it had had its own anticommunist strand. The Catholic Church was indeed undergoing what it considered a period of turpi-tude, such as priests and nuns getting married. Perhaps the most notorious

political involvement was the case of the guerrilla-priest Camilo Torres, a Colombian from the upper class who had taken up arms. He was killed in his first battle with the Colombian army in February 1966 (Rueda 2002). The Ejército de Liberación Nacional (ELN) was formed on July 4, 1964, and is still active in Colombia (in http://www.eln-voces.com/f-todo-eln.html, as of May 28, 2003). Camilo Torres left the priesthood in 1965, pressured by the Catholic hierarchy, and joined the ELN in November 1965 (Rueda 2002, see also Lernoux 1980).

33. Smith also mentions the "literacy campaign promoted in the Santa Cruz del Quiché area" (1990a: 238–39).

34. See Diócesis del Quiché 1994. See also Falla 1980, 1972.

35. Diócesis del Quiché 1994: 78.

36. Ibid.

37. His return was the result of continual political pressure from cooperative activists and Catholic Action mobilization. Campaigning in El Quiché, presidential candidate Julio César Méndez Montenegro, in his quest for votes, promised he would allow Luis back into the country. Once elected in 1966 he was reminded and pressured to fulfill his promise. Luis was told of the promise and did not wait for a letter of invitation from President Méndez Montenegro.

38. One of the best known of these broadcasters was Emeterio Toj Medrano. Toj later joined the EGP. He was captured, paraded in front of the media, forced to confess what the army wanted him to say (mainly that he had been used and brainwashed by the EGP), but then he outfoxed them by performing a daring and spectacular escape—among the few (if any) from the Guatemalan military's hands.

39. Diócesis del Quiché 1994: 158–61. See also Carmack 1988b.

40. Davis and Hodson 1982: 14.

Chapter 2. Settling in the Promised Land

1. The interviews in this chapter were conducted in the Maya Tecún refugee camp in Campeche, July 1990, and in Santa María Tzejá, April 1999.

2. All except Luis had been killed in different incidents by 1980.

3. Sabas, also from El Palmar, and the first to join the EGP from Santa María Tzejá, feels that "everyone is indigenous [todos somos naturales]," using a term Mayas often use to identify themselves: *naturales*. He basically feels, after spending years in the insurgent forces, where he learned Ixil and K'iche', that he is also Maya, but he had lost the culture and language. In the late 1990s he became involved in Coordinación de Organizaciones del Pueblo Maya de Guatemala (COPMAGUA, or Coordination of Organizations of the Mayan Peoples of Guatemala). Miguel Reyes's children, male and female, as well as other Ladinos, have spouses from the K'iche' ethno-linguistic group.

4. AVANCSO 1992: 34–35.

5. Falla 1992: 190n1.

6. Cardamom originated in India and Sri Lanka, and it was introduced to Guatemala early in the twentieth century. By the late 1970s Guatemala had be-

come the largest producer of cardamom in the world, surpassing India—its main competitor. See http://www.guate.net/spice/cardamom.htm (as of July 12, 2002). According to the Bank of Guatemala, in 2000 Guatemala exported $79.4 million worth of cardamom (down from $100.3 million in 1984). See http://www.banguat.gob.gt/estaeco/boletin/envolver.asp?karchivo=.boescu45A (as of July 2002).

7. The military was clearly checking up on Santa María Tzejá and Ixcán more generally. When I returned to the highlands from my first trip to the village in 1973, which included a visit to Mayalán, where Maryknoll priest William Woods was living, I was questioned by soldiers. They wanted to know what had been the purpose of my trip there, why we had stopped in Huehuetenango on the way to the Ixcán. Their questions indicated that my steps had been followed. While the experience was intimidating, and the first of many to come, I did not give it the importance I should have. My Chilean passport in mid-1973 surely fed the military's paranoia.

8. For more on the insurgency and counterinsurgency of the 1960s, see Jonas 1991: 57–72.

9. Payeras 1983: 25.

10. Ibid.: 33.

11. Ibid.: 34–35.

12. The initial fifteen insurgents that entered the Ixcán from Mexico were a "mosaic of ethnic and social backgrounds," as Mario Payeras wrote a few years later (ibid.: 29). Four were Maya Achi' and Kaqchikel, five were from the Pacific coast, two from the eastern zone of the country, four, including the author, were urban and university educated. Some, including Payeras, had studied abroad.

13. Payeras 1983: 36.

14. Cifuentes 1982a: 27–28, 30.

15. The key leaders of the village, such as the president of the cooperative, were told by the guerrilla band that for their own sake it was better to pretend the sale was forced. Their assumption was that either strangers in the village or some settlers themselves may betray the actual reception.

16. Payeras 1983: 71.

17. Ibid.

18. Ibid.

19. See Macías 1998 and Falla 1994.

20. CEH 1999e: 201.

21. Ibid.: 199–203.

22. *El Gráfico*, Jan. 13, 1976: 1 and 3.

23. For a comprehensive analysis of the oil industry in this region, see Losano-Ponciano 2000.

Chapter 3. The War Finds Paradise

1. Most of the interviews in this chapter were conducted in the mid-to-late 1980s. The members of the Committee of Peasant Unity (CUC) were inter-

viewed in Mexico City in 1982, 1983, and 1985. The villagers who were in the refugee camps were interviewed in Modulo 2 in Maya Tecún, Quetzal, Edzná, and Kesté in Campeche 1988, 1989, and 1990, and in Maya Balam, Cuchumatán, and Los Lirios in Quintana Roo in 1988. In Santa María Tzejá most of the interviews in this chapter were done between 1985 and 1990. The former combatants were interviewed in the late 1990s.

2. I make a brief reference to this literature in chapter 7.

3. Weiner 2001.

4. It took several interviews to convince each villager that I was not passing a judgment one way or another about their involvement with, or withdrawal from, the guerrillas' forces. Often people felt that merely asking certain questions implied a point of view on the part of the interviewer.

5. REMHI 1999: xxviii.

6. Ibid.: xxxii

7. Ibid.

8. Ibid.: 220

9. Ibid.

10. Ibid.

11. I interviewed several CUC leaders in Mexico City between 1982 and 1985.

12. Jonas 1991: 128.

13. CEH 1999d: 106.

14. Interviewed in the village in 1998, two years after the demobilization, ideology and personal circumstance intermingled as Braulio reflected on his years in the insurgency. What was at the heart of his recollections was not the horror of combat or the privations of life in the rain forest on the run, but rather the guerillas as a social movement.

15. Everyone in the village knew at that time that those children belonged to the young insurgents. Yet, neither then, nor during the militarization of the village, did anyone ever reveal that the children were not the son and daughter of the older couple. The girl died in the mid-1980s, according to the uncle, because of mistreatment by the grandfather. I photographed the boy throughout the years, seeing him grow. He always posed next to his uncle, who confided dangerous information to me. To the village at large, as with many other delicate matters, I pretended not to know.

16. One of Fabián's sons, Lucio Pérez, came to the United States in the 1980s, studied law, and in 1999 became director of the Guatemalan Maya Center, an NGO that supports Guatemalan immigrants in Florida.

17. There is little doubt that the march was promoted and counseled by the guerrillas. They wanted the demonstration to be peaceful, and thus the people leading the march were civilians such as Miguel Reyes.

18. The workshops on social promotion held at the Jesuit Landívar University started in the 1960s. Father Luis, among others, was an instructor, and the purpose was to train community leaders. Fabián Pérez was one of the first social promoters trained at Landívar. There were several other villagers from Santa María Tzejá that attended these training workshops and received the title "Social Promoters." They then went back to their communities and put into

practice their training, fostering community activities—economic, social, cultural, or political action. One person remarked, "Miguel Reyes was not the only one that went to take those courses at the Landívar University, but he is the one who is always crowing the most!"

19. The military struck one neighboring community after another. Santa María Dolores, a village south of Santa María Tzejá across the muddy Tzejá River, was targeted early on. Rogelio, an old survivor whose memory of these years still consumes him, provided some details of what happened in 1981. The first victim in the village was José Luis Pérez. "It was raining heavily when I heard the gun shots at one [A.M.]," Rogelio recalled. "In the morning, we got word that José Luis Pérez had been killed." The tragedy that night, however, was not limited to José Luis Pérez. "His mother, who lives nearby and heard the commotion, ran to defend her son," Rogelio continued. In the morning, the villagers found her lying on the ground in her own blood and moaning. "She died at ten in the morning of this wound," Rogelio said. "The following day we buried the two of them together." The only explanation Rogelio could think of for the murder was a false accusation. "About every fifteen days the military would come," Rogelio commented. On occasion the troops would drag away peasants such as Manuel Choc and Fractuoso Noriega, who would never be seen again. The arbitrary, random nature of the abductions added to the fear and made everyone feel vulnerable. Fractuoso Noriega was the son of Military Commissioner Feliciano Noriega, underscoring the randomness of some of the killings in the Ixcán. "They were searching for Manuel Choc's son. So, even though it was not him, in the confusion they disappeared Fractuoso all the same."

On Friday, September 14, 1981, Rogelio and his son-in-law were detained by the military along with a number of others. "They captured six of us," he remembered. "Two of us escaped, four were killed." After this ordeal, "I never went back to my house," he said. "I stayed in hiding on the mountain about three hundred meters from my house. My wife would come to bring me food. We kept a plastic tarp for cover and there I slept. I hid there. Later we organized ourselves." Ultimately everyone from Santa María Dolores abandoned the village, probably by late 1981. The women occasionally risked venturing into the village during the day, but all the men remained in hiding.

While many were falsely accused of being insurgents, EGP units did move through the area. In fact, a guerrilla unit came back to Santa María Dolores sometime after the four peasants had been murdered by the military. They killed three people in separate incidents who were the alleged army informants and whom villagers held responsible for deaths and abductions. One of the three, Feliciano Noriega, reportedly is the person who informed on José Luis Pérez, resulting in the death of Pérez and his mother. "Feliciano Noriega worked for the military," Rogelio maintained. "That is why he was murdered. He would go to the military outpost in Copón to give information."

A combatant from Santa María Tzejá who is familiar with Santa María Dolores described other horrors the army inflicted on Dolores. "One of the most painful things that happened to me in the war between 1980 and 1982 were the first bombings and shootings carried out by military Pilatus planes," he said. "Dolores is also where the army began burning homes. Because the population was well organized," he continued, "they had places to hide and because of that the loss of life was reduced considerably. When a murderous column of troops arrived to destroy the village, the people were already hiding, and the only thing the soldiers came across were cattle, mules, and chickens."

20. Preceding the discussion of the village, the manual quotes Nazi minister of propaganda, Joseph Goebbels: " 'Propaganda has only one objective: to conquer the masses; all procedures that lead us to that is good, any methods that hampers it is bad' " (Ejército de Guatemala n.d.: 21).

21. Ibid.: 23–24 (emphasis in the original).

22. The first interview with the widow and her daughter was in the Maya Tecún refugee camp in Campeche, Mexico, in 1989. When I interviewed Rosario at that time, I asked her directly who had killed her husband. She surprisingly replied initially that "the soldiers killed him" and then quickly added, "Well, perhaps not the soldiers, but since we don't know who the soldiers are, but we heard that the soldiers killed him." The daughter interjected that she was only five at the time and her mother was sick that day and stayed home, so she did not know who had been asking for her husband. Rosario fled the army less than two years later, when it destroyed the village and persecuted the villagers. She wound up with the group that remained in hiding in the jungle the longest, for more than a year. Rather than give herself up to the army, as others were doing, she fled with her group to Mexico, where she spent the next twelve years, moving three times. Again, she did not join the group of eight families who returned first from Mexico in 1988. In the camps, Rosario, a K'iche', the widow of a man executed by the guerrillas, was *comadre* of a Ladino family that had several members in the guerrillas. While visiting the Maya Tecún camp, I lived with that elderly Ladino couple. This family spoke very fondly of Rosario, visited her regularly, and cared about her well-being. I had no doubt that since an overwhelming number of refugees had fled the persecution of the army—as she had done—it may have seemed strange to her to indict the guerrillas in a Mexican refugee camp.

23. These tactics are similar to the ones used against the Spanish conquistadores in the 1520s.

24. The burnt, abandoned metal carcass of the plane remains, slowly enveloped by the surrounding foliage. The villagers seem to recall that the pilot's last name was Pacheco.

25. In 1981 the military had prevented an NGO, Wings of Hope, from continuing its use of the cooperative's airplane in flights to the village from the highlands. Thus other than stopping the cardamom buyers flying from Cobán and the villagers flying out with these small planes, the sabotage of the airstrip did not make military sense. However, after Wings of Hope stopped coming, villagers reluctantly supported the guerillas' prevention of all other flights.

26. The village lost more than one thousand head of cattle after the massacre and suffered the total destruction of Santa María Tzejá.

27. La Trinitaria was one of the rural development projects funded by USAID. While USAID learned of the massacre, it did not publicly condemn or acknowledge it, despite receiving a report of the killings and complete destruction of a U.S.-funded project.

28. Some villagers claim that E. Canté and G. Canté, captured probably around San José la 20, were brought along with the soldiers and were presumably forced to guide the troops.

29. Years later, in 1989, I located Ángel's father in a refugee camp in Quintana Roo. He was distraught about the horrors in Santa María Tzejá and heartbroken that Ángel, then a teenager, had gone to the United States. Ángel and his wife, María, were working in a furniture factory in Los Angeles, among the first to migrate to the United States from the refugee camps. They are now back in the village, and both are active members of the cooperative.

30. This account is based on the recollections of Edwin Canil, the only eyewitness survivor, who at the time of the massacre was six years old. It is possible that events unfolded in a somewhat different way than he described. What is certain is that the soldiers murdered everyone—innocent civilians—that grim day.

31. The villagers demanded an official exhumation of the bodies murdered by the army. As of mid-2001, Vicenta Mendoza (killed in February 1982) and Diego Larios (killed in May 1982) had been recovered, but the site of this massacre had not yet been located.

32. The settlers in this village came from Chiantla, a town near the city of Huehuetenango in the highlands, whose eroded fields blanket steep mountain slopes. Father Luis maintains that Kaibil Balam was one of the best-organized villages in the Ixcán and was certainly no stranger to military persecution. The army began making unexpected incursions from the mid-1970s, intimidating villagers in their homes and in their parcels and constantly seeking information about the guerrillas. The first victim of army terror had been a thirty-five-year-old woman who was seized around midnight and was later found dead from a bullet fired at her mouth and exiting through the back of her head. Next was Juan Cifuentes, who was grabbed at three in the morning and, like Santos Vicente Sarat, dragged half-naked in the direction of Santiago Ixcán. He was later found dead with a bullet to his forehead, wearing only his underwear.

33. "The army came from the direction of Santa María Tzejá and entered Kaibil," stated a peasant from Kaibil Balam. "We got the warning the army was coming and about to enter the village. Some of the people were able to escape and go into the jungle, but the army got some others." Almost immediately on entering Kaibil Balam, troops captured a forty-year-old woman, Rosenda, and an eighteen-year-old girl, Catarina, whom they kept alive, sexually abusing them for most of their stay in the center of the village. The army remained for two weeks, repeating many of the gruesome deeds and macabre acts of their shorter occupation of Santa María Tzejá. Soldiers seized all the musical instruments in the village: guitars, violins, and marimbas. Once again, the sounds of marimbas carried through the rain forest at night, and the soldiers feasted on the butchered animals of the villagers. When the army moved on, they left behind the severed heads of fourteen cattle, neatly arranged on some logs.

About a week after the soldiers left, the Kaibil Balam villagers cautiously returned to see what they might be able to salvage. The Catholic church was desecrated with empty tins of military rations strewn over everything. Villagers found the clothing of Rosenda and Catarina buried in a hole near the center of the village, and about five hundred meters away they discovered the naked bodies of both women, who had been raped and then murdered. The remains of the twenty-seven other people who had been killed were left scattered on the ground in a chilling reminder to those who survived. Animals had eaten the bodies, and their bones stood witness to the horror inflicted by the soldiers. From Kaibil Balam the column marched west to Xalbal, clearing a trail through the rain forest rather than following a path. As a result, they stumbled on the family of Santos Gómez in hiding. The soldiers mercilessly murdered all eight people, including an eight-day-old baby, whose body was sliced into pieces and left over a stone. One child managed to survive and tell about the horror that had taken place.

34. Falla 1994: 180. Falla estimates the population of the Ixcán in 1982 between forty-five and fifty thousand. Hundreds of people in the Ixcán would die as a result of illnesses, hunger, and bombing, especially between 1983 and 1985 among the communities of population in resistance (CPR) hiding in the jungle (p. 181). Many died on the journey to Mexico and later in the refugee camps.

Chapter 4. Ashes, Exodus, and Faded Dreams

1. CEH 1999a: 30; Manz 1988a.

2. For more on the Guatemalan refugees in Mexico, see Manz 1984, 1988a, 1988b, 1989; Americas Watch 1984b; Aguayo 1985; Simon and Manz 1992.

3. Most of the interviews for this chapter were done in Campeche in the late 1980s and in Santa María Tzejá and in California in the mid-1990s.

4. CEH 1999f: 285. Ricardo Falla, a Jesuit priest and anthropologist, wrote a moving account of life in the Communities of Population in Resistance (CPR). See Falla 1998. See also Falla 1992, 1994.

5. CEH 1999d: 123.

6. At another point she recalled that soldiers were involved, perhaps also with civil patrollers. She said there was "a lot of firing, bombs, it got dark from so much smoke, the soldiers grabbed a lot of people, and they took us to Playa Grande."

7. I later sent Emiliano several pages of follow-up questions. He responded to all of them at length, using a blue pen and white, unlined legal-size paper. He ended his carefully and painfully hand-written answers with a note: "Beatriz, I ask you to forgive my handwriting, which is very bad. We'll see if you understand some of what I was able to respond. I answered the questions myself but with some concern [pena] that perhaps you will not understand. I wrote every now and again when I came back from working in my parcel. I am working hard so that in ten years I will not still be as I am now with nothing [pelado]. So, I ask you to forgive my handwriting. But as you know I was not even a half-hour in school. The little I know is only because I taught myself with strokes. This is all I want to tell you, your friend, Emiliano Pérez."

8. See Jonas 1991. Jesús still remembered the support for Christian Democratic candidate Ríos Montt and the campaign propaganda lyrics children learned at that time: "Mi papá votará por Ríos Montt. Mi mamá votará por

Ríos Montt. Lástima que yo no puedo votar. Porque votaría también por Ríos Montt." (My father will vote for Ríos Montt. My mother will vote for Ríos Montt. It's too bad I cannot vote. Because I would also vote for Ríos Montt.)

9. Tomasa had given birth to a baby, something that troubled Emilio very much. Their oldest daughter, accustomed to living alone with her father and doing household chores for him, felt uncomfortable with her mother, whom she felt she hardly knew.

In another case, Adelina moved in with her grandparents because she also could not get along with her stepmother. She had been the eldest daughter in Mexico after her mother died and felt quite independent. Girls who came from Mexico often sought to marry later in life, to have few children, and to study for a professional degree. Much too often, however, as with the case of Tomasa's daughter, these girls became pregnant and their bright hopes were dashed.

10. James 1989: 4.

11. Some say a third helicopter came four or five days later.

12. I am not sure if Nicolás was aware that many people know about this incident. During one of my interviews with Nicolás, Bartolo Reyes was standing at a distance (as they always do discretely to allow for confidentiality). When we caught each other's eyes, he broke into silent yet uncontrolled laughter. I knew exactly what he was recalling, and I just tried to keep a straight face. I did not ask Nicolás about it.

13. Eight years later I located the son, Martín, in a refugee camp in Quintana Roo, Mexico, and informed him that his parents and siblings were alive. He was surprised, moved, and overjoyed. His parents were equally thrilled when they found out that their son had survived the army's bullets on that horrid day. Martín later joined the insurgents and remained a combatant until the demobilization in 1996. Alejandro knew well who had led the army to their camp. What he did not envision is that he and others like him later would have to live side by side with informers who had aided in their capture, torture, and misfortune. One person, referring to one of the informers, said, "He committed great sins, because he unjustly denounced some who did not even have much to do [with the insurgency]....It was just vengeance."

14. I have included segments of the following newspaper articles because it was unusual for Guatemalan papers to print articles about this village, especially during this period. More significantly, people in the city read these types of accounts, which were biased toward the army and often contrary to what was really happening. As the saying goes, the first casualty of war is the truth.

It should be pointed out that the job of journalists in Guatemala was not an easy one. More than forty journalists were killed or disappeared in Guatemala during the years of conflict. The military and the government did not want critical reporting nor accurate documentation of what they sought to distort.

The first article, "Campesinos de Ixcán huyen por violencia" (Peasants in Ixcán flee the violence), by Mario Recinos Lima, ran in El Gráfico on June 13, 1982. El Gráfico is no longer in publication.

> Aldea Playa Grande, Zona Ixcán, Quiché. Un total de 279 campesinos, incluyendo mujeres y niños se encuentran en esta localidad bajo protección militar, luego de haber abandonado sus tierras en la aldea Santa María Tzejá, como consecuencia de

los hostigamientos de grupos guerrilleros que operan en esta zona norte del Quiché, informaron oficiales militares.

Durante un mes aproximadamente los habitantes de la aldea Santa María Tzejá convivieron con un grupo de más de 60 guerrilleros en un campamento que estos habían construido en las aproximaciones de la población.

"En este tiempo," relatan los campesinos, "tuvimos un acercamiento fraterno, lo cual fue cambiando paulatinamente conforme ellos," añade uno de nuestros entrevistados, "se fueron apoderando de nuestras gallinas, vacas y otros productos."

Todo esto según afirmaban los jefes guerrilleros pasaba desde ese momento al poder de la revolución. "En parte la actitud asumida por los guerrilleros así como el engaño a que éramos sometidos," indicó otro campesino, "hizo colmar nuestra paciencia, por lo que pedimos nos dejaran regresar a nuestra aldea, a lo cual accedieron." "Desde esa fecha fuimos tildados de orejas y colaboradores," mencionó otro campesino.

The translation of this article is as follows (translated by the author):

Playa Grande village, Ixcán Zone, Quiché. A total of 279 peasants, including women and children, are in this town under military protection after abandoning their lands in the village of Santa María Tzejá due to the harassment of guerrilla groups who operate in the northern zone of El Quiché, military officials stated.

The inhabitants of Santa María Tzejá coexisted for approximately a month with a group of more than 60 guerrillas in a camp that the latter built near the village.

"During this time," the peasants related, "we had fraternal relations, which changed gradually as they took over our chickens, cows and other products," one of our interviewees added.

All this, according to what the guerrilla chiefs stated, became property of the revolution. "In part because of the attitude taken by the guerrillas and the deception they subjected us to," another peasant indicated, they "made us lose our patience, so we asked them to allow us to return to our village, and they agreed." "From that day on, they branded us 'orejas' and 'collaborators,' " another peasant mentioned.

The second article, "Subversión en abierta guerra contra Patrullas Civiles: Indígenas acosados en El Quiché y las Verapaces se defienden" (Insurgents in open war against civil patrols: Indigenous people harassed in El Quiché and Las Verapaces defend themselves), ran in *Prensa Libre* on June 13, 1982; it had no byline. Reprinted with permission.

Doscientos cincuenticinco campesinos, entre hombres mujeres y niños de la aldea Santa María Tzejá, jurisdicción de Uspantán, El Quiché, fueron engañados por delincuentes subversivos para que abandonaran sus aldeas. Posteriormente se dieron cuenta del timo y caminaron por espacio de dos horas para entregarse al ejército en busca de protección.

Dichos refugiados se encuentran actualmente en "Playa Grande" zona de Ixcán, donde existe un campamento militar, huyendo por que sus casas fueron quemadas y no tienen donde protegerse. Se les construyeron unos ranchos y se les proporciona alimentos, mientras que el INTA los reubica en un lugar más seguro.

La agrupación clandestina que opera en esas zonas es el EGP, comandados por líderes internacionales, como el caso del cura párroco de Santa María Tzejá, de nombre Gurriarán que ya abandonó el país y quiso introducir el comunismo.

El mencionado cura, según se supo, observando que nuestros indígenas son idólatras y muy apegados a las religiones, hacia mal uso de la Biblia, indicándoles que el pobre tiene que enaltecerse y el rico ser humillado.

Los refugiados de Playa Grande manifestaron a los medios de comunicación, que un grupo de delincuentes subversivos llegó a la aldea y les dijo que la abandonaran porque llegaría el ejército a matarlos y a quemarles sus ranchos.

Los campesinos, estimando que lo dicho era cierto evacuaron la aldea dejando todas sus pertenencias, incluyendo los animales domésticos que les sirven para la alimentación familiar.

Los subversivos después de hacerlos caminar por la montaña sin darles alimentos, se dirigieron a otras zonas, dejándolos abandonados, por lo que decidieron buscar al ejército para que les diera protección.

Los campesinos al verse atacados por los delincuentes subversivos, con ayuda del ejército han organizado patrullas de autodefensas, entrenados por el ejército y también armados cuando se considere que ya pueden manejar las armas.

Por ejemplo, en la aldea Salaquín de Cobán, Alta Verapaz, el 10 de mayo incursionaron los delincuentes subversivos incendiando 70 viviendas. Los patrulleros civiles repelieron el ataque causándoles 24 bajas.

Dentro de los campesinos de Salaquín, murieron 22 personas entre ellas la esposa del alcalde Reyes González, dos hermanos, dos tíos y otros familiares. Los asaltantes se apostaron desde un cerro donde con ametralladora dispararon contra la población, asesinando a ancianos, mujeres y niños.

The translation of this article is as follows (translated by the author):

Two hundred and fifty-five peasants, including men, women and children from the village of Santa María Tzejá, jurisdiction of Uspantán, El Quiché, were deceived by subversive criminals to abandon their villages. They realized later that they were deceived and walked for 2 hours to hand themselves over to the army, looking for protection.

Many refugees are currently in "Playa Grande," Ixcán zone, where a military base exists, fleeing because their houses were burned and they don't have a place to protect themselves. An encampment was built for them, and they were given food, while the INTA relocates them to a safer place.

The clandestine group that operates in the region is the EGP, commanded by international leaders, such as the case of the priest of Santa María Tzejá, whose name is Gurriarán, who has already left the country and who wanted to introduce communism.

The aforementioned priest, as was known, seeing that our indigenous people are idolatrous and very attached to religion, incorrectly used to the Bible, advising them that the poor should uplift themselves and that the wealthy must be humiliated.

The refugees of Playa Grande told the media that a group of criminal subversives came to the village and told them to abandon it because the army would come to kill them and to burn their houses.

The peasants, thinking that what was said was true, evacuated the village, leaving all their belongings, including their domestic animals, which are used for family consumption.

The subversives, after making them walk in the mountains without giving them food, went to other regions, abandoning them, so they decided to look for protection from the army.

The peasants, seeing that they were attacked by criminal subversives, with the help of the army have organized self-defense patrols trained by the army, and they will be armed when it is deemed that they can use weapons.

For instance, the criminal subversives raided the village Salaquín of Cobán, Alta Verapaz, on May 10, burning 70 houses. The civil patrols counterattacked, killing 24.

Among the peasants of Salaquín, 22 people died, among them the wife of the mayor Reyes González, two brothers, two uncles and other relatives. The assailants were in a hill from where they shot the population with machine guns, assassinating elders, women and children.

The article carried a photo of Don Alejandro Noriega Urízar (father of Sabas and Nicolás) identifying him as sixty-eight years old, with the caption, "He states, they have confused the teachings of the Bible."

15. When I talked to Pedro Juárez Hernantó about the guerrillas killing his son, he said he only had two sons, the rest of his children were daughters. He said both his sons had been killed by the guerrillas. But the eldest had died as a guerrilla combatant. As a fellow *guerrillero* from the village stated, "The brave and heroic *compañero* fell in combat." It was not unusual for people in a militarized village to say either that they did not know who or how a relative was killed or to claim the guerrillas were responsible. Even though I knew the background of this combatant and the circumstances of his death, I did not let on and simply wrote down what the elder said.

Chapter 5. A Militarized Village

1. Destroyed villages retained their names but with the prefix "New." In 1983, I went to the public relations office of the army in Guatemala City to obtain a pass to travel to the countryside. Above my photograph the permit read, "La Nueva Guatemala," March 8, 1983.

2. CEH 1999a: 31.

3. I was not one of Chema Cux's favorite people. He often avoided me to the amusement of the villagers.

4. Most of the *Cobaneros* were from the municipality of Tamahú, Alta Verapaz.

5. Most of the interviews for this chapter were done in Santa María Tzejá between 1985 and 1990.

6. REMHI 1999: 68.

7. CEH 1999a: 31.

8. REMHI 1999: 117.

9. For more on the process of indoctrination by the military see Manz 2003.

10. For more information on the model villages see Manz 1988a.

11. CEH 1999a: 27.

12. Ejército de Guatemala, plan de campaña Victoria 82, Anexo J, capítulo II, cited in CEH 1999f: 189.

13. It took twelve years for the father to be able to recover his land parcel: not until the refugees negotiated their return, which required the *nuevos* to vacate the land. The military (who had given his land to a *nuevo*) did nothing to resolve this land dispute. I remember Candelario patiently looking at this *nuevo* go by with a sack full of cardamom—the cardamom Candelario had planted several years earlier.

14. Since 1985, the constant presence, support, and commitment of outsiders was of great comfort. This was especially true if one was a former acquaintance, in contact with refugees from the village and Father Luis, and had offered positive encouragement even under depressing circumstances. This kept a sliver of hope alive. The correspondence, photos, and news were visibly heartwarming for the villagers. One of the first concrete steps in taking some action was the recovery of the cooperative house in Santa Cruz del Quiché and the attempt to reconstitute the original cooperative. This symbolic action could be in-

terpreted as a claim that the original Santa María Tzejá still existed as a community.

15. CEH 1999f: 187 and 190–191. "Firmeza 83," also known as the Plan de Campaña, was the military campaign plan for 1983.

16. REMHI 1999: 119.

17. Ibid.

18. Ibid.: 123.

19. Ibid.

20. CEH 1999a: 27.

21. Ibid. See also Zur 1998; Green 1999; Hale 1997a; Manz 2002.

22. REMHI 1999: 45.

23. Zur 1998: 93.

24. Ibid.

25. As mentioned in chapter 1, the elites and the military have historically extracted forced labor from the rural population.

26. The patrols were first organized in 1982 and dissolved in 1994.

27. In the militarized village there were several former soldiers who had received a parcel of land after the destruction and displacement. Often former soldiers lived side by side with people who had been tortured. One of the former soldiers from Cobán, a Kaibil, seemed to enjoy displaying his army boots and had no qualms about his participation in the counterinsurgency operations of 1981–83 in the Ixcán region.

28. Valentín was one of those who managed to escape when the army held the villagers in May 1982. He had made the decision after one villager who tried to escape was shot and killed. He stayed in hiding with the others, and eventually went with his wife, Magdalena, to find refuge in Mexico. Both became educators in the camp. Currently he is the director of the school in Santa María Tzejá, and Magdalena is a teacher. All along Magdalena had been considered one of the smartest people in the village. She had studied in the boarding school in Chichicastenango, reaching the highest grade of the group. Sadly, in June 2001, her father, Domingo Us Quixán, also a great leader in the refugee camps, as well as in the village, was killed while working in his land parcel.

29. Xan, who had received severe tortures at the army base, told me in 1987 about the contacts he maintained with the insurgents. He took me to the place where the clandestine meetings had taken place in his parcel. But he disclosed that he no longer had the courage to carry out even the smallest of assignments, such as buying notebooks in Cantabal. He feared the questions of the sales person. He was paranoid while trying to carry out the insurgents' requests. His brother, a combatant at the time, did however come to his house for several days without notice.

30. Years later I obtained several military documents that refer explicitly to the need to check people who had "relations with refugees, evacuated or displaced people" (Ejército de Guatemala 1983: 39). In my case I would have needed to be checked for both since I had relationships with the refugees in the Mexican camps as well as the displaced. My research in the most crucial conflict zone also made me a candidate for observation. Another military document advises to "control people from international entities who arrive in areas of mili-

tary operations" (p. 46). Reviewing several military documents, especially those dealing with "psychological operations," showed that the experiences in Santa María Tzejá had followed the manuals quite closely: talk about nationalism (*doctrina de la Guatemalidad*), life in totalitarian countries, communism; present analysis with the idea that the need comes from the villagers themselves and does not appear imposed; control radios, journalists, teachers, roads, and so on. The guerrillas are mentioned as delinquent terrorists.

31. Oficina de Derechos Humanos del Arzobispado de Guatemala 1998c: 260–61.

32. CEH 1999c: 213.

33. See Kempster 1987.

34. "El Milagro and San Isidro, both within a half-hour or so from the base, were taken over by the insurgents. El Milagro was taken at dawn on Monday April 22, 1987, and San Isidro on Wednesday, April 22, 1987. Informants in those villages gave estimates of guerrilla strength ranging from three hundred to six hundred people. The military commander, Colonel Guido Abdala, confirmed these incidents" (Manz 1988b:63–64). Father Tiziano, the Catholic priest assigned to the area, and I went to El Milagro on Sunday, April 26. He took it upon himself to "evacuate the women and children." The army had not gone to the village, supposedly because they feared an ambush or mines on the road. Tiziano drove a truck and filled it with women and children. As we were driving out of the village, military helicopters flew right over the truck as frightened women screaming and crying displayed white cloth. At one point Tiziano got out of the truck to direct it over a makeshift, perilous bridge. At that point bombs were dropped just ahead, the explosions raising fire behind Tiziano's head while he continued directing the truck. Several days later, a small military unit guided by PACs ambushed a small guerrilla unit near San Pablo just south of Cantabal. Four guerrillas were killed, and two were captured. One soldier was killed.

35. Guatemalan anthropologist Myrna Mack had begun to take field trips to rural areas since her return to Guatemala. After spending some years out of the country she returned toward the end of 1982. In the late 1980s, she conducted research among the displaced population, documenting the reasons for their displacement as well as documenting their lives. Myrna was committed to justice and cared about the future well-being of these people. She was assassinated on Tuesday, September 11, 1990. On the tenth anniversary of her murder I commented that some intellectuals "acquire a public voice without compromise. Myrna Mack was the intellectual of her generation that acquired that public voice with commitment." (Manz, in Fundación Myrna Mack 2000: 9).

36. From Myrna Mack's field notes, Santa María Tzejá, April 23 to May 6, 1987.

Chapter 6. Reunification

1. See Manz 1988b. For a comprehensive analysis of the repatriation effort, see Worby 2002; and AVANCSO 1992: 46–47.

2. The insurgents wanted the refugees to extract as many concessions as possible from the government and the army (even if it meant delaying the return), thereby benefiting the cause of the insurgency.

3. Most of the interviews for this chapter were done in Santa María Tzejá and other places in Guatemala between 1994 and 2002. Deadly disputes over land, or actions preventing recovery of lands by refugees, have become common as a result of land occupations encouraged by the military. For example, the *New York Times* ran a dispatch from the Associated Press on June 27, 2001, which revealed:

> Armed attackers believed to be former paramilitary fighters invaded a village in western Guatemala, burning dozens of homes, raping two women and kidnapping children, neighbors and human rights activists said. Diego Itzep, a resident of a neighboring town, told The Associated Press on Tuesday that about 30 men came into the village of Los Cimientos and "tied up one of the leaders, raped women, then burned 82 of the 86 houses." Itzep and Frank LaRue, of the Center for Human Rights Legal Action, blamed Monday's attack on former paramilitary civilian patrols—residents working for the army against insurgents during Guatemala's 36-year civil war. "We know of two women who were raped and seven children kidnapped by the attackers," LaRue said. In 1982, the army killed two leaders of Los Cimientos, a Quiché Indian community about 200 miles from the capital, prompting residents to flee the village. In 1983, the army handed over the land to its civilian collaborators, while the former owners fled to Mexico to escape massacres that had begun in Guatemala in the 1980s. The original landowners returned and have been fighting for the land since 1994. Guatemalan police said they had sent officers to the site, but had not received any further information.

4. After this unfriendly exchange with Miguel Reyes had become quite loud and heated, and after being ordered by Mexican officials (in an unrelated matter) to leave, it took some time before I returned to the camps. One day in the United States, I received a formal letter signed by several elected officials from Santa María Tzejá living in the camps. It was not only a conciliatory invitation for me to return whenever I wanted, but it asked me to give the refugees enough notice so that they could prepare, organize, and assist me with my research. In thirty years of research, I never had a better organized and more supportive visit. A young woman was put at my disposal to assist me; she acted as a translator if I needed it. Most of the young people in the camps had assignments related to my stay. For example, while I always slept in the same house (of Bartolo Reyes and Dominga Argueta) in the refugee camp, each morning someone came to tell me where I was going to have breakfast. Then another person would come with a list of names and tell me the interview plan for that morning. Someone else came to take me to lunch, and then another person showed up with the list of people to be interviewed that afternoon. Several meetings with all the refugees from Santa María Tzejá were organized for the evenings. They sent word to Kesté announcing my arrival there. It was so well orchestrated that whatever I said or needed was communicated to the elected leaders.

The Mexican government was upset about my visit to Chiapas soon after the forced relocation. Human Rights Watch produced a scathing human rights report (Americas Watch 1984b), the first one on Mexico, denouncing violations and mistreatment of the Guatemalan refugees. The Mexican government officials knew that the condemnatory report was based in large part on my documentation. I was declared persona non grata and asked not to return to Mexico. But I did. As I was entering an elevator in Campeche one day, I found myself literally against the wall of the elevator faced with two men in dark glasses. They did not bother to greet me or ask who I was, simply stating, "You know the way to the airport." I said I sure did. They then elaborated on what they meant by "the way," clarifying they meant the most direct way to the airport, just in case I thought of taking the long way or a detour! I got the message. In 1982 I had gone to the Lacandón jungle looking for refugees and succeeded in getting in and out. But the Mexican government was not at all happy with any outsiders—and by that they meant also Mexicans—to interview refugees. They had kidnapped two nuns and a journalist, Adolfo Aguilar Zinser, who has since become Mexico's ambassador to the United Nations. Aguilar Zinser was kidnapped from his apartment in Mexico City and placed in detention with many others who had been detained illegally. He was freed only after the intervention of several people, including a U.S.-based organization that supported journalists' rights around the world.

During the time when it was difficult for me to enter the camps, I met once with refugees in Villa Hermosa, the capital of the state of Tabasco.

5. The refugees and the people in Santa María Tzejá were also very lucky to have had a real advocate in the United Nations High Commissioner for Refugees. Paula Worby took a particular interest in the future of this village and especially in the reunification efforts.

6. Mexican refugee officials sent a few families who relocated later to two camps in Quintana Roo.

7. The *antiguos* and the *nuevos* did not have the same vision; their cultural and ideological differences were substantial. Despite this, some youth intermarried, and each group tended not to speak openly against the other in front of outsiders.

8. Santa Cruz del Quiché, capital of the department of El Quiché, was no longer the link to the Ixcán that it used to be. After Cantabal had become the established capital of the new municipality of Ixcán, and after roads as well as flights went to Cobán in Alta Verapaz, the new link for marketing and hospitals became Cobán via Cantabal.

9. One example of my caution with Nicolás occurred whenever he would state something quite provocative politically. I would either refrain from responding or I would go along, such as the time he told me the Sandinistas in Nicaragua forced everyone to dress in olive green. I became quite paranoid, thinking that the army was making him say these stupidities. If I told him, "That is not true," I would be reported, and the military could have gone after me. Coincidentally, I was wearing a white cotton shirt with colorful embroidery. I pointed to my blouse and could not resist saying, "Nicolás, let me just say, I bought this blouse in Managua, in a regular store at a market. Women in Nicaragua wear this type of blouse." I was therefore not saying what he told me was untrue, yet I told him people wear different types of clothing.

10. See Manz 1988a.

11. The school is entirely funded by outside sources, especially the Congregational Church in Needham, Massachusetts, and other U.S. donors, as well as funding from Spain. The school has a video machine for viewing films. The Spencer Foundation, located in Chicago, funded two students to attend meetings at their headquarters to present a talk about an environmental project.

12. Montejo n.d.: 115

13. Ibid.: 179.

14. The male returnees also decided that the Permanent Commissions (CCPP) should be disbanded. Otherwise, the symbolism of separate organizations would prolong the divisions.

15. González 2002. Del Cid Vargas also cites a government document about the health conditions in the Ixcán. She quotes the government as saying many of these health problems are preventable, especially regarding mortality (Del Cid Vargas 2000: 13).

16. In 1970 the population of the Ixcán was probably around five thousand. By 1982, at the time of the scorched earth counterinsurgency tactics, the population may have been between forty-five and fifty thousand. According to the census, the population of the Ixcán was 61,448 in 2002. In 1990, according to AVANCSO, there were more than sixty thousand people in the Ixcán (AVANCSO 1992: 63).

17. Del Cid Vargas 2000.

18. The *antiguos* who collaborated with the army and were instrumental in the formation of the civil patrols have now moved to the sidelines. Only one, Miguel Pacheco, remains actively defiant and obstructionist; he continues to intimidate and bully fellow villagers.

After most villagers expressed the desire to use their real names rather than pseudonyms in this book, I went to Rosalío and Miguel Pacheco's house on the evening of February 15, 2003, accompanied by a villager and a person who works for the cooperative. I asked Miguel and Rosalío their preferences on the name issue. Miguel was clearly annoyed by my presence and angrily confronted me using typical military terms, "I will not respond to your interrogations," continuing, "I will not give any declarations." I told him this was simply a courtesy call, that I did not care one way or another how the names would appear. In fact, when I interviewed him on tape years earlier he was using his real name and had not objected to it. Given that he would not express his preference, I opted for using a pseudonym. As I was leaving his house he warned, "We'll see what will happen. I will inform the authorities [military]." And, as if there was a state of siege, he told me in a hostile tone that "it is prohibited to be out at this time; to go to people's houses at this time. We will see what the authorities will do." So it appears that Miguel Pacheco, as late as 2003, still would like to think that the military is in charge and that he can intimidate everyone in the village.

I told my companions that I should have said to "*el teniente* Pacheco" ("the lieutenant," as some villagers have nicknamed him), "The last time I checked the laws of the Republic of Guatemala there was nothing regarding a curfew," and that "I should have asked him what decree he was referring to." It took the villager several hours to stop shaking and perhaps days to recover from the fright.

19. Interview with Paula Worby, Berkeley, 2002.

20. Ibid.
21. Ibid.
22. The boys were left in his care after his wife abandoned him in 1982. They were raised by Nicolás's sister María and the grandparents, Alejandro Noriega and Genara Morales.
23. Goodwin and Skocpol 1989: 489.
24. Ibid.: 490.
25. Quoted in Ibid.: 490–91. See also a very useful anthology, Goldstone 1994. On Latin American peasantry and guerrilla movements, see Wickham-Crowley 1992; Castañeda 1993, 1997; Walker 1994; Singlemann 1981; Paige 1983.
26. See Derecho Indígena Multiétnica Ixcán 1999.

Chapter 7. Treading between Fear and Hope

1. Broder 1999.
2. CEH 1999a: 39.
3. Ibid.
4. Ibid.: 41
5. The thirty-six-year internal war ended with peace accords signed on December 29, 1996.
6. Quoted in Kinzer 2001: 62. See also Jonas 2000.
7. MINUGUA United Nations Verification Mission in Guatemala 2002.
8. For more on lynchings and lawlessness in Guatemala, see Snodgrass-Godoy 2001.
9. Domingo Us Quixán, originally from the highlands municipality of Joyabaj, was a pioneer founder of the village cooperative, serving as president in the 1970s. He was a very active catechist and in the year 2000 had been president of the village's development committee.
10. Kinzer 2001.
11. Smith 1990a.
12. Kinzer 2001: 62.
13. Ibid.
14. Ibid.: 61.
15. I have previously focused on the issues of grief and memory. See Manz 1999, 2002, and 2003.
16. Lira 1994; Malkki 1995; Lambek 1996.
17. Hale 1997a, 1997b; Wilson 1991, 1995, 1997; Warren 1993a; Green 1999; Nelson 1999a.
18. Warren 1998: 86.
19. Zur 1998: 159.
20. Falla 1992; Montejo 1987; Equipo de Antropología Forense 1997.
21. Levi 1988: 23.
22. Ibid.: 27.
23. Ibid.
24. Quoted in Marques, Páez, and Serra 1997: 258.

25. Cifuentes 1998: 89.

26. Arendt 1968: 259.

27. Ibid.: 258, 240.

28. In addition to the cooperative there are now many organizations or committees in the village. The committees are: development projects, Catholic Church, school parents, scholarship program, cardamom drier, transport, vigilance, cooperative education, cooperative purchasing, agriculture, construction, livestock, women's union, fruit juice production, human rights, housing, student association, and former civil patrollers.

29. One adult, who feared for his life when surrounded by a group of drunken youngsters, beat one youth over the chest with a heavy stick, causing his instant death. The mother, Marta Castro, a widow from Joyabaj, accepted the explanation, resigned that she had trouble with her son, who had fallen with the wrong group and felt lost, hopeless, and dejected.

30. For more on Guatemalans in the United States, see Manz et al. 2000; Burns 1993; Chinchilla, Hamilton, and Loucky 1993; Hamilton and Chinchilla 1991, 2001.

31. A front-page article in the *New York Times* in August 2002 reported: "June was the deadliest month ever there, with 67 migrants dying, mostly in the unrelenting heat of the United States Border Patrol's Tucson sector, a barely habitable land that covers most of southern Arizona" (Nieves 2002).

32. According to the INS, 135 people died of heat exposure in 2000. Since Operation Gatekeeper began in 1994, about two thousand migrants have died on the U.S. side of the border. In the month of June 2002, according to the Mexican government, twenty-two migrants died. Mexico does not keep track of Central American deaths. Often the migrants do not have identification papers. They are buried in graves marked "No Olvidado" (not forgotten). See Nieves 2002. On the impact of border buildup, see Reyes et al. 2002.

33. Conversely, Mexicans and Salvadorans have been more exposed to urban life in their country and tend to speak Spanish fluently, both advantages in the United States. Latin American migrants have a tendency to look down on indigenous people. The Guatemalans I met tended to prefer working for a "gringo" (an American), rather than a Latino, because the wages and the treatment in their experience tends to be fairer, a stereotype based on personal experience. While they often feel somewhat uncomfortable around nonindigenous Latinos, they nevertheless frequently attempt to pass as Mexicans in dress, speech, and manners because that makes them less noticeable, and if apprehended by the INS, they would be sent, if lucky, to Mexico, rather than Guatemala. They quickly adopt the stereotypes in the United States, especially in reference to African Americans.

34. MIF/IDB 2003: 4

35. United States Department of State, Congressional Budget Justification for Foreign Operations, The Secretary of State, Foreign Operations, Fiscal Year 2004: 468 (page span 443–97); see also http://www.state.gov/m/rm/rls/cbj/ (as of June 2, 2003).

36. La Moneda 2002.

37. Thompson 2002.

Bibliography

Adams, Richard N. 1970. *Crucifixion by Power: Essays on Guatemalan National Social Structure, 1944–66.* Austin: University of Texas Press.

Aguayo, Sergio. 1985. *El éxodo centroamericano: Consecuencias de un conflicto.* México City: Secretaría de Educación Pública.

Aguilera Peralta, Gabriel, Jorge Romero Imery, et al. 1981. *Dialéctica del terror en Guatemala.* Guatemala City: Editorial Universitaria Centroamericana.

Americas Watch. 1982. *Human Rights in Guatemala: No Neutrals Allowed.* New York: Americas Watch Committee.

———. 1983. *Creating a Desolation and Calling It Peace: May 1983 Supplement to the Report on Human Rights in Guatemala.* New York: Americas Watch Committee.

———. 1984a. *Guatemala: A Nation of Prisoners.* New York: Americas Watch Committee.

———. 1984b. *Guatemalan Refugees in Mexico, 1980–84.* New York: Americas Watch Committee.

———. 1985. *Little Hope: Human Rights in Guatemala, January 1984 to January 1985.* New York: Americas Watch Committee.

———. 1986. *Civil Patrols in Guatemala.* New York: Americas Watch Committee.

Americas Watch and Physicians for Human Rights. 1991. *Guatemala: Getting Away with Murder.* New York: Human Rights Watch.

Amnesty International. 1981. *Guatemala: A Government Program of Political Murder.* London: Amnesty International Publications.

———. 1982. *Massive Extrajudicial Executions in Rural Areas under the Government of General Efraín Ríos Montt.* London: Amnesty International Publications.

———. 1983. *Amnesty International Report 1983.* London: Amnesty International.

———. 1984. *Torture in the Eighties.* London: Amnesty International Publications.

———. 1987. *Guatemala: The Human Rights Record.* London: Amnesty International Publications.

―――. 2002. *Guatemala's Lethal Legacy: Past Impunity and Renewed Human Rights Violations.* London: International Secretariat.

Annis, Sheldon. 1987. *God and Production in a Guatemala Town.* Austin: University of Texas Press.

Antze, Paul, and Michael Lambek. 1996. *Tense Past: Cultural Essays in Trauma and Memory.* New York: Routledge.

Arendt, Hannah. 1968. *Between Past and Future.* New York: Viking Press.

Arévalo de León, Bernardo. 1998. *Sobre arenas movedizas: Sociedad, estado y ejército en Guatemala, 1997.* Guatemala City: Facultad Latinoamericana de Ciencias Sociales (FLACSO).

Arias, Arturo. 1990. "Changing Indian Identity: Guatemala's Violent Transitions to Modernity." In Carol A. Smith, ed., *Guatemalan Indians and the State, 1540 to 1988,* 230–57. Austin: University of Texas Press.

―――, ed. 2001. *The Rigoberta Menchú Controversy.* Minneapolis: University of Minnesota Press.

AVANCSO (Asociación para el Avance de las Ciencias Sociales en Guatemala). 1990a. *Assistance and Control: Policies Toward Internally Displaced Populations in Guatemala.* Washington, D.C.: Hemispheric Migration Project, Center for Immigration Policy and Refugee Assistance, Georgetown University.

―――. 1990b. *Política institucional hacia el desplazado interno en Guatemala.* Guatemala City: AVANCSO.

―――. 1991. "'Vonós a la Capital': Estudio sobre la emigración en Guatemala." Cuadernos de Investigación, no. 7. Guatemala City: AVANCSO.

―――. 1992. *¿Dónde está el futuro? Procesos de reintegración en comunidades de retornados.* Guatemala City: AVANCSO.

―――. 1993. *Agricultura y campesinado en Guatemala: Una aproximación.* Guatemala City: AVANCSO.

―――. 1994a. *El significado de la maquila en Guatemala: Elementos para su comprensión.* Guatemala City: AVANCSO.

―――. 1994b. *Impacto ecológico de los cultivos hortícolas no-tradicionales en el altiplano de Guatemala: Efecto sobre plagas, organismos benéficos y suelo.* Guatemala City: AVANCSO.

―――. 1996. *De la etnia a la nación.* Guatemala City: AVANCSO.

―――. 1997. *La ciudad y los desplazados por la violencia.* Guatemala City: AVANCSO.

―――. 1998. *Imágenes homogéneas en un país de rostros diversos: El sistema educativo formal y la conformación de referentes de identidad nacional entre jóvenes guatemaltecos.* Guatemala City: AVANCSO.

―――. 2000. "Heridas en la sombra": Percepciones sobre violencia en areas pobres urbanas y periurbanas de la Ciudad de Guatemala.* Guatemala City: AVANCSO.

―――. 2001. *Regiones y zonas agrarias de Guatemala: Una visión desde la reproducción social y económica de los campesinos.* Guatemala City: AVANCSO.

Bastos, Santiago, and Manuela Camus. 1995. *Abriendo caminos: Las organizaciones mayas desde el Nobel hasta el Acuerdo de Derechos Indígenas.* Guatemala City: FLACSO.

Belpoliti, Marco, and Robert Gordon, eds. 2001. *Primo Levi: The Voice of Memory*. New York: New York Press.

Black, George, with Milton Jamail and Norma Stoltz Chinchilla. 1984. *Garrison Guatemala*. New York: Monthly Review Press.

Bossen, Laurel. 1984. *The Redivision of Labor: Women and Economic Choice in Four Guatemalan Communities*. Albany: State University of New York Press.

Bounds, Andrew. 2000. "World News: The Americas." *Financial Times of London*, June 17: 5.

Bourdieu, Pierre, and Loic J. D. Wacquant. 1992. *An Invitation to Reflexive Sociology*. Chicago: University of Chicago Press.

Bourgois, Philippe. 2001. "The Power of Violence in War and Peace: Post–Cold War Lessons from El Salvador." *Ethnography* 2 (1): 5–37.

Brandes, Stanley. 2002. *Staying Sober in Mexico City*. Austin: University of Texas Press.

Brintnall, Douglas E. 1979. *Revolt Against the Dead: The Modernization of a Mayan Community in the Highlands of Guatemala*. New York: Gordon and Breach.

Broder, John M. 1999. "Clinton Offers his Apologies to Guatemala." *New York Times*, Mar. 11: A1.

Burgos-Debray, Elisabeth, ed. 1984. *I, Rigoberta Menchú: An Indian Woman in Guatemala*. London: Verso.

Burkhalter, Holly, Juan Méndez, and Pratap Chitnis. 1987. *Human Rights in Guatemala during President Cerezo's First Year*. New York: Americas Watch; British Parliamentary Human Rights Group.

Burns, Allan F. 1993. *Maya in Exile: Guatemalans in Florida*. Philadelphia: Temple University Press.

Cambranes, J. C. 1985. *Coffee and Peasants: The Origins of the Modern Plantation Economy in Guatemala, 1853–1897*. South Woodstock, Vt.: Centro de Investigaciones Regionales de Mesoamérica (CIRMA)/Plumsock Mesoamerican Studies.

Carey, David. 2001. *Our Elders Teach Us: Maya-Kaqchikel Historical Perspectives: xkib'ij kan qate' qatata'*. Tuscaloosa: University of Alabama Press.

Carmack, Robert M. 1968. *Toltec Influence on the Postclassic Culture History of Highland Guatemala*. New Orleans: Middle American Research Institute, Tulane University.

———. 1973. *Quichean Civilization: The Ethnohistoric, Ethnographic, and Archaeological Sources*. Berkeley: University of California Press.

———. 1979. *Historia Social de los Quiché*. Guatemala City: Editorial "José de Pineda Ibarra," Ministerio de Educación.

———. 1981. *The Quiché Mayas of Utatlán*. Norman: University of Oklahoma Press.

———, ed. 1988a. *Harvest of Violence: The Maya Indians and the Guatemalan Crisis*. Norman: University of Oklahoma Press.

———. 1988b. "The Story of Santa Cruz Quiché." In Robert M. Carmack, ed., *Harvest of Violence: The Maya Indians and the Guatemalan Crisis*, 36–69. Norman: University of Oklahoma Press.

———. 1995. *Rebels of Highland Guatemala: The Quiché-Mayas of Momostenango*. Norman: University of Oklahoma Press.

Castañeda, Jorge G. 1993. *Utopia Unarmed: The Latin American Left after the Cold War*. New York: Alfred A. Knopf.

———. 1997. *Compañero: The Life and Death of Che Guevara*. New York: Alfred A. Knopf.

CEH (Comisión para el Esclarecimiento Histórico). 1999a. *Guatemala Memoria del Silencio* (Guatemala Memory of Silence). *Conclusions and Recommendations*. Guatemala City: United Nations Office for Project Services (UNOPS).

———. 1999b. *Guatemala Memoria del Silencio* (Guatemala Memory of Silence). Tomo III. *Las violaciones de los derechos humanos y los hechos de la violencia*. Guatemala City: UNOPS.

———. 1999c. *Guatemala Memoria del Silencio* (Guatemala Memory of Silence). Tomo I. *Mandato y procedimiento de trabajo. Causas y orígenes del enfrentamiento armado interno*. Guatemala City: UNOPS.

———. 1999d. *Guatemala Memoria del Silencio* (Guatemala Memory of Silence). Tomo IV. *Consecuencia y efectos de la violencia*. Guatemala City: UNOPS.

———. 1999e. *Guatemala Memoria del Silencio* (Guatemala Memory of Silence). Tomo VII. *Casos ilustrativos*. Guatemala City: UNOPS.

———. 1999f. *Guatemala Memoria del Silencio* (Guatemala Memory of Silence). Tomo II. *Las violaciones de los derechos humanos y los hechos de violencia*. Guatemala City: UNOPS.

CEIDEC (Centro de Estudios Integrados de Desarrollo Comunal). 1988. *Guatemala, polos de desarrollo: El caso de la desestructuración de las comunidades indígenas*. Mexico City: CEIDEC.

———. 1990. *Guatemala polos de desarrollo: El caso de la desestructuración de las comunidades indígenas*. Vol. 2. Mexico City: CEIDEC.

Central Intelligence Agency. February 1982. "Counterinsurgency Operations in El Quiché." Secret Cable. National Security Archive, Washington, D.C., document 14. www.gwu.edu/~nsarchiv/NSAEBB11/docs/14–01.htm (as of Nov. 12, 2002).

Chinchilla, Norma, Nora Hamilton, and James Loucky. 1993. "Central Americans in Los Angeles: An Immigrant Community in Transition." In Joan Moore and Raquel Pinderhughes, eds., *In the Barrios: Latinos and the Underclass Debate*, 51–78. New York: Russell Sage Foundation.

Cifuentes, Juan Fernando. n.d. *El G-5 en el Ejército de Guatemala*. Guatemala City.

——— 1982a. "Una apreciación de asuntos civiles para la región Ixil." *Revista Militar* (Sept.–Dec.): 26–72.

———. 1982b. "Operación Ixil." *Revista Militar* (Sept.–Dec.): 25–72.

———. 1998. *Historia moderna de la etnicidad en Guatemala. La visión hegemónica: Rebeliones y otros incidentes indígenas en el siglo XX*. Guatemala City: Universidad Rafael Landívar, Instituto de Investigaciones Económicas y Sociales.

Cleary, Edward. 1997. *The Struggle for Human Rights in Latin America*. Westport, Conn.: Praeger.

Coates, Anthony G., ed. 1997. *Central America: A Natural and Cultural History*. New Haven: Yale University Press.

Coe, Michael D. 1999. *The Maya*. New York: Thames and Hudson.

Cohen Salama, Mauricio. 1992. *Tumbas anónimas: Informe sobre la identificación de restos de víctimas de la represión ilegal*. Buenos Aires: Equipo Argentino de Antropología Forense.

COINDE (Consejo de Instituciones de Desarrollo). 1993. *Ixcán: Colonización, desarraigo y condiciones de retorno*. Guatemala City: COINDE.

Cojtí Cuxil, Demetrio. 1997. "Unidad del estado mestizo y regiones autónomas mayas." In Fridolin Birk, ed., *Guatemala: ¿Oprimida pobre o princesa embrujada?* 175–89. Guatemala: Fundación Friedrich Ebert.

Colby, Benjamin N. 1983. Review of *Time and the Highland Maya* (1982), by Barbara Tedlock. *American Anthropologist* 85 (1): 210–11.

———. 1988. Review of *Dreaming: Anthropological and Psychological Interpretations* (1987), by Barbara Tedlock. *American Anthropologist* 90 (4): 991.

Conferencia Episcopal de Guatemala. 1995. "Urge la verdadera paz." Quoted in Quezada Toruño, Rodolfo. 2000. Mensaje de la Comisión de Educación de la Conferencia Episcopal de Guatemala con motivo de la Campaña de Alfabetización. Guatemala. www.riial.org/guatemala/alfabe.htm.

Corradi, Juan E., Patricia Weiss Fagen, and Manuel Antonio Garreton, eds. 1992. *Fear at the Edge*. Berkeley: University of California Press.

D'Andrade, Roy. 1995. "Moral Models in Anthropology." *Current Anthropology* 36 (3): 399–408.

Davis, Shelton H. 1988. "Introduction: Sowing the Seeds of Violence." In Robert M. Carmack, ed., *Harvest of Violence: The Maya Indians and the Guatemalan Crisis*, 3–36. Norman: University of Oklahoma Press.

Davis, Shelton H., and Julie Hodson. 1982. *Witness to Political Violence in Guatemala: The Suppression of a Rural Development Movement*. Boston: Oxfam America.

Del Cid Vargas, Paula Irene. 2000. *Diagnóstico sobre población y medio ambiente en Ixcán*. Guatemala: Red de Población y Medio Ambiente. http://www.poam.org/articulos-estudios/investigaciones/ixcan.pdf (as of July 15, 2002).

Dennis, Phillip A., Gary S. Elbow, and Peter L. Heller. January 1984. *Final Report: Playa Grande Land Colonization Project, Guatemala*. Manuscript.

Department of State. Circa late 1982. "Guatemala: Reports of Atrocities Mark Army Gains." Secret Cable. National Security Archive, Washington, D.C., document 17. http://www.gwu.edu/~nsarchiv/NSAEBB/NSAEBB11/docs /17–01.htm (as of Nov. 12, 2002).

———. 1983. *Country Reports on Human Rights Practices for 1982*. Washington, D.C.: U.S. Government Printing Office.

Derecho Indígena Multiétnica Ixcán. 1999. *El derecho indígena de la Comunidad Primavera del Ixcán (CPR del Ixcán)*. Guatemala City: Coordinación de Organizaciones del Pueblo Maya de Guatemala.

Dickey, Christopher. 1982. "Guatemala Gets Arms From U.S. Despite Ban." *Washington Post/International Herald Tribune,* January 25: 1.

Diócesis del Quiché. 1994. *El Quiché: El pueblo y su Iglesia, 1960–1980.* Santa Cruz del Quiché, Guatemala: Diócesis del Quiché.

Doyle, Kate, and Adam Isacson. 2001. "A New New World Order? U.S. Military Mission Grows in Latin America." *NACLA [North American Congress on Latin America] Report on the Americas* 35 (3): 14–20.

Ehlers, Tracy Bachrach. 1990a. "Central America in the 1980s: Political Crisis and the Social Responsibility of Anthropologists." *Latin America Research Review* 25 (3): 141–55.

———. 1990b. *Silent Looms: Women and Production in a Guatemalan Town.* Boulder, Colo.: Westview Press.

Ejército de Guatemala. n.d. *Manual de operaciones psicológicas.* TE-318–01. Centro de Estudios Militares, Escuela de Comando y Estado Mayor. Guatemala City.

———. 1982a. "Anexo H." *Ordenes permanentes para el desarrollo de operaciones contrasubversivas al Plan de Campaña "Victoria 82."* LEMG-1800. 160800JUL82. Guatemala City.

———. 1982b. *Plan Nacional de Seguridad y Desarrollo.* PNSD-01–82. CEM 01 ABR8 RLHGCC082. Guatemala City.

———. 1983. *Plan de Campaña "Firmeza 83."*

———. 1984a. *Polos de desarrollo.* Guatemala City: Editorial del Ejército.

———. 1984b. "Pensamiento y cultura." *Revista Cultural del Ejército.* Edición especialmente dedicada a la labor institucional del Comité de Reconstrucción Nacional.

———. 1984c. *Las Patrullas de Autodefensa Civil: La respuesta popular al proceso de integración socio-economico-político en la Guatemala actual.* Guatemala City: Editorial del Ejército.

———. 1984d. "Polos de desarrollo." *Revista Militar* 31 (Jan.–Apr.): 75–78.

———. 1985. "Polos de desarrollo." *Revista Cultural del Ejército* (Jan.–Feb.): 1–80.

———. 1986. Comunicado de Prensa No. 0229–86. Comité de Autodefensa Civil de Nebaj. Desalojo a terroristas de la región. Guatemala City: Departamento de Información y Divulgación del Ejército. Ministerio de la Defensa Nacional.

———. 1987. *Foro Nacional.* "27 Años de lucha por la libertad." Una presentación oficial del Ejército de Guatemala. Organizado por el Consejo Empresarial: August 12. Tape transcription.

Episcopado Guatemalteco. 1988. *Carta pastoral colectiva, el clamor por la tierra.* Guatemala City: February, Episcopado Guatemalteco.

Equipo de Antropología Forense. 1997. *Las masacres en Rabinal: Estudio histórico antropológico de las masacres de Plan de Sánchez, Chichupac y Río Negro.* Guatemala City: Equipo de Antropología Forense de Guatemala.

Fabri, Antonella. 1994. "(Re)Composing the Nation: Politics of Memory and Displacement in Maya Testimonies from Guatemala." Ph.D. diss., State University of New York at Albany.

Falla, Ricardo. 1972. "Hacia la Revolución Verde: Adopción y dependencia del fertilizante químico en un municipio del Quiché, Guatemala." *América Indígena* 32 (2): 437–80.

———. 1978. "El movimiento indígena." *Estudios Centroamericanos* 33 (356–57): 437–61.

———. 1980. *Quiché rebelde: Estudio de un movimiento de conversión religiosa, rebelde a las creencias tradicionales, en San Antonio Ilotenango, Quiché, 1948–1970.* Guatemala City: Editorial Universitaria.

———. 1983a. *Masacre de la Finca San Francisco, Huehuetenango, Guatemala: (17de julio de 1982).* Copenhagen: International Work Group for Indigenous Affairs.

———. 1983b. *Voices of the Survivors: The Massacre at Finca San Francisco, Guatemala.* Boston: Cultural Survival and Anthropology Resource Center.

———. 1992. *Masacres de la selva: Ixcán, Guatemala (1975–1982).* Guatemala City: Editorial Universitaria, Universidad de San Carlos de Guatemala.

———. 1994. *Massacres in the Jungle: Ixcán, Guatemala, 1975–1982.* Boulder, Colo.: Westview Press.

———. 1998. *The Story of a Great Love: Life with the Guatemalan "Communities of Population in Resistance": A Spiritual Journal.* Washington, D.C.: Ecumenical Program on Central America and the Caribbean.

Figueroa Ibarra, Carlos. 1991. *El recurso del miedo: Ensayo sobre el Estado y el terror en Guatemala.* San José, Costa Rica: Editorial Universitaria Centroamericana.

Fischer, Edward, and R. McKenna Brown, eds. 1996. *Mayan Cultural Activism in Guatemala.* Austin: University of Texas Press.

Fox, Richard, and Orin Starn. 1997. *Between Resistance and Revolution: Cultural Politics and Social Protest.* New Brunswick, N.J.: Rutgers University Press.

Friedlander, Judith. 1975. *Being Indian in Hueyapán: A Study of Forced Identity in Contemporary Mexico.* New York: St. Martin's Press.

Fundación Myrna Mack. 2000. "Myrna. Décimo aniversario del asesinato de Myrna Mack." Guatemala City: Fundación Myrna Mack.

Geertz, Clifford. 1988. *Works and Lives: The Anthropologist as Author.* Stanford: Stanford University Press.

———. 2000. *Available Light: Anthropological Reflections on Philosophical Topics.* Princeton: Princeton University Press.

Gleijeses, Piero. 1991. *Shattered Hope: The Guatemalan Revolution and the United States, 1944–1954.* Princeton: Princeton University Press.

Glueck, Grace. 1984. "Untouched Mayan Tomb Is Discovered." *New York Times,* May 23: A1, C23.

Gobierno de Guatemala. 1995. *Polos de desarrollo y servicios: Historiografía institucional.* Guatemala City: Editorial del Ejército.

Gobierno de la República. 2001. *El drama de la pobreza en Guatemala: Un informe sobre los rasgos de esta privación y sus efectos sobre la sociedad.* Guatemala City: February, Gobierno de la República.

Goldfrank, Walter L. 1994. "The Mexican Revolution." In Jack A. Goldstone, ed., *Revolutions: Theoretical, Comparative, and Historical Studies,* 115–27. New York: Harcourt Brace College Publishers.

Goldstone, Jack A., ed. 1994. *Revolutions: Theoretical, Comparative, and Historical Studies.* New York: Harcourt Brace College Publishers.

González, David. 2002. "Malnourished to Get Help in Guatemala." *New York Times,* Mar. 20: A3.

Goodwin, Jeff, and Theda Skocpol. 1989. "Explaining Revolutions in the Contemporary Third World." *Politics and Society* 17 (4): 489–510.

El Gráfico. 1976. "Torturada y estrangulada hallan a joven profesora." *El Gráfico,* Jan. 13: 1 and 3.

Graham, Ian. 1981. "On Guatemalan Refugees." *Cultural Survival Newsletter* 5 (4): 15.

Gramajo Morales, Héctor. 1986–87. "Contrainsurgencia en Guatemala: Un caso de estudio." *Revista Militar* 39 (Sept.–Apr.).

———. 1989. *La tesis de la estabilidad nacional.* Guatemala City: Editorial del Ejército.

———. 1995. *De la guerra…a la guerra: La difícil transición política en Guatemala.* Guatemala City: Fondo de Cultura Editorial.

Grandin, Greg. 2000. *The Blood of Guatemala: A History of Race and Nation.* Durham, N.C.: Duke University Press.

Green, Linda. 1999. *Fear as a Way of Life: Mayan Widows in Rural Guatemala.* New York: Columbia University Press.

Hale, Charles R. 1997a. "Consciousness, Violence, and the Politics of Memory in Guatemala." *Current Anthropology* 38 (5): 817–38.

———. 1997b. "Cultural Politics of Identity in Latin America." *Annual Review of Anthropology* 26: 567–90.

Hamilton, Nora, and Norma Stoltz Chinchilla. 1991. "Central America Migration: A Framework for Analysis." *Latin American Research Review* 6 (1): 75–110.

———. 2001. *Seeking Community in a Global City: Guatemalans and Salvadorans in Los Angeles.* Philadelphia: Temple University Press.

Handy, Jim. 1984. *Gift of the Devil: A History of Guatemala.* Boston: South End Press.

———. 1994. *Revolution in the Countryside: Rural Conflict and Agrarian Reform in Guatemala, 1944–54.* Chapel Hill: University of North Carolina Press.

Harris, Marvin. 1995. "Comments." *Current Anthropology* 36 (3): 423–24.

Hawkins, John. 1984. *Inverse Images: The Meaning of Culture, Ethnicity, and Family in Postcolonial Guatemala.* Albuquerque: University of New Mexico Press.

Helms, Mary W. 1975. *Middle America: A Cultural History of Heartland and Frontiers.* Englewood Cliffs, N.J.: Prentice-Hall.

Huxley, Aldous. 1934. *Beyond the Mexique Bay.* London: Chatto and Windus.

Iglesia Guatemalteca en el Exilio. n.d. *Cronología de una experiencia pastoral: Veinte años de vida y de muerte, de fé y esperanza cristianas.* El Quiché, Guatemala. Manuscript.

Immerman, Richard H. 1982. *The CIA in Guatemala: The Foreign Policy of Intervention.* Austin: University of Texas Press.

International Institute for Democracy and Electoral Assistance (IDEA). 1998. *Democracia en Guatemala: La misión de un pueblo entero: Síntesis del informe.* Stockholm: International IDEA.

James, C. L. R. 1989 (1938). *The Black Jacobins.* New York: Vintage Books.

Jelin, Elizabeth, and Eric Hershberg, eds. 1996. *Constructing Democracy: Human Rights, Citizenship, and Society in Latin America.* Boulder, Colo.: Westview Press.

Jonas, Susanne. 1991. *The Battle for Guatemala: Rebels, Death Squads, and U.S. Power.* Boulder, Colo.: Westview Press.

———. 2000. *Of Centaurs and Doves: Guatemala's Peace Process.* Boulder, Colo.: Westview Press.

Jonas, Susanne, and David Tobis, eds. 1974. *Guatemala.* Berkeley, Calif.: North American Congress on Latin America (NACLA).

Kempster, Norman. 1987. "U.S. Copters Fly Guatemala Combat Troops." *Los Angeles Times,* May 6: 1, 7.

Kinzer, Stephen. 2001. "Guatemala: The Unfinished Peace." *New York Review of Books,* June 21: 61–63.

Kita, Bernice. 2000. "Bill Woods Comes Home." *Maryknoll Magazine,* Sept.: 51–54.

Krueger, Chris, ed. 1982. *Guatemala: Government Against the People.* Washington, D.C.: Washington Office on Latin America.

Kruijt, Dirk. 1998. "Reflexiones sobre Guatemala." In Bernardo Arévalo de León, ed., *Sobre arenas movedizas: sociedad, Estado y ejército en Guatemala,* 9–36. Guatemala City: FLACSO.

Kuper, Adam. 1995. "Comments." *Current Anthropology* 36 (3): 424–26.

LaFeber, Walter. 1984a. *Inevitable Revolutions: The United States in Central America.* New York: W. W. Norton and Company, Inc.

——— 1984b. "The Reagan Administration and Revolutions in Central America." *Political Science Quarterly* 99 (1): 1–25.

Lambek, Michael. 1996. "The Past Imperfect: Remembering as Moral Practice." In Paul Antze and Michael Lambek, eds., *Tense Past: Cultural Essays in Trauma and Memory,* 235–54. New York: Routledge.

Le Bot, Yvon. 1992. *La Guerre en Terre Maya: Communauté, Violence et Modernité au Guatemala, 1970–1992.* Paris: Editions Karthala.

Lernoux, Penny. 1980. *Cry of the People.* New York: Penguin Books.

Levenson-Estrada, Deborah. 1994. *Trade Unionists against Terror: Guatemala City, 1954–1985.* Chapel Hill: University of North Carolina Press.

Levi, Primo. 1988. *The Drowned and the Saved.* New York: Vintage International.

Lewis, W. Arthur. 1958. "Economic Development with Unlimited Supplies of Labour." In A. N. Agarwala and S. P. Singh, eds., *The Economics of Underdevelopment,* 400–499. London: Oxford University Press.

Lira, Elizabeth, ed. 1994. *Psicología y violencia política en América Latina.* Santiago: Ediciones Instituto Latinoamericano de Salud Mental y Derechos Humanos (ILAS), Ediciones ChileAmérica, CESOC.

Lira, Elizabeth, and Maria Isabel Castillo. 1991. *Psicología de la amenaza política y del miedo.* Santiago: Instituto Latinoamericano de Salud Mental y Derechos Humanos (ILAS), Ediciones ChileAmérica, CESOC.

Lira, Elizabeth, and Brian Loveman. 1998. *Dilemas éticos y políticos de la reconciliación política en Chile, 1814–1998.* Pittsburgh: Latin American Studies Association.

———. 1999. *Las suaves cenizas del olvido: Vía chilena de reconciliación política, 1814–1932.* Santiago: Ediciones Lom; Dirección Bibliotecas, Archivos y Museos.

Lira, Elizabeth, and Isabel Piper. 1996. *Reparación, derechos humanos y salud mental.* Santiago: Instituto Latinoamericano de Salud Mental y Derechos Humanos (ILAS), Ediciones ChileAmérica.

Lira, Elizabeth, and Eugenia Weinstein. 1984. *Psicoterapia y represión.* Mexico City: Siglo Veintiuno Editores.

Losano-Ponciano, Luis E. 2000. "Efectos económicos y sociales de la actividad petrolera en la Franja Transversal del Norte y Petén, durante el período 1974–1998." *Facultad de Ciencias Económicas.* Guatemala City: University of San Carlos.

Lovell, W. George. 1988. "Surviving Conquest: The Maya of Guatemala in Historical Perspective." *Latin American Research Review* 23 (2): 25–58.

———. 1992. *Conquest and Survival in Colonial Guatemala: A Historical Geography of the Cuchumatán Highlands, 1500–1821.* Montreal and Kingston: McGill-Queen's University Press.

Lovell, W. George, and Christopher H. Lutz. 1994. "Conquest and Population: Maya Demography in Historical Perspective." *Latin American Research Review* 29 (2): 133–40.

———. 1995. *Demography and Empire: A Guide to the Population History of Spanish Central America, 1500–1821.* Boulder, Colo.: Westview Press.

———. 1996. " 'A Dark Obverse': Maya Survival in Guatemala, 1520–1994." *The Geographical Review* 86 (3): 398–407.

———. 2001. "The Primacy of Larger Truths: Rigoberta Menchú and the Tradition of Native Testimony in Guatemala." In Arturo Arias, ed., *The Rigoberta Menchú Controversy*, 171–97. Minneapolis: University of Minnesota Press.

Lutz, Christopher. 1984. *Historia sociodemográfica de Santiago de Guatemala, 1541–1773.* Guatemala City: CIRMA (Centro de Investigación de Mesoamérica).

Lux de Cotí, Otilia. 1997. "La participación representativa del pueblo maya en una sociedad democrática y pluralista." *Guatemala: Cultura de Guatemala, año XVII* (May–Aug.), 1: 29–38.

Macías, Julio César. 1998. *Mi camino: La guerrilla.* Mexico City: Editorial Planeta Mexicana, S. A. de C. V.

Malkki, Liisa H. 1995. *Purity and Exile: Violence, Memory, and National Cosmology among Hutu Refugees in Tanzania.* Chicago: University of Chicago Press.

Manz, Beatriz. 1981. "On Guatemalan Refugees—The Author Responds" (Exchange of letters with Ian Graham). *Cultural Survival Newsletter* 5 (4): 15–16.

———. 1984. "Mayas Celebrated and Mayas Persecuted." *New York Times,* June 1: A30.

———. 1985a. Congressional Record. "The Context for Evaluating Human Rights in Guatemala." In Subcommittee on Western Hemisphere Affairs, Committee on Foreign Affairs, United States House of Representatives, Washington, D.C.

———. 1985b. "Dollars That Forge Guatemalan Chains." *New York Times,* Mar. 18: A19.

———. 1986. "A Guatemalan Dies and What It Means." *New York Times,* July 14: A17.

———. 1988a. *Refugees of a Hidden War: The Aftermath of Counterinsurgency in Guatemala.* Albany: State University of New York Press.

———. 1988b. *Repatriation and Reintegration: An Arduous Process in Guatemala.* Washington, D.C.: Hemispheric Migration Project, Center for Immigration Policy and Refugee Assistance, Georgetown University.

———. 1990. "In Guatemala, No One Is Safe...Why Was Myrna Mack Killed?" *New York Times,* Oct. 27: 15.

——— 1999. *De la memoria a la reconstrucción histórica.* Guatemala City: AVANCSO.

———. 2002. "Terror, Grief, and Recovery: Genocidal Trauma in a Mayan Village." In Alexander Laban Hinton, ed., *Annihilating Difference: The Anthropology of Genocide,* 292–309. Berkeley: University of California Press.

———. 2003. "Reflections on Remembrance: Voices of an Ixcán Village," In Susan Eckstein and Timothy Wickham-Crowley, eds., *What Justice? Whose Justice? Fighting for Fairness in Latin America.* Berkeley: University of California Press.

Manz, Beatriz, Xóchitl Castañeda, Allison Davenport, Ingrid Perry-Houts, and Cécile Mazzacurati. 2000. "Guatemalan Immigration to the San Francisco Bay Area." *Center for Latino Policy Research* 6 (1): 1–25.

Marques, José, Darío Páez, and Alexandra F. Serra. 1997. "Social Sharing, Emotional Climate, and the Transgenerational Transmission of Memories: The Portuguese Colonial War." In J.W. Pennebaker, D. Páez, and B. Rimé, eds., *Collective Memory of Political Events: Social Psychological Perspectives.* Mahwah, N.J.: Lawrence Erlbaum Associates, Publishers.

Martínez Peláez, Severo. 1998. *La patria del criollo: Ensayo de interpretación de la realidad colonial guatemalteca.* Mexico City: Fondo de Cultura Económica.

Mazariegos, Jorge A. 1990. *El Estado, su estabilidad y el desarrollo de una estrategia nacional.* Guatemala City: Editorial del Ejército.

McClintock, Michael. 1985. *The American Connection: State Terror and Popular Resistance in Guatemala.* London: Zed Press.

McCreery, David. 1994. *Rural Guatemala, 1760–1940.* Stanford: Stanford University Press.

Melville, Thomas, and Marjorie Melville. 1970. *Whose Heaven, Whose Earth?* New York: Alfred A. Knopf.

———. 1971. *Guatemala: The Politics of Land Ownership.* New York: Free Press.

Menchú, Rigoberta. 1998. *Crossing Borders.* Ed. and trans. Ann Wright. London: Verso.

MIF/IDB (Multilateral Investment Fund and Inter-American Development Bank). 2003. "Sending Money Home: An International Comparison of Remittance Markets." In http://www.iadb.org/exr/prensa/images/Round TablesFEB2003.pdf (as of June 9, 2003).

Millet, Artimus. 1974. "The Agricultural Colonization of the West Central Petén, Guatemala: A Case Study of Frontier Settlement by Cooperatives." Ph. D. diss., University of Oregon.

MINUGUA (United Nations Verification Mission in Guatemala). 2002. "Comunicado de MINUGUA sobre el sexto aniversario de la firma de la paz." Guatemala City, Dec. 29.

La Moneda. 2002. "Guatemala: Crecen Remesas Familiares." *Moneda: El Periódico Financiero,* Aug. 19–23. In http://monedagt.terra.com/moneda/noticias /mnd8490.htm.

Montejo, Víctor. 1987. *Testimony: Death of a Guatemalan Village.* Willimantic, Conn.: Curbstone Press.

———. 1993. *Testimonio: Muerte de una comunidad indígena en Guatemala.* Guatemala City: University of San Carlos.

———. 2001. "Truth, Human Rights, and Representation: The Case of Rigoberta Menchú." In Arturo Arias, ed., *The Rigoberta Menchú Controversy,* 372–91. Minneapolis: University of Minnesota Press.

Montejo, Víctor, and Q'anil Akab'. 1992. *Brevísima relación testimonial de la contínua destrucción del Mayab' (Guatemala).* Providence, R.I.: Maya Scholars Network.

Morrissey, James. 1978. "A Missionary-Directed Resettlement Project Among the Highland Maya of Western Guatemala." Ph.D. diss., Stanford University.

Nairn, Allan, and Jean-Marie Simon. 1986. "Bureacracy of Death." *New Republic,* June 30: 13–17.

Nelson, Diane. 1999a. *The Finger in the Wound: Ethnicity, Nation, and Gender in the Body Politic of Quincentenial Guatemala.* Berkeley: University of California Press.

———. 1999b. "Rigoberta Menchú: Is Truth Stranger than Testimonial?" *Guatemala Scholars Network News* (Mar.): 5–6.

Nieves, Evelyn. 2002. "Illegal Immigrants Death Rate Rises Sharply in Barren Areas." *New York Times,* Aug. 6: A1.

Nordstrom, Carolyn, and JoAnn Martin, eds. 1992. *Paths to Domination, Resistance, and Terror.* Berkeley: University of California Press.

Nordstrom, Carolyn, and Antonius C.G.M. Robben, eds. 1995. *Fieldwork under Fire: Contemporary Studies of Violence and Survival.* Berkeley: University of California Press.

Oficina de Derechos Humanos del Arzobispado de Guatemala (ODHAG). 1998a. *Guatemala Nunca Más.* Tomo I. *Impactos de la violencia.* Guatemala City: Oficina de Derechos Humanos del Arzobispado de Guatemala City.

———. 1998b. Tomo II. *Los mecanismos del horror.* Guatemala City: ODHAG.

———. 1998c. Tomo III. *El entorno histórico.* Guatemala City: ODHAG.

Oglesby, Elizabeth A. 1995. "Myrna Mack." In Carolyn Nordstrom and Antonius C.G.M. Robben, eds., *Fieldwork under Fire: Contemporary Studies of Violence and Survival*, 254–59. Berkeley: University of California Press.

———. 2002. "Politics at Work: Elites, Labor, and Agrarian Modernization in Guatemala, 1980–2000." Ph.D. diss., University of California at Berkeley.

O'Meara, J. Tim. 1995. "Comments." *Current Anthropology* 36 (3): 427–28.

Orlove, Benjamin S. 2002. *Lines in the Water: Nature and Culture at Lake Titicaca.* Berkeley: University of California Press.

Otzoy, Irma. 1988. "Identity and Higher Education among Mayan Women." M.A. thesis, University of Iowa.

Otzoy, Irma, and Enrique Sam Colop. 1990. "Identidad étnica y modernización entre los mayas de Guatemala." *Mesoamérica* 19 (June): 97–100.

Paige, Jeffery M. 1975. *Agrarian Revolution: Social Movements and Export Agriculture in the Underdeveloped World.* New York: Free Press.

———. 1983. "Social Theory and Peasant Revolution in Vietnam and Guatemala." *Theory and Society* 12 (12): 699–737.

———. 1997. *Coffee and Power: Revolution and the Rise of Democracy in Central America.* Cambridge: Harvard University Press.

Painter, James. 1987. *Guatemala: False Hope, False Freedom.* London: Catholic Institute for International Relations and Latin America Bureau.

Paul, Benjamin D., and William J. Demarest. 1988. "The Operation of a Death Squad in San Pedro la Laguna." In Robert M. Carmack, ed., *Harvest of Violence: The Maya Indians and the Guatemalan Crisis*, 119–55. Norman: University of Oklahoma Press.

Payeras, Mario. 1983. *Days of the Jungle: The Testimony of a Guatemalan Guerrillero, 1972–1976.* New York: Monthly Review Press.

———. 1991. *Los fusiles de octubre: Ensayos y artículos militares sobre la revolución Guatemalteca, 1985–1988.* Mexico City: Editorial Juan Pablos.

Perera, Víctor. 1993. *Unfinished Conquest: The Guatemalan Tragedy.* Berkeley: University of California Press.

Plant, Roger. 1997. "Indigenous Identity and Rights in the Guatemalan Peace Process." Paper presented at the Conference on Comparative Peace Processes, the Woodrow Wilson Center, Washington, D.C., Mar. 13–14.

Popkin, Margaret L. 1996. *Civil Patrols and Their Legacy: Overcoming Militarization and Polarization in the Guatemalan Countryside.* Washington, D.C.: Robert F. Kennedy Memorial Center for Human Rights.

Popkin, Samuel. 1979. *The Rational Peasant.* Berkeley: University of California Press.

Prensa Libre. 1982. "Subversión en abierta guerra contra Patrullas Civiles. Indígenas acosados en El Quiché y las Verapaces se defienden." June 13: 4.

Programa de Ayuda para los Vecinos del Altiplano. 1984. Final Report, USAID project DR-520–84–04. March.

Quigg, David. 1990. "Memorial to Honor Slain Anthropologist." *The Daily Californian,* Sept. 26: 1, 5.

Recinos Lima, Mario. 1982. "Campesinos de Ixcán huyen por violencia." *El Gráfico,* June 13: 7.

REMHI (Recovery of Historical Memory Project). 1999. *Guatemala Never Again!* Maryknoll, N.Y.: Orbis Books.

Reyes, Belinda I., Hans P. Johnson, and Richard Van Swearinger. 2002. *Holding the Line? The Effect of the Recent Border Build-up on Unauthorized Immigration.* San Francisco: Public Policy Institute of California.

Riding, Alan. 1982. "Guatemalans Tell of Murder of 300." *New York Times,* Oct. 12: A3.

Rosada-Granados, Héctor. 1999. *Soldados en el poder: Proyecto militar en Guatemala, 1944–1990.* Utrecht, Holland: Funpadem.

Rueda, Edgar Camilo. 2002. *Biografía Política de Camilo Torres.* In http://www.marxists.org/espanol/camilo/biografia.htm (as of May 28, 2003).

Sam Colop, Luis Enrique. 1983. "Hacia una propuesta de ley de educación bilingüe." Thesis de Licenciatura en Ciencias Jurídicas y Sociales, Rafael Landívar University, Guatemala City.

———. 1990. "Foreign Scholars and Mayans: What Are the Issues?" *Guatemala Scholars Network News* (Feb.): 2.

Sandoval, Leopoldo. 1987. *El problema de la estructura agraria de Guatemala en la coyuntura de un nuevo régimen constitucional en 1986.* Guatemala City: Asociación de Investigación y Estudios Sociales.

Scheper-Hughes, Nancy. 1995. "The Primacy of the Ethical: Propositions for a Militant Anthropology." *Current Anthropology* 36 (3): 409–40.

Schirmer, Jennifer. 1998. *The Guatemalan Military Project: A Violence Called Democracy.* Philadelphia: University of Pennsylvania Press.

Schlesinger, Stephen, and Stephen Kinzer. 1982. *Bitter Fruit: The Untold Story of the American Coup in Guatemala.* New York: Doubleday.

Schoultz, Lars. 1981. *Human Rights and U.S. Policy Toward Latin America.* Princeton: Princeton University Press.

———. 1983. "Guatemala Social Change and Political Conflict." In Martin Diskin, ed., *Trouble in Our Backyard: Central America and the United States in the Eighties,* 174–202. New York: Pantheon Books.

———. 1998. *Beneath the United States: A History of U.S. Policy toward Latin America.* Cambridge, Mass.: Harvard University Press.

Scott, James. 1976. *The Moral Economy of the Peasant.* New Haven: Yale University Press.

———. 1977. "Hegemony and the Peasantry." *Politics and Society* 7: 267–96.

———. 1985. *Weapons of the Weak: Everyday Forms of Peasant Resistance.* New Haven: Yale University Press.

————. 1990. *Domination and the Arts of Resistance: Hidden Transcripts.* New Haven: Yale University Press.

Sereseres, Cesár D. 1985. "The Highlands War in Guatemala." In Georges A. Fauriol, ed., *Latin American Insurgencies*, 97–130. Washington, D.C.: U.S. Government Printing Office; Georgetown University Center for Strategic and International Studies and National Defense University.

Sharer, Robert J. 1994. *The Ancient Maya.* Stanford: Stanford University Press.

Sheehan, Michael A. 1989. "Comparative Counterinsurgency Strategies: Guatemala and El Salvador." *Conflict* 9: 127–54.

Sieder, Rachel. 1997. *Customary Law and Democratic Transition in Guatemala.* London: University of London, Institute of Latin America Studies Research Papers.

Sieder, Rachel, et al. 2002. *Who Governs? Guatemala Five Years after the Peace Accords.* Cambridge, Mass: Hemispheric Initiatives.

Simon, Joel, and Beatriz Manz. 1992. "Representation, Organization, and Human Rights among Guatemalan Refugees in Mexico, 1980–1992." *Harvard Human Rights Journal* 5 (spring): 95–135.

Singlemann, Peter. 1981. *Structures of Domination and Peasant Movements in Latin America.* Columbia: University of Missouri Press.

Sistema de Naciones Unidas en Guatemala. 2000. *Guatemala: La fuerza incluyente del desarrollo humano. Informe de desarrollo humano 2000.* Guatemala City: Programa de las Naciones Unidas para el Desarrollo (PNUD).

Skocpol, Theda. 1982. "What Makes Peasants Revolutionary?" In Robert Weller and Scott Guggenheim, eds., *Power and Protest in the Countryside: Studies of Rural Unrest in Asia, Europe, and Latin America*, 157–79. Durham, N.C.: Duke University Press.

Smith, Carol, ed. 1990a. *Guatemalan Indians and the State, 1540–1988.* Austin: University of Texas Press.

————. 1990b. "Origins of the National Question in Guatemala: A Hypothesis." In Carol Smith, ed., *Guatemalan Indians and the State, 1540–1988*, 72–95. Austin: University of Texas Press.

————. 1993. "Local History in Global Context: Social and Economic Transitions in Western Guatemala." In Daniel H. Levine, ed., *Constructing Culture and Power in Latin America*, 75–118. Ann Arbor: University of Michigan.

————. 1996. "Myths, Intellectuals, and Race/Class/Gender Distinctions in the Formation of Latin American Nations." *Journal of Latin American Anthropology* 2 (1): 148–69.

Snodgrass-Godoy, Angelina. 2001. "Justicia a Mano Propia: The Privatization of Justice in Latin America." Ph.D. diss., University of California, Berkeley.

Starn, Orin. 1991. "Missing the Revolution: Anthropologists and the War in Peru." *Cultural Anthropology* 6 (1): 63–91.

Stoll, David. 1990. *Is Latin America Turning Protestant? The Politics of Evangelical Growth.* Berkeley: University of California Press.

————. 1993. *Between Two Armies in the Ixil Towns of Guatemala.* New York: Columbia University Press.

————. 1999a. *Rigoberta Menchú and the Story of All Poor Guatemalans.* Boulder, Colo.: Westview Press.

———. 1999b. "Rigoberta Menchú and the Last-Resort Paradigm." *Latin American Perspectives* 26 (6): 70–80.

Taylor, Clark. 1998. *Return of Guatemalan Refugees*. Philadelphia: Temple University Press.

Tedlock, Barbara. 1984. "On Colby's Review of Time and the Highland Maya." *American Anthropologist* 86 (2): 425–426.

Thompson, Ginger. 2002. "Vatican Curbing Deacons in Mexico." *New York Times,* Mar. 12: A8.

Trudeau, Robert. 1989. "The Guatemalan Election of 1985: Prospects for Democracy." In John A. Booth and Mitchell A. Seligman, eds., *Elections and Democracy in Central America,* 93–125. Chapel Hill: University of North Carolina Press.

———. 1993. *Guatemalan Politics: The Popular Struggle for Democracy.* Boulder, Colo.: Lynne Reinner.

United States Agency for International Development (USAID). March 31, 1982. "Northern Transversal Strip Land Settlement Project." Office of Rural Development, Report No. 1. (Prepared by David C. Fledderjohn and David C. Thompson).

———. January 1984. "Evaluation of the Ixcán Colonization Project (520-T-026)." Office of Rural Development, Report No. 9. (Prepared by Phillip A. Dennis, Gary S. Elbow, and Peter L. Heller.).

United States Bureau of the Census. 2001. Census 2000, file 1. In http://www.census.gov/prod/2001%20pubs/c2kbr01-3.pdf (as of Nov. 8, 2002).

United States Department of State. 1968. Mr. Vaky to Mr. Oliver, Secret Memorandum, Policy Planning Council, Washington, D.C., Mar. 29. In http://www.gwu.edu/~nsarchiv/NSAEBB/NSAEBB11/docs/05-01.htm (as of April 1, 2002).

———. 1981. Robert L. Jacobs to Mr. Einaudi, Secret Memorandum, Washington, D.C., Oct. 5. In http://www.gwu.edu/~nsarchiv/NSAEBB/NSAEBB11/docs/13-01.htm (as of Mar. 7, 2002).

———. 2004. Congressional Budget Justification for Foreign Operations, The Secretary of State, Foreign Operations, Fiscal Year 2004. Pp. 443–97. In http://www.state.gov/m/rm/rls/cbj/ (as of June 2, 2003).

Veblen, Thomas T. 1977. "Native Population Decline in Totonicapán, Guatemala." *Annals of the Association of American Geographers* 67 (4): 484–99.

Walker, Thomas W. 1994. "The Nicaraguan Revolution: The Economic and Political Background." In Jack A. Goldstone, ed., *Revolutions: Theoretical, Comparative, and Historical Studies,* 147–59. New York: Harcourt Brace College Publisher.

Warren, Jonathan W. 2001. *Racial Revolutions: Antiracism and Indian Resurgence in Brazil*. Durham: Duke University Press.

Warren, Kay B. 1989 (1978). *The Symbolism of Subordination: Indian Identity in a Guatemalan Town*. Austin: University of Texas Press.

———. 1992. "Transforming Memories and Histories: Meanings of Ethnic Resurgence for Mayan Indians." In Alfred Stepan, ed., *Americas: New Interpretive Essays,* 189–219. Oxford: Oxford University Press.

———. 1993a. "Interpreting *la Violencia* in Guatemala: Shapes of Kaqchikel Resistance and Silence." In Kay B. Warren, ed., *The Violence Within: Cultural and Political Opposition in Divided Nations*, 25–26. Boulder, Colo.: Westview Press.

———. ed. 1993b. *The Violence Within: Cultural and Political Opposition in Divided Nations*. Boulder, Colo.: Westview Press.

———. 1998. *Indigenous Movements and Their Critics: Pan-Maya Activism in Guatemala*. Princeton: Princeton University Press.

Washington Office on Latin America, with Chris Krueger and Kjell I. Enge. 1985. *Security and Development Conditions in the Guatemalan Highlands*. Report on a Mission of Inquiry, August. Washington, D.C.: Washington Office on Latin America.

Weiner, Tim. 2001. "In Latin America, Foes Aren't the Only Danger." *New York Times*, Apr. 29: 7.

Weisman, Steven R. 2002. "Abrams Back in Capital Fray at Center of Mideast Battle." *New York Times*, Dec. 7: 1.

Wickham-Crowley, Timothy P. 1992. *Guerrillas and Revolution in Latin America: A Comparative Study of Insurgents and Regimes Since 1956*. Princeton: Princeton University Press.

Wilford, John Noble. 1984a. "Mayan Specialists Hail a 'Fancy Discovery' at Rio Azul Site." *New York Times*, May 23: C23.

———. 1984b. "Professor's Path to Mayan Discovery: The Delight in Finding Time 'Frozen.'" *New York Times*, May 24: C21.

Williams, Robert G. 1986. *Export Agriculture and the Crisis in Central America*. Chapel Hill: University of North Carolina Press.

Wilson, Richard. 1991. "Machine Guns and Mountain Spirits: the Cultural Effects of State Repression among the Q'eqchi' of Guatemala." *Critical Anthropology* 11: 33–61.

———. 1995. *Maya Resurgence in Guatemala: The Q'eqchi' Experience*. Norman: University of Oklahoma Press.

———. ed. 1997. *Human Rights, Culture and Context: Anthropological Perspectives*. London: Pluto Press.

Wolf, Eric R. 1969. *Peasant Wars of the Twentieth Century*. New York: Harper and Row.

———. 1994. "Peasants and Revolutions." In Jack A. Goldstone, ed., *Revolutions: Theoretical, Comparative, and Historical Studies*, 55–63. New York: Harcourt Brace College Publishers.

Worby, Paula. 2002. *Los refugiados retornados guatemaltecos y el acceso a la tierra: Resultados, lecciones y perspectivas*. Guatemala City: AVANCSO.

Yoldi, Pilar. 2000. *Tierra, guerra y esperanza "Memoria del Ixcán" (1966–1992)*. Guatemala City: Diócesis del Quiché. Proyecto Interdiocesano de Recuperación de la Memoria Histórica (REMHI).

Zur, Judith N. 1998. *Violent Memories: Mayan War Widows in Guatemala*. Boulder, Colo.: Westview Press.

Index

Italicized page numbers indicate illustrations.

Abdala, Col. Guido, 171–72, 271n34
Abrams, Elliott, 29, 256n92
Acción Cristiana Guatemalteca (ACG, Guatemalan Christian Action), 134–35
Adela, 128–31
agriculture: collective work in, 130; cooperative for, 53; crops for, 70; destruction of, 143, 149–52; experimentation in, 193; export, 34, 43; fertilizer for, 48; hidden in rain forest, 127, 128; implements of, 37; Mayan tradition of, 34–35; natural fauna vs., 205–6; not allowed by army, 148; pesticide use in, 43; slash-and-burn, 12. See also cardamom; colonization; land; plantations (fincas); Zona Reyna Multiservice Agricultural Cooperative
Aguilar Zinser, Adolfo, 272–73n4
airplanes: in army's terror campaigns, 262–63n19; guerrilla attacks on, 116, 263n24; plantations' use of, for fumigation, 43; tunnels as defense against, 116–17; of Wings of Hope, 66–67, 263n25
Ak Catún, Carolina, 192
Ak'el: attitudes toward, 157–58; on civil patrols, 150–52; on guerrillas' leaflets, 166
Alfaro, Rubén, 110–11
Allende, Salvador, 56, 77
Alta Verapaz region: army repression of, 94; land speculation in, 88; new settlers from, 2, 156; oil drilling in, 90
American Anthropological Association, 7
Americas Watch, 23, 24, 29, 250–51n18

amnesty: army's control and, 142; news of, 135–36; resettlement and, 155
Amnesty International, 3, 23, 24, 250–51n18
Angelina, 135–37, 140
anthropology: active ethnography compared with, 6–7; basic assumptions in, 250n16; cultural and geographical distances in, 15; Guatemalans doing, 12–14; limits of, 8–9; objective and moral models in, 249n12. See also fieldwork; public anthropology
Anthropology Research Center, 250–51n18
anticommunism: of Catholic Church, 50, 258–59n32; of Evangelical Christians, 210; legacy of, 228; rewards for, 78; as U.S. justification, 21–23, 28–29. See also United States
Anti-Communist Unified Party, 78
antiguos (old ones): attitudes of, 183, 184–85, 187, 195–96, 206, 273n7; on author's visits, 169–70; change in leaders of, 274n18; on civil patrols, 163, 165–66; collective memories of, 197, 198, 199; divisions among, 181–82; global changes sensed by, 190; land taken from, 159, 269n13; perspective of, 160, 162; on reforesting, 173; refugees' letters and visits exchanged with, 185, 189; refugees welcomed by, 193; use of term, 156; on war years, 223. See also militarization of village
apprehensions, 226; about the past, in conducting research, 230, 232

Index

of, 4, 17–18, 28, 93, 142–43; targets
of, 1–2, 20, 49; temporary pullback
by, 115, 118; terror campaigns of,
91–93, 95–96, 104, 105, 108–10,
114–15; undercover agents of,
111–12; U.S. aid for, xiii, 10, 21–22,
23, 143, 170, 213, 254n65,
254–55n72; villagers in custody of,
124–26, 127, 128. *See also* destruction
of village; disappearances; militarization of village; murders; torture
Guatemalan Conference of Religious
Orders (CONFREGUA, Conferencia
de Religiosos y Religiosas de
Guatemala), 20–21
Guatemalan Congress, 54–55
Guatemalan government: assistance
from, 39; authoritarianism of, 92, 107;
CEH on role of, 18; evangelical
alliances with, 25–27; land parcel title
issues and, 71–73, 184, 208–9; poor
people disregarded by, 16–18, 49;
URNG negotiations with, 190, 191.
See also economy; elites; politics
Guatemalan highlands: attempted return
to, 135–36; departure from, 58,
59–61; earthquakes in, 34, 93; food
imports of, 39–40; guerrillas in
southern, 97; history of, 34–35;
Ladino lands in, 44, 258n19; survival
in, 37–39. *See also* plantations *(fincas);*
Santa Cruz del Quiché
Guatemalan Mayan Center, 261n16
Guatemalan National Police, 46–47,
258n23
Guatemalan Supreme Court, 251–52n34
Guatemalan United Organized Student
Front (FUEGO, Frente Unido de
Estudiantes Guatemaltecos Organiza-
dos), 86, 87
Guatemalan Widow's Organization, 172
Guatemala Scholars Network (GSN), 7,
250n13, 250–51n18
Guerrilla Army of the Poor. *See* Ejército
Guerrillero de los Pobres (EGP,
Guerrilla Army of the Poor)
guerrillas. *See* Ejército Guerrillero de los
Pobres (EGP, Guerrilla Army of the
Poor)
Guevara, Che, 74. *See also* Ernesto
"Che" Guevara front
Güicho, 102, 214, 220–21
Gurriarán López, Father Luis, 243; on
Acción Cristiana Guatemalteca, 134,
135; background of, 51–52; with
communities of population in
resistance, 182; cooperatives as focus

of, 53–54, 55–56, 65; expulsion of,
54–55; guerrillas' visit to village and,
75–76; influences on, 258–59n32;
initial attitude toward guerrillas, 87;
on military harassment, 70–71; on
people joining insurgency, 107;
radicalization of, 52; on Raisa Girón
Arévalo, 86; return of, 55, 211,
259n37; scholarships from Spain
obtained by, 274n11; on school
graduates, 194; teaching of,
261–62n18; threats against/departure
of, 5, 20, 88, 172; village settlement
and, 4–5, 48, 51–52, 242; on women's
groups, 201; youth group organized
by, 67–68

Halbwachs, Maurice, 230
Harris, Marvin, 249n12
hats: braiding palm leaves for, 39
health care, 205, 274n15. *See also*
disease
Hernández, María (first woman president
of cooperative), 235
Hernández, Roselia, 202; village
reunification and, 186–87; on
women's organizations, 200–204
Herrera, Carlos, 38–39, 68
Ho Chi Minh front, 97, 104, 172
Holiday of Reconciliation and Initiation
of the Reconstruction of the Community, 226
housing: army's burning of, 119, 120,
262–63n19; description of, in Santa
María Tzejá, 69; for plantation
workers, 41–42; rebuilding of,
141–42, 156; shortage of material for,
173
Huehuetenango department, 40, 53
human rights: commitment to, 7, 94,
184; disregard for, 22–24, 27–28;
learning about, 67–68, 197, 218–19;
in refugee camps, 134–35
human rights organizations: absence of,
xiv; military's denunciation of, 172;
Reagan's dismissal of, 23; role of, 250–
51n18. *See also specific organizations*
human rights violations: documentation
of, 3, 11–12; peasants' support for
insurgency and, 92–93; persistence of,
3; protests against, 94–95. *See also*
disappearances; murders; violence
Human Rights Watch, 29, 272–73n4
Huxley, Aldous, 46

IADB (Inter-American Development
Bank), 253n42

DESIGNER: VICTORIA KUSKOWSKI

COMPOSITOR: IMPRESSIONS BOOK AND JOURNAL SERVICES, INC.

INDEXER: MARGIE TOWERY

CARTOGRAPHER: BILL NELSON

TEXT: SABON 10/13

DISPLAY: ITC BRAGANZA, MRS. EAVES

PRINTING AND BINDING: THOMSON-SHORE, INC.